Shanghai

timeout.com/shanghai

Published by Time Out Guides Ltd, a wholly owned subsidiary of Time Out Group Ltd.
Time Out and the Time Out logo are trademarks of Time Out Group Ltd.

© **Time Out Group Ltd 2004**

10 9 8 7 6 5 4 3 2 1

This edition first published in Great Britain in 2004 by Ebury
Ebury is a division of The Random House Group Ltd,
20 Vauxhall Bridge Road, London SW1V 2SA

Random House Australia Pty Limited, 20 Alfred Street, Milsons Point, Sydney, New South Wales 2061, Australia
Random House New Zealand Limited, 18 Poland Road, Glenfield, Auckland 10, New Zealand
Random House South Africa (Pty) Limited, Endulini, 5A Jubilee Road, Parktown 2193, South Africa

Random House UK Limited Reg. No. 954009

Distributed in USA by Publishers Group West
1700 Fourth Street, Berkeley, California 94710

Distributed in Canada by Penguin Canada Ltd
10 Alcorn Avenue, Toronto, Ontario, Canada M4V 3B2

For further distribution details, see www.timeout.com

ISBN 1-904978-22-3

A CIP catalogue record for this book is available from the British Library

Colour reprographics by Icon, Crowne House, 56-58 Southwark Street, London SE1 1UN

Printed and bound by Cayfosa-Quebecor, Ctra. De Caldes, KM 3 08 130 Sta, Perpètua de Mogoda, Barcelona, Spain

Time Out Guides Limited
Universal House
251 Tottenham Court Road
London W1T 7AB
Tel + 44 (0)20 7813 3000
Fax + 44 (0)20 7813 6001
Email guides@timeout.com
www.timeout.com

Editorial

Editor Andrew Humphreys
Consultant Editor Keith Andony
Deputy Editor Natalie Whittle
Listings Checker Sierra Fung, Angeline Liang, Kinono Tang
Proofreader Tamsin Shelton
Indexer Jackie Brind

Editorial/Managing Director Peter Fiennes
Series Editor Ruth Jarvis
Deputy Series Editor Lesley McCave
Guides Co-ordinator Anna Norman
Accountant Sarah Bostock

Design

Art Director Mandy Martin
Art Editor Scott Moore
Senior Designer Tracey Ridgewell
Designers Astrid Kogler, Sam Lands, Oliver Knight
Junior Designer Chrissy Mouncey
Digital Imaging Dan Conway, Tessa Kar
Ad Make-up Charlotte Blythe

Picture Desk

Picture Editor Jael Marschner
Deputy Picture Editors Kit Burnet, Tracey Kerrigan
Picture Researcher Ivy Lahon
Picture Desk Assistant/Librarian Kate Knighton

Advertising

Sales Director Mark Phillips
International Sales Manager Ross Canadé
International Sales Executive James Tuson
Advertising Sales (Shanghai) Ringier Asia
Advertising Assistant Lucy Butler

Marketing

Marketing Manager Mandy Martinez
US Publicity & Marketing Associate Rosella Albanese

Production

Guides Production Director Mark Lamond
Production Controller Samantha Furniss

Time Out Group

Chairman Tony Elliott
Managing Director Mike Hardwick
Group Financial Director Richard Waterlow
Group Commercial Director Lesley Gill
Group Marketing Director Christine Cort
Group General Manager Nichola Coulthard
Group Art Director John Oakey
Online Managing Director David Pepper
Group Production Director Steve Proctor
Group IT Director Simon Chappell

Contributors

Introduction Andrew Humphreys. **History** Spencer Dodington (*The Jewish dynasties* Natalie Whittle; *Peace at the Cathay* Peter Hibbard). **Shanghai Today** Jen Lin Liu. **Architecture** Spencer Dodington. **Where to Stay** Keith Andony. *Additional reviews* Andrew Humphreys. **Sightseeing Introduction** Andrew Humphreys. *Museum reviews throughout the Sightseeing chapters* Peter Hibbard. **The Bund** Peter Hibbard (*Huangpu River* Andrew Humphreys; *To infinity and the Bund* Kath Cummins). **Renmin Square & Nanjing Donglu** Spencer Dodington (*From Park to pyramid* Andrew Humphreys). **Jingan** Spencer Dodington. **The Old City** Peter Hibbard (*To the teahouse* Kath Cummins). **Xintiandi** Spencer Dodington. **French Concession** Spencer Dodington (*Half-arted street* Mary Helen Trent). **Xujiahui, Hongqiao & Gubei** Spencer Dodington. **Pudong** Mary Helen Trent. **Hongkou** Crystyl Mo. **Restaurants & Cafés** Mary Helen Trent, Ulrika Engstrom, Mary Helen Trent (*Brunch bunch, Height Cuisine* Kath Cummins; *Hairy crabs* Mary Helen Trent; *Street eats* Crystyl Mo). **Pubs & Bars** Sam Ailwood, Ulrika Engstrom (*Beyond the Irish bar* Sam Ailwood). **Shops & Services** Mary Helen Trent (*Faking it* Kath Cummins; *Suits you!* Mary Helen Trent; *Mem-Mao-ries are made of this* Sam Ailwood; *Thigh fashion* Lisa Movius). **Festivals & Events** Keith Andony. **Children** Kath Cummins. **Film** Arthur Jones. **Galleries** Ulrika Engstrom. **Gay & Lesbian** Chris McCormick. **Mind & Body** Crystyl Mo (*Invisible touch* Kath Cummins; *Nip, tuck and suck* Ulrika Engstrom and Crystyl Mo). **Music** Lisa Movius. **Nightlife** Sam Ailwood. **Performing Arts** Ulrika Engstrom. **Sport & Fitness** Miriam Rayman (*Hoop and glory* Crystyl Mo; *On track for success* Natalie Whittle). **Getting Started** Olivia Edward. **The Canal Towns** Sam Ailwood (*Sex (but not in the city)* Olivia Edward). **Hangzhou & Moganshan** Olivia Edward. **Suzhou** Sam Ailwood. **Putuoshan** Olivia Edward. **Directory** Keith Andony. *Film* Arthur Jones; *Music* Lisa Movius.

Maps JS Graphics (john@jsgraphics.co.uk).

Photography by Jonathan Perugia, except: page 10 Hulton Archive; pages 13, 17 CPA Media; page 18 Topfoto; pages 50, 51 ImagineChina.com; page 157 Kobal; The following image was provided by the featured establishment/artist: page 84.

The Editor would like to thank Mark DeCocinis, Gadi Farfour, Mark Kitto, Veronica Ann Lee, Hilda Liu, Monica Ma, Tim Robberts, Kelly Sum and Michelle Wan.

Contents

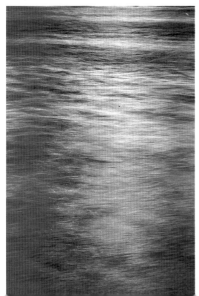

Introduction

Once dubbed the 'Paris of the East' and, less flatteringly, the 'whore of the orient,' Shanghai was a city that prided itself on the variety of vices it offered – from gambling halls and opium dens to bars filled with smiling singsong girls and White Russian 'hostesses.' It was the place that inspired Marlene Dietrich to rasp, 'It took more than one man to change my name to Shanghai Lily,' and where an exasperated missionary once cried out, 'If God lets Shanghai endure, He owes an apology to Sodom and Gomorrah.' That was the city of the 1920s and '30s, but not to worry to worry if you missed out first time around because after a 40-year hiatus under the Communists, Shanghai is back.

While not quite the louche and decadent city of old, this is very much the happening centre of East Asia. Since the Chinese government decided in 1990 that Shanghai would supplant Hong Kong as the financial engine driving China, its residents have been on a spending spree. The lost decades have simply been skipped over as Shanghainese homes have leapt straight from radio to surround-sound flat screen TVs, from no phone to cell phone and from bicycle to SUV. Until as recently as 1988 the tallest building in town was just 22 storeys, now it's 88, courtesy of the Jinmao Tower, a Chinese take on the Empire State building. Soon, rising above it, will be the 101-storey Shanghai World Financial Centre. In just ten years local planners have created an entirely new city of 150 skyscrapers in an area the size of Singapore on what was previously rice fields and marsh land. You can almost hear the roar of redevelopment as Shanghai motors, foot firmly on the gas toward the future.

Conspicuous consumption has reached even dizzier heights with boutiques like Shanghai Tang flogging modern updates on traditional jackets for the equivalent of $200 a pop. In 2004 Armani opened his flagship China store on the city's waterfront, sharing space with a super luxe Evian spa complex and a restaurant owned by and named for darling of the New York dining scene Jean-Georges Vongerichten. Meanwhile at the neighbouring Glamour Bar (an old stager on the city scene at all of five years old) the *jeunesse dorée* gather over frozen Martinis to discuss which opening party to attend that evening. The choice is never easy because with Chinese and South-east Asian business-men and entrepreneurs – not to mention the Americans and Europeans – throwing in the region of $100 billion a year in investment at the city, new bars, restaurants and galleries are opening faster than you can blink.

The city just crackles with energy. Swarms of honking cars zip around on spaghetti loops of elevated highway that are lit up by neon at night. In fact by night the whole hyper-kinetic cityscape twinkles, flashes and ripples with garish lights so that the feeling is of being trapped in some giant video game. It's full on and it's frantic and if this really is the future then boy are we in for some fun.

ABOUT TIME OUT GUIDES

This first edition of the *Time Out Shanghai Guide* is one of an expanding series of Time Out City Guides, produced by the people behind London and New York's successful listings magazines. Our guides are all written and updated by resident experts who have striven to provide you with all the most up-to-date information you'll need to explore the city or read up on its background, whether you're a local or a first-time visitor.

THE LOWDOWN ON THE LISTINGS

Above all, we've tried to make this guide as useful as possible. Addresses, telephone numbers, websites, transport information, opening times, admission prices and credit card details are all included in our listings. And, as far as possible, we've given details of facilities, services and events, all checked and correct according to the information we were given as we went to press. However, owners and managers can change their arrangements at any time. Arts and events programmes are particularly prone to last minute changes and cancellations in Shanghai, while bars, clubs and restaurants open and close with baffling frequency. Before you go out of your way, we would advise you to phone and check opening times, ticket prices and other particulars.

While every effort has been make to ensure the accuracy of the information contained in this guide, the publishers cannot accept responsibility for any errors it may contain.

PRICES AND PAYMENT

We have noted where venues such as shops, hotels and restaurants accept the following credit cards: American Express (**AmEx**), Diners Club (**DC**), MasterCard (**MC**) and Visa (**V**). Many shops, restaurants and attractions will also accept other cards, including JCB, as well as travellers' cheques issued by a major financial institution (such as American Express).

Prices in this book are given in Chinese *reminbi* (RMB). At the time of going to press exchange rates were around RMB 8.3 to the US dollar or RMB 15 to the pound sterling.

The prices we've supplied should be treated as guidelines, not gospel. If prices vary wildly from those we've quoted, please write and let us know. We aim to give the best and most up-to-date advice, so we always want to know if you've been badly treated or overcharged.

THE LIE OF THE LAND

Shanghai is simply massive but the areas of interest covered by this book are restricted to a manageable few square kilometres of the city centre, either side of the banks of the Huangpu River. This central district is easy to fathom, and small enough to explore on foot. For further details of the city's geography, *see p47*.

Street signs are in both English and Chinese. Because many streets are so long they are often prefixed by 'north', 'south', 'east', 'west' or 'central'. So the main highway Yanan Lu progresses from Yanan Xilu (West Yanan Road) to Yanan Zhonglu (Central Yanan Road) to Yanan Donglu (East Yanan Road). Maoming Lu is either Maoming Nanlu (South Maoming Lu) or Maoming Beilu (North Maoming Lu).

Travelling around on public transport is made difficult by the language barrier, but the metro is partially signed in English so we've included metro details with each listing. For more information on getting around and the various transport options, *see pp214-16*.

TELEPHONE NUMBERS

The international dialling code for China is 86 and the code for Shanghai is 021 (drop the zero if calling from overseas). Follow with the eight-figure number as given in this guide.

Advertisers

ESSENTIAL INFORMATION

For all the practical information you might need for visiting the city, including visa and customs information, advice on disabled facilities and access, emergency telephone numbers and local transport, turn to the Directory chapter at the back of the guide. It starts on page 213.

MAPS

The map section at the back of this guide includes a useful overview map of the city, as well as tiled street maps. Map references throughout this guide indicate the page number and square for every venue. Additional street maps appear within the Sightseeing chapters. There's also a street index on page 250.

LET US KNOW WHAT YOU THINK

We hope you enjoy the *Time Out Shanghai Guide* and we'd like to know what you think of it. We welcome tips for places that you consider we should include in our future editions, and take note of your criticism of our choices. You can email us on guides@timeout.com.

There is an online version of this book, along with guides to 45 other international cities, at **www.timeout.com**.

Londoners take when they go out.

Time Out
London

EVERY WEEK

In Context

History

Gatecrashers, warlords, gangsters and money-makers –
the Shanghai party has been anything but dull.

There are no terracotta warriors or Ming
Dynasty tombs in Shanghai. In fact, beyond
the exhibits in the Shanghai Museum, there's
nothing of antiquity at all, for the simple reason
that the city is too young. For a metropolis of a
comparable age, think Sydney or Los Angeles.
In its relatively short years, however, Shanghai
has experienced enough glory and turbulence
to make many other older cities look positively
two dimensional.

Like other young metropoli, Shanghai is
a hybrid beast created by new blood from
domestic and international immigrants. And
my, how it's grown in such a short time. In
1843 the population stood at around 250,000.
By 1930 it was over three million. Today best
guesses put it at somewhere in the region of
20 million, while forecasts estimate that with
continued urbanisation of the surrounding
rural areas there will be over 30 million
Shanghainese within another decade.

Throughout its history the city has been
shaped by lucrative trade, cheap and plentiful
labour and relative calm compared with the
rest of China. While wars and unrest plagued
interior China for most of the late 19th and
early 20th centuries, Shanghai was largely
safeguarded by business-motivated Chinese-
Western coalitions. This gave the Shanghainese
– the collective name for both Chinese and
resident foreigners – an aloof feeling that they
were impervious to the ills of the rest of China.
Indeed, were they part of China at all?

TRADE, OPIUM AND WAR

Prior to 1842 Shanghai was a prosperous but
slightly isolated Chinese town. Its position on
the Yangtze River delta with a safe harbour on
the tributary Huangpu River guaranteed its
importance as a trading port. Rice, cotton and
other crops were brought to Shanghai to be
carried on barges and sampans up the Yangtze

and its tributaries or to be shipped down the coast and thence inland again along China's extensive canal network.

Shanghai at this time was apparently a pleasant sight: a bustling modestly sized centre of commerce encircled by a wall three and a half miles in circumference. Local leaders had built the city walls in the 16th century to protect themselves from Japanese coastal raiders. On the flat marshy delta that stretched around were numerous fishing and farming villages, but otherwise, the landscape was featureless.

Unlike most cities built upon trade, Shanghai, along with China's other ports, remained exclusively Chinese. It had long been the desire of the ruling Qing Dynasty (1644-1912) to keep its borders sealed from the outside world. Opinion at the Beijing court was that foreigners were uncivilised, thus there could be no reason to interact with them.

Undeterred by Qing isolationism the British asked for permission to trade and even reside in Shanghai under the terms of the peace settlement that ended the First Opium War in 1842. This conflict had centred around the right of the British to import Indian-grown opium into China. Over the preceding decades the British East India Company and other traders had exported Chinese tea, silks, porcelain and other goods to Britain, without having anything of equal value to sell to China. To redress this situation the enterprising, if unprincipled, British decided to capitalise on the Chinese penchant for opium smoking. They introduced an Indian-grown product that was more refined than the Chinese version. In a short spell of time, the balance of trade was reversed.

Unable to curb the increasingly widespread opium addiction among its populace, the Qing court instead concentrated on shutting down the drug industry. Britain responded by sending gunboats under the premise of protecting free trade. The expected results were swift: a few skirmishes on the coast were followed by Chinese acquiescence to all British demands at the 1842 Treaty of Nanking. Among those demands was the British right to trade and reside in five Chinese cities: Ningbo, Amoy, Fuzhou, Guangzhou and Shanghai. In 1843, the first British traders arrived in Shanghai and were allotted 140 acres of muddy riverbank, just north of the walled city.

SETTLING IN

The British called their land the British Settlement, reflecting the fact that it was neither a leased territory nor a government-controlled colony. The muddy stretch of riverfront was named the Bund, a Hindi word the traders brought with them from India. They set up

shop and began trading opium and British manufactured goods in exchange for the exotic oriental goods their home markets desired. These early traders governed themselves under the laws of their own country, a right called extraterritoriality. The US and France jealously claimed the same concessions from the beleaguered Qing court. The Americans settled north of Suzhou Creek while the French were sandwiched in between the British Settlement and the Chinese walled city to the south.

> ### 'The city was a "hardship post", with bitter winters and stifling summers, pestilent mosquitoes and an absence of European females.'

As late as 1848, there were fewer than 100 resident foreigners in Shanghai. Their mudflat settlements resembled the colonial bungalow style favoured in South-east Asia and India. Wide, Roman arch-bordered verandas shaded the buildings from the heat of summer. The city at this time was a 'hardship post', complete with bitter winters and stiflingly hot summers, regular flooding, pestilent mosquitoes and foul stenches, plus an almost complete absence of European females. Because Chinese were not allowed to reside within the settlements, foreign men found sexual solace in service professionals from the Philippines and elsewhere. Otherwise, leisure conformed to the traditional British Empire pursuits of horses and shooting. Early expatriates constructed Shanghai's first racetrack just inland from the Bund (later to be superseded by a larger track on the site that's now Renmin Square).

In spite of the humble form of these early settlements, the pioneers of Asia's largest British trading firms were quick to Shanghai. Jardine & Matheson, Butterfield & Swire, and Hutchison Whampoa all started as competitors in the opium trade. Over time they diversified

Shanghai'd

Shanghai'd, the verb, entered the English language in the 1870s to describe the act of drugging and kidnapping sailors for compulsory service aboard ships bound for China and specifically the treaty port of Shanghai.

into all sectors of Chinese trade. Although tough Scots and Englishmen had founded firms, their Baghdadi-Jewish employees were ultimately to make an equally great impact on business in Shanghai. These were the Sassoons, Kadoories, Hardoons and others, who used their close contacts with the foreign elite and deep understanding of international trends to build Shanghai's first real estate empires (*see below* **The Jewish dynasties**). Their palatial ex-residences and former properties still dot the city today.

REBELS AND REAL ESTATE

Small and under-populated, the foreign settlements found themselves at risk from the rising tide of the Taiping Rebellion. One of the bloodiest conflicts in history, this was a clash between China's imperial rulers and those inspired by Hong Xiuquan, a mystic and 'God's Chinese Son' – a Christian convert. Around 20

to 30 million people are believed to have died. In 1860 and 1862 Taiping forces menaced Shanghai, but were repulsed by British and French expeditionary forces temporarily stationed in the settlements. Their force, combined with eventual support from the Qing court, put an end to the Taipings in 1864.

The rebellion irrevocably altered Shanghai. Before the insurrection, the foreign-controlled part of Shanghai had been dwarfed by the larger Chinese city. By the end of hostilities the reverse was true. Foreign militias had proven their overwhelming strength and ability to protect property and civilians. Not so in the Chinese city where gangsters known as the 'Small Swords', as well as militant factions allied to either Qing or Taiping, were destroying property and terrorising residents. The foreign settlements took pity on the Chinese and offered shelter – but at a price.

The Jewish dynasties

David, Elias and Victor. Or rather, Sassoon, Sassoon and Sassoon. Three men, one family business and, between them, a huge pot of cash. The Sassoons were the first of several Iraqi-Jewish families to arrive in Shanghai, all of which left an indelible impression.

The Sassoon wealth was not of the quick-buck or gold-rush variety. When Victor began to load up his portfolio with lucrative Shanghai real estate in the 1930s, he was continuing a tradition of enterprise that had been upheld by previous generations. The family was from Baghdad but had outposts all over the world, trading in, among other things, cotton and opium. The founder of the business, David Sassoon, had set up a trade axis between Bombay and China. His son Elias improved the business in Shanghai before handing the baton to Victor.

Already a man of some repute due to his extravagant approach to business in Bombay, Victor arrived in the city to great excitement. Shanghai at this time was in cash-rich party mode and Victor upped the ante on the social scene by building the Cathay Hotel (now the Peace Hotel, *see p14* **Peace at the Cathay**) and using its eighth-floor ballroom for a series of legendary soirees. But when World War II struck and the Japanese seized the city, Victor moved elsewhere. The Sassoon fortune eventually passed to Victor's wife, an American who had nursed and wed him in his anecdotage.

The other Iraqi-Jewish families synonymous with Shanghai wealth, the Hardoons and Kadoories, both began on the bottom rung of the Sassoon ladder. Silas Hardoon started as a rent collector for Sassoon & Sons. The job gave him a taste for real estate and, after a few false starts, Hardoon set up his own highly successful business. He won seats on the Municipal Councils of the French Concession and the International Settlement, but remained fascinated by Chinese culture. This aspect of his personality baffled the British and he was perceived as deeply eccentric when he married a Eurasian and took to Buddhism. One visible fruit of his wealth was the Beth Aharon Synagogue near Suzhou Creek, which he built in honour of his father. Later it was used as a shelter for Polish Jews escaping Europe. Unfortunately, it no longer exists.

The head of the Kadoorie dynasty, Elly, was born in Baghdad and started his career in Bombay working for Sassoon & Sons. He was transferred to Shanghai where he became rich through merchant banking, real estate and rubber manufacturing. The Kadoorie family now lives in Hong Kong, using its wealth for good causes. Their most ostentatious legacy in Shanghai is a residence that was once known as the Marble Hall – it survives today as the Children's Palace in the downtown district of Jingan (*see p67*).

Opium – the root of all old China's problems and the solution.

Driven by Chinese demand the cost of an acre of land soared from £50 in 1850 to £20,000 in 1862. Shanghai's first fortunes were amassed by an emerging elite of property barons. Global interest sharpened.

At this time Shanghai's foreign settlements now housed some 300,000. In 1863, alarmed by the Taiping episode, the Americans joined with the British to form one International Settlement. The new unified Settlement governed itself through the auspices of the Shanghai Municipal Council, which was made up of a small number of representatives of British and American landowners. Leaders of the French Concession declined to join the English-speakers, instead formalising their governing body as an extension of the French colonial government in Hanoi. Both the International Settlement and the French Concession took advantage of their superior military strength in the face of Qing weakness to expand their respective territory into the surrounding Chinese countryside. By the early 20th century the two territories occupied no less than 12 square miles.

EARLY LABOUR PAINS

Throughout the second half of the 19th century the International Settlement and French Concession prospered. Increasingly settled

and self-confident, residents built ever more handsome structures backed by an impressive infrastructure. Shanghai boasted not only China's best roads and hotels, but also its first gaslights (1865), telephones (1881), electric power (1882), running water (1884), cars (1901) and trams (1908).

Shanghai's next great change came in the aftermath of the Sino-Japanese war of 1895. Acceding to victorious Japan's terms, the Qing court granted Japan similar rights to those it had allowed the Western powers earlier in the century. Japan, however, asked for one other concession: the right to open factories in Shanghai. The Western powers valued the city for its market and raw materials; the Japanese saw greater potential in its cheap and pliable labour. Other countries copied, taking the line that a concession to one was a concession to all.

The city's Chinese population was employed to spin silk, mill grain, roll cigarettes… Workers' conditions were grim and wages pitiful – so much so that already in 1905 there were the first stirrings of organised unrest. This moment can be seen as the beginning of modern Shanghai – even modern China. On the one hand were the rich foreign capitalists, on the other the masses of uneducated but increasingly organised labourers.

Peace at the Cathay

In much the same way that the landmark Oriental Pearl Tower heralded the awakening of new ambitions for Shanghai in the early 1990s, the Cathay Hotel epitomised 1930s modernity and symbolised the increasing prosperity and importance of Asia's number one metropolis.

The building was the personal vision of Sir Victor Sassoon (*see p12* **The Jewish dynasties**) who, having moved the opium-enriched family fortune from Bombay, set out to transform Shanghai into a modern cosmopolitan city with a spectacular new skyline. The hotel was designed by the British architect 'Tug' Wilson and opened in August 1929.

Almost from its sensational opening night the Cathay became Shanghai's premier rendezvous – the 'Claridge's of the Far East'. Then, as now, the eighth floor was the main public area, in particular the extravagant Chinese grill-room. For many tourists the grill-room provided their only taste of China. Since the mid '20s world cruising had become a fashion for a predominantly rich American clientele. As visitors gingerly alighted from their tenders, the European buildings of the Bund would confound those anxiously looking for the prescribed (and fictional) opium-smoking, pigtailed Chinaman. They were more likely to

bump into a fellow American, wishing to catch up with news from home. Conversely, the Cathay's grill-room (added in 1933), with its dragon-motif ceiling fashioned after door panels from the former imperial palace in Beijing, contained all the treasures they expected to see in China.

The eighth floor also housed the main dining room and ballroom. Rose-tinted curtains and carpets splashed with gold, dull silver and gold walls, white birch furniture, a white maple dancefloor and a liberal show of Lalique lighting fused together to create one of the most beautiful dining rooms in the world. It also provided the setting for Sir Victor's legendary fancy dress parties, which were customarily perverse in nature. He could be seen yielding a whip or cane at his circus or school parties whilst respectable local figures, half-clad, ran amok though the hotel. The ballroom routinely received celebrated callers including Douglas Fairbanks, Ronald Coleman, Charlie Chaplin and, possibly, Noël Coward, although he may have been too busy penning *Private Lives*, which was written in his Cathay suite.

Unfortunately, the heyday of the Cathay was short-lived. Commencing with the bombing incident known as 'Bloody Saturday' in August 1937, the hotel's fortunes fell with those of the city. The parties continued, however, right up to the Japanese occupation of Shanghai in 1941. After the war, the hotel played host to the American and British military, only to be usurped by the Nationalists and made redundant by the Communists. The building resumed its former duty when it was paired with the neighbouring Palace Hotel to become the Peace Hotel in 1956.

As the Peace it hosted 'friendship groups' and official delegations, largely from the Soviet block. The hotel remained open during the Cultural Revolution when, although guests were thin on the ground, staff numbers climbed to over 300. They spent their redundant days being rolled through political and technical education and endured endless hours cleaning and re-cleaning the hotel.

The hotel became commercial again under the aegis of the Jinjiang Group Holding Company following the opening of China to tourists in 1978. While the hotel did not suffer at the hands of the Red Guards, with staff even going as far as to put a plain false ceiling below the dragon designs on the eighth floor, it has suffered some ungracious modernisation in the years since. Perhaps the greatest indignity was the total despoliation of Sir Victor Sassoon's personal suite at the apex of the building in 1995. The hotel remains a popular tourist haunt (*see p32*), and is usually full, even though it is a pale shadow of its former self.

In 1912 the feeble Qing Dynasty gave way to a fledgling republic headed by the revolutionary figure of Sun Yatsen. In short order Sun and his followers were ousted from Beijing by a power-hungry rival and, forming a new Nationalist Party, or Kuomintang, they relocated to the southern city of Canton. Attracted by the safety of the Settlements, Sun also kept a house in Shanghai's French Concession (*see p78*), which he shared with his bride Soong Qingling (*see p19* **Soong of the century**).

THE WHITE RUSSIANS

Shanghai saw no fighting during World War I but 1917 was significant for events that happened thousands of kilometres away but ultimately had great impact on this city. The Communists' victory in the Russian Revolution resulted in the flight of the defeated 'White Russians'. Over 40,000 made their way overland to eastern Siberia and Vladivostok (where they made one of their final stands), which was only a few days' sail from Shanghai. As many as could afford the passage made the Chinese city their new home.

The Russians altered life in various ways. They introduced a new cosmopolitanism with their music, food and fashion. Parts of the French Concession, in particular around the central expanse of Avenue Joffre (now Huaihai Zhonglu), took on a Slavic air with bakeries, dance and music studios, as well as restaurants and cafés. But not all foreigners were pleased with the Russian influence. Many came bereft of belongings and funds and were forced to take the most menial or unsavoury work to survive. The men took jobs as rickshaw coolies and bodyguards, the women as nannies, nightclub hostesses and prostitutes. Some simply begged. Shanghailanders – the city's long-term foreign residents – resented the Russians for destroying the myth of the omnipotent foreigner: for the first time the Chinese could see Caucasians performing the same sort of demeaning tasks that up until then had been exclusively the lot of Asiatics.

COMMUNISM AND EXTERMINATION

Distant Shanghai was also buffeted by one other significant repercussion of the war in Europe. Under the terms of the concluding Treaty of Versailles, the Chinese territories belonging to defeated Germany were to be handed over to Imperial Japan. Offended Chinese student leaders led anti-Japanese and anti-Western strikes accompanied by boycotts of foreign goods. This was part of a general wave of protest that came to be known as the 4 May (1919) Movement. Leftist-leaning leaders of the Movement formed links with international communism and in 1922 Mao Zedong and others held the first meeting of the Chinese Communist Party in a small lane house in the French Concession (*see p74*).

Order in Shanghai was increasingly difficult to maintain for its foreign rulers. Strikes were becoming more disruptive. In 1925 a Japanese foreman shot a striking Chinese worker in a Shanghai textile mill, triggering mass protests on the streets. On 30 May a mob surrounded the headquarters of the Municipal Police hoping to free students held inside; police shot directly into the crowd instantly creating 11 martyrs.

> ## 'Though not exactly prostitutes, the girls would become concubines to the men with money to pay for them.'

Anti-foreign sentiment was channelled into mass support for the Kuomintang under its new leader Chiang Kaishek, who had succeeded Sun Yatsen on his death in 1925. On a mission to unite China and rid the country of imperialists the Kuomintang marched north out of Canton. In 1927 the 'Northern Expedition' reached Shanghai where the Communists, in alliance with the Kuomintang, had organised a city-wide strike. But what the Communists didn't know was that Chiang had struck a deal with arch-capitalist-cum-gangster Du Yuesheng (*see below* **Big Eared Du**) and together the two parties had agreed to do the dirty work of the beleaguered Shanghai Municipal Council and leaders of the French Concession and rid the city of its disruptive Communist elements.

On 12 April 1927 Green Gang thugs and Nationalist soldiers rounded up thousands of suspected Communists and strike leaders and executed the lot. Chiang's motive for partaking in the massacre was to win the support of the wealthy bankers, traders, property barons and industrialists of Shanghai. Job done, the Kuomintang retreated to headquarter in Nanjing where money from Shanghai poured into Nationalist coffers.

SHANG-HIGH LIFE

With the political uncertainties and labour unrest of the 1920s out of the way, the Shanghailanders and Shanghainese could concentrate on what they did best: making money. The average man in the street was untroubled by the collusion of Shanghai municipal leadership, Chinese military power and Shanghai organised crime. All they knew was that the economy was stable. Over the next

Big Eared Du

Du Yuesheng (aka Big Eared Du) was the quintessential Chinese power lord, with his personal financial interest and reputation involved in everything that went on in the French Concession. His not-so-secret triad, the Green Gang, controlled every organised labour group – from beggars, to stevedores and on up – including the Chinese municipal employees. Du also ran a handful of respectable businesses, notably the Chung Wai Bank, one of the largest Chinese financial concerns of the day, but his real power lay in the money he made from his monopoly of the opium business. Du created this empire through his own initiative and beneficial relationships with many powerful men, like Huang Jinrong, the boss of the Green Gang, and Chiang Kaishek, the Nationalist leader.

Whether or not any of Du's activities were legal was not the point; the Chinese Nationalist or foreign 'legal' power in Shanghai respected and sometimes relied upon someone who could control the city.

One of his most impressive feats of negotiation was the Nationalist/Communist split in 1927. Du was able not only to convince the International Settlement's Shanghai Municipal Council and French leadership to agree to aid the Nationalist warlord, Chiang Kaishek, but he ensured Chiang's lightning-like destruction of the Chinese Communists in Shanghai. For his efforts he was allowed even more breadth in his control of the Shanghai underworld.

Du ran his empire from his well-defended properties throughout the former French Concession, including what's now the Donghu Hotel. His power lasted as long as capitalistic ambition was respectable in Shanghai. When the Communists won the battle for control of the mainland in 1949 Du, like others, fled to Hong Kong to escape China's new leadership, who would have remembered his complicity in the 1927 slaughter of their brethren. He lingered in Hong Kong in ill health for another two years, but lavish gangster-like spending and drug habits meant that he died poor.

White Russian girls on stage in Shanghai.

decade, despite unprecedented aggression from Japan just outside Shanghai's borders, cultural and business life within the city was at its apex. In pursuit of profit Shanghai became the most international metropolis ever seen.

An article published in US magazine *Fortune* in 1935 describes Shanghai as 'the fifth city of the earth, the megalopolis of continental Asia, inheritor of ancient Baghdad, of pre-War Constantinople, of nineteenth-century London, of twentieth-century Manhattan.' It ascribes to Shanghai the tallest buildings outside the American continent, 50,000 junks at the city's wharves and the 'greatest concentrated silver hoard on earth'.

This vast wealth is 'justly claimed', according to *Fortune*, by 'just a few thousand white men,' which, broken down by nation, included 9,331 British, 3,614 Americans, 1,776 French and 1,592 Germans.

Life for the Shanghai elite (known as *taipans*) revolved around the club, the most exclusive of which was the great, gloomy Shanghai Club

with its Long Bar, of which, Noël Coward said, laying his cheek on it he could see the curvature of the earth. Then there were the races, dinners, fancy-dress balls and nightclubs, particularly the Chinese dance palaces with their 'taxi dancers' – slim girls clad in *qipaos* slit to the hip whose company on the dancefloor was bought with a ticket. Though not exactly prostitutes, the girls would become concubines to the men with money to pay for them.

During the 1920s and '30s the city became a legend. It was the city of money, gangsters, drugs, warlords, brothels and spy rings but, above all, also of opportunity. In addition to Coward, other famous figures flocked to see for themselves this so-called 'whore of the orient', including Christopher Isherwood, WH Auden and George Bernard Shaw and Charlie Chaplin. Wallis Simpson, the woman for whom a future king of England would give up his throne, was apparently doing the rounds appearing in a series of saucy postcards posing in nothing more than a lifebuoy.

Japanese troops parade along the Bund in 1942.

It was also in the 1920s and '30s that the Bund, the ultimate account of Shanghai's foreign-dominated wealth, took its familiar shape; 1923 saw the completion of the grandoise domed Hongkong & Shanghai Bank building, while the imposing brown-stone cliff-face of the Cathay Hotel was added in 1929 (see *p14* **Peace at the Cathay**).

Even as the rest of the world suffered in the lead-up to World War II, Shanghai experienced its greatest exuberance. Its citizens must have thought that the magic that had so far blessed their city would shield it forever. However, Japan had other ideas.

JAPANESE RULE

China's political weakness – as proved by its inability to form a strong national government since the fall of the Qing Dynasty – was an irresistible temptation to natural resource-poor Japan. It had already seized Manchuria from China in 1931 by creating its puppet 'Last Emperor' regime. From there it menaced Beijing and Tianjin. In 1932 Japanese troops had invaded the Chinese-run parts of Shanghai following anti-Japanese rioting. International condemnation, however, had forced them to relinquish their gains. Events were to prove more dangerous a second time around.

Soong of the century

Charlie (Chiaoshun) Soong was born in 1866 in Hainan, China. At age 14 he stowed away on a sailing ship and began a career as a trader in Boston, Massachusetts. It's here that he developed a strong friendship with an American evangelist who sent the bright Chinese to university and seminary in the American South. Returning to China, Charlie moved to Shanghai. After six years of unrewarding preaching to a sceptical public, he embarked upon a successful career as a bible publisher, a flourmill comprador and machinery agent. In the 1890s he met another Western-educated Chinese, Sun Yatsen, and joined the young revolutionary in his anti-Qing Dynasty movement. The friendship changed Charlie's fortunes and those of his family dramatically.

Charlie's legacy is chiefly remembered for his four children. His three daughters, Soong Ailing, Qingling and Meiling, and his son, TV, were to become some of the most influential people in 20th-century China. Ailing married one of the wealthiest Chinese of the day, HH Kung, who would go on – as would TV Soong – to hold office as China's finance minister. The second daughter, Qingling, married her revolutionary idol Sun Yatsen. Charlie's third daughter wed Chiang Kaishek.

Charlie's second and third daughters continue to inspire intense love and hate, respectively. Qingling was made honorary president of the People's Republic before her death in 1981. Her name graces children's bookstores and countless children's awards bestowed upon the gifted throughout China. Her former home in Shanghai's French Concession (see p84) is something of a shrine. Meiling, on the other hand, earned China's undying enmity for her loyalty to husband Chiang Kaishek, the man responsible for the wholesale massacre of Communists in 1937; the unhappy couple fled together to Taiwan in 1949.

By 1937 Japanese forces had conquered much of northern China. As they menaced Shanghai, Chiang Kaishek mobilised his forces in the Chinese quarters of Shanghai. The ensuing fighting brought heavy casualties to both sides and almost total destruction to Chinese Shanghai (these events form the backdrop to Kazuo Ishiguro's haunting novel *When We Were Orphans*). Death also came to the International Settlement when Chinese pilots mistakenly dropped bombs on the Bund's Palace Hotel and on entertainment complex Great World (see p62), where Chinese refugees fleeing the Japanese had taken shelter – over 1,000 were killed and another 1,000 wounded in the largest ever death toll from a single bomb until Hiroshima.

The Japanese were victorious and this time no amount of international pressure could get them to relinquish their territorial gains. With control over a large part of the International Settlement, Japanese leaders pressured the Municipal Council for a greater role in city politics. The more prescient could see that swallowing only part of Shanghai would not sate Japanese hunger. Many civilians left the city and ominously Britain and America began to scale back their military presence, citing the overwhelming Japanese numerical superiority.

On the morning of 8 December 1941, almost the same time as Japanese bombers were destroying Pearl Harbor, Japanese forces attacked the two remaining gunships of the Anglo-Saxon powers, at moor off the Bund (an event powerfully described in the opening chapters of JG Ballard's *Empire of the Sun*), and invaded the International Settlement. (The French Concession, under the nominal authority of the Nazi-collaborationist French Vichy government, was already technically a Japanese ally.) All Allied nationals – up to 5,000 men, women and children – were required to register with the new rulers. In early 1942 Allied nationals were interned in several detention centres around Shanghai, the largest being at Longhua to the south-west of the city. They were to remain there for the next three years, until the Japanese surrender in the summer of 1945.

Other than the fact that basic staple items became hard to find, life remained much the same for Shanghai's large masses of non-combatant Chinese.

THE CALM BEFORE LIBERATION

Imperial Japan surrendered to the Americans on 15 August 1945. The US navy moved to occupy Japan in late 1945, also taking the reins in Shanghai. During the war both the International Settlement and the French Concession had ceased to exist – control of the areas had passed to Chiang Kaishek. Thus the Americans filled a power vacuum in the first-ever united Shanghai, created by Japan's defeat.

Although the American occupiers were in control of the city for only a year before handing over to Chiang, they left one lasting result: the switch in driving from the left to the right side of the road, bestowed on a surprised public on Christmas Day 1945.

From the end of 1945 until 1948 Shanghai attempted to rebuild its former glory. Returning industrialists invested in new factories and built new homes. However, with the foreigners gone, Shanghai could no longer partition itself off from political changes sweeping the rest of China. By late 1948 Chiang's government was on its last legs, having lost countless military campaigns to the Communists. The Nationalists started to plan for an evacuation to Taiwan, the capitalists headed for Hong Kong. Believers in the 'New China' stayed put. On 25th May 1949, in an event known as the 'Liberation', the Communists marched silently into a Shanghai that had already been abandoned by the Nationalist leadership and its army.

> **'By the early 1970s, when President Nixon visited Shanghai, the city that had enjoyed the first electricity in China was completely dark at nightfall.'**

Most Shanghainese accepted the new state of affairs with their usual pragmatic stoicism. The middle classes – still donning their business suits and hats for another day in the office on the day of Liberation – presumed that nothing much would change. At first what change did occur took place slowly. Those foreign and Chinese industrialists who had chosen not to abandon their businesses found themselves gradually pressed with crippling demands, as comparatively prosperous Shanghai was milked to finance schemes in the rest of China. Then in 1953 the Communists announced that all Shanghai companies were henceforth to be 'owned by the people'. The last group of Westerners left. Surviving dance halls and privately owned villas were converted into 'cultural palaces' and the stylish apparel that the peacocks of the former 'Paris of the East' were known for was traded in for grey unisex tunics and caps.

In 1966 Mao launched his Cultural Revolution aimed at consolidating his own power by exposing those leaders and Party members who did not follow the Maoist line. Shanghai was the headquarters for a group later termed the 'Gang of Four' – Zhang Chunqiao, Yao Wenyuan,

Wang Hongwen and Mao's wife, Jiang Qing. They were fervent supporters of Mao's policies and exerted great control over the activities of the new revolutionary, militant Red Guards who attacked all manifestations of bourgeois Western culture. Before marrying Mao Jiang Qing was a second-rate Shanghai actress and used her new-found power to settle more than a few grudges against people who had snubbed her in the past. Shanghai's streets were renamed (the Bund becoming Revolution Boulevard), buildings were destroyed (notably Jingan Temple, while Xujiahui Cathedral had its spires lopped off) and large numbers of Shanghainese – who the average Chinese viewed as tainted with Western decadent ways – were forced into demeaning public self-criticism sessions before being locked up.

By the early 1970s, when President Nixon visited Shanghai for his historic meeting with Zhou Enlai, the city that had enjoyed the first electricity and cars in China was completely dark at nightfall. Shops that had held all the goods the world could offer were empty. The city's residents were cowed and had to watch what they said in case someone overheard and reported them. The vibrant, decadent capitalist paradise of the 1930s had been put to death.

DEATH AND REBIRTH
The start of the rebirth came in 1976 with the death of Mao. A more moderate Communist Party leadership arrested the reviled Gang of Four. A shell-shocked Shanghai reopened its schools and factories. In 1978 Deng Xiaoping became China's new leader and launched a new era of reform. The benefits were slow to come to Shanghai. The city's industries were still harnessed for the greater good of greater China and over 80 per cent of all revenues were still directed to Beijing. With no investment the city was stagnant. In 1988 the tallest building in town remained the Park Hotel (*see p59*) built in 1934. But there was one event with irrefutable impact: this was the Anglo-Chinese Joint Declaration in 1984 agreeing the handover of the British colony of Hong Kong. Now there would be a city in China that was even more foreign and tainted than Shanghai.

In 1990 the government in Beijing decreed that Shanghai was to become the country's new economic powerhouse. The city government was allowed to use fiscal revenues to develop long-neglected infrastructure. Pudong was set up as an investment-friendly Special Economic Zone and furnished with a first skyscraper, the Oriental Pearl Tower.

While South-east Asia experienced crisis and new-returnee Hong Kong stumbled, the 1990s were a boom time for Shanghai. The skyline

毛主席万岁！

中国共产党万岁！

欢呼毛主席万寿无疆

坚决到底

跟阶级文化大革

伟大领袖毛主席万

革命委员会

囍

Chairman Mao, bestselling author of a little red book.

changed beyond recognition (*see pp27-30* **Architecture**) as the city attempted to make up for, in a decade, the 40 years that it had lost under Communism.

COSTS OF PROGRESS

On the surface, Shanghai at the beginning of the 21st century appears very much like the modern city it would much like to be. The Gap crowd bars and cafés of designer heritage mall Xintiandi and the Rolls Royce dealership at the

po-mo Westin hotel offer visible proof to support all the rosy statistics touting the city's rediscovered economic might. But such rapid growth doesn't come without its associated growing pains and the average citizen is paying for his or her modernity. The rich are most certainly getting richer but at the foot of shining skyscrapers elderly beggars rummage through garbage bins – a city in which everyone once cycled to work in identical blue overalls now has a society that almost rivals

Brazil as the most unequal on earth. While the speed of growth is exhilarating (go away for two weeks and you are guaranteed to find a new building on your return) such rapid urban development comes at the expense of the city's rich architectural heritage as the government seems hell bent on demolishing all pre-war structures to replace them with skyscrapers and urban parkland. Increased wealth is attracting ever increasing numbers of migrants from the hinterland who need to be provided with ever more housing, which, in turn, sends the city sprawling outwards with more roads, more congestion, more pollution. The positive aspect here, though, is that ordinary citizens are aware and do express open concern at the cost of their city's race to wealth.

In such a climate of hyper capitalism and open discussion, it's easy to forget that all of this is being overseen by a Communist government. Clues remain, however, in a fondness for sloganeering and finger-wagging. The red banners have gone but they've been replaced with enamelled plaques warning against the 'Seven no-nos'. These range from SARS-sensible 'No spitting' to the prissy 'No foul language'. According to the government this is necessary to bring Chinese behaviour in line with that of 'global citizens'.

Global citizens? In the headlong rush to the future it seems the government has forgotten Shanghai's past – this is, after all, the place that arguably invented the concept of the modern global city in the first place.

Key events

1684 Following Emperor Kangxi's green light to maritime trade, Shanghai flourishes as a nexus of trade along the Yangtze River.
1839 British and Chinese forces clash in the First Opium War.
1842 The embattled Qing Court signs the Treaty of Nanjing, giving Britain the right to trade and settle in Shanghai.
1843 A British settlement is established on a muddy patch of ground near the Huangpu River and Suzhou Creek. The Brits name it the Bund.
1849 The French negotiate the same rights as the British, and set up the French Concession.
1853 Taiping Rebellion forces capture Nanjing and begin a campaign of violence against Shanghai. Settlement troops defend the city.
1863 The British and American settlements combine to form the International Settlement.
1895 The Qing Court is defeated in the Sino-Japanese war. The Japanese win the right to trade, settle and open factories in Shanghai.
1905 First organised labour protest.
1911 The weak Qing Dynasty concedes power to early Republican forces.
1917 An international decree makes opium illegal; Shanghai is filled with smugglers.
1919 The Treaty of Versailles awards Germany's Chinese territories to Japan. Chinese students protest and spark labour unrest.
1922 The first meeting of the Chinese Communist Party takes place in a small lane house in the French Concession.

1927 Gangster Du Yuesheng strikes a deal with Nationalist leaders to kill off the Communist faction in Shanghai. The coalition is a success and fosters economic prosperity.
1937 Japanese troops take increasing control of China, including Shanghai.
1941 On the same morning they bomb Pearl Harbor, the Japanese seize the International Settlement. The French Concession is already captured by default of the Vichy Government.
1945 American forces occupy Shanghai following Japan's surrender.
1946 Chiang Kaishek's Nationalist government is reinstalled in Nanjing.
1949 The Communist People's Liberation Army marches into Shanghai. Mao forms the People's Republic of China.
1966 The Gang of Four, which includes Mao's wife, instigates the bloody Cultural Revolution.
1976 Mao dies and the Gang of Four is arrested and tried.
1978 Deng Xiaoping pledges to reform and open up the Chinese economy.
1989 The Tiananmen Square anti-government protests leave Shanghai largely unaffected.
1990 Shanghai is earmarked by the government as the economic hope for China. Pudong is declared a Special Economic Zone.
1993 The Oriental Pearl Tower goes up and becomes an icon of the new Shanghai.
2002 The city makes a successful bid to host the 2010 World Expo.
2003 The Maglev, the world's fastest train, goes into service running between Pudong International Airport and the city.

Shanghai Today

The city that wants its future now.

In the early years of the 20th century, the British, American and French made their way to Shanghai to seek their fortunes at the frontier port city famously dubbed the 'whore of the orient'. They built elegant neo-classical buildings, made money for their empires and took beautiful Chinese women as mistresses. Strangely enough, all of these things hold true in Shanghai today. With the rush of foreigners pouring into the city once again, around a century later, it's irresistible to compare the current boom with that of Shanghai's colonialist heyday.

Since emerging from the dark days of the Cultural Revolution in 1976, Shanghai has been on the upswing, and things seemingly get better year after year. Even as the rest of the world experienced economic downturn and the threat of terrorism, Shanghai has continued to enjoy a streak of luck that few other cities can claim. It even managed to escape 2003's SARS scare: as other Chinese cities such as Beijing and Hong Kong took the brunt of the disease, Shanghai remained relatively calm, with much lower infection rates.

EASTERN PROMISE

Shanghai today, as in the past, draws both the high rollers and the disenfranchised. All are trying to escape the traditions and constraints of where they came from. Whether it's a migrant from China's central Sichuan province trying to eke out a living as a butcher or an American selling mobile phones to the world's largest market, Shanghai is a city where everyone is from somewhere else. It's a place where people come to better their lives, whether that means something as modest as making enough money to eat, live and save a few bucks for relatives back in the Chinese countryside or something as ambitious as becoming the next real estate mogul and living the cigar and cognac, Humvee-driving high life.

As a port city, Shanghai has always thrived on contact with the outside world. This has unarguably made the Shanghainese more open-minded than the average Chinese person. They're willing to try new things – particularly if they're Western. While most Chinese shun any kind of cuisine that's not from within their national borders, the Shanghainese will eagerly wait in long lines to sample Mexican fare at somewhere like the recently opened Taco Bell Grande, a sit-down, cloth-napkin version of the American fast-food chain.

BEST FACT FORWARD

It's easy to forget just how rapidly Shanghai has evolved over the past decade. Since the height of colonialism, the city has lived several lifetimes, having survived an invasion by the Japanese, the distrastrous rule of Chairman Mao and the economic reform of President Deng Xiaoping. As China steadily progresses down the road of capitalism, government officials are proud to boast of Shanghai as the nation's home-grown economic powerhouse, one that they can truly claim as their own. (The same can't be said of Hong Kong, which was under British rule during its boom time.)

City officials like to talk about economic growth in percentage terms. But such figures are rarely accurate – don't forget we're still dealing with authoritarians here. Here's a better way of looking at it: a decade ago, the city was beginning to build its first skyscrapers. Now, the city has more than 2,000 buildings of more than 20 storeys, with an average start-to-finish time of two years. Few, if any Shanghainese, owned cars ten years ago – now hundreds of thousands are behind the wheel. Families are moving out of old communal housing allotted through the socialist model of planning and into high-rise buildings. The goal of more affluent families is to buy a second or third home, a phenomenon that many government officials worry is leading to a property bubble.

SHOOTING UP

Shanghai remains connected to its colonial past in a visual sense too. Plane trees that were originally imported from France more than 100 years ago canopy the streets of Puxi, the area west of the Huangpu River. Art deco buildings and European villas dot the city streets. Street vendors push wheelbarrows chock-full of wares and bicyclists whiz by, as if from an earlier era. But there is also visual proof that shows Shanghai moving away from its colonial past. To the foreign visitor, the changes might seem a bit disheartening. But in the eyes of most Shanghainese, the changes are a source of pride. They show that the city, held back during the country's experiment with socialism, is catching up with the rest of the developed world. In Pudong, the area east of the Huangpu River, space-age skyscrapers with gaudy baubles and shiny exteriors occupy prime waterfront lots. Cars and motorcycles now hog much of the road space, leading to congested and polluted streets. On virtually every block, Shanghai's historic architecture is being bulldozed to make way for the latest

Keeping up with the Guinnesses

Given Shanghai's inclination to measure its achievements in speed, height and distance, you'd be forgiven for thinking that it had some sort of an inferiority complex. The city could be content with simply having the fastest train in the world, the German-built Maglev. Its top speed reaches 430kmh (266mph), easily surpassing the Japanese bullet train (*see p90* **Badly trained**). But apparently, that's not enough and other records are being chased.

The problem is that other cities are spoiling the fun. Take, for example, the plan to build the world's largest Ferris wheel. The city announced its plans in the summer of 2002 to build a super-sized fairground ride 200 metres (656 feet) high in time for the Shanghai World Expo in 2010. The Ferris wheel will be taller than the current record holder, the London Eye, by 65 metres (213 feet). Little more than a year after the Shanghai plan was announced, Beijing said that it has decided to build a bigger wheel.

A Shanghai contender for the world's longest bridge, spanning 35 kilometres (21 miles) over a bay, began construction in July 2003 and is estimated to cost $1.9 billion. But engineers should have taken out the tape measures before beginning. In Louisiana the bridge that holds the current Guinness World Record is a few thousand metres longer at 38.6 kilometres (24 miles).

Shanghai broke ground last year with what's intended to be the tallest skyscraper in the world, the Shanghai World Financial Center. The building, which was originally planned to be 94 storeys and 460 metres (1,510 feet) tall, was revised so that it will top out at 101 storeys and 472 metres (1,548 feet). But even with the growth spurt, the skyscraper will still be shorter than the recently completed Taipei Financial Centre, which is 509 metres (1,670 feet) high.

Shanghai may not have the world's tallest or longest anything, but it certainly sets a record for simply trying.

commercial or residential high-rise development. Investors from all over Asia and now the West are pouring into Shanghai to invest in real estate and other ventures.

In the government's ideal model of urban planning, every piece of land would be given a specific function. Pudong's Lujiazui district is the most obvious example of a newly invented zone, with officials concentrating on developing it into the city's new financial centre with wide, curving streets that make it unfriendly to pedestrians. In other parts of Pudong, former parcels of farmland have been zoned into 'high-tech parks' with clusters of software and biotech campuses. Meanwhile, in the centre of the city, certain streets have been designated 'art streets' while others are promoted as 'bar streets', where pubs blare out Top 40 hits and young women wear dresses that double as beer advertisements (or at least they do until some government official buys a house in the neighbourhood, decides it's too noisy and indulges in a little rezoning).

Tear it down, build it up.

PROTEST VOICES

It is slightly ironic that the changes Shanghai is experiencing are a result of the city's growing status on the world scene, aided by the rush of foreigners, and yet it is the foreigners who are decrying the city's transformation. The number of foreigners is still small – only 80,000 residents hold overseas passports in a city estimated to have a population of anything between 16 and 20 million. But, like nearly everywhere else in the developing world, foreign influence on Shanghai – through the media, new products and direct contact – is rapidly transforming the city and keeping the city's identity in constant flux.

> **'Despite authoritarian rule, Shanghai residents enjoy more personal freedoms than in the West.'**

Still, it's the Chinese not the foreigners who are running the place. The Shanghai government likes to say that it's kinder and more transparent than other Chinese local governments, many of which are notoriously corrupt. But there's evidence to the contrary, particularly on the issue of relocating residents in the name of urban renewal. The government claims that it is properly reimbursing residents for being relocated. Most residents disagree, claiming the money is rarely enough to buy a comparable home. Critics accuse officials of working with property developers to evict residents in the city centre, where land is increasingly in demand. Last year, a lawyer was sentenced to three years in prison for daring to defend residents who had been evicted from their homes.

TIES AND BLIND EYES

Despite the authoritarian rule, Shanghai residents enjoy a fair amount of freedom in everyday life, with fewer laws or enforcement of laws that limit personal freedom in the West. Cars or motorcycles rarely abide by traffic rules. Many residents work under the table, get paid in cash and avoid paying taxes. Prostitution, though officially outlawed, happens in every pink-lit barber shop with the girls in push-up bras only doubling as hairdressers. Cannabis is for sale at some restaurants around the city, and patrons at swanky nightclubs regularly do cocaine in the toilets and ecstasy on the dancefloors.

Every so often, the police will get fed up, afraid that the city's international image is being tarnished, and initiate a feeble drive to crack down on a particular problem. Many of these crackdowns turn out to be comical. At one point, officials in 2001 outlawed the hanging of laundry from windows because they thought the sight of grandma's bloomers hanging from apartment buildings would be unsightly to foreigners. That law was never enforced, and seems to have quietly disappeared.

Mini-crackdowns aside, most citizens have a large amount of personal freedom so long as they choose not to engage in political affairs or activities that 'undermine the authority of the Communist Party', in the words of officials.

Fortunately for the government, most of the Shanghai populace remains startlingly apolitical, choosing to concentrate on making money, not trouble.

THE LURE OF BIG BUSINESS

As was true of the old colonial days, businessmen are in Shanghai to take advantage of China's cheap labour costs. But these days, they're coming from an array of places other than the typical Western nations. Japanese companies constitute 40 per cent of one the businesses in one industrial area of Shanghai. Nearly a dozen Indian information technology companies have set up shop in the port city, hoping to bring their successful out-sourcing model to China. In the nearby town of Yiwu, buyers from places as far-flung as the Middle East, Africa and Australia mingle and strike deals for bulk orders of any sort of widget you could imagine.

Foreigners in the 1930s came for trade and that's still what makes the city tick. It's easier to make business partners here than friends. Practically every lunch is a business lunch, complete with the trading of business cards (this is a city in which business cards are traded like hellos). Old retired men check their stocks at local trading centres that look like the off-track betting parlours in America. At bookstores, the hottest selling books fly off the business and management shelves with translated titles such as *Rich Father, Poor Father*, or *Who Moved My Cheese?*. Show a Shanghainese person something you bought and the typical response is 'Where'd you buy that? I can get it cheaper.'

EMPEROR'S NEW CLOTHES

The contrast between those who have struck it rich since Shanghai's economic revival and those who have not is growing ever more apparent. Just outside Plaza 66, where name brands such as Hermès and Louis Vuitton have set up shop, homeless beggars approach pedestrians, waving paper cups. Across from Xintiandi, a new complex of high-end shops and restaurants, families live in quarters the size of closets. The combined monthly salary of a family might cover two courses at one of Xintiandi's ritzy restaurants.

Other urban ills have begun to appear – increasing pollution, crime, traffic and, most worryingly, unemployment. The relaxing of the *hukou*, or residential permit, system nationwide means that more rural folk have been flooding into Shanghai looking for work. Meanwhile, middle-class Shanghainese workers are getting laid off, as nearby factories are shut down and moved to the countryside. Recent university graduates, no longer the rarity they once were, complain that it's increasingly difficult to find jobs that match their skill levels.

But still, most Shanghainese would say that life has got better year on year since China began its economic reforms. Since that time, Shanghai has been experiencing a renaissance that far surpasses the boom of the colonial era of the 1920s. In fact, the city's current flush has also been compared to the California Gold Rush of the mid 19th century. So will this bubble burst? It's anybody's guess. Given China's growth rate, which hovers at around eight per cent a year, and the country's increasing engagement with the rest of the world, Shanghai's fortunes will rise so long as China remains in the world's spotlight. And that could be a very long time indeed.

A city driven by commerce.

Architecture

It's a boom time for building, but the jury's still out on the architecture.

Shanghai is one huge construction site. Of its 3,924 square kilometres (1,515 square miles), it seems there isn't anywhere that the cranes don't lean into or crowd the cityscape. In fact, during the latter half of the 1990s it was reckoned that Shanghai laid claim to around one third of all the world's high-rise construction sites. Now, with more than 12,000 buildings over 18 storeys, including several of the planet's tallest structures either already built or under construction, it would seem that Shanghai's hopes to be a new 'world city' have indeed been realised. This is not the ossified city that greeted the first visitors to the newly emerging China back in the 1980s.

Unfortunately, construction is not necessarily the same thing as architecture. A good number of critics – and the general populace – see Shanghai's new skyline as an eyesore. It's not hard to see their point. There is an oft repeated, though possibly apocryphal story about one of the old Concession-era villas being designed by the 12-year-old daughter of its millionaire owner: well, it looks like the city might have taken this unorthodox method as its guiding principle. How else to explain the vast number of ridiculous, nay grotesque, skyscrapers topped variously by crowns, flying saucers, giant balls, pincers (as at the Tomorrow Square building, *above*)…? And the sky-high pile-up of silver and pink balls that is the landmark Pearl Oriental TV Tower? A pre-pubescent with a box of crayons is about the only credible way to explain it.

There is a degree of inevitability to all this. Property investment in any boomtown results in low-budget projects designed for quick returns. And, as is true of all socialist state-planned economies, development in Shanghai is subject to an intense design-approval process, which in this case favours simplicity over innovation. Added to which, architecture, while respected, is a young profession in China.

It seems that Shanghai is committing the same ugly development mistakes made by the West in the 1950s and the rest of East Asia in

Ladislaus Hudec

In 1918 a young Hungarian, Ladislaus Hudec, escaped from a Siberian prison camp and came to Shanghai. Trained as an architect in what was then Czechoslovakia, he began his new life in this new city at an American architecture firm, RA Curry. At this time there were fewer than 20 architectural practices in the city and, given the wealth of building work around, it wasn't long before Hudec was striking out on his own.

Although his name is little known outside of East Asia, Hudec was hands-down Shanghai's most remarkable pre-war architect. His meticulous attention to detail and human comfort – wide stairwells, high ceilings, multi-planar views – bucked the local trend for building functional boxes and slapping a bit of decoration on the outside. He also eschewed the easy route of repetitive projects for a few choice clients and instead cultivated an extraordinarily diverse portfolio including villas and mansion blocks, churches and hospitals.

The superior nature of Hudec's work has ensured that much of it has survived, notably the **Moore Memorial Church** (*see p60*) and the **Park Hotel** (*see p59*), both on Renmin Square, and the **Museum of Arts and Crafts** building in the French Concession (*see p82*).

Shanghai's present focus on architecture has brought the Hungarian latter-day fame too, and he's one of the few pre-Liberation Westerners who is officially lauded by the Shanghai People's Government. Fame, though, only counts for so much; the house he designed for himself and his family was razed to make way for a flyover in 1998.

---

the '60s and '70s. Thus the city is becoming stuck with an increasing number of bathroom-tiled towers that look shabby as soon as they are constructed, with interiors fashioned from brittle concrete and buckling wood, and uninsulated structures that waste dam-fulls of electric power in both summer and winter. However, there are some notable improvements being made to this state of affairs, and the city's new-builds should only get better.

Any discussion of architecture in Shanghai is, thankfully, not limited to modern blunders. The city is a repository of brick and stone treasures, mostly from the Settlement era (late 19th century through to the 'Liberation' by the Communists in 1949), but also from the recent past. These riches can roughly be divided into three categories: the commercial centre of the Bund; pre-Liberation residential architecture (including humble *shikumen* terraces and lavish villas); and the better of the towers that are currently adding their flourishes to Shanghai's signature skyline.

THE BUND

The Bund, the waterfront commercial centre of pre-Liberation Shanghai and the current real estate hotspot, has been witness to much of the city's turbulent history. Built in the first half of the 20th century by Shanghai's industrial magnates, it was intended to be the social and financial centre of all China. The buildings continue to impress. Erected between 1906 and 1937, they display most early 20th-century Western architectural styles, with neo-Gothic structures abutting beaux-arts blocks and vertical, stucco-covered art deco squeezed against neo-classical piles of granite.

In further disregard for local architectural traditions, whereas most Shanghai structures face south for feng shui reasons – as well as to catch precious winter sunlight – the Bund's proud façades face east towards the city's harbour, which was the entry point for most newcomers to the pre-war city.

> **'When it comes to development, the favoured method is simply to send in the bulldozers.'**

These waterfront monoliths were built with the best engineering methods of the time. Some are early examples of steel-frame construction, and they all float: Shanghai has no shallow bedrock like Manhattan and the Bund's buildings sit on brick rafts bedded in mud. Construction firms exacted strict control over all details, importing Italian artisans to handcraft marble and terrazzo, and English or American engineers to install plumbing, electricity and heating. Rare indigenous elements on this most prestigious bit of real estate were limited to the Chinese renaissance-style Bank of China, with its lattice-work façade and blue-tiled cap, and to the usage of 'Shanghai concrete', a local cocktail of natural materials containing a high percentage of pebbles, which was heavily employed in non-exterior structural elements.

Despite the widely held view that the buildings of the Bund were first and foremost 'architectural hymns to white omnipotence' (as denounced by Harriet Sergent in her city biog, *Shanghai*), post-Liberation city rulers let them stand (although they also left them to rot). In more recent times, the city municipality has gone a step further and decided to reverse the neglect. This prompted heated public debate, especially when city planners applied for UNESCO-sponsored World Heritage status for the Bund in 2003. Plans are now under way to renovate the entire promenade. Morbid state-owned enterprises are slowly being shunted to new digs elsewhere, as municipal leader/landlords let the buildings to more dynamic local companies and overseas conglomerates. Most surprisingly, officials have announced plans to lease several properties to foreign-controlled upscale hotels. One project will construct a Bund museum/park in the remaining vacant spot along the waterfront, between the former Bank of Communications and the Shanghai Gold Exchange. The city has accepted designs from four local architect firms for this project; the final selection had not been made at the time of going to press. Clearly, the Bund will continue to be a keystone in Shanghai's architectural landscape (*see p52* **To infinity and the Bund**).

Shikumen lane in central Shanghai.

SHIKUMEN LANES

Shanghai has long been compact and densely populated. Even during the Concession era, when Shanghai presented a Westernised face to the world, most of the residents were Chinese – and there were a lot of them. Urban planners and developers had to find a way to incorporate their requirements, such as ancestor-worship halls and south-facing gardens, into dense, middle-class neighbourhoods. The result was the *shikumen*, or 'stone-gated' house, grey and brown two-storey tenements arranged in terraces. The appearance is more northern England mill town than China. The houses typically had five rooms upstairs and five down; family members had the best rooms, while servants and paying lodgers took the undesirable north-facing rooms and roomlets off rear staircases. Gardens were often minuscule and paved.

Because they were so densely squeezed together, developers built the *shikumen* in south-facing rows with common bathing facilities at the ends of the lanes. The *shikumen* model was standard throughout Shanghai, and by the 1930s almost every part of town was gridded with them.

Sadly, economic pressure to develop Shanghai has had a harsh impact on the *shikumen* lanes. In spite of the fact that most Shanghainese were born and raised in these neighbourhoods, little has or is being done to protect this key part of the city's shared heritage. Most are overcrowded and poorly maintained by non-owning occupants (most residents only have usage rights from the government) which only favours the pro-development lobby. And when it comes to development, the favoured method is simply to send in the bulldozers. Finding creative ways to preserve the architecture is rarely an option, although there is the odd exception, notably **Xintiandi**, where several dilapidated blocks of housing have been overhauled and restyled to create a ritzy mixed-use development that even incorporates a small museum devoted to *shikumen* living. Even here, however, there was no attempt at retaining the original community and tens of thousands of long-term residents were evicted in the process. To see a good example of *shikumen* in their original state, visit 200-303 Maoming Beilu, which is between Nanjing Xilu and Weihai Lu, close to Shimen Yilu metro station.

VILLAS AND MANSION BLOCKS

While *shikumen* were built for the more modest of Shanghai's residents, the wealthy – both Chinese and Western – preferred much more privacy. In the days when Shanghai was less crowded, tycoons built palatial mansions within the city and on its western fringes. But even as late as the interim period between the close of World War II and the Communist Liberation, the über-rich were building detached, multi-storey residences on expensive downtown property. Reflecting both the occupants' desire for comfort and to appear more Western than they perhaps were, these houses were almost exclusively built in European styles. (For the movie of JG Ballard's *Empire of the Sun* the producers had no problems finding a double for the author's childhood Shanghai home in the leafy English suburbs around Shepperton Studios where the film was being shot.)

By the 1930s, not only had Shanghai become less safe for the wealthy – with kidnapping rampant and military skirmishing around the edges of the International Settlement – but its urban elite now considered low-maintenance, high-rise living as the height of fashion. Introduced in the early 1920s, the mansion block, filled with middle-class and upscale flats, became immensely popular in the following decade. All were built with lifts and detached servants' rooms leading off back stairwells. Today there are over 80 surviving examples of pre-war mansion blocks. Interestingly, these almost completely ignored the feng shui principles followed for *shikumen* and villas; instead of a south-facing garden orientation, most blocks face street intersections. Although this is supposed to bring bad luck for the residents, the buildings remain in fair shape.

Styles vary. The **Embankment Building** (400 Beisuzhou Lu), built by Sir Victor Sassoon in the early 1930s, is English Streamlined Moderne, with nautically inspired curves and railings and even a crowning tower that suggests a captain's bridge. Further striking examples include the stepped art deco masterpieces of **Shanghai Mansions** (*see p50*), on the north side of Suzhou Creek, and **Hamilton House** (*see p54*), on Fuzhou Lu near the Bund. Most of these residences are privately owned and thus well preserved.

SIGNATURE SKYLINE

Shanghai's better examples of modern architecture are mostly skyscrapers. The best by far is the **Jinmao Tower** (*see p89*) in Pudong, the new business district east of the river. Although designed by a French firm, the building incorporates oriental pagoda-like geometric detailing in its protruding eaves, stepped structure and delicate roof. Feng shui masters were also drafted in to help with the planning and design – there are, for example, 88 floors because the sound of the word eight in Chinese also sounds like the word for good luck.

Under construction since August 1997 on a site next to the Jinmao is what, when finished, was to be the highest building in the world, the **Shanghai World Financial Centre** (or Mori Building). Was to be because its 101-storey height has already been pipped by a Taipei building with a higher antenna. But that doesn't change the fact that it is a stunning design (by new York-based Kohn Pederson Fox Architects) of a twisting prism with a giant cylindrical hole punched out of the tapering top to relieve wind pressure. It's scheduled for completion in October 2007.

> ### 'It took New York 50 years to achieve its distinctive Manhattan skyline; Shanghai might do it in ten.'

Less than a mile from the construction site that is the SWFC is the **Jiushi Headquarters** building, the first by Norman Foster and Partners on the Chinese mainland. Completed in 2001, it's a 40-storey tower with a curving glass frontage overlooking the Huangpu River.

Over on the other side of the water, top American architect and designer of Disney hotels, Michael Graves, recently masterminded the renovation of a 10,000 sqm historic structure built in 1916 on the Bund. Christened **Three on the Bund** it features two striking atria and a grand stairway clad in alabaster. Nearby Renmin Square also has a number of unique structures. These include the circular **Shanghai Museum** and, on the north side of Nanxing Xilu, the Dutch-designed, cantilevered **Ciro's Tower**, the design of which cleverly references a Settlement-era nightclub of the same name, which formerly occupied the site.

There's plenty more to come. In 2010 Shanghai will host the World Expo and before then entire swathes of the city will have been reshaped and remodelled: a shipyard will become a yachting basin, an old quarter of *godowns* (warehouses) will become an ocean-going passenger terminal, and the city's lesser riverbanks will be remade as parks with abutting multi-functional structures.

Just as in the early 20th century, when some of the most adventurous architects found their way to Shanghai (for example, Ladislaus Hudec, *see p28*), the early years of the 21st century have the appearance of being an historic time for the shaping of the city. As one visiting architect commented, it took New York 50 years to achieve its distinctive Manhattan skyline; it looks like Shanghai might do it in ten. Carbuncles and all.

Where to Stay

Where to Stay

Shanghai doesn't really do budget, so pay your money and pick your view.

Shanghai's hotel scene is on a roll. The single-digit hotel occupancy figures of the 2003 SARS crisis are now a nightmare long over. In the current heady climate, peak season runs for a full 365 days a year.

But booming doesn't mean dynamic. Hotels are emphatically geared towards the business traveller, and new properties overwhelmingly take the form of foreign-managed four- and five-stars, with a few state-owned chains just to make the competition look good. Alternatives are few. There are a handful of revamped golden oldies, notably the **Peace Hotel** and the **Metropole**, but standards of service fail to live up to the august surrounds and rooms show their age.

Mid-range and budget travellers are poorly catered for. Most of the hotels in these lower price brackets are Chinese run and very often unattractive by Western standards – in the following pages we list the best of what's available, but it's a poor showing.

Part of the problem is that the idea of small, independently run hotels has yet to gain currency. Only as recently as late 2003 did Shanghai get its first boutique accommodation, in the form of the **Old House Inn**, a very attractive little place that makes great use of a traditional *longtang* (alley) house. Its instant popularity suggests that it may only be a matter of time before other investors follow suit.

Much of the city's accommodation is in the area of the Bund or in the neighbourhood of the French Concession. The former is convenient for the Old City, Renmin Square and the business district of Pudong, just across the water, while the latter is good for dining and nightlife. Be warned, grinding traffic can make a room in the wrong part of town a real frustration.

The best Hotels

For old-school luxury
The **Portman Ritz-Carlton** – impeccable service and delicious food. *See p39.*

For boutique shelter
The **Old House Inn**, a converted lane house, puts the chic into antique. *See p42.*

For the sky-high life
88 storeys into the clouds and unbelievable river views at the **Grand Hyatt**. *See p44.*

For plain sailing
The **Captain's Hostel** – straight-cut budget digs close to the river. *See p35.*

For escaping the madness
Soak up the calm and sophistication at art deco gem **#9**. *See p42.*

For business class
The **Westin** has more deluxe facilities than you can shake a briefcase at. *See p34.*

For the visitors' book
Madame Mao loved **Taiyuan Villa**. *See p43.*

For the city pulse
Top bars, restaurants and shops are a room key's toss from **88 Xintiandi**. *See p41.*

BOOKING INFORMATION

Given the high occupancy rates, booking a room in advance is absolutely essential. Hotels in the budget category – and even some of the mid-range places – are unlikely to have an English-speaking reservation line. The best bet is to email where possible, or to fax with a request that the hotel acknowledges receipt. Alternatively, for ease of booking and some genuinely good accommodation rates try **www.english.ctrip.com**.

In this guide the listings are divided into the following categories: **Expensive** upwards of $200 (RMB 1,660) for a standard double room; **moderate** $60-$200 (RMB 500-1,660); and **budget** under $60 (RMB 500). We give rates in US dollars for ease of reference, although bills will be presented in RMB. Payment can usually be made in RMB, dollars or any other hard currency. In most hotels in the moderate and expensive categories, room rates are subject to a 15 per cent surcharge.

The Bund

Expensive

Peace Hotel
20 Nanjing Xilu, by Zhongshan Dongyilu (6321 6888/ fax 6329 0300/www.shanghaipeacehotel.com). Metro Henan Lu. **Rates** $108-$160 double; $230-$900 suite. **Credit** MC, V. **Map** p243 J4.

Westin.
See p34.

Shanghai's most famous hotel claims an illustrious history of decadence and debauchery (*see p14* **Peace at the Cathay**). But these days the state-run Peace is something of a washout. Rooms overlooking the river are OK but many others face into the internal courtyard with its pollution-darkened walls and wind-whipped trash. And while the lobby remains elegant, the top-floor ballroom has suffered a disastrous revamp. The house restaurants should also be given a miss. Staff are generally scowling and uninterested and the service is reputedly extremely poor. Persistent rumours link the Peace with a takeover from one of the top international chains but until then we recommend popping in for a drink on the rooftop terrace or catching the jazz band at the Hotel Bar (*see p177*), which proudly proclaims the average age of its musicians as 75, and then departing to a more welcoming bed elsewhere.
Hotel services *Bar. Business services. Concierge. Disabled: adapted rooms. Gym. Parking. Restaurant.* **Room services** *Air-conditioning. Internet access: wirelss. Mini-bar. Room service. TV: satellite.*

Westin

Bund Centre, 88 Henan Zhonglu, by Guangdong Lu (6335 1888/fax 6335 2888/www.westin.com/shanghai). Metro Henan Lu. **Rates** $320-$345 double; $395-$750 suite. **Credit** AmEx, DC, MC, V. **Map** p242 H4.

Part of the Bund Centre complex (dominated by a central 50-storey tower with a crown on top), the Westin fills the pair of smaller (26 floors) secondary towers with 301 guest rooms and suites, plus long-term residences. It's the stylish end of corporate, and carries off the business of bed and board with panache. The dramatic main atrium turns on the razzle dazzle with pertrified palms, mirror pools and a Vegas-style cantilevered glass staircase with computer-programmed lighting. Subtle it ain't. Rooms are done out in cherrywood and come with heavenly beds and big, big bathrooms fitted with rainforest showers. Italian restaurant Prego does great pizzas, Eest serves excellent Chinese, Japanese and Thai, while the Stage restaurant hosts the most popular brunch in town (*see p110*). Also on the premises is the Banyan Tree spa (*see p172*).
Hotel services *Bar. Business services. Concierge. Disabled: adapted rooms. Gym. Parking. Restaurants. Spa. Swimming pool (indoor).* **Room services** *Air-conditioning. Internet access: broadband. Mini-bar. Room service. TV: satellite.*

Moderate

Panorama Hotel

53 Huangpu Lu, by Wuchang Lu (5393 0008/www.panorama-sh.com). **Rates** $110-$170 double; $120-$190 suite. **Credit** AmEx, DC, MC, V. **Map** p243 K3.

A modern four-star, affiliated with the Accor group, the Panorama is aptly named: its riverside site affords excellent views over the water toward Pudong and the Bund. Unfortunately, these tend to

be monopolised by the suites, which come decked out with Persian-style carpets, comfortable sofas and, in the bathrooms, raised bathtubs on white marble bases that shoot out strong jacuzzi jets. The hotel also has serviced apartment suites. It's a swish, well-designed place with a complete range of services and offers a good deal for the money – the only drawback is the location, north of Suzhou Creek and not convenient for anywhere except the cruise ship terminal.
Hotel services *Bar. Business services. Gym. Parking. Restaurant. Sauna.* **Room services** *Air-conditioning. Internet access: broadband. Mini-bar. Room service. TV: satellite.*

Seagull Hotel

60 Huangpu Lu, by Wuchang Lu (6325 1500/www.seagull-hotel.com). **Rates** $99 double; $150 double or suite with river view. **Credit** AmEx, DC, MC, V. **Map** p243 K3.

Right on the river's edge just east of the Garden Bridge, rooms at the Seagull come with excellent views of the Huangpu River and its traffic, as well as Pudong and the Bund skyline. So who cares if the hotel's public spaces are decked out in a rather naff '70s style with white marble and gold? Standard rooms are more restrained with simple pastel colour schemes (suites, by contrast, are overloaded with busy wallpaper and taupe-coloured faux-Victorian furniture). Business suites come with PCs and printers. The hotel is often referred to as the Epson because of the neon sign on the roof. See the review of the Panorama, above, for comments on the location.
Hotel services *Bar. Business services. Gym. Parking. Restaurant. Swimming pool (indoor).*
Room services *Air-conditioning. Internet access: broadband. Mini-bar. Room service. TV: satellite.*

JW Marriott. *See p37.*

Shanghai Mansions

20 Beisuzhou Lu, by Wusong Lu (6324 6260/
fax 6306 5147/www.broadwaymansions.com).
Rates $116-$155 double; $130-$167 double with
view; $158-$218 suite. **Credit** MC, V. **Map** p243 J2.
Unlike other historic Shanghai buildings (for the
colourful life and times of this former mansion block,
see p50), this one has not yet been overwhelmed by
taller skyscrapers. Even sandwiched between the
raised highway of Wusong Lu and the girder frame
of the Garden Bridge it remains an imposingly solid
affair. Sadly, as is often the case, the interior has
been stripped of dignity and appears to have been
made over by somebody's half-sighted octogenarian
aunt. If you do stay here (and again, it's a fringe location), insist on a Bund view, as rooms to the rear
overlook nothing more than asphalt and concrete.
Hotel services *Bar. Business services. Gym.*
Parking. Restaurant. **Room services** *Air-*
conditioning. Internet access: broadband. Mini-bar.
Room service. TV: satellite.

Budget

Captain's Hostel

37 Fuzhou Lu, by Sichuan Zhonglu (6323 5053/fax
6321 9331/www.captainhostel.com.cn). Metro Henan
Lu. **Rates** $6.60 dormitory; $54-$66 double; $145
suite. **Credit** (doubles & suites only) DC, MC, V.
Map p243 J4.
This is just about the only proper backpackers' in
town. While there are a handful of cheapo flop-
houses around, this is the only place where the
words Lonely Planet will elicit a glimmer of recognition. The place is simple but clean, rooms basic
but smart. The dormitories each have several sets

of bunk beds and share bathroom facilities, which
include hot showers. The doubles are equivalent to
those found in any comparable mid-range hotel – ie
they come with en suites, air-con and all other con-
veniences. The location is grand, an attractive 1920s
block just a sailor's hornpipe from the Bund and not
much further to the Old City, Nanjing Lu or Renmin
Square. There's a decent top-floor bar, Noah's (*see*
p120), on-line terminals in the foyer and the management rents bikes. Nautical, but nice.
Hotel services *Bar. Business services. Internet access.*
Restaurant. **Room services** *Air-conditioning. TV.*

JJ Inn

33 Fujian Nanlu, by Jingling Zhonglu (6253 5577/
www.jj-inn.com). Metro Henan Lu. **Rates** $23 single;
$28 double. **Credit** MC, V. **Map** p242 H5.
JJ Inn has multiple locations around town but we
favour this one for its strategic siting between the
Bund and the Yu Gardens. With a slogan in the
lobby announcing the chain's intention to 'create a
VIP experience for the masses', the JJ is pitching to
the budget-conscious Chinese business traveller. It's
a VIP experience that stops short of red-carpet treatment but it does stretch to clean, well-managed
establishments. Decor is functional, amenities simple
and the beds are hard by Western standards, but the
price and location are certainly crowd pleasing.
Hotel services *Business services. Payphone.*
Restaurant. TV. **Room services** *Air-conditioning.*
Room service.

Metropole Hotel

180 Jiangxi Zhonglu, by Fuzhou Lu (6321 3030/
fax 6329 8662/www.metropolehotel-sh.com). Metro
Henan Lu. **Rates** $36-$96 double. **Credit** MC, V.
Map p243 J4.

While not as famous as its sibling, the nearby Peace, this 1932 hotel, just two blocks inland from the Bund boasts a strikingly angular exterior fit for Fritz Lang's *Metropolis*. Unfortunately, the lobby is both poky and chintzy; rooms are also on the small side and have been renovated into blandness. They're nevertheless comfortable. The cellar bar, with its heavy wooden tables and dim lighting, still looks every bit the old colonial den, and it is sometimes used as a film set – hotel guests (mainly Chinese) are occasionally invited to ham it up as extras.

Hotel services *Bar. Business services. Gym. Internet access. Laundry. Parking. Restaurant. Swimming pool.* **Room services** *Air-conditioning. TV: satellite.*

Pujiang Hotel

15 Huangpu Lu, by Garden Bridge (6324 6388/fax 6324 3179/www.pujianghotel.com). **Rates** $6.60 dormitory; $50-$82 double; $106 'celebrity' room. **Credit** MC, V. **Map** p243 K3.

Shanghai's perennial backpacker favourite was once the haunt of the champagne set. Then it was called the Astor House Hotel and held tea dances in the clover-shaped Winter Garden ballroom. The city's first electric lights and the first telephone also debuted at the Astor House. The lobby displays B&Ws of distinguished former guests (both Charlie Chaplin and Albert Einstein boarded here), and staff are knowledgeable on local history. Sadly, recent decades of guests are more likely to have been Dirk from Copenhagen on a six-month trip round the world and Shaz looking for work teaching English to fund the coming winter in Chang Mai. Dorms and double rooms retain some original Victorian detailing and the place is well maintained overall.

Hotel services *Bar. Internet access. Parking. Restaurant.* **Room services** *Air-conditioning. TV.*

Xinxietc

*398 Beijing [...]
2888). Met[...]* **Credit** Am[...]

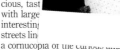

A modern [...] close to the [...] cious, tast[...] with large [...] interestin[...] streets lin[...] a cornucopia of the curious and [...]

Some of the architecture around here, in the back streets behind the Bund, though faded is still quite striking. Note that most of the hotel staff do not speak English, but there is usually someone around who can help with translation problems.

Hotel services *Bar. Business services. Gym. Parking. Restaurant.* **Room services** *Air-conditioning. Internet access: broadband. Mini-bar. Room service. TV: satellite.*

Renmin Square

Expensive

JW Marriott

Tomorrow Square, 399 Nanjing Xilu (5359 4969/ fax 6375 5988/www.marriotthotels.com/shajw). **Metro** Renmin Park or Square. **Rates** $320-$380 single/double; $470-$490 suite. **Credit** AmEx, DC, MC, V. **Map** p242 F4.

Opened on 1 October 2003, the Marriott occupies the upper part of the 60-storey rocket ship that is the Tomorrow Square development on the north-west corner of Renmin Square (a location convenient for just about everywhere). The lobby and check-in are

Bath before bed

Scrubbing up is the usual procedure at the Sea Cloud Bathing House, but bedding down is also an option – it's a spa and a place to stay, all rolled into one no-nonense package. Provided you're feeling adventurous and game for a uniquely Chinese experience, there's not a great deal to be intimidated by – men and women have separate, luxurious spa and pool areas, and relaxing treatments include a jade steam room, Chinese herbal saunas and ginseng baths. It is, however, worth noting that when attendants in the bathing area give guests expert and thorough exfoliation treatments, they will get rid of any dead skin cells no matter where they are located. Skip this one if you don't fancy the idea of the attendant's washcloth going to places where the sun don't shine.

After a good soak and scrub guests can slip on matching pyjamas and go upstairs for a massage, beauty treatments, mahjong and karaoke followed by an overnight snooze in a room filled with comfy lazy-boy recliners. The Sea Cloud also has a restaurant, where you can enjoy the novel sight of a room full of diners wearing the same outfit. For those who might not feel comfortable sleeping in a room full of snoring Chinese businessmen, there are private VIP rooms available at a marginal extra fee. Payments for services are signed for using the number on the locker key where guests' clothing is stored until they leave.

Sea Cloud Bathing House

888 Panyu Lu, by Hongqiao Lu, Hongqiao (6407 0011). **Rates** RMB 60. **Credit** MC, V. **Map** p240 B3.

88 Xintiandi.
See p41.

on the 38th floor with two floors of restaurants and bars above and, above them, 342 guest rooms. These are a cut above the five-star norm ('JW' is the Marriott's premier league brand), spacious and with power massage jets in the showers. Best of all are the simply fantastic views over the city, made the most of courtesy of massive picture windows with bench-like sills. This is not a hotel for vertigo sufferers. In addition to all the usual facilities, the JW also boasts a small library on the uppermost floor, reached by a winding staircase, and a branch of the renowned Mandara Spa (*see p173*).

Hotel services *Babysitting. Bar. Business services. Concierge. Gym. Parking. Restaurants. Spa. Swimming pools (indoor & outdoor).* **Room services** *Air-conditioning. Hi fi. Internet access: broadband. Mini-bar. Room service. TV: satellite.*

Moderate

Park Hotel

170 Nanjing Xilu, by Huanghe Lu (6327 5225/fax 6327 6958/www.parkhotel.com.cn). Metro Renmin Park or Square. **Rates** $65 single; $75 double; $140 suite. **Credit** MC, V. **Map** p242 F4.

Today it is dwarfed by skyscraping neighbours but when it opened in 1934 this was the tallest building in Asia. Then it overlooked a racecourse, now it addresses the park and cultural institutions of Renmin Square; it remains a good location, convenient for sightseeing and the shops of Nanjing Lu. Although the exterior is still imposing, don't expect great shakes from the interior: modernisations in 1998 stripped away much of the original art deco character. Rooms are furnished in identikit fashion, while the public spaces now look bland and tawdry. The hotel hosts lots of delegations and groups. **Hotel services** *Bar. Business services. Concierge. Gym. Parking. Restaurant.* **Room services** *Air-conditioning. Internet access: dataport. Mini-bar. Room service. TV: satellite.*

Yangtze Hotel

740 Hankou Lu, by Yunnan Zhonglu (6322 6075/ www.e-yangtze.com). Metro Renmin Park or Square. **Rates** $50-$55 single; $55-$65 double; $100 suite. **Credit** MC, V. **Map** p242 G4.

Dating from the same year as the nearby Park Hotel, 1934, the Yangtze is of a comparable size but less architecturally distinguished. It has a similarly good location, one block east of Renmin Square and close to the museums, the Bund and the Old City. Like the Park, it underwent extensive renovation in the 1990s, re-emerging as what the management claims is the first internet and e-commerce hotel in Shanghai. That's a bit of flimflammery – lots of hotels in town have broadband access from every room – but few, if any, offer the service at such cheap rates. **Hotel services** *Bar. Beauty salon. Business services. Gym. Parking. Restaurant. Sauna.* **Room services** *Air-conditioning. Internet access: broadband. Mini-bar. TV: satellite.*

Jingan

Expensive

Four Seasons

500 Weihai Lu, by Shimen Yilu (6256 8888/fax 6287 1004/www.fourseasons.com). Metro Shimen Yilu. **Rates** $305-$350 single/double; $400-$1,000 suite. **Credit** AmEx, DC, MC, V. **Map** p249 E5.

Fans of the particular brand of elegance and sophistication usually associated with the name Four Seasons may find themselves a bit nonplussed by the chain's Shanghai property, a purpose-built 37-storey twin-spired tower. The cavernous lobby and adjacent atrium café are pleasant enough but they really aren't anything too special – this could be a Radisson, it could be a Hilton. The same is true of the rooms, which are large but lack that extra oomph that usually sets the Four Seasons apart. Neither is the location too great: the hotel is within walking distance of most places but the immediate surroundings are distinctly lacking in glamour. **Hotel services** *Babysitting. Bars. Business services. Concierge. Gym. Parking. Restaurants. Spa. Swimming pool (indoor).* **Room services** *Air-conditioning. Internet access: broadband. Mini-bar. Room service. TV: satellite.*

Portman Ritz-Carlton

Shanghai Centre, 1376 Nanjing Xilu (6279 8888/ fax 6279 8800/www.ritzcarlton.com). Metro Jingan Temple. **Rates** $350-$430 single; $370-$460 double; $530-$750 suite. **Credit** AmEx, DC, MC, V. **Map** p248 C4.

As part of the Shanghai Centre, the Portman is at the heart of expat life; ranged around the forecourt are various airline offices, the City Shopping supermarket, café-cum-deli Element Fresh (*see p102*) and the Long Bar (*see p121*). The hotel itself, entered across a bridge over a fish-filled water feature, offers 578 rooms over 50 floors – spacious, if standard five-star accommodation. Bonuses include one of the city's top Italian restaurants, the Palladio (*see p107*), a good bar with nightly jazz (*see p177*) and a gift shop with some unusual items including motorcycles and sidecars. Service throughout is exemplary, although what really wins favour is that despite being the oldest of the city's international five-stars (opened 1 January 1998), the Portman still feels like the most vibrant and essential place to stay in town. **Hotel services** *Babysitting. Bar. Beauty salon. Business services. Disabled: adapted rooms. Gym. Parking. Restaurants. Spa. Swimming pool (indoor).* **Room services** *Air-conditioning. Hi fi. Internet access: broadband. Mini-bar. Room service. TV: satellite.*

Old City

Moderate

Shanghai Classical Hotel

242 Fuyou Lu, by Liushi Lu (6311 1777/ www.laofandian.com). **Rates** $50 single/double; $100 suite. **Credit** MC, V. **Map** p245 J5.

With its yellow walls, curved tile roofs, red lanterns and ornate Chinese windows, this Qing Dynasty-styled hotel offers discount Disney boarding. It's right beside the Yu Gardens, which makes it very convenient for exploring the Old City but a little far from the nightlife action of the French Concession. It has 66 comfortable and modern guest rooms and a restaurant serving Shanghainese cuisine. The rooftop bar has fine views of the gardens below, which look especially pretty during the annual Lantern Festival (*see p152*). **Hotel services** *Bar. Business services. Restaurant.* **Room services** *Air-conditioning. Room service. TV.*

Shanghai YMCA hotel

123 Xizang Nanlu, by Yanan Donglu (6326 1040/ www.ymcahotel.com). Metro Renmin Square. **Rates** $15 dormitory; $55 single; $64-$68 double; $145-$180 suite. **Credit** AmEx, DC, MC, V. **Map** p242 G5.

The location couldn't be better: on the edge of the Old City and French Concession and just five minutes' walk from both Renmin Square and Xintiandi. The hotel itself is a 1929, 11-storey, Chinese-style building with a startling variety of rooms (165 of them), ranging from backpacker dorms to deluxe suites. Facilities are slightly run-down – if you are going to spend $145 on a room, we would recommend spending it elsewhere – but the view from the rooms has improved greatly since the municipality built a park across the road. The fitness facility often schedules classes in traditional Chinese exercise. **Hotel services** *Bar. Business services. Gym. Restaurant.* **Room services** *Air-conditioning. TV.*

*M*ake *Your* City
Discovering Simple

Ramada Plaza Shanghai, boasting of unparalleled location with a stone's throw to every major tourist and shopping attractions in downtown city, offers the guests the quintessential vibrancy of Shanghai's nightlife

With comfortable and elegantly appointed guestrooms and lounges, plus all business amenities like broadband and wide working desk, it is mostly tailor-made for these modern business travelers who like to mix a little business and shopping to sooth & revive the nerve after a busy day.

For more demanding and perceptive travelers . . . . . .

RAMADA.
PLAZA
SHANGHAI
南新雅华美达大酒店

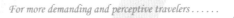

Address: NO.700 Jiujiang Road, Shanghai, P.R.China 200001
Tel: (8621)6350 0000 Fax: (8621)6350 6666 Email: nxysales@sh163.net Website: www.ramadainternational.com
Worldwide toll free number for room reservation: (Mainland China) 100 800 852 0469   (Hong Kong) 852 2525 9966
(Taiwan) 00 801 855 316   (Thailand) 001 800 852 2435   (Tokyo) 81 3 3239 2303   (Australia) 1 800 25 12 59

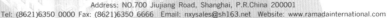

Xintiandi

Expensive

88 Xintiandi

380 Huangpi Nanlu, by Taicang Lu (5383 8833/fax 5383 8877/www.88xintiandi.com). Metro Huangpi Nanlu. **Rates** $258 single/double; $298 single/double with lake view; $328 suite. **Credit** AmEx, DC, MC, V. **Map** p244 F6.

Part of the massively ambitious Xintiandi complex, 88 is a boutique-style guesthouse aimed primarily at the wealthy business traveller. Its beautifully appointed rooms sport an updated Chinese art deco look, and come with all the requisite creature and technological comforts. The best rooms overlook the artificial lake; the others address a busy shopping plaza. Guests have access to both the private clubhouse across the street and the Alexander fitness club within the shopping complex.

Hotel services *Parking.* **Room services** *Air-conditioning. Internet access: broadband. Mini-bar. Room service. TV: satellite.*

French Concession

Expensive

Jinjiang Hotel

59 Maoming Nanlu, by Changle Lu (6258 2582/ ax 6472 5588/www.jinjianghotelshanghai.com). Metro Shanxi Nanlu. **Rates** $195-$235 single; $205-$245 double; $290-$360 suite. **Credit** AmEx, DC, MC, V. **Map** p247 E6.

Constructed in 1931 as plush residences for the French, the Jinjiang is now a three-star, state-run facility with ambitions to recapture some of that golden-era flair. Topped by an imposing red turban, the Sikh doorman harks back to the days when Indians were just one of the multitude of nationalities that found plentiful employment in boomtown Shanghai. Careful management has retained choice elements of the building's original interior, such as the moulded fireplaces. Rooms can be cramped but at least the beds are comfortable. Across the lawn is the 'Jinjiang gourmet street' and Yin (*see p114*), one of the city's best MSG-free Chinese restaurants.

Hotel services *Bar. Beauty salon. Business services. Gym. Parking. Restaurant.* **Room services** *Air-conditioning. Mini-bar. Room service. TV: satellite.*

Okura Garden Hotel

58 Maoming Nanlu, by Changle Lu (6415 1111/fax 6415 8866/www.gardenhotelshanghai.com). Metro Shanxi Nanlu. **Rates** $160/$180 single/double; $180/ $200 single/double with garden view. **Credit** AmEx, DC, MC, V. **Map** p247 D6.

The Okura Garden looks a bit like a miniature White House, complete with lawn, which has had a great 33-storey concrete monstrosity land on top of it. The classically styled building is what remains of the old Cercle Sportif French Club. It's gorgeous, with two grand lobbies with sweeping staircases and deco detailing and the original 1926 oval ballroom with stained-glass dome ceiling. The new block contains the accommodation – 500 guest rooms that are comfortable if undistinguished. As part of the Okura group the hotel is geared to travellers from Japan – staff speak Japanese, the rooms have kimono-style robes, slippers and green tea, and there's a fine Japanese restaurant, Yamazato.

Hotel services *Bars. Beauty salon. Business services. Garden. Gym. Parking. Restaurants. Swimming pool.* **Room services** *Air-conditioning. Internet access: broadband. Mini-bar. Room service. TV: satellite.*

The chain gang

Shanghai's booming economy has attracted the global chains in numbers. In addition to the places reviewed in the main text and below, other internationals who have set up shop include Accor, Hilton, Holiday Inn, Howard Johnson, Novotel, Ramada, Sheraton, Sofitel and St Regis; check the group websites for details. Don't expect great character, but do rest assured that you'll get the same standard of service and comfort that you last found at the same chain's outlet in Dallas, Kuala Lumpur, Zurich...

● The well-equipped **Marriott Hongqiao** (2270 Hongqiao Lu, by Jianhe Lu, 6237 6000, www.marriott.com) is a low-rise that welcomes guests with bronze statues and palm trees. Its Champions sports bar is a hangout for expats. Excellent fitness facilities include tennis courts. The drawback is its edge-of-town location.

● The **Pudong Shangrila** (33 Fucheng Lu, by Yincheng Donglu, 6882 8888, www.shangri-la.com) is the largest hotel in Pudong. Much marble creates a luxurious ambience, especially in the lobby overlooking the river. Rooms are comfortable and spacious. The basement houses the popular BATS bar.

● The **Radisson Plaza Xingguo** (78 Xingguo Lu, by Huashan Lu, French Concession, 6212 9998, www.radisson.com) is set in six hectares (15 acres) of beautiful gardens. Relatively small, the hotel has a boutique feel. The Clark Hatch fitness group manages the pool, gym, bowling alley and squash courts.

Moderate

City Hotel

5-7 Shanxi Nanlu, by Yanan Zhonglu (6255 1133/ fax 6255 0211/www.cityhotelshanghai.com). Metro Shanxi Nanlu. **Rates** $74-$100 single/double; $144 suite. **Credit** AmEx, DC, MC, V. **Map** p249 D5.

A standard four-star that's a little aged (it's more than 20 years old now) and lacking in character but has ample compensations in the form of a fine location (midway between the restaurants and nightlife of the French Concession and Jingan) and some very competitive rates. The guest rooms and suites (of which there are 274 over about 30 floors) are fine and dandy: modern, attractively furnished and well maintained. Request one facing south for sun and views down bicycle-thronged Shanxi Nanlu.

Hotel services *Bar. Beauty salon. Business services. Gym. Parking. Restaurant. Swimming pool (indoor).* **Room services** *Air-conditioning. Internet access: broadband. Mini-bar. TV: satellite.*

Donghu Hotel

70 Donghu Lu, by Huaihai Zhonglu (6415 8158/fax 6415 7759/www.donghuhotel.com). Metro Changshu Lu or Shanxi Nanlu. **Rates** $87-$113 single/double. **Credit** AmEx, DC, MC, V. **Map** p246 C6.

The Donghu is a collection of mansion blocks in walled grounds, dating from the 1920s and '30s, and formerly home to infamous gangster Du Yuesheng *(see p12* **Big Eared Du)** and his sundry mistresses. In their current demobbed incarnation the assorted buildings offer 118 guest rooms, which come equipped with all the usual facilities. The real draw is the garden setting, lush with trees and flowers and with a large outdoor swimming pool – a real rarity in Shanghai. There is a good Korean restaurant on the premises, as well as an excellent bar in the Seven *(see p126).* The Donghu also benefits from a good location, with the Xiangyang fake market just over the road and a great cluster of bars and restaurants a couple of minutes' walk west down Huaihai Zhonglu.

Hotel services *Bar. Business services. Gym. Parking. Restaurant. Swimming pool (outdoor).* **Room services** *Air-conditioning. Internet access: dataport. Mini-bar. Room service. TV: satellite.*

Hengshan Moller Villa

30 Shanxi Nanlu, by Yanan Zhonglu (6247 8881/ fax 6289 1020/www.mollervilla.com). Metro Shanxi Nanlu. **Rates** $80-$95 double; $105-$220 suite. **Credit** AmEx, DC, MC, V. **Map** p249 D5.

Popular mythology has it that this fantastic villa was built to a design drawn by the 12-year-old daughter of a wealthy Norwegian businessman. It seems a plausible enough explanation for the steeples, spires, pointy red gables and patterned brickwork that give the place the look of a gaudy Gothic castle. The fun continues inside, with rooms that are all-out high camp with dangling chandeliers, faux-Louis XIV furniture and extravagant drapes. No wonder that the villa is a popular photo-op spot for Chinese

newly-weds. When booking, specify that you want to stay in the house itself, and not the cheaper but personality-free concrete box next door.

Hotel services *Bar. Parking. Restaurant.* **Room services** *Air-conditioning. Mini-bar. Room service. TV: cable.*

Jingan Hotel

370 Huashan Lu, by Changshu Lu (6248 1888/ fax 6248 2657/www.jcbus.co.jp/jingan/index_e.htm). Metro Jingan Temple. **Rates** $90-$96 single; $108-$133 double; $145-$242 suite. **Credit** MC, V. **Map** p248 B5.

Nowadays the Jingan is hidden behind the bulk of the Hilton, but when it was built in 1935 its Spanish stylings of curved arches, whitewashed adobe walls and tiled roof must have made quite an impact. In recent times the guest rooms have been refitted and, in the process, have been denuded of any original character, but the function rooms still have that wow factor, particularly the ninth-floor banquet hall with ornate pillars, wall carvings and Chinese lanterns. The hotel is popular with music lovers for Sunday afternoon chamber recitals held in the 'San Diego' room. When booking avoid the modern wing, added in 1985 specifically to cater for Japanese tourists.

Hotel services *Bar. Beauty salon. Business services. Gym. Parking. Restaurant.* **Room services** *Air-conditioning. Mini-bar. Room service. TV.*

#9

9 Jianguo Xilu, by Taiyuan Lu (6471 9950/fax 6433 2123). Metro Hengshan Lu. **Rates** $80-$160 single; $90 double; $120-$160 suite. **No credit cards.** **Map** p246 C8.

This beautiful art deco B&B is run in laid-back (albeit slightly exclusive) style, shunning press and soliciting most of its reservations through word of mouth alone. Entering through large wooden gates, the lucky few (there are only four bedrooms) immediately get a sense that this is more private residence than hotel. Exquisite antique furniture and Buddhist sculptures engender an air of class and tranquillity, as do the peaceful garden and secluded balconies. #9 also has a restaurant, with a menu based on fresh ingredients from the market across the street. The management sees its guests as friends, but fussy diets, noisy kids and bad attitudes are not tolerated.

Hotel services *Garden. Restaurant.* **Room services** *Air-conditioning. Internet access: broadband.*

Old House Inn

No.16 Lane 351, Huashan Lu, by Changshu Lu (6248 6118/fax 6249 6869/www.oldhouse.cn). Metro Changshu Lu. **Rates** $48 single; $72 double. **Credit** MC, V. **Map** p246 B6.

The first of its kind in Shanghai, the Old House is a small independently run boutique hotel. It's a conversion of an old lane house, undertaken by Shanghainese architect-owner Wu Haiqing (who also has a practice in the United States). A dozen guest rooms – all doubles, bar one single – with wooden floors, elegant Ming Dynasty-style furniture and the most gorgeous Zen-like bathrooms are

connected by creaking stairs and rickety corridors. A stylish ground-floor restaurant (Shanghainese cuisine) and bar leads to a serene courtyard garden. It's the kind of highly individual place that Shanghai needs more of and we can't recommend it enough.
Hotel services Bar. Garden. Restaurant.
Room services Air-conditioning. Internet access: broadband. TV.

Ruijin Guesthouse

118 Ruijin Erlu, by Fuxing Zhonglu (6472 2277/fax 6473 2277). Metro Shanxi Nanlu. **Rates** $85 single; $150 double. **Credit** MC, V. **Map** p247 E7.
What's now a guesthouse used to be the Morriss Estate, home to an eccentric newspaper tycoon and his pack of racing hounds (*see p80*). In its current form the place is composed of five old villas, with rooms decked out in a Chinese take on Olde English style, all surrounded by lawns, wooded gardens with a small lake. What could be an amazing boutique hotel remains slightly underwhelming due in large part to poor service and mismanagement. Still, the setting can't be beat, especially given that what's arguably the city's best bar (Face Bar, *see p124*), with accompanying upstairs Thai restaurant (La Na Thai, *see p116*) and an excellent Shanghainese (Xiao Nan Guo, *see p113*), are all within the grounds.
Hotel services Bar. Business services. Garden. Parking. Restaurant. **Room services** Air-conditioning. Room service. TV: satellite.

Taiyuan Villa

160 Taiyuan Lu, by Yongjia Lu (6471 6688/fax 6472 2618). Metro Hengshan Lu. **Rates** $60 single; $60-$362 double/suite. **Credit** MC, V. **Map** p246 C8.
This state-owned mansion, built in 1920 by a French nobleman, is best known as the former digs of General George Marshall, who was chief mediator between Nationalist Chinese leader Chiang Kaishek and Communist leader Mao Tsetung. After the Communist victory, it became Madame Mao's favourite *pied à terre* in Shanghai. Decked out in Chinese furniture, it has a nostalgic, characterful atmosphere. It lacks amenities (there's no restaurant, gym or business centre) but the history, architecture and lovely garden go a long way to making up for any shortcomings. Note that government delegations often book up the whole villa.
Hotel services Garden. Parking. Restaurant.
Room services Air-conditioning. Mini-bar. TV.

Budget

Shanghai Dramatic Arts Centre

288 Anfu Lu, by Wulumuqi Lu (6474 8600 ext 100/ fax 6437 3573/www.china-drama.com). Metro Changshu Lu. **Rates** $18. **No credit cards**. **Map** p246 B6.
The Arts Centre (*see p187*) has a limited number of guest rooms, which are typically used by visiting performers, but if they're vacant, management is happy to accommodate non-theatrical types. The rooms are fitted out in a similar fashion to those

Hengshan Moller Villa. *See p42.*

found in any nondescript three-star with all the requisite facilities. Boredom should be unlikely here with live performances downstairs. The hotel also offers a state-of-the-art exercise room that guests can use for free. Rooms are single-sex.
Hotel services Gym. Restaurant. **Room services** Air-conditioning. TV.

Grand Hyatt – and that's just the lobby bar. *See p44.*

Xujiahui

Expensive

Cypress Hotel

2419 Hongqiao Lu, by Huqing Pinglu (6268 8868/ fax 6268 1878/www.cypresshotel.com). **Rates** $110 standard; $190 executive; $210 suite. **Credit** AmEx, DC, MC, V. **Map** p240 A3.

Situated in the grounds of the former estate of Shanghai tycoon Sir Victor Sassoon, this is more country lodge than hotel. The residences are surrounded by extensive lawns and wooded gardens landscaped with ponds, streams, pavilions and bridges. The guest rooms are fairly unexceptional though supremely comfortable; executive rooms have separate office areas. Although some distance from the city centre, the hotel is close to Hongqiao (domestic) airport and the zoo.

Hotel services *Bar. Business services. Garden. Gym. Parking. Restaurant. Swimming pool.* **Room services** *Air-conditioning. Internet access: broadband. Mini-bar. Room service. TV: satellite.*

Moderate

Manpo Boutique Hotel

660 Xinhua Lu, by Dingxi Lu (6280 1000/ sales@manpo.cn). **Rates** from $86. **Credit** AmEx, DC, MC, V. **Map** p240 B3.

Don't be misled by the name: this is in no way a boutique hotel, although with just 76 guest rooms, it is considered small for Shanghai. What it is, is a modern four-star situated in an exclusive area along a tree-lined road that leads to the state guesthouse, where visiting dignatories stay when in town. It's a brutal looking thing from the outside but inside is reasonably grand with lavish use of marble. It has a good clutch of extras – suites come equipped with kitchenettes, there is a small gym on the ground

floor and a billiards room. The hotel also has two restaurants, one of which specialises in shark-fin dishes. The proximity to the Hongqiao (domestic) airport, and the Shanghai Mart and Intex expo/ conference centres may make this a useful option for business travellers.

Hotel services *Bar. Business services. Gym. Parking. Restaurants.* **Room services** *Air-conditioning. Internet access: dataport. Room service. TV: satellite.*

Pudong

Expensive

Grand Hyatt

2 Century Boulevard, by Yincheng Lu (5049 1234/ fax 5049 1111/www.shanghai.hyatt.com). Metro Lujiazui. **Rates** $107-$604 single/double. **Credit** AmEx, DC, MC, V. **Map** p243 L4.

Shanghai's one true destination hotel, the Grand Hyatt occupies the top 34 floors of the skyscraping 88-storey Jinmao Tower, thus claiming the title of the world's highest hotel. As if that wasn't enough, the design is stunning. The central atrium, which rises 33 floors from the hotel lobby, is a sci-fi spectacular of circular galleries rising away to infinity (or at least what looks like it). The 555 guest rooms and suites are some of the most spacious in town, with floor-to-ceiling windows to make the most of the incredible views; those facing the river on the 40th to 50th floors offer the finest panoramas. The hotel also boasts a clutch of excellent restaurants (including Cucina, *see p118,* with inventive modern Italian cooking) and a dream of a bar in the appropriately named Cloud 9 (*see p128*).

Hotel services *Bars. Beauty salon. Business services. Gym. Parking. Restaurants. Swimming pool (indoor).* **Room services** *Air-conditioning. Internet access: broadband. Mini-bar. Room service. TV: satellite.*

Sightseeing

duction

Forget creaking cultural institutions, historical monuments and ancient temples and tombs. Shanghai doesn't really do any of that. This is a young city – and getting younger by the minute as vast swathes of the old (by which the locals mean pre-1990) are replaced by the newer than new. Which is not to say that there is nothing to see and do here – far from it – it's just that the quintessential Shanghai experiences differ from those of other cities.

For instance, our list of Shanghai highlights starts with eating. For the top things to do during your visit, check out *p97* **The Best Restaurants**. We can't conceive of a finer introduction to the city than an evening at Bao Luo, 1221 or Yin, gorging on dish after dish of local specialities (snake, eel and jelly fish, optional), bombarded by the cacophonous jabbering of groups of fellow diners.

The next essential experience is to shop. It doesn't matter if the activity is normally anathema to you, in Shanghai it's a whole different ball game – in fact, it's not a ball game at all, it's a blood sport. Don't believe us? Then try haggling at Xingyang Market, a wonderland of $10 Rolexes, two-for-one Gucci and one-dollar DVD box sets of *Lord of the Rings 4* (what do you mean, it's a trilogy?).

After that, nights should be spent in orgies of old colonial indulgence, sipping Gin Twists on the verandah of a villa that once belonged to a 1920s opium lord. There are plenty such venues to chose from: *see p121* **The best bars**.

Shanghai in a day… or two

Beyond eating, drinking and shopping, here are a few suggestions for what to do in 48 hours or less:

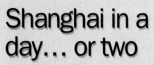

- Stand on **the Bund** and look over at **Pudong**, then cross the river to Pudong and look back at the Bund for Shanghai past and future. *See p50.*
- Skip the crowds at the Oriental Pearl Tower for similar, if not better, views from the **Grand Hyatt** (and check out that foyer!). *See p89.*
- Visit **Three on the Bund** for Michael Graves' quirky new atrium and a glimpse of the future of Shanghai's past. *See p52.*
- Swing by the **Urban Planning Centre** on Renmin Square for a glimpse at the Shanghai city masterplan. *See p59.*
- Scour the stalls of **Dongtai Lu** for a copy of Mao's Little Red Book or posters of ruddy-cheeked peasants. *See p75.*

SHANGHAI GEOGRAPHY

Shanghai is divided into a multitude of local municipalities with unpronounceable names. For the most part, we've ignored these and divided the city up into geographical areas that make the city more easily digestable for visitors. Thumbnail sketches of these areas might read:

- **The Bund & Beyond** – heart of colonial Shanghai with a grand waterfront promenade.
- **Renmin Square & Nanjing Donglu** – museums and a busy shopping street.
- **Jingan** – the central business district with top-end malls and two plastic temples.
- **The Old City** – the original Chinese bit with beautiful gardens, temple and bazaar.
- **Xintiandi** – a modern redevelopment of an old quarter, now a top spot for shopping, dining and entertainment.

● **French Concession** – low rise, tree-lined and pretty with little to see, but lots of shopping, dining and drinking.

● **Xujiahui, Hongqiao & Gubei** – far-flung western suburbs with a real temple, gardens and a bloody history.

● **Pudong** – east of the river financial district with rapidly sprouting skyscrapers.

● **Hongkou** – largely residential but with sites of cultural and Jewish significance.

Shanghai operates on an east-west axis. Its two main streets are Nanjing Lu and Huaihai Lu. The first connects Jingan with Renmin Square and the Bund, the other the French Concession with Xintiandi and the Old City. Both are pedestrian-friendly and many of the city's sights are located on or just off one or the other. Running parallel between the two is Yanan Lu, an elevated highway for fast moving traffic. At night this expressway is lit in neon pinks and blues (see the cover of this guide) – trust Shanghai to make a feature of a flyover.

GETTING AROUND

Despite the immense size of the greater city, the districts that will most interest visitors are closely grouped and manageable in size. Getting around on foot is easy. There's also a good, modern metro system, although it can be crowded and what English-language signage there is is not easy to spot. We recommend that you make use of taxis, which are both plentiful and cheap. For more information, *see p216.*

TOURS AND CRUISES

Jinjiang Tour Buses leave from just outside the Okura Garden Hotel on Maoming Lu every 45 minutes from 9am to 4.15pm daily. They pass by Renmin Square en route to Pudong and the Oriental Pearl Tower before returning over the Nanpu Bridge, passing by the Old City and Yu Gardens. Tickets cost RMB 18 and you can hop on and off the buses all day.

The **Huangpu River Cruise** (239 Zhongshan Donglu, 6374 4461) company offers a one-hour river cruise up to the Yangpu Bridge (RMB 35) or a much better three-and-a-half-hour, 60-kilometre (37-mile) round trip up to the Yangtze River. Tickets cost from RMB 45 to RMB 100; the more expensive tickets include refreshments. Departure times vary but there is usually one sailing in the morning, one in the afternoon and one in the evening. The times are posted at the Jingling Pier (this is also where you get tickets and where the boats depart from), which is just south of the Bund, beyond the Meteorological Tower.

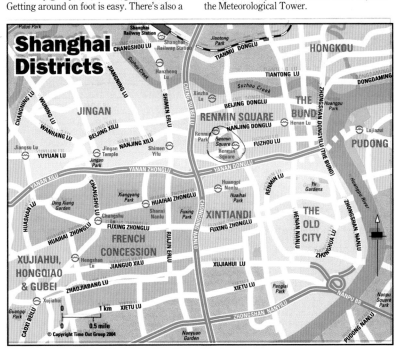

The Bund & Beyond

A time capsule of colonial-era glories that's set to flourish again.

Tai chi on the **Bund promenade**.

Map p243

The Bund (or Waitan to the Chinese) is quintessential Shanghai. It is the history of the city writ in stone: a curving sweep of the most magnificently pompous buildings, the former headquarters of foreign – particularly British – banks and institutions, their halls and corridors largely dormant for most of the last half century, but now slowly stirring back to life.

The word Bund, often mistaken for a German expression, derives from the Hindustani word *band*, meaning an artificial causeway or embankment. The area was given its name by the British, even though it was little more than a muddy towpath when they first arrived in the 1840s. That changed in the 1880s when the Shanghai Municipal Council decided to create an esplanade along the entire waterfront. The Bund was further widened in the early 1920s, assuming its present state in the mid 1990s. It now has a wide, raised promenade, a magnet for sightseers, especially at night when the buildings are spectacularly illuminated.

Apart from their diverse architectural styles, which range from neo-Grecian to Italian Renaissance and art deco, the buildings are impressive in terms of scale and height – a number of them have at some point claimed the (quickly conceded) title of the tallest in Asia. Amazingly, the bulk of the materials used for their construction and decoration were imported, including tons of rare Italian marble, granite from Japan and just about everything from toilets to pre-moulded ceilings from England. The buildings have seen little outward change over the last 60 years, apart from some despoilation during the Cultural Revolution, though many of their grand interiors have been lost.

Until the early 1990s most of the buildings served as government offices. However, in the new supercharged economic climate, the city government is happy to 'sell off' the Bund and some former occupants have moved back, while other buildings are getting smart new tenants: *see p52* **To infinity and the Bund**.

Meanwhile, in the streets behind, stately old banks and commercial concerns still survive among a pot-pourri of small shops offering everything from hardware and mechanical instruments to underwear.

North of Nanjing Donglu

Most visitors approach the Bund along Nanjing Donglu. Where it meets the Bund is as good a place as any to start a tour of the area. On the northern corner is the magnificent landmark edifice the **Peace Hotel** (*see p32*), formerly Sassoon House, incorporating the Cathay Hotel. The Peace is famed for its nightly offerings of unpolished pre-war swing performed by an almost octogenarian ensemble in its original English Tudor-style bar (*see p177*). The foyer is splendid and it's also worth going up to the roof garden for the views of the river and beyond, although a hefty cover charge is demanded whether you take a drink or not.

Walking northwards, the neighbouring **Bank of China**, again in art deco style and partly designed by the same architect, stands a few metres lower than the hotel. Original plans for a twin-towered bank building climbing over 20 metres (66 feet) higher than the hotel had to be scrapped as Sir Victor Sassoon wouldn't tolerate anything outdoing his triumphal showpiece. The building, completed in 1939, was built on the site of the Club Concordia, a German club that was a favourite entertainment centre for all nationalities before World War I.

Next door at No.24, the **Industrial & Commercial Bank of China** occupies the former Yokohama Specie Bank building, opened in 1924. Successfully blending neo-Grecian with Eastern designs, it was liberally adorned with granite sculptures and bronze work featuring Japanese warriors; only two defaced sculptures have survived above the ground-floor windows. The neighbouring building, No.26, was built for the Yangtsze Insurance Association in 1916 and is now used by the **Agricultural Bank of China**.

No.27, the **Foreign Trade Building**, opened in 1922 as the EWO Building, HQ for Jardine Matheson, one of the most influential British companies in Asia. The company was presided over by two pillars of British society, the Keswick brothers. Tony Keswick acted as chairman of the Shanghai Municipal Council and was chief of underground operations in the Far East during World War II.

Crossing Beijing Donglu, the northernmost stretch of the Bund includes the former buildings of the Glen Line shipping company (1922), the Banque De L'IndoChine (1914) and the plain façade of the NYK shipping company

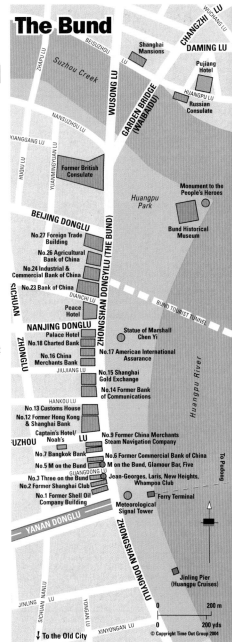

The Bund

The Bund, Huangpu River and Pudong.

(1926). All of these buildings have been totally gutted. The grassed compound at the end of the Bund contains some off-limits buildings that were part of the **former British Consulate**. This area is scheduled for major redevelopment.

HUANGPU PARK

The underpass at Beijing Donglu surfaces near the entrance to the psychedelic **Bund Tourist Tunnel** (*see p88*), which takes visitors across to Pudong, and the entrance to **Huangpu Park**. The area was originally created as the Public Gardens in 1868 – with the definition of 'public' excluding those of Chinese origin. However, the infamous and frequently mentioned sign that supposedly read 'No Dogs or Chinese Allowed' never actually existed. The Chinese were finally allowed to enter the park in 1928.

Council records reporting this change in regulation are to be found in the underground **Bund Historical Museum** (*see below*), which is located at the base of the **Monument to the People's Heroes**, an ugly concrete monolith designed by a local university professor.

The northern perimeter of the park is bounded by Suzhou Creek, which is crossed by way of the **Garden Bridge** (Waibaidu), built by the British in 1907 and originally paved with wooden blocks and traversed by tramlines.

Bund Historical Museum

1 Zhongshan Dongerlu, Huangpu Park (6321 6542). *Metro Henan Lu*. **Open** 9am-4pm daily. **Admission** free. **Map** p243 K3.

A small, subterranean museum with a reasonably interesting collection of historical photographs.

North of Suzhou Creek

The northern side of Suzhou Creek, which used to be known as the Broadway, is dominated by the mighty art deco **Shanghai Mansions**, which used to be Broadway Mansions. When completed in 1933, the 19-storey block was the highest building in Asia. Its British owners made a fortune with its opportune sale to a Japanese government company in 1939. After the war it was a popular residence for foreign correspondents – they had the best spot in the city from which to observe the triumphant Communist troops parading along the Bund in 1949. It now functions as a poor tourist hotel.

A block east is another hostelry, the **Pujiang Hotel** (*see p37*), which now largely caters for budget travellers. The first hotel on the site was opened in 1858 but the present building, which is in English Renaissance style, opened in 1911. As the Astor House, it was one of the best hotels in Asia; it's still worth a visit for a glimpse at the old lobby and ballroom (which

accommodated post-reform China's first
securities exchange until its move to Pudong
in 1998), and a cheap beer at the bar.

In front of the hotel, where its gardens once
unfolded, is one of the few surviving German-
designed buildings in the city. The **Russian
Consulate** was built in 1917 and is still in use
in its intended role. East of here many further
remnants of the early 20th century survive in
the form of shabby but charming wooden-
framed houses and warehouses. **Jiulong Lu**,
in particular, is a fine timewarp of a street.
However, the whole area, known as 'North
Bund' is set to be transformed into a waterfront
showpiece with hotels, a world trade plaza, an
international terminal for cruise ships and a
'cultural street' featuring a 200-metre (656-foot)
high Ferris wheel – by comparison, the London
Eye is a paltry 135 metres (443 feet) high.

Along Suzhou Creek west of Shanghai
Mansions, the building with a clocktower was
built as the **Chinese Post Office** in 1924 and
continues to function as such. A little further
down the creek the elongated ten-storey art
deco apartment block known as **Embankment
House** was the largest of its time when it
opened in 1932. A few years later it was used as
a processing centre for Jews escaping the Nazi
regime. It's now a fashionable expat address.

Huangpu River

Prior to the age of the aeroplane, visitors
would approach Shanghai by sea and dock
just north of the Bund. The Bund waterfront
was itself lined by jetties from which
masses of coolies hauled crates into the
trading houses. Those scenes are long
gone, although Shanghai is still China's
biggest port and river traffic remains
heavy. The best place to watch the passing
river steamers, barges, tankers, sampans
and even the odd junk, is from the
waterfront promenade, which also offers
fine panoramic views of Pudong across
the water.

A **ferry** across to Pudong is one way of
getting out on the river; these leave from
a terminal just south of the Meteorological
Tower. They depart every 15 minutes
throughout the day and the fare is RMB 8
eastbound, free westbound. Alternatively,
there are also regular **river cruises**
departing from the Jinling Pier, which
is just 200 metres south of the ferry
terminal; for further details, see p47.

...hapu Lu ...as formerly ...ices and ...e remains, ...st west of ...hou Lu and ...as the ...stern ...n film ...aqiu Lu was formerly known as Museum Road because of the foreign-run Shanghai Museum at No.20, housed in the Royal Asiatic Society building; you can still see traces of the 'RAS' sign up on its crown.

South of Nanjing Donglu

The building on the south side of Nanjing Donglu at the Bund began life as the **Palace Hotel** (it's now an annexe of the neighbouring

Peace). It is the oldest surviving hotel building in Shanghai – though despite a keystone displaying the date 1906, it didn't fully open until 1908. The building was scheduled to be demolished in 1939 but was saved by the advent of World War II. Despite its gaudy redecoration, the ground-floor Chinese restaurant retains many of the features that made it the place to hang out in '30s Shanghai.

The former **Chartered Bank building** at No.18, dating from 1923, was at the time of writing being converted into a glamorous multi-level complex for dining and shopping (*see below* **To infinity and the Bund**). Magnificent Italian marble columns and facings have been preserved on the ground floor.

Next door at **No.17**, American International Assurance has reclaimed a property it originally occupied in 1927 – it was one of the first of the Bund's former tenants, who left en masse in 1949, to return. Back then it shared the

To infinity and the Bund

The Bund is Shanghai's most famous bit of real estate and its skyline the city's historical signature, but also a bit of a headache.

After the colonial powers fled China in 1949, this most visible symbol of their former rule over Shanghai suffered neglect under its new Communist masters. The grand European façades fell into disuse and disrepair; the once lush riverside boulevard was overlaid with a noisy highway.

When foreign investment returned to Shanghai in the 1990s it shunned the Bund in favour of other better maintained districts such as Jingan and the old French Concession. But the lure of the riverfront remained. Some original owners tried to buy their old buildings back. (Most famously, the Hong Kong Shanghai Bank, which found the price demanded by the Shanghai municipality too expensive and instead set up in a new HSBC tower across the river.) Architects, meanwhile, weighed the enormous cost of draining the damp Venetian-like foundations (drill down a metre and a half and you hit the river) and refitting the creaky, near-100-year-old buildings for the demands of today. Only one business, the M on the Bund restaurant, managed to win through: in 1999 it staked a claim to Shanghai's former 'best address' and eternally stunning river views.

Then in 2002 a nominal law that zoned the Bund for finance and shipping was dropped in favour of one supporting culture and

entertainment. Since then, a clutch of the world's most famous retail, hotel and hospitality brands have been vying to get a piece of what they believe will be the Madison Avenue of China. Already hundreds of millions have been spent. Following an internal revamp by star American architect Michael Graves, **Three on the Bund** opened with Armani, the Evian Spa, a top-flight gallery and a clutch of restaurants and bars, including one under the helm of celebrated New York restaurateur Jean-Georges Vongerichten (*see p99*). Next up is **Bund 18**, which will open in October 2004 with Cartier, Zegna and the first restaurant in China to be run by Michelin three-star chefs (Jacques and Laurent Pourcel of Montpellier's Le Jardin des Sens). The Rockefellers and the Peninsula Hotel Group have a hotel and luxury retail arcade in the pipeline, and the old Peace Hotel may yet be restored to its former glory.

But will the world's elite really stroll down the Bund the way people used to before eight lanes of grimy traffic roared between them and the river? Even the biggest boosters of the Bund agree, that longterm, the traffic will have to be diverted, or somehow go underground through the marshy and unstable banks of the river. It's an architectural and financial challenge that may prove too ambitious, even for Shanghai's planners. As one ambitious foreign architect put it, 'Life is too short.'

premises with the offices and printing presses of the *North China Daily News*, aka 'the Old Lady of the Bund', which ran from 1864 to 1951 and was the mouthpiece of the municipality. Over the ground-floor windows is a series of three fine Italian marble panels and the chiselled motto of the old newspaper: 'Journalism, Art, Science, Litterature [sic], Commerce, Truth, Printing'.

Continuing southwards are three institutions in three very different architectural styles: at No.16 the **China Merchants Bank** is the neo-Grecian former Bank of Taiwan (1927); No.15, the **Shanghai Gold Exchange**, is the former Russo-Asiatic Bank (1902) in Italian Renaissance style; and No.14 is the former **Bank of Communications** in art deco style.

At No.13 the **Customs House** boasts a huge clocktower that once housed a bell that chimed in the fashion of Big Ben (hence its nickname 'Big Ching'). The bell was dismantled during the Cultural Revolution and replaced with loud speakers playing a taped version of 'The East is Red', the anthem of the People's Republic. Since 1986 the tower has once again chimed. The building remains a customs house, so entry is denied to the public, but you can take a peek at the entrance vestibule with its faded mosaics depicting Eastern shipping and commerce. The portico wall is splashed with some revolutionary zeal in the form of a sculpture commemorating the Communist seizure of the city in 1949.

THE LIONS OF SHANGHAI

The most opulent pile on the Bund is No.12, the **former Hongkong & Shanghai Bank**. Architects Palmer & Turner were given the simple instruction 'Dominate the Bund' and when completed in 1923 the resulting bit of stone boastfulness was considered the 'finest building east of Suez'. It's distinguished by – among other things – two bronze lions flanking the entrance. These represent Protection and Security and reputedly bring good luck if you rub their paws. They disappeared during the Japanese occupation and it was assumed that they'd been melted down until they turned up in the 1980s in the basement of the Shanghai Museum. The lions outside the bank are replicas but locals rub them just the same. Just inside (the building is now occupied by the Pudong Development Bank and is open to the public) is a rotunda decorated with fine Italian mosaics depicting the eight cities in which the bank had its branches in 1923. Similarly splendid is the grand banking hall, while the **Bonomi Café** on the second floor, with its terrace overlooking the bank's quadrangle, is a great place for a breather.

Huangpu Park. See p50.

Among the larger buildings between Fuzhou Lu and Guangdong Lu, No.7, the **Bangkok Bank**, was built in 1908 for the Great Northern Telegraph Company, which had introduced the telephone to Shanghai as early as 1881 (Britain had to wait until 1884). Next but one, at No.5, the former HQ of a Japanese shipping line is now best known as the address of one of the city's most celebrated restaurants, **M on the Bund** (*see p99*). The entrance is on Guangdong Lu, which is also where you'll find the huge **Shanghai Antiques and Curios Store** (*see p133*), in business for over a century.

No.3 is – logically – **Three on the Bund**, the swanky new development that's spear-heading the city's waterfront regeneration. Its current airs and graces echo the history of the adjoining building, No.2, best known as home of the **Shanghai Club**, a great British bastion of old boy snobbery that denied membership to women and Chinese. It was the place for toast and marmalade at breakfast over freshly ironed newspapers, pink gins before lunch and martinis at six. But nobody took a drink unless invited. There's a story, most likely apocryphal, that relates how a young banker was caught in the crossfire between Japanese and Chinese soldiers skirmishing on the Bund. He ran for the nearest cover, which happened to be the Shanghai Club, and was promptly ordered off the premises because he wasn't a member. The club's famed Long Bar, which ran over 35 metres (110 feet), has long gone. The building

The **Metropole Hotel**.

later housed the Seaman's Club, with Mao's portrait replacing that of King George VI, then the Dongfeng backpacker hotel and even – oh, the ignomy – a Kentucky Fried Chicken outlet. It's currently empty.

No.1 the Bund was built by the McBains, a wealthy British trading family, but was more associated with the Shell Oil Company. Diagonally opposite the building is the old **Meteorological Signal Tower**, built in 1907 and now home to the very modest **Bund Museum** (*see below*) on the ground floor and a terrace café on the upper level, with good views of the Bund sweep. The tower was moved over 20 metres from its original site in 1995 as part of the waterfront redevelopment.

YANAN DONGLU

At the southern end of the Bund, the elevated highway Yanan Donglu delineates what was once the boundary between the French Concession and the International Settlement. Three blocks inland, quaking at the traffic thundering by at first-floor level, is the musty **Natural History Museum** (*see below*), while tourist souvenirs and similar inessentials are peddled at the neighbouring **Shanghai Friendship Store** (*see p129*). The stone and red brick art deco building directly south of the Yanan Donglu freeway was formerly the Chung

Wai Bank, owned by Shanghai's most famous mobster turned respectable civic dignitary, Du Yuesheng. The building to its right used to house the French police headquarters where Du's accomplice Huang Jinrong acted simultaneously as chief of the Chinese detective squad and as a king of the underworld.

Tracking back northwards into the streets behind the Bund, the skyline is dominated by the crowned peak of the **Bund Centre**, a hulking new office complex. Its restaurant and bar, **CJW** (*see p100*), is 50 floors up and has some of the best views in town. A block north again, the intersection of Fuzhou Lu and Jiangxi Zhonglu is dominated by the Bund Centre of its day, an early 20th-century grouping of imposing corner buildings. The two matching 19-storey art deco monoliths on the west side were built by Sir Victor Sassoon as the **Metropole Hotel** and **Hamilton House** in 1932. The former remains a hotel (*see p37*), while the latter houses various offices, as it was intended to. The squat building on the north-west corner (built 1922) is occupied by government offices, much as it was in days gone by, when it hosted the offices of the British-dominated Shanghai Municipal Council.

Further north on Jiangxi Zhonglu, the red-brick former **Holy Trinity Cathedral**, built in the late 1860s, looks very much the part of an English city cathedral (although to the Chinese, it's the Hong Miao, or 'Red Temple'). Its Gothic-inspired architecture was based on the designs of Sir George Gilbert Scott, one of England's most celebrated Victorian architects. The cathedral is set to reopen for worship in 2006.

Bund Museum

Meteorological Signal Tower, Zhongshan Dongyilu, by Yanan Donglu (6321 6542). Metro Henan Lu. **Open** 9am-6pm daily. **Admission** free. **Map** p243 J4.
Housed in a 49m-high (161ft) tower that once delivered typhoon warnings to local shipping, the Bund Museum has little more than a small collection of old prints and a replica 1855 map of the area.

Natural History Museum

260 Yanan Donglu, by Henan Zhonglu (6321 3548). Metro Henan Lu. **Open** 9am-4.50pm Tue-Sun. **Admission** RMB 5. **No credit cards**.
Map p242 H5.
The magnificent 1920s building (converted to its current use in 1950) exhibits the same signs of age as its poorly displayed stuffed exhibits. The main hall's impressive display of dinosaur skeletons stinks of prehistory, while the original mosaic floors, woodwork and stained-glass windows tell of the city's more recent fall from grandeur. An extensive display of invertebrates, fish, birds and mammals fills the upper two levels, while a pair of locally discovered Ming Dynasty mummies rests on the ground floor.

Renmin Square & Nanjing Donglu

Racecourse, prison camp, now cultural pride and joy.

Renmin Square adds sparse greenery to the concrete and stone cityscape.

Map p242

Renmin Square, or 'People's Square', is the sinkhole at the centre of Shanghai. It sucks in traffic and people. Never imperial, regal or grand, it's a great formless space – part park, part concrete plaza, barely hemmed in by a fringe of ragtag buildings and a stretch of elevated highway. In recent years it has gained a clutch of grand cultural edifices – each designed in a strikingly modernistic fashion emphasising Shanghai's ambitions and the apparent ease with which it accepts and blends Chinese and Western influences, but all swallowed up and rendered insignificant by this vast ragged absence at the heart of the city.

The square's perimeters are loosely defined by two of the city's main east-west arteries, Nanjing Donglu (Shanghai's Oxford Street) and Yanan Donglu; there's a bus station at its north-eastern corner and two metro lines cross beneath, served by a pair of stations. It's a Mecca for commuters, and hundreds of thousands pass through daily. Visitors are drawn by the square's three museums, which include the truly excellent Shanghai Museum, and also by the green spaces, which provide a little respite from the relentless urbanism beyond the park fences.

RACEY BEGINNINGS

Renmin Square started life as the Shanghai racetrack. It was built by the British in 1862 and races were held in the spring and autumn of each year right up until the Japanese occupation in 1941. In the off-season the ground was used for training, riding and games of polo.

The city gentry raced short-nosed Mongolian ponies and laid bets (ladies wagered fans, gloves and bonnets). It was the Far Eastern equivalent of Ascot, a gathering of power and wealth and a high-society spectacle, only on a weekly basis. It was a source of gossip, intrigue,

From Park to pyramid

IM Pei is the world-renowned Chinese American architect who created the Rock and Roll Hall of Fame and Museum in Cleveland, Ohio, the sleek Bank of China building in

Hong Kong and, most famously, the Louvre's glass pyramid. But it was apparently Shanghai's Park Hotel that first inspired his passion for buildings.

Born in 1917 in Guangzhou, Pei grew up in Shanghai. In his memoir he recalls an occasion shortly after the hotel had been completed when he and his uncle had just seen a movie at the nearby Grand Theatre. On stepping out, Pei saw the new hotel and was spellbound. He took out a pencil and sketched the building on the spot. Pei's father wanted him to go to Britain and study banking after his schooling but instead he opted for America and architecture.

Although Pei has always maintained strong links with China (funding, out of his own pocket, a scholarship programme for young Chinese architects to study in the US) his building in the country has been limited to just two projects, both in Beijing. Shanghai's Pei heritage was until recently limited to the architect's childhood home, a three-storey mansion on Huangpi Nanlu, just south of Renmin Square. It remained occupied by Pei's relatives until 2000 when, despite several handwritten letters of protest to the government from Pei himself, the building was demolished. (Ironically, the same fate befell the Shanghai home of the architect of Pei's inspiration: *see p28* **Ladislaus Hudec**.)

outrage and more, including the occasion when a Japanese general with a bee in his bonnet about the lack of Nipponese representation on the Municipal Council shot the city's leading British citizen, Sir William Keswick, during post-race celebrations at the clubhouse.

In 1941, when the Japanese seized Shanghai, the racecourse became a holding pen for enemy nationals – Jim, the young protagonist in JG Ballard's *Empire of the Sun,* is briefly intered here. Following the 1949 Communist takeover, the racecourse was ploughed out of existence. During the Cultural Revolution the site was a venue for pro-government propagandising. The Red Guard used the open area for enforced self-criticism sessions by notorious 'criminals'. It's only in recent years that the joint square and park has taken on a more attractive face, with the turning point perhaps being in the mid 1990s when the municipal government moved into a new home here, abandoning its former HQ of the old Hongkong & Shanghai Bank building on the Bund.

Museums & parks

The races, horses and stables have gone but the clubhouse survives at the corner of Nanjing Xilu and Huangpi Beilu. Built in 1934, it's distinguished by a grand clocktower. The rooftop is now occupied by bar-restaurant **Kathleen's 5** (*see p100*); on the way up note the insignia of the SRC (Shanghai Race Club) above the main door, the brass plaque on the first floor honouring the club members who died in the Great War and also the cast-iron horses' heads worked into the design of the balustrade. Back outside, there's a lovely sculptural grouping of loafing locals, a nod to one of the building's other current tenants, the **Shanghai Art Museum** (*see p59*).

The clubhouse was imposing in its time but is now dwarfed by the neighbouring **Tomorrow Square** development, with its signature angular glass tower crowned with four pincers grasping at the sky. It's the tallest building this side of the river and should be

Sightseeing

home to a Bond villain, but instead it houses the **JW Marriott** (*see p37*). The management won't thank us for suggesting this but you could take the lift up to the 38th floor reception for some fantastic views over the square.

Equally emblematic of the new Shanghai is the striking industrial-orientalism of the **Shanghai Grand Theatre**, which takes the form of a plinth with a rocker on top. It was designed by French architect Jean-Marie Charpentier, who explains his creation thus: 'the layout is a geometrical square, the perfect shape in Chinese which symbolises Earth. The curved roof is a segment of a circle representing the Sky'. Whatever. It is undeniably gorgeous at night thanks to some very effective lighting. The soaring foyer is also quite magnificent and generally open to the public. The three auditoria can be visited as part of daily guided tours – or you could attend a performance (*see p185*).

Beside the theatre is the yawning avenue **Renmin Dadao**, of a width tailored to mighty parades of massed armies and rocket-carrying trucks (except that doesn't happen any more). On the north side is **City Hall** (closed to the public) and the space-module that is the **Urban Planning Centre** (open to the public and well worth a visit, *see p59*). To the south is Renmin Square's centrepiece, the world-class **Shanghai Museum** (*see p59*) with its highly distinctive

profile inspired by the cooking vessel. For d were denied access to calligraphy, bronzes now it's open to all.

For less culture ar a **walled garden** v corner, beside Nanjing Xilu. Early ... fills with folk practising tai chi. The open plazas around City Hall and the Shanghai Museum are softened with manicured gardens and flowerbeds, as well as a musical fountain. They are constantly busy with strollers, bench-sitters and kite flyers (kite flying is banned in most parts of the city). Between City Hall and the Grand Theatre is what's known as **English Corner**, where eager citizens gather to practise their spoken language on acquiescing Westerners. Those who want to practise Japanese – the second most common foreign language studied in Shanghai – gather in the walled garden.

Not all activity is above ground. Below the square is the **Hong Kong Shopping Centre** (*see p132*), or D-Mall, which fills a vast former air-raid shelter burrowed in the 1960s in the wake of the Sino-Soviet split. Now it's filled with bargain basement beauty parlours, cheap accessories stalls and gaming arcades. It's a teenagers' paradise.

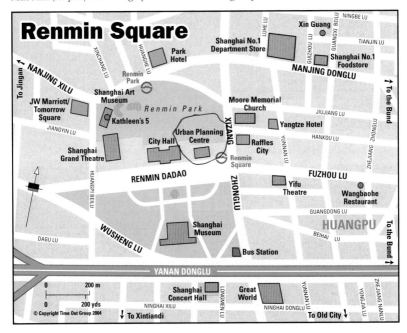

Sleek **Tomorrow Square** dwarfs the squat **Shanghai Art Museum**.

Shanghai Art Museum

325 Nanjing Xilu, Renmin Square (6327 4030).
Metro Renmin Park or Square. **Open** 9am-4.45pm
daily (last entrance 4pm). **Admission** RMB 20;
RMB 5 under-16s. **No credit cards. Map** p242 F4.
The museum houses traditional Chinese artworks
as well as a fine collection of contemporary art,
which predominates in the exhibition areas. The
romantic landscapes are dull but the patriotic daubings are a hoot, particularly the image of Bush and
other world leaders in Chinese tunics at the APEC
meeting in Shanghai in 2001. Permanent collections
are supplemented by hangings of international
artists and the building also hosts the prestigious
Shanghai Biennale (*see p163*). Unfortunately, there
is little English-language explanation and despite
signs advertising an audio tour, no such thing exists.
The museum has a good shop (*see p135*).

Shanghai Museum

201 Renmin Dadao, Renmin Square (6372 3500).
Metro Renmin Park or Square. **Open** 9am-5pm daily
(last entrance 4pm). **Admission** RMB 20; RMB 5
under-16s. **No credit cards. Map** p242 G5.
The Shanghai Museum was established in 1952 and
originally operated in an old bank building down
near the Bund. This distinctive new building,
opened in 1996 at a cost of around $50 million, was
designed by Shanghai architect Xing Tonghe. Six
stone lions and a pair of mythical beasts guard the
entrance and the granite walls are decorated with
designs inspired by those found on ancient bronze-
ware. The 120,000 or so pieces on show span Chinese
history from the Neolithic age to the present day.
Superb collections of sculpture, furniture, calligraphy, coins, ceramics, jade-ware, minority ethnic
handicrafts and particularly ancient bronzes are displayed in state of the art fashion.

All the major displays are annotated in English
and an excellent Acoustiguide commentary is available (RMB 40, plus leave your passport or RMB 500

as a deposit), as are free double-page guides to each
of the museum's collections. In addition, the museum also hosts quality international touring exhibitions, such as an astounding display of Cartier
masterpieces, shown in 2003. The museum shop has
an excellent range of replicas from the various collections and is the best source of books on Shanghai
and Chinese arts and culture.

Urban Planning Centre

100 Renmin Dadao, at Xizang Zhonglu, Renmin
Square (6318 4477). Metro Renmin Park or Square.
Open 9am-5pm Mon-Thur; 9am-6pm Fri-Sun.
Admission RMB 25; RMB 5 under-16s. **Credit**
AmEx, DC, MC, V. **Map** p242 G4.
A showcase of the city's ongoing architectural
development, the centre evokes past, present and
future through models, dioramas and multimedia.
A countdown clock, displaying the days left until
the 2010 World Expo, to be held here in Shanghai,
hammers home the message that this is a city with
definite goals and ambitions. These are set out for
all to see in what's billed as the largest of its kind in
the world – a huge model of how the central part of
the city should look come 2020. It can be viewed at
eye-level on the third floor or from above on the
fourth. The fourth floor also highlights a series of
key projects for future growth, including 11 spectacularly massive new town projects in the suburban districts. The basement exit area contains a little
frequented and rather tepid mock-up of a 1930s
street – better to go to the Municipal History
Museum in Pudong (*see p89*) for that sort of thing.
The hall has a number of good bookstores and an
audio tour is available.

Around Renmin Square

High-rise hotels and shopping complexes
surround the square – which is just as it has
always been. Today the JW Marriott dominates

Travelling theatre

If the demolition of the Pei house (*see p56* **From Park to pyramid**) had preservationists tearing out their hair, the saving of the Shanghai Concert Hall has them scratching their follically devastated pates in bafflement.

It opened as the Nanjing Theatre in the early 1930s and specialised in screening first-run Hollywood films. After 1949 it became the home of the Shanghai Symphony Orchestra, an arrangement that persisted until the opening of the new Shanghai Grand Theatre in the late 1990s. As a piece of architecture, the 70-year-old concert hall is not particularly representative of its era. Rather than art deco, which was the currency of the time, it's executed in a classical revival style with Chinese detailing for local flavour.

However, when in 1998 the city's first elevated highway (Yanan Donglu) was constructed less than 30 metres from the front door and the constant vibration of passing traffic threatened to destroy the building, city planners decided to make the theatre a showpiece of preservation. Brick by brick they took the theatre to pieces and reconstructed it on a new site some 60 metres to the south (in the process, razing a block of housing that had stood in the way).

Given the past record of the Shanghai municipality, which, according to the Shanghai Historic House Association, has already destroyed more than 50 per cent of the city's old neighbourhoods, why go to all this trouble (not to mention the cost of $8.45 million) over this one fairly undistinguished building? Apparently, the reason is because the theatre was designed by Chinese architects – unlike most of the rest of the buildings of the era, which were almost all the work of foreigners.

Fair enough. Except the relocated theatre has yet to open. Since the move, construction has begun on an extension of the underground metro system and a new line passes just east and under the theatre. Once again, the building is plagued by the shakes. Whoops. Preservation, it seems, is a whole lot harder than demolition.

but it used to be the **Park Hotel**. Built by Ladislaus Hudec (*see p28*) in 1934 and rising 22 storeys, the Park was the tallest building in Shanghai until as recently as 1988. Because of this distinction, distance from Shanghai is still measured from its main entrance. The rust-coloured tiled exterior remains a monument to vertical art deco design but the top-floor dance club with retractable roof is now defunct.

Running north beside the Park is **Huanghe Lu**, which looks exactly like everyone's idea of 'Chinatown': a narrow street crowded with tall neon signs, washtubs of writhing things on the pavement and tables of people eating cooked formerly writhing things in myriad tiny restaurants. It's colourful, exotic and fun: go with an appetite and lose it.

What is now the Shanghai Athletics Association building, next to the Park Hotel, was the interrogation centre for enemies of the state during the Cultural Revolution. It was here that the daughter of author Nien Cheng (*Life and Death in Shanghai*) was beaten to death by overzealous Red Guards.

At the north-east corner of Renmin Square twin spires mark another Ladislaus Hudec design, the red-brick **Moore Memorial Church**, built in the late 1920s and named for Texan Arthur J Moore, who donated funds for its construction. Then as now it serves a large community of Chinese Christians.

Nanjing Donglu

Nanjing Donglu has traditionally been regarded as 'China's number one shopping street'. While the Bund symbolised British imperial might, *da malu* (literally, the 'big road'), was always far more egalitarian. Throughout the 20th century shoppers of all nationalities and class thronged its department stores, where, in addition to the finest and most expansive selection of foreign and domestic goods, the retailers competed for attention with rooftop garden terraces and restaurants, in-store cinemas, amusement halls, radio studios where shoppers could watch local singing sensations, and even, in one case, an in-store hotel.

Today the road holds little of the cachet it once did and Shanghai's best shopping is most definitely elsewhere. However, as a spectacle of the crowded, gaudy, neon-lit China of coffee-table photo books it is unbeatable. Evening strollers can expect to be approached with offers of massage and other services from 'Chinese ladies', as well as hash and money (rent) boys. If you don't fancy walking, there's a free silly little electric 'train' that runs up and down plastered with ads for McDonald's.

Look out for the **Shanghai No.1 Department Store** (800 Nanjing Donglu), which for many years was the largest in China

Shanghai Museum. *See p59.*

Nanjing Donglu by night. *See p60.*

and boasted the country's first escalators.
Next door, across Guizhou Lu (the corner with
Nanjing Donglu is the site of the 30 May
Massacre, where in 1925 British police killed
11 Chinese anti-Japan protestors: *see p15*), is the
unmissable **Shanghai No.1 Foodstore** (*see
p142*). At **No.635**, corner of Zhejiang Zhonglu,
is the former Wing On, a department store that
once boasted two whole floors of
entertainments, while **No.429** used to be
Sincere, so named because it was the first store
to feature fixed prices. It was also the first
department store on Nanjing Donglu, opened in
1917. Ahead is the Bund, but it's also worth
diverting to explore the streets to the south.

SOUTH OF NANJING DONGLU

Once known for its brothels and bars, **Fuzhou
Lu** is home to the city's best bookshops. These
range from the tiny suppliers of stationery and
paper to the mighty state-owned booksellers.

For English-language titles try **Book City**
or the **Foreign Languages Bookstore** (for
both, *see p136*). One block south, **Guangdong
Lu** specialises in small shops selling beauty
supplies. Come here for anything from Chinese
opera make-up to a new camphor wood comb.

The building tiered like a wedding cake at
the corner of Xizang Zhonglu and Yanan
Donglu was, prior to 1949, the hub of Shanghai
nightlife. Billing itself as **Great World**, it was
an adult amusement palace and, in the words
of city biographer Stella Dong, 'No one
establishment said more about Shanghai during
the last decades of semicolonialism than this
hodgepodge of the most déclassé elements of
East and West'. Quite innocuous when it was
opened in 1916 by a local pharmacist who'd
made his fortune with a cure-all tonic, the place
become notorious after its takeover by arch-
gangster 'Pockmarked' Huang in 1931. Its six
storeys offered sing-song girls (whose clothing
got more revealing with each successive floor),
whores, cabaret and gambling. The rooftop
reportedly lacked a safety rail offering a quick
way out of debt for chronic losers. Josef von
Sternberg visited in the early '30s while
scouting locations for *Shanghai Express*, a
movie that, as Stella Dong writes, 'had film
audiences all over the world – except perhaps in
Shanghai – wondering what Marlene Dietrich
really meant when she said, "It took more than
one man to change my name to Shanghai Lily".'
During the Communist years the building
survived as a wholesome 'youth palace'; it is
currently closed, awaiting redevelopment.

Immediately west is the transplanted
Shanghai Concert Hall (*see p60* **Travelling
theatre**), while running down the east side
of Great World is aromatic **Yunnan Nanlu**
(*see p115* **Street eats**).

Discount tickets

Serious sightseers might consider
investing in combined tickets for Renmin
Square's attractions. For RMB 60 you can
get one ticket good for admission to the
Shanghai Museum, the Shanghai Art
Museum and either the Urban Planning
Centre or a tour of the Grand Theatre.
Be warned, however: the ticket is valid for
just one day and that's a lot of sightseeing
to cram into only a few hours. Perhaps a
better option is the combined Art Museum
and Urban Planning Centre ticket for
RMB 45. Get the tickets from the
relevant box offices.

Jingan

Temples to commerce, temples to wealth, temples to Buddha.

Map p248 & p249

The district is named for the Jingan Temple, a local Buddhist landmark – but the only god worshipped with any fervour in this part of town is Mammon. Jingan is Shanghai's 'downtown', home to prime office and retail space. The main street is Nanjing Xilu, the western extension of Nanjing Donglu (*see p60*), which is just about the most exclusive business address in town, home to a premier league line-up of swanky malls twinkling with top-end retailers such as Burberry, Louis Vuitton, Moschino and Prada.

Despite the intense redevelopment, among all the mirrored glass and polished terrazzo, pockets of a far older Shanghai remain. Jingan was absorbed into the International Settlement in 1899 and retains some evocative reminders of its colonial-era heritage. It's an area easily explored on foot, starting at Renmin Square and heading west along Nanjing Xilu.

BUBBLING WELL ROAD

What's now Nanjing Xilu was formerly the charmingly named Bubbling Well Road. It ran from the Shanghai racetrack – today's Renmin Square – to the western end of what was then the International Settlement, the boundary of which was marked by the Jingan Temple. The neighbourhood of the temple was the quieter, leafier, suburban end of the Settlement, so it was where the wealthiest *taipan* (foreign community leaders) – and Chinese – built their town mansions.

By the 1930s this section of town was suburban no longer; it had been swallowed up by the rapidly expanding city. The population density sent land prices sky-high with the result that many owners sold or razed their mansions and erected exclusive clubs, dance halls and residential tower blocks along Bubbling Well and other nearby thoroughfares. Some of Shanghai's most celebrated clubs of that era – including DD's and the Majestic – indulged in their particular brand of hedonism just up the road from where the Portman Ritz-Carlton stands today. Fashionable types moved into new apartments like the Medhurst and the Continental, not just because they were close to the night-time hotspots, but because the strict police force of the International Settlement provided a veneer of safety during the violent years leading up to World War II.

High flyin' **Nanjing Xilu**.

Nanjing Xilu

Walking from Renmin Square, after passing under the Chengdu Beilu flyover, a garden centre-style façade on the north side of Nanjing Xilu announces the **Antiques, Bird and Plant Market**. While not the largest such market, it does have heaps of atmosphere with two central courtyards surrounded by shops specialising in old light fittings, vases and furniture. Just north of the antiques section is a small area devoted to seasonal plants and songbirds. The best time to visit is Friday afternoon when the courtyards fill with up-country peasants who spread their meagre wares on mats for inspection.

Close by the market, a small road slips off the south side of Nanjing Xilu taking a roughly parallel arc; this is the former Love Lane, once full of dance halls before the Liberation, but as **Wujiang Lu**, one of Shanghai's busiest centres of alfresco dining (*see p115* **Street eats**).

Jingan – where new Shanghai bosses the old.

Employees of the tumble of tiny restaurants hawk their menus to passers-by. Go for the fried dumplings (*shengjian*), which are sold at several places in the middle of the first block approached from Renmin.

Beyond the junction with Shimen Yilu, Wujiang goes upscale. In place of the small, almost makeshift mom-and-pop venues (good food, if a little doubtful on the hygiene front) is a host of more polished Cantonese and other regional restaurants. This stretch of the road is wider and newly resurfaced, and also off limits to traffic (including bicycles). The westernmost stretch of Wujiang Lu is the haunt of street sellers flogging all manner of knock-off items from DVDs to perfume and designer bags. Weekends are the busiest time. At the point where Wujiang rejoins Nanjing it's worth a quick detour south down **Maoming Beilu** for some particularly good examples of *shikumen* tenement housing (*see p29*).

Also down here, among the grid of tiny cramped lanes strung with washing, where women squat the doorsteps peeling veg while cigarette-sucking, middle-aged gents putter by on noisy motor scooters, is the little-visited **Chairman Mao's Residence** (*see below*).

Chairman Mao's Residence

Nos.5-9 Lane 583, Weihai Lu, by Maoming Beilu (no phone). Metro Shimen Yilu. **Open** 9.30am-4.45pm daily. **Admission** RMB 5. **No credit cards. Map** p249 E5.

This was the most frequently used of three houses that Mao kept during his early years in Shanghai. He shared it with his wife, their two children and his mother-in-law. The well-preserved grey- and red-brick *shikumen* dwelling features spartan bedrooms and a large exhibition of photos and letters. The displays are annotated in English.

Shanghai Centre

In an astonishing contrast that says more about the dynamics of Shanghai today than any amount of written analysis, just one turn of a corner is a leap of a century, from the *National Geographic* world of the *shikumen* of Maoming Beilu to the 21st-century mall culture of central Nanjing Xilu. The scenes of hanging washing and women hunched over pots and pans are replaced by high-heeled, pencil-skirted misses and their dark-suited male counterparts scooting between appointments, streaming rapid-fire speech into palm-sized mobiles. The backdrop is the sheet-glass walls and rounded contours of the **Westgate Mall**, the **CITIC Square** mall and the precisely named 66-storey **Plaza 66** mall, three large monuments to high chic and high spending. If *Sex and the City* went Shanghai, this is where you'd find the girls. For shopping specifics, *see p130*.

North along Shanxi Nanlu is the old **Ohel Rachel Synagogue** (No.500), built in 1920 by Jacob Sasoon and the spiritual home of the city's wealthy Sephardic Jewish community until their departure in 1949. The building was subsequently used as a stable, warehouse and Communist centre, until then-US First Lady Hillary Clinton and Secretary of State Madeline Albright asked to visit the building during a 1998 visit to China. The city cleaned up and painted the building. Now local preservationists in league with the remaining Jewish community are trying to get the city to allow the synagogue to reopen as a regular place of worship.

One block west of Plaza 66 is the granddaddy of the city's commercial developments, the **Shanghai Centre**, which is all of 15 years old.

Also known as the Portman, after its American architect (he's also responsible for the Bund Centre and Tomorrow Square), this was one of the first foreign-backed property ventures in the city since the Communist takeover of 1949. It opened in 1989, just after Tiananmen. While most other foreigners were cutting ties with China in protest at the unfair matching of tanks vs students, the money behind the Portman honoured its commitment. Because of this, the development has certain unique special rights such as its own telephone exchange (operated by the US-based BellSouth), the only one in all China. It also boasted the first HSBC automatic teller machine in Shanghai.

The central section of the complex is anchored by the **Portman Ritz-Carlton** (*see p39*); also here is the **Shanghai Centre Theatre**, which is home to the Shanghai Acrobats (*see p134*); one of the best grocery stores is on the ground floor, close to a dry cleaner's, a bank and a Starbucks. Around the forecourt are ten airline offices, several consulates (including that of the United Kingdom) and chambers of commerce, plus numerous office suites.

While the Portman represents Shanghai's embracing of US-style market capitalism, directly across Nanjing Xilu is a monument to an earlier ideological union, that between China and the USSR, in the highly Muscovite form of the **Shanghai Exhibition Hall**. It was the early 1950s and the Chinese Communist Party had just 'saved' the country from the evil Nationalist 'Kuomintang' Party. China had also recently helped North Korea beat back the 'imperialist' Americans. To show off the first fruits of the newly won socialist paradise, the city government decided on a grand monument to international communism, which – oh sweet revenge – was built on a site formerly occupied by a villa belonging to one of the Concession era's wealthiest foreigners, Silas Hardoon.

With communism firmly out of fashion, the Exhibition Hall is largely empty. For a few *yuan* visitors can wander in and look around. Most of the rooms have long been denuded of their Proletariat-lauding mural work, but the Soviet influence remains pervasive in the odd mixture of baroque Bolshevik-cum-beaux arts architecture and crowning red star.

Temples

A short walk west of the Portman and Exhibition Hall, past the excellent dim sum restaurant **Bi Feng Tang** (*see p104*), is the attractive expanse of greenery that is **Jingan Park**, formerly Bubbling Well Cemetery. Now it boasts a scenic lake overlooked by the **Bali**

CITY
WEEKEND
城 市 周 报
Pick up
City Weekend magazine
Sign up at
cityweekend.com.cn
for email updates
What's on in
Shanghai
this
week?

Laguna restaurant (*see p107*) and a copy of an old tram car that is used as a snack bar. There's also a re-creation of the well that gave the cemetery and road its name; the original spring was just outside the cemetery gates, at what is now the junction of Nanjing and Wanghang Lu. It was paved over in 1919.

The well dated back to at least the third century AD, which is around the time that the first place of worship was erected on the site now occupied by the **Jingan Temple** (Temple of Tranquillity). That first temple collapsed in 1216 to be rebuilt in something similar to the form in which you see it today. 'Something similar' because not a bit of the old structure remains, having being pulled down in the 1990s to be rebuilt again from scratch as part of an ongoing Chinese programme to demolish its historic structures and replace them with concrete-based, gussied-up lookalikes. In this case, the temple comes with an all-new shopping mall. As such, it's of limited interest except during festivals, when the place is busy with worshippers rather than tourists.

West again along Nanjing Lu, just before the junction with Wulumuqi Zhonglu, the imposing white structure on the south side of the road is the Jingan **Children's Palace**. Each municipal district has one of these institutions, where gifted children recieve special tutoring and perform for visiting dignitaries. Talent-show brats aside, what's interesting about the Palace is its former incarnation as the fabled 'Marble Hall'. Built for wealthy Shanghai Jew Sir Elly

Kadoorie, the mansion took six years to complete. Its name derived from the massive amounts of Italian stone imported to ornament the fireplaces. It was the first house in the city to have air-conditioning and boasted a 19-metre-high (65-foot) ballroom with 5.4-metre (18-foot) chandeliers. Amazingly, the ballroom and its chandeliers have survived and can be viewed by anyone, as long as they turn up as part of a group and submit to a minder.

A ten-minute walk north of Nanjing Xilu is the district's other major religious foundation, the **Jade Buddha Temple**, or Yufo Si. It was completed around 1920 and houses a 1.9-metre-high (six-foot) seated Buddha. According to one of the temple guides, however, this is a new Buddha sculpted in the early 1990s. Apparently, the guardians of the temple thought a bigger Buddha would be more impressive to visitors. Where the smaller original Jade Buddha is the guide couldn't say. Also in this part of town, a couple of blocks north of the temple, is the warehouse district of **Moganshan Lu** (*see p162* Alt art).

Jade Buddha Temple

Corner of Jiangning Lu & Anyuan Lu (no phone). Metro Shanghai Railway Station. **Open** 8am-4.30pm daily. **Admission** free. **Map** p248 C2.

Jingan Temple

Nanjing Xilu, by Wanghang Lu (no phone). Metro Jingan Temple. **Open** 7.30am-5pm daily. **Admission** RMB 5. **No credit cards**. **Map** p248 B5.

Religious rights

Shanghai remains nominally Communist-run. However, the more open nature of the Party of today means that Chinese citizens are allowed to partake in religious activities – as long as they respect the primacy of the Communist Party and allow all activities to be supervised by Party representatives. There's also a further caveat, which is that rights of worship are extended to a handful of state-approved religions only.

The list of acceptable religions is compact. The Chinese authorities recognise the Western religions of Christianity, in both its Catholic and Protestant forms, and Islam, plus the Eastern religions of Buddhism or Taoism. One venue for the worship of each of these religions is permitted per municipal district. The authorities allow no room for the different sects within these complex groups (so no Baptists, First Adventists or

Methodists, and no Shia or Sunni divisions). They also limit some services to 'passport holders', by which they mean non-Chinese. Neither are the Catholic or Protestant churches allowed communication with their own higher authorities – so no chats with the Pope or flying visits from the Archbishop of Canterbury.

Despite the major role the Jews have played in the development of Shanghai, the Party only sanctions one working synagogue for the entire city. That's on paper: in practice, neither of the city's two surviving synagogues (from a one-time total of seven) is in use. The Ohel Moshe (*see p94*) is a museum, while the Ohel Rachel (*see p65*) remains in the hands of the city government, which allows Shanghai's Jewish community – of approximately 300 – to use the building for services only a few times a year.

The Old City

Chinatown vs toytown.

Temple of the City God. See p70.

Map p245

Look at a map of Shanghai and it's easy to
identify where the original settlement once lay:
it's the yolk in the egg white of the city. The
defining, near circular line of the old walls –
demolished in 1911 but now traced by Renmin
Lu/Zhonghua Lu – rebuffs the cartesian grid
of the modern city.

Previously known as Nanshi (Southern City),
this site has been occupied for around 2,000
years and was well established as a small
fishing town long before foreigners first arrived
to create Concession-era Shanghai. A five-
kilometre (three-mile) circuit of walls and a
moat were added in the 1550s to keep Japanese
pirates at bay. With the arrival of the foreign
powers, the Old City remained a wholly Chinese
ghetto, squalid and mysterious, and a place
where few Westerners ever ventured.

Thomas Cook, the company patriarch, led the
first group of tourists from England to the Old
City in 1872. Despite his adverse impression of
its choked and offensive streets, it subsequently
became a must on all sightseeing itineraries. It

remains so today, presenting as it does a
curious anomaly of a Chinatown in a Western-
looking Chinese city. Crowds perpetually
swarm its narrow store-lined lanes, stuffed
to the hilt with arts and crafts, antiques,
jewellery, foodstuffs and all manner of other
items, desirable and not so desirable.

Despite classic appearances, most of the bits
of the Old City that draw the tourists have been
restored or even completely rebuilt over the last
decade or so, in a fusion of mock Ming and Qing
Dynasty styles. Many visitors are also under
the impression that the Yu Gardens and
neighbouring bazaar are all that there is of
interest. This is not so – there's a lot more of
local and historical interest to be discovered
within walking distance, although the Yu
Gardens does make a good spot from which
to begin any visit.

Yu Gardens & Bazaar

The most visited part of the Old City is a tightly
defined block bounded by Jiujiaochang Lu to
the west, Fangbang Zhonglu to the south,
Fuyou Lu to the north and Anren Lu to the east.
Taking up a large part of this area is Shanghai's
number one tourist attraction, the **Yu Gardens**
(Yuyuan; open 8.30am-5pm daily, admission
RMB 30), or Garden of Leisurely Repose. It
was originally created for the governor of the
Sichuan province, Pan Yunduan, in the 16th
century. Neglect followed his demise before
the gardens were rescued and restored in the
middle of the 18th century. These days the
Yu Gardens are resplendent, with a design
that embodies an artistic vision of the world
in miniature, ingeniously mingling over 30
pavilions with hillocks and picturesque bridges,
stairs, winding paths and carp-laden lotus
ponds. Each section of the gardens is separated
by curvaceous white walls crowned with the
head and body of a dragon.

One of the key features to look out for is the
Exquisite Jade Rock, which stands in front
of the Hall of Jade Magnificence. The rock was
supposedly destined for the imperial park in
Beijing, during the reign of Emperor Hui Zong,
but by misfortune its cargo boat sank and it
ended up languishing at the bottom of the
Huangpu River. It was later rescued by the
creators of the Yu Gardens.

Of the pavilions, the **Three Ears of Corn Hall** is the largest; symbols of plenty (rice ears, millet, wheat seedlings, melons and fruit) adorn the doors and windows. The nearby **Hall for Viewing the Grand Rockery** is a beautiful two-storey building overlooking a pond. Upstairs is the 'Chamber for Gathering the Rain', which derives its name from a Tang Dynasty poem by Wang Bo. The 'Corridor for Approaching the Best Scenery' (aren't these just the greatest of names?) leads to the heart of the gardens, the **Grand Rockery**, built with 2,000 tons of yellow stone quarried from Zhejiang province; the whole thing is cemented together with rice glue. At the foot of the rockery is the Pavilion for Viewing Frolicking Fish and neighbouring 200-year-old wisteria, while a gingko tree, reputed to be 400 years old, stands in front of the Ten Thousand Flower Pavilion. Also worth a look is the **Hall of Mildness**, which houses a century-old set of furniture skillfully carved from banyan tree roots.

Note that the gardens can get uncomfortably crowded. Our advice is to get there early or visit during the relatively quiet lunchtime period.

Yu Gardens Bazaar

Just outside the entrance to the Yu Gardens is a large ornamental lake, teeming with carp and crossed by the wonderfully batty **Bridge of**

Nine Turnings, which zigzags across the water in lightning-flash fashion. It's built like this to halt evil spirits, which are, apparently, unable to turn corners. At the centre of the lake sits the **Huxinting Teahouse**, patronised by presidents and queens, and immortalised on dinner plates worldwide as the Willow Pattern Teahouse (*see p72* **To the teahouse**).

There are a number of speciality eateries in the vicinity, notably **Nan Xiang** (*see p107*), a famous little dumpling shop near the gardens entrance selling delicious steamed dumplings – easy to spot by the snaking queues of salivating customers. Nearby in a Ming Dynasty-style pavilion, **Lu Bo Lang** (*see p107*) does inferior but decent dumplings – the safest bets are those filled with crabmeat.

Around the lake area is the **Yu Gardens Bazaar** (Yuyuan Shangsha), an area of narrow lanes filled with over 100 small stores. The architecture is traditional in style but modern in execution and the whole thing comes across as a sort of Disneyfied version of 'ye Olde Shanghai'. Of the few places of genuine interest, look out for **Liyunge Shanzhuang**, at 35 Yuyuan Laolu, which is a shop specialising in fans that's been around since 1880, and also the city's oldest medicine store **Tong Hang Chun Traditional Chinese Medicine Store** at 20 Yuyuan Xinlu (*see p145*), where you can stock up on bear bile and preserved antlers.

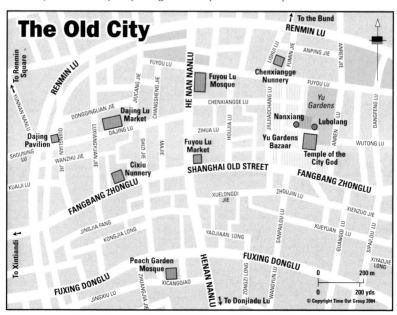

Temple of the City God

At the heart of the Yu Garden Bazaar area is what in days gone by was the focal point of the town, the **Temple of the City God** (Chenghuang Miao; open 24hrs daily, admission RMB 5) originally built in 1403. The temple was traditionally a venue for fairground activities where entertainers and vendors would gather at festival times. It was believed that the City God had charge of all the other spirits who had once been embodied in the citizens of Shanghai. Following years of neglect and prior use as a factory and shop, the temple has recently been restored and people still seek advice on private and business matters from the City God.

Fuyou Lu & Shanghai Old Street

North of the Yu Gardens area is Fuyou Lu, address of a missable array of warehouse-like jewellers and 'antique' stores and Western fast-food joints. More worthy of attention is the **Chenxiangge Nunnery** (open 7am-4pm daily, admission RMB 5) on Lishui Lu, which was part of the estate of the gardens' original owner. It was rebuilt as a temple in the early 19th century and, like all religious edifices in the area, ignobly converted into a factory workshop during the Cultural Revolution. Following five years of careful restoration, it reopened as a place of worship in 1994. Visit for the massed figurines of the 348 disciples that adorn the surface of a vault enclosing a gilded statue of Buddha.

A few minutes' walk west, the **Fuyou Lu Mosque** is one of the oldest surviving buildings in the area. Consisting of three interconnecting halls in traditional Chinese style, it was built in 1870 and reopened in 1979.

South of the Yu Gardens, the street known to locals as Fangbang Zhonglu is marketed to visitors as '**Shanghai Old Street**'. It's a picturesque alley of two-storey shop-houses, some of which are around 100 years old and most of which were renovated when the street was given a tourist-friendly makeover at the turn of the millennium. Just east of the junction with Jiujiaochang Lu is the **Hua Bao Building** with an interesting, if expensive, basement antique market. Continue in this direction and, as the street narrows, the renovated buildings give way to genuine old Shanghai, a ramshackle, unprettified mass of apothecaries, grocers and food stalls that lines the route all the way until Zhonghua Lu.

Travelling west from the junction with Jiujiaochang Lu, Shanghai Old Street is lined with antique, curio and craft stores, one of which, at No.361, is the endlessly fascinating **Seal Military** (*see p136* **Mem-Mao-ries are made of this**). Shanghai's largest and most lively antique market, the **Fuyou Lu Market**, is housed on the north side in the Cang Bao Building, just before the *pailou*, or ceremonial

Yu Gardens. *See p68.*

arch, that frames the street. The market comes alive at weekends, and especially on Sundays, with an astounding array of antiques and knick-knacks spread over its four levels. It's best to get there early as many stallholders tend to pack up mid afternoon. Just before dawn a large 'ghost' market (it only appears at certain times), sprawls along this stretch of the street.

Also on this section of Shanghai Old Street are several teahouses including the **Old Shanghai Teahouse** (385 Fangbang Zhonglu, 5382 1202, open 8.30am-11pm daily), which doubles as a small museum, with 1920s artefacts and memorabilia including clothing, paintings, photos, posters and old maps.

West of Henan Lu

To escape the tourist version of Old Shanghai, continue west on Fangbang Zhonglu across major north-south thoroughfare Henan Nanlu. About 100 metres along are the ochre-coloured walls of the new part of the **Cixiu Nunnery**. Running north beside the nunnery is a small lane called **Zhenling Jie**, replete with joss-stick vendors and residents with open-air kitchens, preparing food and doing their washing in outside sinks. The older and more interesting part of the nunnery is back here, sited behind the new. There's a richly decorated small courtyard temple, built in 1870, with a prayer hall on one side and dormitories for the nuns opposite. Visitors are welcome.

A left at the top of the lane leads past a row of imposing *shikumen* (stone-frame-door) housing from the 1920s and to a magnificent old school building. A couple of twists north is splendid **Dajing Lu Market**, one of the city's biggest food markets, packed with sellers of unfathomable varieties of vegetables, fish and assorted aquatic creatures, as well as steamed dumplings and other appetising munchies. Visit while you can because with the present mania for redevelopment streets like this one won't be around for much longer.

Also on Dajing is the imposing **White Cloud Taoist Temple**. It looks like it's seen a bit of history, but was actually only completed in 2004. It serves as a stage for the daily rituals of Taoist monks. The temple possesses seven unique Ming Dynasty bronze statues. The neighbouring **Dajing Pavilion** adjoins the only surviving section of the Ming Dynasty city wall. It's a three-storey tower that originally served as a battlement from which archers could fire on marauding Japanese pirates in the 16th century. It was subsequently converted into the Guangong Temple and today houses a rather primitive exhibition dedicated to the native city. A small model of the old town and a short series of Chinese annotated visuals chronicling the area's history can be found on the second floor.

Over across main Renmin Lu, hawker-lined Yunnan Lu (*see p115* **Street eats**) makes a beeline north for central Renmin Square.

Confucious Temple

South on Zhonghua Lu – the lower half of the Old City 'ring road' – a ceremonial arch marks the entrance to Wenmiao Lu. This is the site of the only **Confucious Temple** (Wenmiao Lu; open 9am-5.15pm daily) to have survived in the city. The temple's present appearance dates from 1855, the days of bloody tempest when it was occupied by the gangster Small Swords Society during its assault on the city (*see p12*). However, much more damage was done to its majesty and riches during the Cultural Revolution, only some of which was righted during extensive restoration that took place in the mid 1990s.

The centrepiece is the 20-metre-high (66-foot) Kuixing Pavilion, which overlooks the 'Sky and Cloud Reflection Pool' and once commanded views over the whole of the Old City (it's now dwarfed by a rash of neighbouring 20-plus storey dwellings). The temple features a number of exhibition halls with exhibitions of Chinese crafts, including a teapot museum.

As well as being a centre for worship, the compound was also a place of learning. It housed the National Library of Shanghai in the 1930s. Students hoping for success in the June national examinations still tie red ribbons around the camphor trees in front of the temple. The main courtyard of the temple also hosts a large and lively parasol-shaded **second-hand book market** each Sunday. While most titles are in Chinese, a good rummage will turn up revolutionary and pre-revolutionary offerings in English. Outside, the street is busy with vendors peddling pirated CDs and DVDs. There's also a large **book market** north-east of the complex, just off Xuegong Lu.

A few streets north and east, close to the junction of Fuxing Lu and Henan Lu, is the **Peach Garden Mosque** (Xiaotaoyuan; 52 Xiaotaoyuan Lu, open 8am-7pm daily), tucked down an alley of the same name. Completed in 1927, this imposing historic building with Western, Chinese and Islamic architectural adornments is the major centre for the city's growing Muslim population and serves as the headquarters for the Shanghai Islamic Association. Like everything else around here, it has been recently restored to something like its previous state.

To the teahouse

Seeking refuge at the bottom of a tea cup can be a particularly soothing pursuit in China. At traditional teahouses, whole afternoons can be whiled away with a fragrant succession of green and flower teas, while the locals play chequers, study for exams and share gossip. Tea is an integral part of Chinese eating and drinking, with its own deities, folklore and customs, and it's not just tourists who are drawn to teahouses.

Sadly, these old institutions are under serious threat from relentless commercial development, as well as from the arrival of Western-style cafés and bars, including the ubiquitous Starbucks (of which, at last count, the city had no fewer than 36 – four times as many as Miami, Florida).

But there is still a handful of places where you can enjoy the teahouse experience. The etiquette can vary a lot, but in most places you pay for your pot of tea once (usually about RMB 15-30) and it will be endlessly refilled with hot water. The more modern the teahouse, the more likely that soft drinks, beer and snacks will also be available.

The most famous traditional teahouse is the ornate multi-storey **Huxingting** on the lake inside the touristy Yu Gardens (257 Yuyuan Lu, Old City), which boasts Bill Clinton and Queen Elizabeth as previous visitors. Another beautiful old-style teahouse packed with antique furniture and curios is **Tangyun** (down the alley at 119 Hengshan Lu, French Concession). The **Mingren** (9 Duolun Lu, 5696 4368) or 'celebrity teahouse' in the historic Hongkou district is worth visiting if you're in the area. Housed in a three-storey colonial villa, it's a popular locals' afternoon haunt for a game of mahjong.

Sophia's (480 Huashan Lu, French Concession) serves as both a restaurant and a teahouse, and its sunny balcony on the second floor is a small oasis amid the traffic and construction.

The most popular teahouses among locals are, however, the more modern chain variety (the curiously named Be For Time Tea Houses, for example; try the one at the corner of Huaihai Zhonglu and Wuxing Lu in the French Concession). These tend to fill up with students and young office workers so don't be surprised if they approach you wanting to practise their English. The gentle slurping and game-counter clacking are accompanied by the less soothing noises of TV soap opera and/or karaoke.

Chenxiangge Nunnery. *See p70.*

Dongjiadu & Nanpu

South-east of the Old City (as defined by the line of the old walls) is Dongjiadu Lu, site of the city's famed **Fabric Market**. It's a vast place with over 200 stalls and small shops parading rolls of cashmere, silks and assorted tailoring fabrics (*see p130*).

Just up the street, **Dongjiadu Cathedral** is Shanghai's oldest and perhaps most beautiful place of worship. It was founded in 1849 by a Bishop Besco and a band of Jesuit missionaries. In recent times its magnificent Spanish Baroque-style façade and interior have been meticulously restored. The bas-relief on the upper sections of the walls adopts traditional Chinese emblems and the bell tower still holds all four original bells. The surrounding area once housed a huge Catholic community, with its own police force and fire brigade – something like China's very own Vatican – which survived until the early 20th century. Mass is held every morning. At other times just ring the bell; visitors are welcome. A 1914 school building, once attached to the cathedral, stands across the road.

A short walk south of Dongjiadu is one of the city's most photographed modern landmarks, the **Nanpu Bridge**. Completed as recently as 1991, this was the first bridge over the Huangpu River. Previous to this, everything crossed by ferry. Cars ascend a spiralling access road to reach its distinctive cable-suspended structure; pedestrians and tourists take the lift up to the main span for great views up-river and across the city (open 8.30am to 4pm daily). The area to the south of the bridge, down to the new Lupu Bridge, is to be razed to accommodate one of the main sites for the 2010 World Expo.

One hopes that the authorities have sense enough to avoid the destruction of the **Sanshan GuildHall**, a precious bit of history that lies in the way of the Expo. Up until the 1920s, guilds were very important associations for regulating the economic and social life of migrant workers living in Shanghai. Sanshan, one of the few surviving guildhalls, was built in 1909 for its Fujianese community. The magnificent red-brick, stone and wood courtyard building was restored in 2002 and now serves as the **Shanghai Museum of Folk Collectibles**. Its central feature is an opera stage with an intricately carved roof, plus of course the exhibits (*see below*).

Shanghai Museum of Folk Collectibles

1551 Zhongshan Nanlu, by Nanchezhan Lu (6314 6453). **Open** 9am-4pm daily. **Admission** RMB 5. **No credit cards. Map** p244 H9.
The exhibition halls display temporary exhibitions from private collections and offer an intriguing insight into the history of Shanghai through such everyday items as cosmetics, cigarette lighters and cases from the 1920s and '30s, small shoes for bound feet, furniture, porcelain, clocks and family photos. There are also some more general examples of Chinese arts and crafts on display.

Xintiandi

Where Chinese Communists first conspired, cappuccino culture reigns.

Map p244
You are unlikely to find the name Xintiandi (pronounced 'shin-tien-dee') on too many maps, least of all any maps published longer than three years ago. That's because it's a modern appellation, possibly dreamt up in some marketing boardroom (it translates as 'New Heaven and Earth'), which very specifically applies to a spanking new city centre development. It's a mix of retail, entertainment, commercial office space and residential units, and it has won renown and, indeed, widespread favour through its innovative recycling of traditional architecture. In business since 2001, Xintiandi is already a leading fixture on the Shanghai city sightseeing list. Not bad going for what is essentially an open-air mall.

It helps that Xintiandi is just a ten-minute walk south of central Renmin Square, and just off central Huaihai Zhonglu, with its clustered malls and department stores, visited by hundreds of thousands of shoppers daily.

For commerce of a less brassy nature, a brief walk east of Xintiandi is the antique and curios market on Dongtai Lu and side streets, which offers an authentic slice of Old Shanghai sans redevelopment – although it's only a matter of time. The bulldozer engines are idling.

Xintiandi

If the Bund was the showpiece of early 20th-century Shanghai, then Xintiandi is arguably its 21st-century counterpart. But whereas the structures lining the Bund were all about bombast, Xintiandi is a celebration of modern Shanghai's ability to fuse old and new, East and West. Its 28 buildings, grouped into North and South blocks, are all examples of renovated or wholly reconstructed *shikumen*, or 'stone-gated' lane houses (*see p29*). They're a photogenic fusion of 19th-century English terrace housing, with south-of-the-Yangtze traditional Chinese residences. They were originally built in the 1920s and '30s to house the Chinese middle classes. As part of the redevelopment, exteriors were retained – or rebuilt anew – while the interiors were gutted and refitted to modern requirements. Between the buildings run tiny *nontang*s (alleys) that connect with large open-air plazas suitable for European-style alfresco dining and drinking.

The development is subject to the most meticulous touches, such as buttermilk treatment to help grow moss on bricks and monthly inspection of manhole covers to ensure their proper alignment.

Sadly, for all the care and the veneration of traditional architectural forms, the result resembles little more than a high-end mall, a Potemkin village of pretty façades aimed at seducing affluent visitors and parting them from their money. Its 100 or so units are filled with ritzy boutiques such as Cheese & Fizz, where Romeo y Julieta brand Cuban cigars cost $12 each, and the likes of Starbucks, Häagen-Dazs, a Vidal Sassoon salon and an Alexander City Club fitness centre.

There are some worthwhile places: we very much like the deli **KABB** (*see p108*), superior lunch venue **Simply Thai** (*see p117*) and, for top-end dining, **T8** (*see p109*), which are all in the North Block. The South Block has dim sum-specialist **Crystal Jade** (*see p108*) and the **UME International Cineplex** (*see p159*). Other than the cinema, cultural representation is limited to the **Shikumen Open House Museum** (*see p75*) and, irony of ironies, the **Museum of the First National Congress of the Chinese Communist Party** (*see below*) – the humble meeting room in which Chinese communism was founded now anchors the North Block of this most bourgeois of developments.

East across Huangpi Nanlu is a fabricated but quite beautiful **lake**. This is also part of the Xintiandi development – which when completed will cover 52 hectares (128 acres), or 23 blocks, at the heart of the city. This section is designed for the well-heeled long-term leaseholder and is flanked by modern residential towers (Lakeville at Xintiandi) and grade A office buildings (set out on the chillingly named Corporate Avenue). The area east of the lake is pencilled in for more upscale shopping but is currently occupied by real traditional housing, an antiques street market (Dongtai Lu, *see p75*) and a Buddhist temple. Visit while you still can.

Museum of the First National Congress of the Chinese Communist Party

374 Huangpi Nanlu, by Xingye Lu (5383 2171).
Metro Huangpi Lu. **Open** 9am-4pm daily.
Admission RMB 3. **No credit cards.** Map 244 F6.

Here on 23 July 1921 the Chinese Communist Party was formed in reaction against foreign domination. A large upstairs exhibition area sets the historical context displaying hated imperialist, Concession-era icons, such as the seat used by the chairman of the Shanghai Municipal Council. The centrepiece is a lifelike wax diorama immortalising the historic First Congress, with Mao centre-stage. It's then down to a small red-brick lane house to see where this gathering of Mao, 12 other delegates and two Comintern representatives actually took place. The gift shop has some excellent memorabilia.

Shikumen Open House Museum

No.25, Lane 181, Taicang Road, North Block, by Xingye Lu (3307 0337/www.xintiandi.com). Metro Huangpi Nanlu. **Open** 10am-10pm daily. **Admission** RMB 20; RMB 10 under-12s. **No credit cards. Map** p244 F6.

A small museum devoted to the traditional vernacular architecture of the kind seen around Xintiandi. Exhibits take the form of photographs and models, with labelling in Chinese and English. The museum foyer doubles as a visitor information centre with assorted bilingual publications on Xintiandi, flyers, brochures, free magazines and maps of Shanghai.

Dongtai Lu Antique Market

Just a few twists south and east of Xintiandi's lake and park is one of Shanghai's most popular markets. Over 100 booths and shop-houses line the neighbouring streets of Dongtai Lu and Liuhekou Lu, all filled with a mix of antiques (fresh-from-the-factory and the genuine article), kitsch and trash. Browse for Mao memorabilia, vintage furniture and locally printed old Tintin books in Mandarin. It's a popular spot with tourists and although many of the pieces can be found across China, it's a good place to hunt for fragments of Shanghai's past.

One block east of Dongtai is the **Wanshang Bird and Flower Market** (open 7am-7pm daily), which is where locals come to buy pets – rabbits, hamsters, puppies, kittens. Purchased animals are dropped into plastic bags to be taken home like supermarket buys.

At the southern end of the antique market, where Jian Lu meets Fuxing Zhonglu, is the **Fazangjiangsi Buddhist Temple**. Built in 1923, it boasts a huge main hall split into two levels. On the lower level worshippers join with monks in prayer, while the upper hall houses giant Buddhist statues and fine bas-relief murals. Around 1,000 devotees can be accommodated at any one time. Apart from the infectious atmosphere, what sets this temple apart from others is that the interior and exterior design and decoration is a melange of Western art deco and traditional Chinese styles. The temple was restored and reopened to the public in 1999 – after years of neglect and, you've guessed it, use as a factory. The temple adheres to the teachings of the Pure Land Sect, worships Amitabha Pusa and believes in reincarnation in a Pure Land similar to Heaven.

Sightseeing

Chilling on the North Block. *See p74.*

Huaihai Zhonglu. *See p80.*

French Concession

Dining, drinking and boutique hopping.

Map p246 & p247

It lacks the monuments of the Bund and the photogenic Chinese scenes of the Old City. It cannot compete with Renmin Square for important cultural institutions. It is less dynamic than Pudong and bettered by Jingan for shopping… Yet there's something about the French Concession that makes it by far the most appealing part of Shanghai.

It's certainly the most pleasing on the eye: predominantly low rise, cut through with winding, tree-lined streets. Elegant European-styled mansion blocks and villas are flavoured by assorted restaurants and coloured by a host of small boutiques. Early mornings are soundtracked by shuffling street hawkers and the setting up of dawn markets; late nights echo with chattering revellers crawling the area's bar streets. This is Shanghai's Marais, its Greenwich Village, even its Soho – but less crowded and prettier.

The Concession is where the fortunate and wealthy of Shanghai reside; the fortunate being the Chinese who were allotted residences here by the People's Government after 1949, the wealthy meaning any Chinese or foreigner with the funds to rent or buy in an area where property values are ever on the rise. It's beloved of expats, who like to note that they share an area address with the neighbourhood's most famous resident, China's former premier, Jiang Zemin, whose retirement abode takes up most of an entire city block in the Concession's leafy south-west corner.

SHAPING THE CONCESSION

The French presented their claims for Shanghai territory to the imperial Qing court in 1844, pressing for the same generous rights the British had gained the previous year in the aftermath of the First Opium War. The court allowed the French a muddy plot of just over a mile in breadth south of the International Settlement (now the Bund area) and east of the old walled city of Shanghai. Over the course of the next 70 years 'Frenchtown' expanded westward, eventually taking up about 18 square kilometres (seven square miles). But the Frenchness of the Concession was far from absolute. By the 1930s there were fewer than 10,000 French nationals within its boundaries, compared to 12,000 English subjects, 30,000 Russians and more than half a million Chinese.

Even so, there was a distinctly Gallic air about the place. The exclusively French municipal government (Conseil Municipal Français, or CMF) lined each street with French plane trees and enforced zoning regulations designed to make their part of the city more liveable. It's the legacy of these bits of localised legislation that gives today's French Concession a more bucolic and genteel air than much of the rest of the city.

There were, though, other less attractive aspects of Frenchtown that contributed heavily to its character. By the beginning of the 20th century Anglo-Saxon sensitivities had largely forced the rampant trades in opium and prostitution out of the International Settlement, so the criminal element, run by rival Chinese gangs, decamped to the more permissive sphere of French rule. The result was that the French Concession became the crime headquarters of Shanghai, if not all of China.

Yet more colour was provided by the White Russians, large numbers of whom began arriving in Shanghai after fleeing their own country's 1917 revolution. Many of the newly arrived Slavs settled along central Huaihai Lu, where they opened shops and businesses and greatly added to the cultural life of the city (*see p13*).

The gangsters are long gone, ruthlessly suppressed after the Communists took over in 1949. Neither has much of the Russian presence survived. There are two onion-domed Orthodox churches but both now provide no more than exotic settings for fine dining.

EXPLORING THE CONCESSION

The Chinese no longer recognise the term 'French Concession', but it still has currency among foreign residents, who consider it to mean the area below Yanan Lu from the Old City to Xujiahui, including Xintiandi, which for the purposes of this guide we cover in its own chapter (*see pp74-6*). It's a big area, and one that could easily absorb two or three days' worth of shoe leather. Our coverage goes from east to west, beginning at Fuxing Park.

Fuxing Park

The French municipality set aside the land for **Fuxing Park** (foo-shing) in the early 20th century. It spreads over almost ten hectares. Its northern boundary was the Collège Français, one of the city's top public schools, while the central expanse was – and still is – a long rectangle delineated by arcades of tall plane trees. Turn up when the park gates open at 6am to watch the legions of tai chi enthusiasts, or come later to observe games of chess or cards or the gentle waltzing of the veterans and pensioners who gather here daily. Fellow observers include comrades Engels and Marx, or at least their granite-hewn likenesses. In the north-west corner of the park exit is a well-tended rose garden with circular fountain, which is overlooked by several posh eateries and nightclubs, including **Guandii** (*see p179*) and **Park 97** (*see p179* **California Club**; *p128* **Upstairs at Park 97**), as well as one of the city's best galleries, **ShanghArt** (*see p163*).

Running from the park's north-west gate is Gaolan Lu, dominated by the golden dome of the former Russian Orthodox **Church of St Nicholas**, built in 1933 and dedicated to the murdered last Tsar. During the Cultural Revolution it was saved from destruction at the hands of the Red Guard by a canny priest who added a Mao fresco above the doorway. It's still there, although the church is now a French restaurant, the **Ashanti Dome** (*see p114*).

Connecting with Fuxing Park's south-west gate is Xiangshan Lu (formerly rue Molière), spiffy address of the **Former Residence of Sun Yatsen**. This is just one of several 'former residences' for the man considered the father of modern China; the house is open to visitors (*see below*). Running north-south beside the house is **Sinan Lu** (née rue Massenet), one of the city's most attractive thoroughfares, which idly meanders between arcades of plane trees. Little surprise that as well as Sun Yatsen, several other dignitaries chose to make their homes here, including Yuan Shikai, the general who assumed the presidency and proclaimed himself emperor in 1912, while at No.73 is the **Former Residence of Zhou Enlai**, which is also open to visitors (*see below*). As with most houses around here, from its external appearance this freestanding, stuccoed home could just as easily originate in northern Europe or America.

Former Residence of Sun Yatsen

7 Xiangshan Lu, by Sinan Lu (6437 2954/www.sh-sunyat-sen.com). Metro Shanxi Nanlu. **Open** 9am-4.30pm daily. **Admission** RMB 8. **No credit cards**. **Map** p247 E7.
Sun Yatsen (1866-1925), founder of the Kuomintang Party that sought to replace the ailing Qing Dynasty with democratic leadership, lived here with his wife, Soong Qingling, from 1919 to 1925. It's a fairly modest house with simple furnishings but the place was witness to innumerable historic meetings, including that between Madame Sun's sister, Meiling, and her future husband, Chiang Kaishek. The place is

stuffed full of memorabilia, from a fascinating library of over 2,700 volumes to family photos and a Suzhou embroidery of a cat. Recorded English commentaries play in the main rooms.

Former Residence of Zhou Enlai

73 Sinan Lu, by Fuxing Zhonglu (6473 0420). Metro Shanxi Nanlu. **Open** 9-11am, 1-5pm daily. **Admission** RMB 2. **No credit cards**. **Map** p247 E7.
Precociously placed in an established Nationalist area, Zhou and his wife, Deng Yingchao, managed and promoted Shanghai's underground Communist movement from here in 1946-47. Meetings were held in the ground-floor reception room, while the upper floors contained offices and dormitories for Party workers, including the bedroom of Dong Biwu, who went on to become a leading Party figure.

South of Fuxing Park

At its very southern end Sinan Lu intersects with **Taikang Lu**, a short, narrow lane on which lots of hopes are riding. Since the day several years ago when a local entrepreneur turned a derelict sweet factory into low-rent studios for artists and designers, developers and fledgling creatives have seized space in neighbouring buildings in an attempt to transform the area into some kind of alternative, low-rent Xintiandi. It has yet to pay off fully (*see p81* **Half-arted street**) but is nonetheless worth a nose around.

Five minutes' walk south of Taikang Lu is the morbid yet absorbing **Museum of Public Security** (*see below*), with a gun collection that's reputed to be the largest in the world; just west and north is **Shaoxing Lu**, which is the home of the Shanghai publishing world. Numerous publishers have their offices here and most have bookshops attached. Of course, it's all in Chinese. For reading matter in English visit the **Old China Hand Reading Room**. Nominally a business, this is also a museum of 1930s Shanghai memorabilia (*see p80*).

Museum of Public Security

518 Rihui Donglu, by Xietu Lu (6472 0256). **Open** 8.30am-4pm Mon-Sat. **Admission** RMB 8. **No credit cards**. **Map** p247 E9.
Opened in 1999, the museum chronicles the history of the city's security services, going back to the establishment of its first police department in 1854 – though the emphasis is on post-1949 achievements. Only the introductions to the exhibition areas are in English but little interpretation is required for the 3,000 items on display, which run from graphic photos of real life murders to a huge armoury of weapons that includes some fascinating period pieces, such as a cigarette case weapon made for mobster/police chief Huang Jinrong and an ebony pistol that belonged to Sun Yatsen.

If it can be done in the open air then it's done in **Fuxing Park**. *See p77*.

Two wheels good on **Fuxing Zhonglu**.

Old China Hand Reading Room

27 Shaoxing Lu, by Shanxi Nanlu (6473 2526/
www.han-yuan.com/shudian/huodong-e.htm).
Metro Shanxi Nanlu. **Open** 10am-midnight daily.
Admisson free. **No credit cards. Map** p247 D8.
Glass-fronted cabinets contain masses of volumes
on Shanghai and China in general, many of which
are published by the Old China Hand Press, a joint
venture between photographer/collector Deke Erh
and writer/historian Tess Johnston. Together the
two specialise in documenting the architectural heritage of the Concession-era. The space is decorated
in Ming Dynasty fashion and is peppered with
antiques and curios.

Huaihai Zhonglu

Huaihai Zhonglu, formerly avenue Joffre,
is a great bisecting slash across the French
Concession. Its four lanes are perpetually heavy
with traffic, its pavements every bit as crowded
with shoppers. The pre-Liberation apartment
blocks that line much of its length rise above
street-level boutiques catering predominantly
to middle-class Chinese. The busiest area is
around the junction with Ruijin Erlu. Towards
Changshu Lu, the commerce fades and several
consulates occupy large villas around here.
Finally, at its western extreme, Huaihai is home
to local restaurants and small shops as it slides
into the neighbouring municipality of Xujiahui.
   The following ruled subheads are all major
north-south streets that intersect with Huaihai.

Ruijin Erlu

Two blocks south of Huaihai are the imposing
entrance gates of the **Ruijin Guesthouse**, a
walled compound of several buildings in a fine
garden setting. This was formerly the town
estate of HE Morriss Jnr, whose father had
made his money as founder and owner of the
North China Daily News, the largest English
newspaper in China. Within this compound the
son raised horses and greyhounds to run at the
nearby Canidrome (*see p81*). The grounds are
still lovely and are open to passers-by. The
former red-brick main residence is now a posh
guesthouse (*see p43*), with snippets of local
history presented on the foyer walls. Another
building serves as the Shanghai offices for *The
Economist*, while other tenants include the **Art
Deco Garden Café** (*see p109*), the fabulous
Face Bar (*see p124*) and restaurants **Lan Na
Thai** (*see p116*) and **Xiao Nan Guo** (*see p113*).
   A gateway at the rear of the guesthouse
grounds leads on to Maoming Nanlu.

Maoming Nanlu

Maoming Nanlu (Maoming Lu, for short) is best
known – infamous even – for the boozy-going-
on-sleazy nightlife strip at its southernmost
end. The busiest hour to be around here is any
time gone midnight. By day it's a far quieter
proposition. Slip down the alleyway by a club
called Babyface to arrive at a well-worn, huge

building completely covered in panes of glass. Before Liberation this was the **Canidrome** – the dog track – plus ballroom and boxing arena, built in 1928 and financed by Felix Bouvier and notorious gangster Du Yuesheng. The original structure burnt in the 1940s but was quickly rebuilt for a gambling-happy public. The dogs are long gone, replaced by blooms: part of the Canidrome is now the **Jinwen Flower Market** (see p132), though the north-west corner still has its spectator stands. The ballroom also survives and is occasionally used as a government function hall.

Maoming north of Fuxing Zhonglu boasts a handful of small, quality tailors, as well as the enchanting **1931** restaurant (see p113), while lording it over the junction at Huaihai Zhonglu is the **Cathay Theatre**, very obviously a creation of the 1930s, with its vertical lines over a heavy marquee entrance and topped by an art deco spire. It's now a cinema showing Chinese-language movies.

North again Maoming appears very much as it must have done in the days when this was rue Cardinal Mercier. On the west side of the road is the former **Cercle Sportif Français**, one of the most popular clubs in Concession-era Shanghai. Ignore the distraction of the looming concrete tower block (added in the '80s when the club became the **Okura Garden Hotel**, see p41), and take a walk around the gorgeous gardens and then pop inside for the ballroom and splendid staircase lobbies. Have a drink on the roof of the south-facing porte cochère, and picture the lawn below filled with 20 tennis courts – and below those a reinforced concrete

nuclear bunker, a hidden reminder that the premises were used as a private guesthouse by Chairman Mao on his visits to Shanghai.

Directly across Maoming Lu is the **Jinjiang Hotel** (see p41), formerly Sir Victor Sassoon's **Cathay Mansions**. Built in 1928 this was the first mansion block in the Concession. It's best known now as the venue in which then-US President Richard Nixon and Chinese Foreign Minister Zhou Enlai signed the Shanghai Communiqué in 1972, the first step toward normalising US-China relations. Flanking the entrance to the hotel grounds is pop chinoiserie boutique **Shanghai Tang** (see p137) and, in the small lane behind the store, highly regarded Shanghainese restaurant **Yin** (see p114) and upstairs Jap sibling **Zen** (see p116).

Facing the Jinjiang across Changle Lu, the **Lyceum Theatre** was built in the 1930s as the home of the British Amateur Dramatic Society. Margot Fonteyn danced here as a girl. She was born in England but at the age of eight her father's work took the family to Shanghai. She studied ballet here before returning with her mother to the UK when she was 14. Her father stayed in Shanghai and was interned by the Japanese during World War II.

Shanxi Nanlu

Shanxi Nanlu lacks the charm of neighbouring streets. The junction with Huaihai is dominated by modern shopping plazas while touts haunt the pavements delivering tugs and rapid-fire pitches of 'Bagwatchshoesdvd*looklooklook*!!!'. For a bit of escapism, veer north for the

Half-arted street

It all kicked off in 1998 with the conversion of a former sweet factory. It was gutted and scrubbed before being re-let and subsequently called the **International Artists' Factory**. The idea vaguely caught on and the four-storey space is now home to a handful of design and marketing studios as well as fashion and interiors outlets. Highlights include **Jooi Design** (see p139) and **Marion Carsten Silver Jewellery** (see p139).

The bottom end of the little alley (Lane 210) on which the Artists' Factory sits is anchored by the **Deke Erh Art Centre** (see p161), which also acts as an informal information centre for the area. Further along is the Kommune courtyard, fringed with high-end boutiques, such as Tibetan jeweller **Jo Ma Arts** and lingerie store **Studio IFF**. Also worth checking

out are the real pashmina and cashmere shawls at **Sunlight**. There are a few small art galleries, a couple of pottery studios and, complementing the shopping, a bunch of bars and cafés – which we hesitate to namecheck because of their blink-and-miss-it life spans.

The whole area has been branded the 'Taikang Lu Art Street' and various interested parties have been trying to promote it as the home for Shanghai's underground culture. However, they are slowly wising up to the fact that you don't create an 'underground scene' through zoning and property development. What the city has got, rather, is a promising little boutiquey enclave for the newly emerging middle classes. Clean up the facilities and get a Starbucks in here and they'll be on to a winner.

fairytale stylings of the **Hengshan Moller Villa** (*see p42*): it's a guesthouse but management doesn't mind non-guests taking a peek inside. Also up this way, facing small Xianyang Park, is the former Russian Orthodox **Cathedral of the Holy Mother of God**, built in 1931. It used to hold 2,500 worshippers but now it's a fairly indifferent restaurant.

Back on Huaihai the touts increase in numbers as you approach the **Xiangyang Market** or, as it's more commonly known, the 'fake market' (*see p132*). A haggler's wet dream, Xiangyang is brimming with Gucci bags, Nike trainers, DVDs… The latter go for around a dollar a piece, while a $2,000 Rolex can be yours for as little as RMB 100 ($12), depending on your bargaining skills. The origins of the merchandise are as ambiguous as the prices.

One block south and west on **Fenyang Lu** is an attractive old villa behind tall trees: this is the Arts and Crafts Research Institute, a part of which is the **Museum of Arts & Crafts** (*see below*). The building itself is in a neo-classical style and was designed by Ladislaus Hudec (*see p28*) as the residence of the manager of the French municipal bus lines. It was later the home of Shanghai's first Communist mayor.

Fenyang connects with Taiyuan Lu, which, back in the rum old days, as rue Delastre, boasted not only a French-styled château but also a resident count and countess. The Count de Marsoulies was a lawyer who, along with several community leaders, had a falling out with local mobster Du Yuesheng when they asked him to remove his opium business from the Concession. To show that there were no hard feelings, Big Du invited the Frenchmen to dinner. Within the month several of the dinner guests were dead of a mysterious illness. Rumour was that Big Du had poisoned the mushrooms. The widowed countess remained in the house until 1940. After the war the US army rented the château and it's where General George Marshall stayed while attempting to broker a treaty between the Communists and the Nationalists. Today the château is the **Taiyuan Guesthouse** (*see p43*).

Back where Fenyang meets Yueyang is one of Shanghai's only monuments to a non-Chinese individual, a **statue of Pushkin** (Puxijin), erected in 1937 by the Russian community on the centenary of the poet's death.

Museum of Arts & Crafts

79 Fenyang Lu, by Taiyuan Lu (6437 3454). Metro Changshu Lu. **Open** 9am-5pm daily. **Admission** RMB 8. **No credit cards. Map** p246 C7.
High-quality arts and crafts exhibits form only a small part of the museum. The villa in which the museum sits has been the home of an arts and crafts research institute since 1960 and visitors can

observe artisans involved in carving, embroidery and paper-cutting. Much of the work is for sale and there is also an antique store in the basement.

Changshu Lu & west

As Huaihai dips into the westernmost part of the French Concession the buildings become grander with plenty of villas and mansions in extensive gardens. This was the 'country manor' part of town. Some of the properties now fly international flags as consulates, many are bars and restaurants; places such as **Ambrosia** (*see p116*), **Le Garçon Chinois** (*see p115*), **Sasha's** (*see p126*) and **Yongfu Elite** (*see p128*) should be visited for the setting alone. A little out of the way but worth the effort is **Swire House**. George Warren Swire was company chief of Butterfield & Swire, one of the first companies to set up operations in Shanghai. In 1934 he commissioned a new residence from celebrated Welsh architect Clough Williams-Ellis – creator of Port Merion on the Welsh coast, immortalised as the setting for '60s cult TV series *The Prisoner*. The architect never visited China, rather he sent drawings and samples by post. The resulting property was sufficiently magnificent to earn it the nickname of 'the palace'. Post-1949, of course, it became a state guesthouse. Today the house is part of the **Radisson Plaza Xingguo Hotel** (*see p41* **The chain gang**) and available for hire.

Also in the neighbourhood, just north of the Dingxiang Garden, buried in the basement of one of a group of residential tower blocks, is the **Propaganda Poster Art Centre** (*see p84*) – a must for enthusiasts of political kitsch.

Back on Huaihai Zhonglu is the **Shanghai Library** (corner of Gaoan Lu), which is Asia's largest book repository. It's not much use if you don't read Chinese but pass by around 8am to see the library staff out front doing their tai chi exercises before starting work. Further west is the striking red-brick **Normandie Building**, which is a dead-ringer for New York's Flatiron Building, only on a smaller scale. On the ground floor (enter from Wukang Lu), is café-bar-restaurant **Arch** (*see p123*).

South across the busy intersection from the Normandie is an evocative slice of social and political history in the shape of the **Former Residence of Soong Qingling** (*see p84*), while a short walk further west it's commerce and industry celebrated at the **CY Tung Maritime Museum** (*see p84*), which is housed in a refurbished 19th-century dormitory on the campus of the prestigious **Jiatong University**, China's second-oldest secular educational institution.

Two wheels better on **Yueyang Lu**.

Fans of JG Ballard's autobiographical novel *Empire of the Sun* might like to stroll up Xinhua Lu, which angles off Huaihai Xilu north of the university: this is Amherst Road where both Ballard and his fictional alter ego Jim spent their childhood years.

CY Tung Maritime Museum

Jiatong University Campus, 1954 Huashan Lu, by Huaihai Xilu (6293 2403/www.cytungmm.com). Metro Xujiahui. **Open** 1.30-5.30pm Tue-Sun. **Admission** free. **Map** p246 A8.

The ground floor plots China's often understated maritime history from Neolithic times to the present day. Exhibits highlight the silk and porcelain maritime route of the Middle Ages and China's leading role in naval innovation during the 15th century. The first floor is dedicated to the activities and manifold interests of Shanghai-born shipping tycoon Mr Tung and includes the ship's bell from the ill-fated *Queen Elizabeth*; Tung acquired the old Cunard liner in 1970 only to see her destroyed by fire in Hong Kong two years later.

Former Residence of Soong Qingling

1843 Huaihai Zhonglu, by Yuqing Lu (6347 6268). Metro Hengshan Lu. **Open** 9am-4.30pm daily. **Admission** RMB 8. **No credit cards. Map** p246 A7.

This is the house in which Soong Qingling (*see p16* **Soong of the century**) grew up and where she returned to live following Sun Yatsen's death in 1948. The sitting and dining rooms contain a photographic record of Mao's visit to the house and a large selection of gifts received from foreign dignitaries. Don't miss the garage and its two limousines, a Chinese 'Red Flag' and a Russian 'Jim' presente by Stalin in 1952. A neighbouring hall contains an outstanding collection of artefacts ranging from books and family photos to personal correspondence and written exchanges with Mao, Nehru and Stalin. The statue outside was completed in 2003 to commemorate the 110th anniversary of her birth.

Propaganda Poster Art Centre

Basement, Building B, 868 Huashan Lu, by Wukang Lu (6211 1845). Metro Changshu Lu. **Open** 10am-3pm daily. **Admission** RMB 20. **No credit cards. Map** p246 A6.

The brainchild of Yang Peiming, the PPAC is two basement rooms in a residential tower block hung floor to ceiling with a stunning collection of original posters from 1949 to 1979. Mr Peimang delights in leading visitors through the collection (there are at least a couple of hundred pieces) explaining each bit of artwork. The fact that you may not understand Chinese and he has only four words of English is no impediment. When he comes to the images of ruddy-cheeked Chinese peasants crushing imperialist Uncle Sams underfoot you worry that he's going to damage himself from laughing so hard. Some of the posters are also for sale. Can there be a better souvenir of Shanghai?

Propaganda Poster Art Centre.

Xujiahui, Hongqiao & Gubei

Shanghai's middling south-west.

Longhua Temple and **Pagoda**. *See p87.*

Map p240 & p246
Xujiahui (pronounced 'shoe-jah-way'), Gubei ('gub-ey') and Hongqiao ('hong-chow') make up the great suburban mass that is Shanghai's urban south-west. Connecting the city proper with its rural hinterland, these districts allow residents to keep one foot firmly in the urban and the other placed somewhere that's a little more tranquil. While the 'burbs do not often make it on to tourist hitlists, they do have a bit of history and the odd intriguing landmark that may make the schlep worthwhile – although it's a good idea to plan an excursion carefully.

Bordering the old French Concession, **Xujiahui** is one of Shanghai's transportation hubs, a lattice of highways dotted with long-distance bus terminals. Its road intersections are the unnatural home of great hulking shiny malls

which, unlike the malls in Jingan with their high-end fashion labels, actually sell things the average Chinese person might need, like white goods, electronics and household items. Cinemas, sports complexes and other entertainments offer shoppers distraction once the purchasing is done. Most of the activity is centred on the neighbourhood of Xujiahui metro station.

Hongqiao begins where old Settlement-era Shanghai ends (roughly where Zhongshan Xilu runs today) and extends west to the city's domestic airport. The part closest to town is forested with strikingly modern high-rise office developments, residential complexes and hotel towers, while the further reaches are divided into gated housing estates known locally as 'villa communities'. Hongqiao is also home to Shanghai Zoo (*see p155*).

South of Hongqiao and west of Xujiahui lies the relatively new district of **Gubei**. Its rows of residential tower blocks – mostly investment properties owned by overseas Chinese – are home to much of Shanghai's non-Chinese, east-Asian population. Restaurants and businesses here tend to be Japanese, Korean or Taiwanese.

GETTING THERE

The most convenient way to get out west is to take Metro Line 1, which stops at Xujiahui. For Longhua Park and temple, get off at Caobao Lu. Metro Line 2 is currently being extended out to Gubei and Hongqiao. By foot, from the French Concession walk south down Hengshan Lu.

Xujiahui

Characterised by suburban towers and shopping malls, Xujiahui is the site of Shanghai's oldest Western settlement – a Jesuit centre started by a Chinese Catholic, Paul Xu, in the early 17th century. Xu was a high-ranking Ming official and a committed scholar, who had converted to Catholicism. He donated some of his land in Xujiahui (meaning 'gathering place of the Xu family') to the Church and invited Jesuit missionaries to take up residence.

The nuns and priests held on to various mission buildings throughout the intervening centuries until the Cultural Revolution, at which time they were 'resettled' elsewhere. Some of the structures – all of which were built by orphans under the wing of the Jesuits – are still standing, but many are being pulled down to make way for new towers. The most prominent extant building is the Catholic cathedral, **St Ignatius** (158 Puxi Lu, by Caoxi Beilu, 6438 2595), built

Longhua Temple. *See p87.*

in 1910 on the site of earlier churches dating back to 1608. The more permissive political climate today allows the Chinese Catholic diocese to hold masses there for foreign and Chinese Catholics (for service times, *see p226*).

Xu was also a keen astronomer/scientist and he operated a meterological observatory that could transmit its findings to the tower on the Bund (*see p54*). To this day, Shanghai's central weather observatory is still in Xujiahui.

Longhua & south

Just south of central Xujiahui is the bold yellow **Longhua Temple** (*see p87*), named for the longhua tree where Buddha reached enlightenment. Adjacent to the temple is urban Shanghai's only **pagoda**, which stands an impressive 44 metres (145 feet) high, with delicate pointed eaves at each of its seven levels on which hang countless small bells.

Tranquil as it appears, the park in which the temple stands has witnessed much bloodshed. In the 19th century Shanghai it was the site of countless public executions. Under the philosophy of 'kill the chicken to frighten the monkeys', prisoners would be led through the streets to be spat at and pummelled by spectators. Once at Longhua they would receive further gruesome and lengthy torture. During the 'White Terror' of 1927 when Kuomintang forces set about brutally exterminating their Communist rivals in Shanghai (*see p16*), thousands were led to Longhua where, out of sight of the general public, they were executed (these brutal weeks are the background to André Malraux's novel *Man's Estate*).

On the same site during World War II the Japanese ran their largest civilian internment camp in China for British, American and other Allied nationals. The camp – and the pagoda – feature in JG Ballard's book (and Spielberg's movie adaptation), *Empire of the Sun*. The Japanese military airstrip portrayed in the story is the adjacent **Longhua Airport**, its lovely Streamline Moderne terminal presently mothballed and awaiting development by its owners, Chinese Eastern Airlines.

Nearby, **Longhua Martyrs Cemetery** (Lieshi Lingyuan) commemorates the lives of the murdered Chinese Communists. A graceful tree-lined walkway leads up to a pyramidal Memorial Hall, while landscaped gardens are dotted with bizarre statues, such as an enormous torso of a man, half buried in the earth but with one arm reaching desperately for the sky. The park also houses picnic-perfect lawns.

There's more greenery about two kilometres (1.2 miles) further south at the little visited **Shanghai Botanical Gardens** (*see p87*).

Longhua Temple

2853 Longhua Lu, Longhua Park (6456 6085).
Metro Cabao Lu, then taxi. **Open** 7am-4pm daily.
Admission RMB 6. **No credit cards.**
Map p240 C4.

Shanghai's only fully functioning temple and monastery is scented with incense and contains the usual collection of gold-crusted Buddhas. The star piece is a gargantuan 6,500kg (14,300lb) bell, which, legend has it, brings good fortune when struck three times (try your luck: RMB 10). Each New Year's Eve the bell is struck 108 times, to address the 108 troubles of Buddhist philosophy. The temple is also the venue for numerous other festivities including the Birthday of the Queen of Heaven (*see p149*) and the Longhua Temple Fair (*see p149*).

Shanghai Botanical Garden

111 Longwu Lu, Xinlonghua (5436 3369). Metro
Shanghai South Railway Station. **Open** 8am-5pm
daily. **Admission** RMB 8. **No credit cards.**
Map p240 B5.

Whereas most of Shanghai's green spaces are filled with seasonal flowerbeds and rows of French-inspired plane trees, the Botanical Garden is at once lush and varied, with ponds, fields, bonsai gardens and greenhouses. It's a very popular picnic ground – arrive early with your rug and basket to claim your spot. Pack toys and sporting gear for letting off steam after lunch, or have a go at kite-flying. The only unfortunate aspect is its distance from Shanghai proper. From a central location such as the Portman Ritz-Carlton, it's a long-ish cab ride that will cost around RMB 50 (better to take the metro).

Hongqiao Lu & south

Running directly west from central Xujiahui is Hongqiao Lu. In the Concession-era this street was lined with the country estates of the stinking rich. One of the most famous of these belonged to Sir Victor Sassoon (*see p12* **The Jewish dynasties**). His Tudorbethan villa is now the Cypress Hotel (*see p44*), and sits out near to Hongqiao Airport. Although the government has maintained this house and several dozen others as VIP accommodation, most such opulent reminders of the 1920s and 1930s have either been razed or left to deteriorate slowly. Some former residents have petitioned the government to return the properties to their original owners, but the development frenzy of the past decade has made the land too valuable to relinquish. Only a few villas will survive the next ten years. None are open to the public, except several that are now antique furniture shops (*see p132*).

Just to the south of Hongqiao Lu is the **Soong Qingling Mausoleum** (*see below*). The site was formerly the Wanguo Cemetery, the resting place of many Shanghai notables. The revered Soong Qingling (*see p19* **Soong of**

Longhua Martyrs Cemet...
See p86.

the century) died in 1981; after her body was interred the city changed the name of the cemetery in her honour (her infamous sister Meiling declined to return to China for the funeral; she died in the USA in October 2003, aged 105). This is also the burial ground for members of Shanghai's wealthy Jewish families, such as the Kadoories and Sassoons. The original Jewish cemeteries in other parts of town were destroyed during the Cultural Revolution. Grave-lingering aside, the park surrounding the mausoleum is also popular as a social venue. Moon-gazing parties are held here during the Moon Festival, or Mid-Autumn Festival (*see p151*), and a Japanese-English-Chinese language exchange group also meets in the park at the weekends.

Soong Qingling Mausoleum

Song Qingling Lingyuan, 21 Songyuan Lu, by
Hongqiao Lu (no phone). Metro Homngqiao Lu.
Open 8.30am-5pm daily. **Map** p240 B3.

Civil and women's rights activist Soong Qingling was made an honorary president shortly before her death and was buried next to her parents in the Soongs' own burial ground – the Wanguo Cemetery. The tomb of her beloved maid, Li Yane, lies alongside. A well-presented exhibition room portrays her life and dedication with old school exercise books, clothing and an epitaph for her friend, the author Edgar Snow. A foreign and a Chinese cemetery are also housed within the park.

Sightseeing

...ui, Hongqiao & Gubei

...:ast.

...buildings on
...an eastern
...ireless
marshy fields with some snabby warehousing
fringing the water's edge. Flash forward just
over a decade and today it's a sci-fi landscape
of spaceship towers, 88-storey pagodas, giant
globes the size of rogue meteorites and golden
skyscrapers where the whole side of the
building acts as a giant video screen. Modern
Pudong is the key to Shanghai's bid to become
the most important international economic and
trading centre in 21st-century East Asia.

Located on the east side of the Huangpu,
the 530 square-kilometre (205 square-mile) area
extends from the river all the way out to the
coast of the East China Sea. It includes the
Lujiazui Financial and Trade Zone, Pudong
International Airport and numerous other
developmental zones. While for non-business
types the best aspect of Pudong is its striking
– if slightly ludicrous – skyline, it is also
certainly worth crossing the river, if only for
the opportunity to look back at the equally
splendid spectacle of the western city skyline.

GETTING THERE
Easily the most entertaining way to get over to
Pudong is to take the **Bund Tourist Tunnel**
(5888 6000, open 9am-9.30pm daily, tickets RMB

30). Glass-enclosed capsules whizz along a 647-
metre (2,123-foot) tunnel of strobing lights. It's
a trip in every sense of the word.

Otherwise, the most appealing way to cross
(and the cheapest at under one *yuan*) is by ferry.
Boats leave every 15 minutes from the terminal
at the southern end of the Bund, beside the
ramp road connecting with Yanan Donglu.

By taxi, the ride from Renmin Square or
thereabouts takes 15 to 20 minutes and costs
RMB 20-25. At rush hours the tunnel is closed
to cabs. Buses Nos.3 and 518 (tickets RMB 2)
depart from opposite the Shanghai Museum
and drop off in front of the Jinmao Tower.

The riverfront

The most popular visitor activity in Pudong is
to stroll the **Riverside Promenade**. This
currently stretches for 2.5 kilometres (1.5
miles) along the waterfront and has plenty of
concessions (a Starbucks, a Häagen-Dazs) with
outdoor seating. Midway along the Promenade
stands the gloriously gaudy **Oriental Pearl
Tower** (*see p89*) where three high-altitude
observation decks are perpetually thronged by
megaphone-toting tour guides and their groups.
The views just might be worth it. At basement
level is the highly recommended **Shanghai
Municipal History Museum** (*see p89*).

Bund Tourist Tunnel.

Pudong's sci-fi skyline viewed from the Bund.

In opposing corners of the park that surrounds the Oriental Pearl Tower are two animal-world attractions: west is the **Natural Wild Insect Kingdom** (*see p155*), with over 200 different kinds of things that creep, crawl and flit, while east is the **Ocean Aquarium** (*see p155*), one of the largest of its kind in Asia.

South of the park is Lujiazui metro station and beside it **SuperBrand Mall**, a ten-storey, Thai-owned shopping centre with top-brand fashion outlets. For a spectacular night-time view of the Bund, reserve a windowside table at Sichuan restaurant **South Beauty** (*see p113*) up on the top floor. For greater elevation, one block east is the **Jinmao Tower** with the most jaw-dropping views from its observation deck on the 88th floor (5047 5101, open 8.30am-9pm daily, admission RMB 50). The tallest building in China (until the completion of its 101-storey neighbour, the Shanghai World Financial Centre, *see p30*) accommodates offices on its lower floors and the luxurious **Grand Hyatt** (*see p44*) on the 54th to the 87th floors. Spare yourself the mayhem of the public observation and instead spend the 50 yuan on a drink at the Hyatt's 87th floor bar **Cloud Nine** (*see p128*) or put it towards a meal at one of the hotel's 56th-floor restaurants (which include **Cucina**, *see p118*). As impressive as the views beyond is the view upwards from the Hyatt's **Patio Bar**, also on the 56th floor. For more on the architecture of the Jinmao, *see p30*.

Oriental Pearl Tower

1 Shiji Dadao (5879 3003). Metro Lujiazui.
Open 9am-9pm daily. **Admission** RMB 100.
No credit cards. Map p243 K4.

Completed in 1994, the Pearl Tower is a 468m (1,535ft) Shanghai icon, the highest TV and radio tower in Asia and the third highest in the world. It's instantly recognisable by its two 50m (164ft) diameter pink spheres, which are connected by concrete tubing. Visitors can get inside the bubbles, for panoramas of Puxi and Pudong on clear days. RMB 150-180 will buy you a Chinese/Western buffet in the rotating restaurant inside the second bubble.

Shanghai Municipal History Museum

Gate 4, Oriental Pearl Tower, 1 Shiji Dadao (5879 3003). Metro Lujiazui. **Open** 9am-9pm daily. **Admission** RMB 35. **No credit cards. Map** p243 K4.

Stacked with historical artefacts, life-size dioramas, models, photos and paintings, this museum puts the spotlight on all aspects of life in post-1840s Shanghai, from the city's famous cinema industry to its opium houses and curious forms of criminal justice. In a hall focusing on Shanghai's 1920s and '30s heyday (charmingly entitled the 'Metropolis Infested with Foreigners') is one of the precious bronze lions that once guarded the Hongkong & Shanghai Bank on the Bund. The city's life is brought up to date with a small display of SARS - related documents and photographs. An excellent audio tour is available.

Badly trained

With a maximum cruising speed of 430kmh (266mph), Shanghai's Maglev is the world's fastest commercially operated train by a long shot. Maglev stands for 'magnetic levitation': in this German design, the wheels and rails of conventional trains are replaced by giant magnets that keep the carriage hovering a finger's width above the flat tracks. As the train glides effortlessly out of the station, large digital speedometers at either end of the carriages keep passengers transfixed with their climbing numbers.

But despite the slick ride, the short history of the Maglev has been anything but smooth. Pet project of former PM Zhu Rongji, the original plans were for a high-speed service between Shanghai and Beijing. What currently exists is a short 30-kilometre (20-mile) run between Pudong and its international airport; further expansion plans have been scrapped. Some blame the recent changing of the guard among China's top leadership, but the $1.2 billion price tag for a seven-minute journey must also have been a major factor.

Flagging ticket sales due to steep fares forced operators to slash prices just one month after regular service began in March 2004. And now there are reports that the track is sinking due to the soft ground on which it's laid (although the government staunchly defends the system's safety).

But the worst problem of all is the Maglev's no-man's land western terminus. Coming in from the airport the line irrationally ends at the Longyang Lu metro station in Pudong, which is a 15-minute taxi ride from the Grand Hyatt and 25 minutes from the city centre. It is possible to transfer to the metro but this involves long walks and multiple escalators.

Whether this latest chest-thumping exercise will eventually inspire awe rather than just irritation is yet to be seen. Ride the Maglev for the thrill of it, just don't expect it to go anywhere. For practical details, *see p215*.

Lujiazui

For a one-stop tour through Pudong's past, present and future, visit the **Lujiazui Development Museum** (*see below*), which is just a few minutes' walk east of the Jinmao Tower. It occupies what was once one of the largest residences in Shanghai. Around the back of the house, a red cobblestoned path leads right into the heart of **Lujiazui Central Green** (also known as Lujiazui Park), 100,000 square metres (1 million square feet) of evergreen grass, a large variety of trees and plants, fountains, and a man-made lake.

From the Green, eight-lane **Shiji Dadao** (Century Boulevard), which is modelled after the Champs-Elysées, apparently, runs southeast and arrow-straight for four kilometres (2.5 miles) to pull up at **Century Park** (passing en route the **Science & Technology Museum**, *see below*). Meant to be Shanghai's answer to Central Park, this is the city's largest spread of greenery and includes woods, lakes, an open-air theatre, a children's amusement park, a fishing area and lots and lots of grass.

On the far (southern) side of the park is the Longyang Lu metro station, terminus for Shanghai's much-hyped super train, the Maglev: *see above* **Badly trained**.

Lujiazui Development Museum

15 Lujiazui Lu, by Shiji Dadao (5887 9964). Metro Lujiazui. **Open** 10am-5pm daily. **Admission** RMB 5. **No credit cards. Map** p243 L4.

The exhibits here are a curious mix of the antique and the modern, with old furniture displayed alongside contemporary landscape photography and a crystal model of present-day Pudong.

Science & Technology Museum

2000 Shiji Dadao (6862 2000). Metro Shanghai Science & Technology Museum. **Open** 9am-5pm Tue-Sun. **Admission** RMB 60. **Credit** MC, V. **Map** p241 F3.

A RMB 1.75 billion glass-and-steel facility with hundreds of interactive, state-of-the-art attractions that draw on the research of 22 scientific institutes and universities. These include an indoor (plastic) rainforest, sound and light shows, and two IMAX 3D cinemas (shows six times a day, tickets RMB 30). It's all huge fun for kids, but note that there is no English-language labelling.

Hongkou

The former Jewish ghetto has history in spades and buildi...

At the ea⁵
addition
of the ⁴
belⁱ
⁻

Map p241

Suzhou Creek, tributary of the Huangpu River, marks the boundary of visitors' Shanghai. The neighbourhoods across the waterway appear to be a mass of grey, run down, residential blocks; the view doesn't inspire much enthusiasm to explore, yet there's much history in the district of Hongkou. It was on swampy lands here that in 1853 the Americans set up their consul and founded the American Settlement, which a decade later merged with the British Settlement to form the International Settlement. By the beginning of the 20th century the district had gained 30,000 Japanese residents, earning it the nickname 'Little Tokyo'. After the Japanese invaded Manchuria, unrest in Hongkou led to them also seizing Shanghai. In 1931-2 Suzhou Creek was the battle line drawn between Chinese and Japanese forces. A few years later upheavals elsewhere in the world sent European Jews fleeing persecution; some 20,000 landed in Shanghai settling on the north bank of the Huangpu, just east of Hongkou.

GETTING THERE

Most of what's interesting lies in the vicinity of Duolun Lu (which is just off Sichuan Beilu) and Lu Xun Park; to get here take Metro Line 3 from Shanghai Railway Station to East Baoxing Lu. Bus No.21 runs by Duolun from Sichuan Zhonglu, one block in from the Bund. A taxi to Duolun Lu picked up around Renmin Square will cost around RMB 15.

Duolun Lu & Lu Xun Park

Once the home of several famous writers (most notably the 'father of modern Chinese literature' Lu Xun), L-shaped Duolun Lu has recently been spruced up and bestowed with the nebulous designation of 'Cultural Celebrities Street'. Passing between rows of charming *shikumen* lane housing, the street forms a pedestrianised thoroughfare laid with cobblestones set in geometric patterns. The street furniture includes gleaming bronze statues of said cultural celebrities.

Sightseeing

Suzhou Creek

Further north from Renmin Square is Suzhou Creek. At this point in the city it runs vaguely parallel to Nanjing Donglu, emptying into the Bund next to the old British Consulate. Early European traders called it Suzhou Creek because that's where they thought it might take them. Unfortunately, like the mythical but hoped for ice-free ocean across northern North America, this just isn't the case. Today maps call the waterway the 'Wusong Creek' but locals still use the Concession-era term.

Before urban development restarted in the early 1990s, the creek was lined with neo-Gothic and art deco *godowns* (warehouses). Today few remain; those fortunate enough to survive now house posh loft flats and design studios. Most of the rest of the creek is given over to new high-rise tower blocks. Also remaining from the 19th century are the low gunwale barges that transported goods to and from Shanghai along the peaceful waterway. Families now live in them and grow herbs and flowers on the top decks.

As little as five years ago the entire stretch was, according to municipal authorities, a stinky and murky thoroughfare devoid of most forms of life – aquatic or human. Since then a considerable amount of time and money has been poured into a rejuvenation project that is only partly finished. The first phase closed most liquid effluent-producing menaces along the bank and diverted sewage lines, thus instantly improving water quality. Subsequent phases included height restrictions on all new construction, as well as generous provision of green space on both sides of the creek for strolling, recreation and environmental benefits.

To date much of the south bank has been revamped with footpaths and groves of flowering trees. More bridges too have been added to alleviate the heavy traffic congestion on both sides. The ultimate goal is, apparently, to remake Suzhou Creek into one of the most picturesque waterfronts in the world. No faulting the ambition.

...tern end of Duolun is a welcome ...to the city's arts scene in the form ...Doland **Modern Art Museum** (see ...w). Although the institutional grey cubist ...rchitecture doesn't do much for the scenery, the exhibits tend to be refreshingly provocative. At the point at which the street curves north are two fine old mansions, both of which are now cafés – the **Old Film Café** (see below), which is at No.23, is the most famous java house in the area. The nearby **Reading Room Café** at 195 Duolun Lu is also worth a visit.

The ground floors of many of Duolun's houses have been turned into **art and antique stores**, heaped high with collections of old magazines, crockery, watches, posters and assorted aged miscellania. A shop run by Guo Chunxiang at **Nos.179-81 Duolun Lu** has one of the finest collections of memorabilia from early 20th-century Shanghai and the Cultural Revolution years. Duolun Lu also has several mini-museums devoted variously to chopsticks (No.191), porcelain (No.185) and, at No.183, Wang Zaoshi's collection of 10,000 Mao badges – which some zealous revolutionaries wore pierced into their skin as proof of their loyalty.

A little to the north-east of Duolun is the **Former Residence of Lu Xun** (see below), the creator of modern Chinese vernacular literature – as opposed to age-old classical Chinese literature, which has always been unintelligible to most ordinary people. A supporter of the Chinese cause against foreign exploitation, Lu Xun (1881-1936) was also one of the masterminds behind the Nationalist May 4th Movement (see p15). It's in this elegant 1924 mansion that the Chinese League of Left-wing Writers was founded in March 1930. Walk out into the courtyard garden to see a quintet of statues of young writers, looking very earnest and revolutionary among the bushes. The five were secretly murdered by Nationalists in 1931.

A short walk from Duolun is **Lu Xun Park**, also known as Honglou Park, which is one of the city's most pleasant green spaces. In addition to a couple of lovely lakes it contains the **Tomb of Lu Xun**, fronted by a giant seated bronze of the writer and with memorial calligraphy inscribed by Chairman Mao himself. There's also a museum, the **Lu Xun Memorial Hall** (see below).

Doland Modern Art Museum

27 Duolun Lu, by Sichuan Beilu (6587 6902).
Metro East Baoxing Lu. **Open** 9am-5pm daily.
Admission RMB 10. **No credit cards.**
Map p241 D1.
The first state-owned museum in China devoted entirely to modern art is an impressive seven-storey affair. Run by the culture bureau of the Hongkou district it opened in 2003 but has already become one of the city's most active cultural institutions. The permanent collection is supplemented by regularly changing temporary shows as well as music events.

Former Residence of Lu Xun

No.9, Lane 132, Shanying Lu, by Duolun Lu
(no phone). Metro East Baoxing Lu. **Open** 9am-5pm daily. **Admission** RMB 5. **No credit cards.**
Map p241 D2.
Replete with original furniture and a collection of Lu Xun's belongings. Conspicuous by their absence are his books – the writer's secret library was housed elsewhere and found a final home in Beijing.

Lu Xun Memorial Hall

Lu Xun Park, 146 Dongjiangwan Lu (6306 1181).
Metro Hongkou Stadium. **Open** 9am-5pm daily.
Admission RMB 5. **No credit cards.**
Map p241 D1.
This spacious new museum opened in 1999. The second level displays a voluminous collection of his books, letters, hand-scripted essays and personal artefacts, including his hawks-bill-rimmed glasses and a plaster cast death mask still embedded with a few strands of his facial hair. Signs are in English and Chinese. The museum shops sells Lu Xun's books in English-language editions.

Old Film Café

123 Duolun Lu, by Sichuan Beilu (5696 4763).
Metro East Baoxing Lu. **Open** 10am-1am daily.
Admission free. **No credit cards. Map** p241 D2.
The place justifies its name with framed black and white shots of Golden Age movie stars. An old carved wooden serving counter, deep red curtains and comfy chairs speak of decades of refined indolence over cups of English and Chinese teas. Coffee, wines and spirits are also available. The veranda area is pleasant given the right weather.

Jewish Shanghai

Not much has been done to mark Shanghai's historic Jewish ghetto, where almost 20,000 Jews fleeing the Holocaust once found unlikely refuge under the strict but comparatively benevolent eye of the occupying Japanese. The six-block area in Hongkou now looks like any other crowded Chinese neighbourhood. But the Jewish history is there if you know where to look for it. Now is a good time to go looking because the city government's North Bund is set to raze the area as part of the colossal facelift for the 2010 World Expo.

Jews first arrived in Shanghai in the late 19th century on the coat tails of the British. This first community numbered only around 800 souls – although the impact they made on the city was far out of proportion to their small number (see p12 **The Jewish dynasties**). In the early 20th century came another wave – this time Russian Jews fleeing the pogroms and service in the Tsar's army and, shortly after

Doland Modern Art Museum. *See p92.*

A Chinese Jewish resident of Hongkou.

that, when the Tsar had been defeated, fleeing the vindictiveness of the Red Army. They were doctors, musicians, writers and intellectuals who had left almost everything behind and they found a cheap residential area in Hongkou's townhouses. The third and last influx was that of the Holocaust refugees. They fled central and eastern Europe to Moscow and from there took the Trans-Siberian railway to Vladivostok and thence passage on a ship to Shanghai.

In July 1942 the Nazis sent Josef Meisinger to present to their Japanese allies a 'Final Solution' plan for Shanghai that involved mass drowning of the city's Jewish citizens. The Japanese refused to implement the plan. However, they did herd all the city's Jews into the one designated area in Hongkou.

ORGANISED TOURS

Dvir Bar-Gal (1300 214 6702/www.shanghai-jews.com), an Israeli based in Shanghai, gives an insightful tour of Jewish Shanghai, including the Hongkou district; call for further details.

Huoshan Lu

The heart of Jewish Shanghai is Huoshan Lu – not to be confused with Huashan Lu, which is in the French Concession. Get here by crossing the Garden Bridge then walking east along Dongdaming Lu (map p243 L2) or take a taxi from the Bund area.

At 65 Huoshan Lu is what was once the **Broadway Theatre**, which had a Jewish-owned roof garden called the Vienna Café.

Now the big neon sign in Chinese reads 'Broadway Disco'. East along the street are some charming brick townhouses with small gardens in front; this was formerly Jewish housing. **Huoshan Park** (open 6am-6pm daily), a nondescript leafy area, has the distinction of bearing the city's one public monument to the area's historic role as a Jewish haven; the inconspicuous stone engraved in English, Chinese and Hebrew alludes to the Hongkou neighbourhood as a 'designated area for stateless refugees'.

Across the street, **No.119 Huoshan Lu** was once the offices of the Joint Distribution Community (JDC), an international organisation that helped support Jewish refugees.

Zhoushan Lu is one of Huoshan's crossroads; its brick townhouses with arches over the windows are lovely, if run-down. Michael Blumenthal, the US Secretary of the Treasury from 1977-79 and now director of the Jewish Museum Berlin, once lived at **No.59**.

Follow Zhoushan Lu north to Changyang Lu and track back west for the **Ohel Moshe Synagogue**. Built in 1927 Ohel Moshe was run by Meir Ashkenazi, the spiritual leader of the Russian Jewish community and chief rabbi of Shanghai from 1926 to 1949. Step in to the hollow and empty ground floor for a small display of grainy black and white photos of Jewish buildings from Shanghai's past. Out back is a small exhibit donated by Canadian artists of Jewish or Chinese descent to honour the friendship between the Jews and the Chinese. The third floor is now the only **Jewish museum** in China (it's also probably the smallest museum in China). The only interesting aspect of the museum may be the elderly Mr Wang who oversees the exhibits and speaks fluent English and Japanese.

Back on Zhoushan Lu, north of Changyang Lu is a shabby **pet market** soundtracked by the pitiful twittering of caged birds and the incessant chirruping of crickets. On the east side of the street a high wall hides a jail built in 1901 by the British and later used by Japanese for military intelligence. Now it is once again an active jail, allegedly holding 20,000 inmates.

Jewish Refugee Museum

63 Changyang Lu, by Dalian Lu (6541 5008).
Open 9am-4.30pm daily. **Admission** RMB 50.
No credit cards. Map p241 E2.
The former Ohel Moshe Synagogue reopened in 1992 as a small museum dedicated to the Jewish refugees who were forced to leave their homes in other parts of the city to endure a life of squalor in the Hongkou ghetto between 1943 and 1945. There are period photos, a historical video and books on the Jews in Shanghai – but keep in mind that other bookstores stock them at less inflated prices.

Eat, Drink, Shop

Restaurants & Cafés

Menus on streamers, noise levels on high and chefs on form: step up to the Shanghai banquet.

Eat, Drink, Shop

Bao Luo. *See p110.*

Shanghai often boasts that it is China's most 'international' city, with the best global dining in the country to prove it. But the rich scope of eating here is not created by foreign flavours alone. As the hub of internal migration in China, Shanghai has an indigenous restaurant scene influenced by immigrants from more than 30 provinces, plus Hong Kong and Taiwan. These self-styled 'New Shanghainese' (*xin shanghairen*) move to the metropolis to seek their fortunes, and increasingly, so it seems, find them by running restaurants.

This makes Shanghai a one-stop culinary tour of Greater China, a place to sample the best of the regional cuisines – from the frosty north to the steamy south, the new cosmopolitan east and the Chinese development frontier out west.

Obviously, not all are good. Inexperienced owners out to make a quick buck often deliver inconsistent food and service. There is also a tendency to blow the budget on decor, at the expense of food or good staff. In a similar vein, some of the restaurants housed in Shanghai's old colonial villas, for example, benefit from stunning settings but are run by people with powerful connections, not skilful chefs.

The best in dining is concentrated in the **French Concession**, particularly on and around Huaihai Zhonglu and Hengshan Lu. But perhaps the most exciting developments are down on the riverfront. Until recently there was only **M on the Bund** (*see p99*), but this past year has seen a rush of new arrivals to fill the former colonial properties by the water, most notably superchef Jean-Georges Vongerichten's **Jean-Georges** (*see p99*). Autumn 2004 will see another international French culinary export as twins Jacques and Laurent Pourcel set up shop, also on the Bund.

With world class cooking comes world class prices; dining in Shanghai can be an expensive business. If the truth be told, when it comes to European, Japanese and other international cuisines, many visitors are disappointed by the quality vs the price. Our advice? Stick to Chinese in all its myriad flavours and you're unlikely to be disappointed

DINING ETIQUETTE

The do's and don'ts of dining in Shanghai are not as elaborate as you might imagine, but there are a few points still worth observing. Your coat won't be taken, so just hang it on the back of your seat – a plastic covering will be slid over to protect it. Most meals will be served communal-style, with platters in the centre of the table, so usually only one menu is given to the host to order for everyone. Your plate is for food that you serve yourself with chopsticks from the main dishes, and for scraps. The bowl and spoon is for soup and for dishes that are difficult to eat with chopsticks, such as slippery tofu. For anyone who finds chopsticks awkward, there is no shame in asking for a fork (*chazi*) or spoon (*shaozi*).

Cold dishes come first. Next come meat and vegetable dishes, followed by fish. Soup comes last. Shanghainese are big fans of soup, and if you don't order it the waitstaff may prompt you to do so. Rice is average everyday food, and most locals won't order it in restaurants. Tea is refilled as many times as you drain your cup. Dessert is usually a plate of watermelon slices to cleanse the palate. Toothpicks will be provided to clean your teeth.

Except at extremely formal official dinners, dining Chinese-style is casual. People will smoke or talk on mobile phones while eating. The only real no-nos are superstitions in nature. For example, don't stab your chopsticks into a pile of food or bowl of rice and leave them there – this evokes funeral incense sticks. Don't turn a whole fish over – this is like a boat capsizing. Don't reach across the table for food and never take the last piece from a dish – bad manners in any part of the world, really.

If you are being treated to dinner by locals, remember that a host always pays for his (rarely her) guests, and do try everything you are offered because to leave a dish untouched implies that your host did a poor job of ordering. You won't offend if you leave something on your plate that you didn't like. If you are offered *baijiou*, the extremely strong rice spirit used here for toasting, you may have to toss it down when your host shouts out '*Gang bei!*' ('touch glasses'). You can plead illness (*wo bu shufu*) if you really don't want to drink any more.

For more on general issues of attitude and etiquette, *see p218*.

MENUS AND PRICES

While most of the restaurants listed in this guide have English menus, some local places will not. Our advice in this case is simply to point to the things you see on other tables. It's what the locals do.

For the listings in this guide we give the average price one person would pay for a meal without drinks; that might be two courses at a French restaurant or a single share of a table piled high at some local joint.

The best Restaurants

Bao Luo
Arguably the ultimate authentic Shanghai city dining experience. Go as a group, preferably with someone who knows a bit about the local cuisine, and fill the table with the strangest sounding dishes you can find on the menu – 'You ordered what?!'. *See p110.*

Crystal Jade
Never mind the location (upstairs in a half empty, soulless mall), it's got a buzzing atmosphere, superb service and, best of all, fantastic dim sum. You won't find a better HK barbeque combination plate – with roast duck and suckling pig – this side of Canton. *See p108.*

Jean-Georges
If he's good enough for Manhattan... Stylish and sexy, the latest 'most talked about restaurant in town' actually lives up to the hype. Go for the desserts, which include a heavenly strawberry and rhubarb Napoleon crème brûlée. Just like the decadent days of old. *See p99.*

Jishi
Another good bet for down-home Shanghai cuisine. It's loud, it's smoky and the Chinglish menu is a model of garbled syntax but just point and shout – everybody else does. Try the jellyfish heads with vinegar. *See p111.*

1221
The modern face of eating Shanghainese, this is the place to go local without getting down and dirty. It's smart, it's stylish, there's a very decent wine list and the food, of course, is tip-top. Go for crispy duck. *See p104.*

Shintori
Purists argue that you can get better Japanese food elsewhere, but there's nowhere else with an interior that has anything like the wow factor of Shintori. The tuna-avocado paste appetiser is a bit of a knockout too. *See p116.*

Yin
For a taste of 1930s Shanghai: a room divided by wooden screens, a long bar, cocktail waitresses in slinky *qipaos*, live jazz and very fine food. *See p114.*

Eat, Drink, Shop

BRAZILIAN CHURRASCARIA SALAD BAR, ALL YOU CAN EAT

The most fantastic barbeque and salad bar, you tried in Brazil, you can find the same here

LUNCH MENU

Lunch "Special" All you can eat, including the largest variety of meats served on your table, unlimited servings at the buffet, including hot dishes, salads, soup and desserts.

RMB **55** / person (11am - 4pm)

DINNER MENU

Dinner "Samba Style" All you can eat, selected meat cuts of cow, chicken, sheep, and pork served on your table, unlimited servings at the buffet.

RMB **66** / person (4pm - 11pm)

上海市南京西路1649号
1649 Nanjing Xi Road
(across from Jing An Temple)
Tel: 86 21-6255 9898

上海市淮海中路1582号
1582 Huaihai Zhong Road
(across from Shanghai Library)
Tel: 86 21-6437 7288
www.brasilsteakhouse.net
www.brasilsteakhouse.cn

OPENING TIMES AND BOOKING

The Chinese tend to eat early by Western standards. Most local restaurants will serve lunch between 11am and 2pm, and dinner between 5pm and 8pm. Some kitchens will close even earlier than that. For popular places it's always advisable to book (*youding*), but many local restaurants won't take bookings for dinner after 6.30pm, or 7pm at the latest.

CREDIT CARDS AND TIPPING

Credit cards are accepted in most international restaurants, but otherwise Shanghai is largely still a cash economy, so you should always carry enough currency to cover a meal. Tipping is not necessary in local places, although the custom of 10% or 15% is creeping in at top-end venues. Most hotel restaurants will add a 15% service charge to the bill.

The Bund

The grid of streets back from the waterfront is full of small eateries but the action on the Bund is all about high-end dining. For less formality try the paninis, espressos and fresh juices at **Bonomi Café** (Room 226, 12 Zhongshan Dongliyu), situated in the former Hong Kong and Shanghai Bank building, right on the Bund. **Zhapu Lu**, just north of the Bund across Suzhou Creek, is an excellent food street with dozens of small restaurants. There's also a branch of **Shanghai Uncle** (*see p118*) near the Natural History Museum.

Chinese

Whampoa Club

5th floor, Three on the Bund, 3 Zhongshan Dongyilu, by Guangdong Lu (6321 3737/www.threeonthebund. com). Metro Henan Lu. **Open** 11.30am-2.30pm, 5.30-11pm daily. **Average** RMB 250-300. **Credit** AmEx, DC, MC, V. **English menu. Map** p243 J4.
Shanghainese
One of Asia's pre-eminent chefs, Jereme Leung, breathes new life into traditional Shanghainese cuisine at this dazzling modern deco setting created by celebrated Hong Kong designer Alan Chan. The extensive menu features everything from soups and seafood to shark's fin dishes and Leung's signature slow-cooked Australian abalone. His adaptations of classic dishes include drunken chicken with Shaoxing wine, shaved ice and house-smoked tea eggs. Leung also breaks new ground with dishes such as almond and cocoa fried spare ribs and seared goose liver on glutinous red dates. If you can afford it, the five-course tasting menu (RMB 550) is the way to go. Diners can also choose from over 50 special teas for a traditional ceremony served tableside or in one of the opulent private tearooms. Reservations are required for dinner.

Fusion

Jean-Georges

4th floor, Three on the Bund, 3 Zhongshan Dongyilu, by Guangdong Lu (6321 7733/www.threeonthebund. com). Metro Henan Lu. **Open** 11.30am-2.30pm, 5.30-11pm daily. **Average** RMB 300-400. **Credit** AmEx, DC, MC, V. **English menu. Map** p243 J4.
Jean-Georges being Jean-Georges Vongerichten, the Alsace-born hotshot chef, lauded for his New York restaurants Vong and 66. Long a fan of Shanghai cuisine, in April 2004 he put the money where his mouth had and introduced the city to his fragrant Chinois take on trad French cuisine. The location is the Michael Graves-designed setting of Three on the Bund (*see p54*). Decorated with eel-skin sofas and pony leather armchairs, the restaurant is part Gothic Shanghai gentlemen's club, part Manhattan martini bar. Diners can order à la carte, or select one of two seven-course tasting menus. Start with crisp foie gras brûlée, juicy scallops with a caramel caper-raisin sauce, or divine red snapper sashimi with fresh wasabi and rose gêlée. Exquisite mains include lobster infused in lemongrass and fenugreek broth. Alternatively, the RMB 188 lunch menu is a less painful way to introduce yourself to the Jean-Georges experience. Reservations are required for both lunch and dinner.

Laris

6th floor, Three on the Bund, 3 Zhongshan Dongyilu, by Guangdong Lu (6321 9922/www.threeonthebund. com). Metro Henan Lu. **Open** 11.30am-2.30pm, 5.30-10.30pm daily. **Average** RMB 450-500. **Credit** AmEx, MC, V. **English menu. Map** p243 J4.
The prevailing trend in restaurant decor is retro-chic and a taste of 'Old Shanghai', but not at Laris – this place is all about 'new Shanghai' and the money that goes with it. It's the first signature restaurant of the energetic David Laris, formerly executive chef of Terence Conran's Soho flagship Mezzo, and it taps into the nouveau Shanghainese love of lux: cue bright marble interiors and fat velvet couches, cocktails in the sexy Vault Bar, followed by fresh oysters, lobster and Russian caviar at the marble Claws, Wings & Fins bar. An inventive dining menu includes the likes of wild chicken with herb gnocchi and five-spiced venison with Vietnamese banana blossom salad. There is also a chocolatier on the staff whose windowed workshop is by night a private dining room.

M on the Bund

7th floor, 20 Guangdong Lu, by Zhongshan Dongyilu (6350 9988/www.m-onthebund.com). Metro Henan Lu. **Open** 11.30am-2.30pm, 6.15-10.30pm daily. **Average** RMB 138-218 (lunch); RMB 500 (dinner). **Credit** AmEx, DC, MC, V. **English menu. Map** p243 J4.
Before Jean-Georges (*see above*) there was M on the Bund. Named after the city's networking tour de force Michelle Garnaut (founder of Hong Kong's M on the Fringe), M has been a bellwether for

Bi Feng Tang. *See p104.*

contemporary Asian *and* Western, so it takes in both Thai-inspired deep-fried fish with chilli jam and good old Anglo fish and chips, as well as salads, burgers and steaks. Reservations are required for dinner. In the evening the place operates as a bar with house DJs: *see p120.*

International

CJW
50th floor, Bund Centre, 222 Yan'an Donglu (6339 1777). Metro Henan Lu. **Open** 11.30am-2.30pm, 6-10.30pm daily. **Average** RMB 88 (lunch); RMB 300-350 (dinner). **Credit** AmEx, MC, V. **English menu.** Map p243 J4.

The most sweeping river view of any eatery on the western side of the city, CJW gives you the Pudong towers and the arc of the Huangpu River – from the new high-rise riverside apartment blocks to the south, all the way to the cranes loading at to the port to the north. CJW is 40-odd floors above the rest of the competition in the area, so go here if you want to see the city planners' perspective. The food is less impressive. The menu reads and tastes like that of the average hotel: Caesar salad, oysters kilpatrick, ribeye steak and grilled sea bass, mostly served with tired vegetables. When you consider that prices are in the same range as M and New Heights, where the cuisine is innovative and the ingredients market fresh, it feels overpriced. Lunch is probably the best value – two or three courses for RMB 88/188 – especially if you book a table near the window. The open terrace is great for a drink with a view.

Shanghai's giddy economic growth since opening in 1999. It's the haunt of deal-makers and doyennes and so popular with them that it turns over tables three times a night. The art deco revival venue is stunning, with sweeping views of the historic Bund and the Pudong skyscrapers across the river. The new North African-meets-Mediterranean menu is hearty at dinner (suckling pig, salted lamb, charred vegetable platter with yoghurt), and lighter at lunch (lamb pinenut pastries, goat's cheese with walnut mint salad). Toast the Shanghai skyline with a glass of champagne or raise a pinky at Sunday high tea. Late cocktails and desserts are accommodated at the Glamour Bar (*see p120*) across the hall. *See also p104* **Height cuisine** and *p110* **Brunch bunch**. Reservations required for lunch and dinner.

New Heights
7th floor, Three on the Bund, 3 Zhongshan Dongyilu, by Guangdong Lu (6321 0909/www.threeonthebund. com). Metro Henan Lu. **Open** 10am-1pm, 5.30-10.30pm daily. **Average** RMB 300. **Credit** AmEx, DC, MC, V. **English menu.** Map p243 J4.

New Heights occupies the uppermost floor of the new Three on the Bund development. Bully for it: it also gets the roof with a 180-degree panorama of the river and the eastern city (the rooftop clock tower is for hire). Inside is all casual minimalism, with the accent on the casual. Unlike Jean-Georges and the Whampoa Club downstairs (for both *see p99*), this is intended as a place to just drop by for a leisurely lunch or a quick cappuccino (a library of Western magazines is provided for browsing). The food is

Renmin Square

As a main bus and metro terminus, Renmin has a clutch of cheap noodle joints, Western fast-food outlets and Japanese and Chinese chain restaurants plus, in season some prime crab outlets (*see p109* **Hairy crabs**). **Huanghe Lu**, beside the Park Hotel, has plenty of small eateries, as does **Yunnan Nanlu** (for both, *see p115* **Street eats**). For more upmarket fare, there's a branch of **Xiao Nan Guo** (*see p113*) just north of the square

Kathleen's 5
5th floor, Shanghai Art Museum, 325 Nanjing Xilu, by Huangpi Beilu, Renmin Square (6327 2221). Metro Renmin Park or Square. **Open** 11.30am-11.30pm daily. **Average** RMB 80-100 (lunch); RMB 200 (dinner). **Credit** AmEx, DC, MC, V. **English menu.** Map p242 F4.

This stunning site atop the Shanghai Art Museum offers the best city views outside the Huangpu riverfront. A modern, glass-enclosed and neon-lit dining area is fused with the neo-classical architecture of the former racecourse clubhouse, affording an unobstructed panorama of glittering Renmin Square. The menu's basic but modern American cuisine uses fresh ingredients and homemade condiments, and

Jean-Georges at **Jean-Georges**.
See p99.

leans toward seafood (fishcakes, steamed clams, Cajun-seared scallops with potato cakes, and cod with garlic and tomato purée. The best seats are actually up at the bar (*see p121*), while VIPs can request those in the clocktower. Reservations are required for both lunch and dinner.

Jingan

In addition to the places listed below, Jingan has branches of Sichuan restaurant **Darling Harbour** (*see p118*) and the ever-popular Shanghainese **Xiao Nan Guo** (*see p113*). The city's most vibrant streetfood locale is here at Wujiang Lu (*see p115* **Street eats**). As expat central, Jingan also has plenty of Western-

friendly restaurants, particularly around the neighbourhood of the Shanghai Centre/Ritz-Carlton. At the Centre itself is rib and burger joint **Tony Roma's**, with more diner fare at **Malone's** (*see p121*) around the corner. The **Brasil Steakhouse** (1649 Nanjing Xilu) is just up the street, opposite the Jingan Temple.

Cafés & snacks

Element Fresh

Room 112, Shanghai Centre, 1376 Nanjing Xilu, by Xikang Lu (6279 8682). Metro Jingan Temple. **Open** 7am-11pm Mon-Thur, Sun; 7am-midnight Fri, Sat. **Average** RMB 100-200. **Credit** AmEx, DC, MC, V. **English menu. Map** p249 D4. **Bistro**

Eat, Drink, Shop

Chinese cuisines

Chinese people have a well-deserved reputation for eating practically anything. But each region is different. The Cantonese certainly aren't picky (civet cat, anyone?), while northerners do, in fact, eat dog, believing it keeps them warm in winter. Shanghainese diners, meanwhile, are notoriously fussy, and do not like to be thought of as indiscriminating eaters. Still, it's all relative: delicacies such as crab sperm, snake's blood and turtle shells are all considered Shanghainese specialities and served at many restaurants.

Just as in the West nobody would ever say 'Let's go eat European', but instead specify French, Italian or whatever, the Shanghainese don't go out for a Chinese – they eat Cantonese, Shanghainese or Sichuan. Cuisines from most provinces of China are available in Shanghai, although some are more popular than others.

SHANGHAINESE

As you'd expect, this is the most popular cuisine in town, rich both in flavour and texture. Heavy, unctuous brown sauces are used for braising meats such as pork shanks or knuckle, or to simmer fatty pork balls with vegetables. Dumplings are popular, and very different from the lighter Cantonese variety. The most famous Shanghainese dumplings are *xiao long bao*, which are filled with pork and flavourful broth made solid with gelatine. The gelatine melts in the heat of the steamer and fills the interior of the dumpling with liquid. They're then dipped in a sauce made with Shanghainese brown vinegar and shreds of ginger. This unusual vinegar is an essential flavouring to other dishes – it's an ingredient

in some braising sauces and stir-fries and is drizzled over seafood, including delicate freshwater shrimp.

While the main starch of Chinese from the south is rice, the Shanghainese prefer bread. The poetically named 'silver threads' bread (so called because the interior dough is formed into long, thin strands and then wrapped in a flat sheet of dough) is subtly sweet and comes either steamed or fried; the former is better for sopping up juices.

Shanghainese also specialise in so-called 'cold dishes', which are not actually cold, but room temperature or tepid. They're most often eaten as an appetiser but are so delicious and varied it's easy to make an entire meal of them. They include jellyfish flavoured with sesame oil, mashed soybeans with preserved vegetables, sweet and crispy fried eel, and 'drunken' chicken or pigeon, which has been marinated in rice wine until the flavour permeates the meat.

Shanghai means 'by the sea' and the region's own peculiar sea cucumber is served braised with shrimp roe. Similarly, shark's fin soup is usually served with braised chicken and ham giving it a curious taste (one not enjoyed by all).

For Shanghainese dining *see* **Bao Luo** (*p110*); **Jishi** (*p111*); **Lu Bo Lang** (*p107*); **Meilongzhen** (*p104*); **Nan Xiang** (*p107*); **1931** (*p113*); **Shanghai Lao Zhan** (*p117*); **Shanghai Uncle** (*p118*); **Sophia's Tea Restaurant** (*p113*); **1221** (*p104*); **Whampoa Club** (*p99*); **Xiao Nan Guo** (*p113*); **Xia Wei Guan** (*p114*); **Yè Shanghai** (*p108*); **Yin** (*p114*); and **Yuan Yuan** (*p114*).

The brainchild of a young American entrepreneur, this modern deli is pure San Francisco or LA. It's always packed with young professionals tucking into generous servings of Asian, Western and Middle Eastern dishes. The pastas are average, but everything else on the menu is great, including sushi, gourmet sandwiches, bagels and salads. It also does a good breakfast and the juice bar is the best in the city. Having eaten a virtuous, vitamin-packed meal you can retire to the terrace with a beer or cocktail. *See also p110* **Brunch bunch**.

Red Door (Xiamien Guan)

5th floor, Plaza 66, 1266 Nanjing Xilu, by Shanxi Beilu (6288 1217). Metro Shimen Yilu. **Open** 11am-9.30pm daily. **Average** RMB 20-100. **Credit** AmEx, DC, MC, V. **English menu. Map** p249 D4. Noodles

On the fifth floor of posh Plaza 66 (*see p130*), overlooking several levels of newly rich Shanghainese ladies shopping for Escada, Lanvin and Celine, Red Door is a noodle restaurant designed in the fashion of a sushi bar – all clinically white and complete with conveyor belt delivery. Servings come in lovely large white bowls (you'll want ot take them home) and include classics such as beef noodles (RMB 38) and an in-house special of seafood noodles. It's a little pricey at RMB 68, but excellent.

Wagas

Room LG12A, Underground Floor 1, CITIC Square, 1168 Nanjing Xilu, by Shanxi Beilu (5292 5228). Metro Shimen Yilu. **Open** 7.30am-10pm daily. **Average** RMB 60-100. **No credit cards. English menu. Map** p249 D4. Sandwich bar

CANTONESE

Cantonese is the cuisine of the south, exported worldwide via Hong Kong. In this type of cooking, the freshness of ingredients is paramount and cooking techniques (especially steaming) are evolved to highlight the freshness. Because subtlety of flavours is so important, Cantonese cooks use a light, delicate hand with seasonings. To those who prefer more robust flavours, Cantonese food might seem bland.

Traditional Cantonese cooking techniques include steaming and stir-frying – which seals in the flavour of food by cooking it quickly over high heat for no more than a minute – producing dishes such as delicate rice noodles, dumplings and a variety of deep-fried savoury pastries.

For Cantonese dining *see* **Bi Feng Teng** (*p104*); **Crystal Jade** (*p108*); and **Nan Xiang** (*p107*).

DONGBEI

Dongbei is the name of the cuisine from Beijing and the north-east region of China. It is rich and oily with plenty of meat, vegetable and aubergine dishes, all flavoured with lashings of spring onions and garlic. Lamb and mutton are popular, and stir-fried slivers of meat and vegetables are frequently served stuffed into pockets of sesame-coated baked breads. The cuisine's most famous dish is Peking duck. It is always served with great ceremony by a white-gloved waiter carving off the deep, mahogany-coloured skin, wrapping the pieces in a thin pancake with a dab of plum sauce and a sliver of spring onion. When it's good, the skin is the best part of the duck – it should be crisp, flavourful and with just a hint of fat.

For Dongbei dining *see* **Dongbei Ren** (*p111*).

HUNANESE AND SICHUAN

China's western spice belt provinces of Hunan and Sichuan have similar base ingredients, but the source of the spice is different. Hunanese dishes use chilli, but Sichuan mixes dried chillies with gum-numbing, metallic-tasting pink peppercorns harvested from prickly ash trees. Sichuan food is hearty and rich, with sauces that ideally blend sweet, sour and spicy flavours. Hot and sour soup is probably the Sichuanese dish best known in the West – it combines vinegar, pepper and chillies to make a powerful, sinus-clearing broth. Dumplings and breads are also popular. Steamed buns are usually served with tea-smoked duck; meat dumplings look similar to Cantonese won ton, but instead of being served in a subtle broth, they're smothered in a sauce of soy, garlic and chillies.

For Hunanese and Sichuan dining *see* **Darling Harbour** (*p118*); **Di Shui Dong** (*p111*); **Guyi** (*p111*); **Pin Chuan** (*p113*); and **South Beauty** (*p113*).

XINJIANG

The autonomous region of Xinjiang is situated south-east of Kazakstan and Afghanistan, thus the influences in the Xinjiang cuisine are more Central Asian than Chinese. Lamb stews and skewers are combined with nan bread, spicy salads, dark beer and live entertainment.

For Xinjiang dining *see* **Uighur Restaurant** (*p113*).

Eat, Drink, Shop

A prime lunch-on-the-run venue, Wagas is a big hit with time-strapped office workers. The fare is all healthy – fresh salads, great pastas, soups and sandwiches, plus daily blackboard specials, as well as fresh juices, non-dairy frappes and smoothies. The coffee's excellent, and there's always a good selection of cakes. Breakfast is also served daily. The interior is smart and clean, its utilitarian nature softened by couches and magazines for browsing.

Chinese

Bi Feng Tang
1333 Nanjing Xilu, by Tongren Lu (6279 0738). Metro Jingan Temple. **Open** 10am-5am daily. **Average** RMB 40-100. **Credit** AmEx, DC, MC, V. **English menu. Map** p248 C4. **Cantonese**

Height cuisine

As Shanghai climbs ever higher, the opportunities for vertiginous dining increase.

CJW
A superb aerial-postcard view of the Huangpu River and the Pudong skyline from the 50th floor of the Bund Centre. Food is basic, but drinks on the open terrace are something else. *See p100.*

Cucina at On56
Go head-to-head with Pudong's skyscrapers by reserving a window table at the Hyatt's modern Italian restaurant, located on the 56th floor of the world's fourth tallest building. *See p118.*

Kathleen's 5
A glasshouse plonked on top of the Shanghai Art Museum with superb views of the area around Renmin Square. Casual or formal dining, or a pre-dinner drink. *See p100.*

M on the Bund
From M's terrace overlooking the Huangpu watch the old barges make their way through the murky waters against a backdrop of dazzling skyscrapers. The lights on the Bund turn on at 6.30pm – be there to raise a toast when they are turned off at 10.30pm. *See p99.*

New Heights
Next door to M and one floor higher, New Heights has indoor and alfresco dining perfect for cooing over the twinkling lights of Pudong, across the river. *See p100.*

The local answer to McDonald's, BFT is a city-wide chain that draws round-the-clock crowds with cheap Cantonese dim sum and similar savoury snacks. This particular branch is hugely convenient for guests at the Ritz-Carlton, which is just over the road. It's kitted out like a traditional fishing village, with an outdoor seating area of small wooden huts draped with fishing nets and festive pin lights. Expect all the usual dough-wrapped suspects from steamed shrimp and pork dumplings to barbecue pork buns. Various congees are also available and, for dessert, baked egg custard tart. Late-night clubbers make up a significant portion of the custom at the 24-hour Changle Lu branch, *see below.*
Other locations: 175 Changle Lu, by Ruijin Yilu, French Concession (6467 0628).

Meilongzhen
1081 Nanjing Xilu, by Jiangning Lu (6253 5353). Metro Shimen Yilu. **Open** 11am-2pm, 5-10pm daily. **Average** RMB 100-200. **Credit** AmEx, DC, MC, V. **English menu. Map** p249 D4. **Shanghainese**
The kitchens at Shanghai's most famous local restaurant have been churning out dishes since 1938. The building was once home to the Chinese Communist Party and the restaurant remains a state-run operation. Its rooms feature classic decor with mahogany and marble furniture, carved wood panels and paper lanterns. Sichuan dishes are prepared in Shanghai style (that's to say, blander and oilier). Highlights include Meilongzhen special chicken, deep-fried sweet and sour fish and crabmeat and shark's fin (RMB 150). First-timers might enjoy the Sichuan convention of serving tea at several paces by means of a long-spouted teapot. The quality of food and service deteriorates as the night wears on, so an early booking is advised.
Other locations: Westgate Mall, 97 Jiangning Lu, by Nanjing Xilu, Jingan (6255 6688).

1221
1221 Yanan Xilu, by Fanyu Lu (6213 6585). Metro Jiangsu Lu. **Open** 11.30am-2pm, 5-11pm daily. **Average** RMB 100-150. **Credit** AmEx, DC, MC, V. **English menu. Map** p240 B3. **Shanghainese**
A perennial favourite among expats for its consistently delicious food, excellent service and an extensive and reasonably-priced wine list. In looks, the place is simple but classy with white starched tablecloths, chalkboard-black floor and a couple of great big daubings of modern art for colour. Owner Michelle Liu was raised by Shanghainese parents in Hong Kong and her mixed background is expressed in a diverse menu of local and Cantonese dishes. It's hard to go wrong ordering but the best of the offerings include shredded chicken with peanut sauce, crispy duck with taro, sautéd beef with fried dough sticks and, for dessert, fried sticky rice with red bean paste (although it's unlikely you'll make it that far). Note that the restaurant is remotely located some way from central Jingan, down a small alley off main artery Yanan Xilu; a taxi is really the only convenient wat to get here.

Eat, Drink, Shop

Eat, Drink, Shop

The serene Indo-China scene at **Bali Laguna**. *See p107.*

European

Palladio

1st floor, Portman Ritz-Carlton, 1376 Nanjing Nanlu, by Xikang Lu (6279 7188). Metro Jingan Temple. **Open** 11am-2pm, 6-10.30pm Mon-Sat; 6-10.30pm Sun. **Average** RMB 250-500. **Credit** AmEx, DC, MC, V. **English menu**. **Map** p248C4. Italian

Did Italy import the notion of spaghetti noodles from China via Marco Polo or was the exchange in the reverse direction? Either way, the bond secured by those long, thin strips of dough remains strong, and Shanghai has more than its fair share of Italian eateries, in all price categories. For the top-drawer experience, check the balance on the credit card and head to Palladio. Its location at the Portman Ritz-Carlton makes it a favourite with the Nanjing Lu CBD crowd for high-power business lunches. At dinner, the hotel's guests mix with local glamour as moneyed city residents dress up for chef Giovanni Terracciano's seriously divine dishes such as nutty risotto and squid ink pasta. Alternatively, test the limits of your plastic on veal with goose liver and black truffles. Further trappings of *la dolce vita* are offered in the form of grappa and cigars.

South-east Asian

Bali Laguna

189 Huashan Lu, within Jingan Park (6248 6970). Metro Jingan Temple. **Open** 11am-2.30pm, 6-10.30pm daily. **Average** RMB 150. **Credit** AmEx, DC, MC, V. **English menu**. **Map** p248 C5. Indonesian

Scented blooms, exotic statuary and carved teak furniture in a pretty residence beside a lily-carpeted lake in the middle of Jingan Park – this place makes a fair stab at the notion of a Balinese island paradise. No wonder, then, that it's a big hit with local *langman* (romantic couples). On warm summer nights they favour the open-air café, but if it's cold or raining the second-floor dining hall, with its views of tree tops, is hardly less attractive. Dishes include plenty of seafood and pork with coconut and sweet potato flavourings. Waitstaff – pretty in brightly coloured sarongs – are slow but the atmosphere is so chilled that nobody seems to mind. Reservations are required for dinner.

Old City

Dining in the Old City is synonymous with touristy dumpling restaurants, although many such places have seen better days and are overpriced. As an alternative to KFC and the other Western fast-food franchises that are prevalent round here, visit Yunnan Nanlu (*see p115* **Street eats**), a great place for cheap eats with a wealth of small stalls and restaurants specialising in regional cuisines.

T8 (diners and food not shown). *See p109.*

Chinese

Lu Bo Lang

115-131 Yuyuan Lu, south shore of the teahouse pond, Old City (6328 0602). Metro Henan Lu. **Open** 7am-10am, 11am-2pm, 5pm-midnight daily. **Average** RMB 80-250. **Credit** AmEx, DC, MC, V. **English menu**. **Map** p243 J6. Shanghainese

Housed in a classical Ming Dynasty-style pavilion overlooking the Yu Gardens and the teahouse pond (*see p69*), this place has the tourists flocking in to soak up the history and gawk at the admittedly impressive decor. They are in good company: previous rubberneckers have included Bill Clinton, Queen Elizabeth and Fidel Castro – their visits are commemorated in photos gracing the walls of the second- and third-floor corridors. However, as is true of most state-run enterprises in China, the service and food are entirely underwhelming. House speciality is dim sum; order individually from a vast menu or opt for a set meal (RMB 50-100).

Nan Xiang

85 Yuyuan Lu, Yu Gardens, Old City (6355 4206). **Open** 10am-9pm daily (1st floor); 6.30am-8pm daily (2nd floor); 10.45am-6.30pm (3rd floor). **Average** RMB 8-100. **Credit** AmEx, DC, MC, V. **English menu**. **Map** p243 J6. Dumplings

At the heart of the Yu Gardens and Bazaar, this three-storey shrine to *xiao long bao* (dumplings) is possibly the city's most famous eaterie. It features

Hunanese hotpot to share at **Di Shui Dong**. *See p111*.

on the itinerary of every visitor, as evidenced by the permanent, lengthy queues that stretch from its doorway. The basic dumpling varieties are steamed pork and crabmeat, but the higher the floor, the more elaborate the offerings; the third floor is where you go for the crab roe filling. We prefer the second floor, which boasts the best views of the nearby lake and zigzag bridge.

Xintiandi

In addition to the places listed below, Xintiandi also boasts a branch of the excellent **Simply Thai** (*see p117*) and Shanghainese favourite **Jishi** (*see p113*).

Cafés & snacks

KABB
House 5, North Block, Lane 181, Huangpi Nanlu, by Taicang Lu (3307 0798). Metro Huangpi Nanlu. **Open** 6.30am-midnight Mon-Thur, Sun; 6.30am-2am Fri, Sat. **Average** RMB 150-200. **Credit** AmEx, DC, MC, V. **English menu. Map** p244 F6. **Diner**
American-style casual dining with a bit of Mexican and Italian thrown in. Go for sizeable snacks such as club sandwiches, pork ribs with BBQ sauce and Mexican nachos, or go the whole hog with lasagne, beef burgers or grilled rib-eye steak. KABB also boasts one of the best locations at Xintiandi and its outdoor tables are the perfect place to while away a summer's afternoon over rich desserts and a glass of wine. It gets far more lively at night: *see p123*.

Chinese

Crystal Jade
Unit 12A & 12B, 1st floor, House 6-7, Lane 123, Xingye Lu, South Block, by Zizhong Lu, Xintiandi Plaza (6385 8752). Metro Huangpi Nanlu. **Open** 11.30am-3pm, 5-11pm Mon-Sat; 10.30am-3pm, 5.30-11pm Sun. **Average** RMB 70-100. **Credit** AmEx, DC, MC, V. **English menu. Map** p244 F7. **Cantonese**
Part of a Singaporean chain, this place is wildly popular for the inexpensive but incredibly good Cantonese and Shanghainese dim sum. Top picks are the baked barbecue pork bun, the fried turnip cake, the Shanghainese steamed pork dumplings and the spicy wontons. The regular menu features superb Hong Kong barbeque fare, especially the suckling pig and roast duck combination. Break off from eating to watch the mesmerising performance of kitchen staff making noodles entirely by hand (it's all in the wrist), observable through a long slot of a window at the entrance to the massive dining room. Bookings are essential for both lunch and dinner.

Yè Shanghai
House 6, North Block, Lane 181, Taicang Lu, by Huangpi Nanlu (6311 2323). Metro Huangpi Nanlu. **Open** 11.30am-2.30pm, 5.30-11pm Mon-Thur, Sun; 11.30am-2.30pm, 5.30pm-midnight Fri, Sat. **Average** RMB 250-280. **Credit** AmEx, DC, MC, V. **English menu. Map** p244 F6. **Shanghainese**
Named after a hit song of the 1940s, recorded by popular local songstress Zhou Xuan, Yè Shanghai ('Shanghai Night') is a nostalgia trip of red lanterns, antique furniture and sepia-toned images of old

Bubbling Well Road and the pre-war era racecourse. The menu features such typical Shanghainese dishes as drunken chicken and steamed pork dumplings, as well as chef's specials such as sautéd river shrimp and king prawns with chilli sauce.

Fusion

T8
House 8, Lane 181, Taicang Lu, North Block, by Huangpi Nanlu (6355 8999). Metro Huangpi Nanlu. **Open** 11am-11.30pm Mon, Wed, Thur; 6.30-11.30pm Tue; 11am-4am Fri; 4pm-4am Sat; 4-11.30pm Sun. **Average** RMB 400-500. **Credit** AmEx, DC, MC, V. **English menu**. Map p244 F6.
T8 looks South-east Asian, has an Australian chef in the kitchen and tastes Mediterranean. Hefty slate slabs laid over fish-filled pools make for a striking entrance, while the main dining area is all sleek lacquered furniture with warm seagrass and cane accents. Central to the action is the large open kitchen, where half a dozen young chefs sear, sauté and flash-fry in front of diners seated at counter tables. With flavours that punch their weight – as

seen in dishes such as lamb and Sichuan high pie, or basil-rich beef carpaccio – the food is worthy of the superlatives it frequently attracts. Accompany with something from a fine Australian-accented wine list. Reservations are required for dinner.

French Concession

In addition to the places listed below, the Concession also has branches of Cantonese dumpling-fest **Bi Feng Tang** (*see p104*) and the Sichuan specialist **Darling Harbour** (*see p118*). **Sasha's** (*see p126*) also serves decent food, as does **O'Malley's** (*see p125*).

Cafés & snacks

Art Deco Garden Café
Building 3, Ruijin Guesthouse, 118 Ruijin Erlu, by Maoming Nanlu (6472 5222 ext 3006). Metro Shanxi Nanlu. **Open** 8.30am-1am daily. **Average** RMB 30-60. **Credit** AmEx, DC, MC, V. **English menu**. Map p247 E7. **Café**

Hairy crabs

It's called the hairy crab (*da zha xie*) but it is, in fact, hairless. The name comes from the woven bamboo trap (zha) in which the crustaceans are caught. And caught they are, in vast numbers. As the autumn winds begin to blow, crab connoisseurs from all corners of Asia make their annual pilgrimage to Shanghai to feast on the region's most famous delicacy. The season runs from the ninth through the tenth lunar month (roughly early October through November), during which the roe-filled females mature in the first half, and the fleshy, spermatic males in the second.

For the uninitiated, eating the crabs is a challenge. The first step is to remove the top shell by sliding either a fingernail or fork under the belly flap and prying it open. Females will reveal a hard reddish or orangey mass of roe, while males will contain a sticky, grey substance – the most prized part for gourmets. Next, the legs are pulled off and snapped in two, allowing a chopstick to be pushed inside to dislodge the meat. Finally, the body can be broken in half and all the flesh inside eaten, minus the air sacs and other internal organs.

As crab is considered a 'cold' food according to the precepts of Chinese medicine, it's traditionally accompanied by 'warm' condiments (black vinegar and fresh

ginger) and drinks – Shaoxing and yellow wine is often drunk with the meal and sweet ginger water is usually served at the end.

Wangbaohe Restaurant
603 Fuzhou Lu, by Zhejiang Lu, Renmin Square (6322 3673). Metro Renmin Park or Square. **Open** 11am-1pm, 5-8.30pm daily. **Credit** AmEx, DC, MC, V. **Map** 242 G4.
A block east of Renmin Square, this is the most famous place in town for the hairy crab feast boasts 'secret' ingredients for the seasoning. Set menus include a wide range of cold and hot dishes, starting at around RMB 300. Reservations are recommended.

Xin Guang
512 Tianjin Lu, by Guangxi Beilu, Renmin Square (6322 3978). Metro Renmin Park or Square. **Open** 11am-2pm, 5-10pm daily. **Credit** AmEx, DC, MC, V. **Map** 242 G4.
Xin Guang employs teams of women to do the dirty work of picking the meat from the shell. The RMB 400 set meal includes a succession of dishes, from leg meat sautéd with asparagus to chicken broth with tiny crab won tons. Intrepid diners should try the platter of pure roe and sperm tossed with bean thread noodles. Reservations are essential.
Other locations: 1591 Hongqiao Lu, by Shuicheng Lu, Hongqiao (6219 7788).

Eat, Drink, Shop

A charming café with a gorgeous location beside the lush but carefully manicured gardens of the Ruijin Guesthouse. Even so, it's rarely busy – although the gardens themselves are popular with wedding photographers. In addition to teas and coffees, light snacks, fruit and desserts are available for parsimonious appetites. Booze is served too and, if the weather's right, there's no finer place for a late afternoon cooler than a chair on the lawn.

La Casbah

1554 Huaihai Zhonglu, by Hunan Lu (6471 2821). Metro Hengshan Lu. **Open** 8am-10pm Mon-Fri; 8am-11pm Sat, Sun. **Average** RMB 30-50. **No credit cards**. **English menu**. **Map** p246 B7. **Café**
A tiny café just a dictionary's heave from the Shanghai Library. It's ideal for a pitstop on a walk around the French Concession, especially if you're not keen on paying the expat prices of the eateries on Hengshan Lu. Casbah does good basic lunch fare such as generously sized, thin-crust pizzas with

Brunch bunch

Crystal Jade

Brunch Chinese-style doesn't get better than this: rice dumplings, rice noodles, taro cakes, steamed buns and pork ribs served from 10.30am until 3pm weekends. *See p108.*

Element Fresh

This is the recharge-the-batteries brunch, stacked with healthy options and fantastic juices and smoothies. Order eggs, toast, fruit and grills from the placemat menu. *See p102.*

M on the Bund

Brunch at M is a Shanghai institution. Two courses and a cocktail cost a reasonable RMB 188, or tuck into three courses for RMB 218 (all served from 11.30am to 3pm Saturday and Sunday). *See p99.*

Mesa

Go healthy with Bircher muesli and yoghurt or get a full service with eggs Benedict, chorizo sausages and the perfect Caesar salad. Served weekends from 9.30am to 5pm. *See p116.*

Westin

The most popular hotel brunch in Shanghai. The house speciality is top-grade lobster, crabs and sashimi – served in a seemingly endless procession from 11.30am until 3pm for RMB 298, all in. Booking is essential. *See p34.*

meat and vegetarian toppings, plus salads and grilled sandwiches on toasted breads. Fresh juices, good coffee and ice teas are also available. Service is friendly and staff speak some English.

Planet Shanghai

1428 Huaihai Zhonglu, by Fuxing Lu (6473 5996). Metro Changshu Lu. **Open** 10.30am-1am daily. **Average** RMB 80. **Credit** AmEx, DC, MC, V. **English menu**. **Map** p246 B7. **Bistro**
Now eclipsed by venues such as Wagas (*see p103*) and Element Fresh (*see p102*), Planet Shanghai was the one-time first choice for a non-pricey lunchtime burger or pasta in the French Concession. The good-quality burgers and pasta are still in place (the lunch deal is RMB 38 and includes a drink, throw in a salad for RMB 6), but be aware that many of the desserts include a dollop of fake cream, as do many of the 'cocktails'. Seats near the window are sunny (weather permitting) and good for people-watching on Huaihai Lu, as well as the comings and goings of the US Consulate over the road.

Chinese

Bao Luo

271 Fumin Lu, by Changle Lu (5403 7239). Metro Changshu Lu. **Open** 11am-6am daily. **Average** RMB 50-60. **No credit cards**. **English menu**. **Map** p246 C6. **Shanghainese**
Packed day and night, Bao Luo is brash, loud, smoky Shanghai dining at its best. A true rags to riches story, the restaurant that international super chef Jean-Georges Vongerichten regards as the best in town began as a fried rice and noodle shop opened by a man running a small bike repair stand out front. It has since expanded to hold 300 in one cavernous dining hall and a warren of tiny rooms upstairs. Waitstaff dash and rush beneath massive metallic trays delivering heaps of typical Shanghai fare

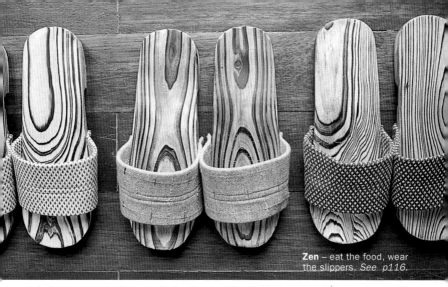

Zen – eat the food, wear the slippers. *See p116.*

including pot-stewed crabmeat and minced pork, stir-fried river shrimp and steamed mandarin fish. Other house favourites are the Swiss steak, which is spicy beef barbecued in a mayonnaise sauce, and the 'aubergine sandwiching patty' (as it's described in the manual-thick menu) with minced pork and rice pancakes. Fantastic flavours and a truly exhilarating experience. Bookings are essential.

Di Shui Dong

2nd floor, 56 Maoming Nanlu, by Changle Lu (6253 2689). Metro Shanxi Nanlu. **Open** 11am-1am daily. **Average** RMB 100. **No credit cards. English menu. Map** p247 D6. **Hunanese**
A veteran of the Shanghai restaurant scene, Di Shui Dong is a throwback to dining in the days before 'design'. Expect oily floors, menu items written in big characters on streamers pasted to the wall and large tables with checkered cloths. Dishes are helpfully listed on a bilingual menu, although for some reason those in English are often unavailable. Try spicy staples such as fried chicken with a mountain of chillis, sour beans with minced pork or sweet and spicy twice-cooked pork in red sauce – apparently Chairman Mao's favourite comfort food. The lack of humidity in the Hunan region is good not only for drying chillis, but also favours citrus fruits, so pitchers of freshly squeezed orange juice are served in season. Reservations are required for dinner.

Dongbei Ren

1 Shanxi Nanlu, by Yanan Zhonglu (5228 9898). Metro Shanxi Nanlu. **Open** 10.30am-10pm daily. **Average** RMB 50-60. **No credit cards. Map** p249 D5. **Dongbei**
In Chinese there is a word, *renao*, that means warm, noisy and hearty, all at the same time. Renao is the concept that the owners of Dongbei Ren ('the people from Dongbei') would appear to have based their business on. On a recent visit we were greeted by the waitress with a cry of '*Waiguo pengyou lai le*!'

('Foreign friends coming in!'). As we ordered she proceeded to share the information with the surrounding tables. Not a place for shy, retiring types then. Nor for those with less than hearty appetites; typical Dongbei dishes include *jiaozi* (heavy dumplings) and *guo bao rou* (fatty, crispy pork in a tasty sweet and sour sauce). Wash it all down with the excellent northern dark beer Snow.
Other locations: 555 Shuicheng Lu, by Tianshan Lu, Gubei (6233 0990).

Guyi

87 Fumin Lu, by Julu Lu (6249 5628). Metro Jingan Temple. **Open** 10.30am-2pm, 5.30-10.30pm daily. **Average** RMB 70-80. **Credit** AmEx, DC, MC, V. **English menu. Map** p248 C5. **Hunanese**
Guyi is one of a few restaurants equally popular with (affluent) locals and with expats. It's always packed, so if you turn up without a reservation be prepared to wait anything up to an hour (pass the time with a drink at nearby Manifesto, *see p124*). The decor juxtaposes traditional China with modern Shanghai and creates a classy setting for classic spicy Hunanese fare. Standouts include the spicy beans with ground pork and the king-sized grilled shrimp. Portions are sized to share, so bring friends. Fresh lemon sodas nicely take the edge off the chilli.

Jishi

41 Tianping Lu, by Huaihai Zhonglu (6282 9260). Metro Hengshan Lu. **Open** 11am-midnight daily. **Average** RMB 100-150. **Credit** AmEx, DC, MC, V. **English menu. Map** p246 A8. **Shanghainese**
Dishing up superb home-style Shanghainese cuisine, this no-frills, two-storey shack now has a side annexe to accommodate the throngs of lively locals. Chatty diners sit elbow-to-elbow while the efficient waitstaff shout orders as they stomp up and down the narrow rickety staircase. No oil, sugar or MSG is spared and must-eats include air-dried eel with horsebean paste, deep-fried bamboo shoots, wild

Eat, Drink, Shop

Eat and drink your way around the world

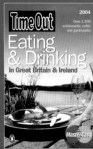
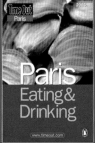

herbs with beancurd, jellyfish heads with vinegar and house speciality pork knuckle, which is braised for five hours in soy sauce, sugar and salt. Reservations are required for dinner.
Other locations: Building 9, Lane 169, Taicang Lu, by Huangpi Lu, Xintiandi (6336 4746).

1931
112 Maoming Nanlu, by Nanchang Lu (6472 5264). Metro Shanxi Nanlu. **Open** 11.30am-midnight daily. **Average** RMB 100. **Credit** AmEx, DC, MC, V. **English menu. Map** p247 D7. **Shanghainese**
Possibly the city's most romantic dining room, 1931 feels like the posh but intimate parlour of a house belonging to some Shanghai-French madam back in the days when this city swung. Sadly, the food struggles to live up to the surrounds. There are two menus to choose from – one regular and the other seasonal (changed monthly). Favourites include fried pork dumplings, spicy tofu and the house speciality '1931 brand pancake', which comes with duckling skin, lamb or pork. Portions are small, which makes the place best suited to lunch or a light dinner (reservations are required for both).

Pin Chuan
47 Taojiang Lu, by Wulumuqi Nanlu (6437 9361). Metro Changshu Lu. **Open** 11am-2.30pm, 5-10pm daily. **Average** RMB 100-120. **Credit** AmEx, DC, MC, V. **English menu. Map** p246 B7. **Sichuan**
In world cuisine terms, Sichuan is the new Thai – or so the food writers tell us – and Pin Chuan is the best place in town to try it. It sits opposite the US Consulate in an old Shanghai house made bright with paint and manned by friendly waiters, some of whom speak enough English to offer novices guidance in this spiciest of Chinese cuisines. All the classics are here, including fish with sliced beef in chillies and peppercorn oil, cold peppery noodles and claypot spicy bean with beef and pork. Reservations required for dinner.

Sophia's Tea Restaurant
480 Huashan Lu, by Wulumuqi Zhonglu (6249 9917). Metro Jingan Temple. **Open** 11.30am-2.30pm, 5.30-11pm daily. **Average** RMB 150. **Credit** AmEx, DC, MC, V. **English menu. Map** p246 B6. **Shanghainese**
Tucked into a modest terrace house, just around the corner from the Hilton, Sophia's bucks the Shanghai trend for cavernous food palaces with large tables and boisterous patrons. Its intimate atmosphere makes it a favourite for low-key business lunches or quiet family dinners. Diverse Chinese dishes have their stronger flavours toned down for the Shanghainese palate, and the chefs go easy on the oil. Standouts include a hearty northern-style pancakes with aubergine or chicken, and subtly spiced Sichuan-style lemon fish. The prawns are also good: try them crisp and deep-fried with longjin tea leaves, or fat, steamed and juicy with rose petals. There's an excellent range of teas, too. Reservations required for both lunch and dinner. *See also p72* **To the teahouse.**

South Beauty
28 Taojiang Lu, by Baoqing Lu (6445 2581). Metro Changshu Lu. **Open** 11am-10pm daily. **Average** RMB 150-180. **Credit** AmEx, DC, MC, V. **English menu. Map** p246 C7. **Sichuan**
If you want to know where regional Chinese cuisine is headed, South Beauty shows the way. The setting reeks of understated affluence, from the chauffeured motors in the car park to the sleek glass and concrete interior. The airy main dining area downstairs and light-filled private rooms upstairs both overlook a bamboo garden. Despite Shanghai's reputation for being spice-shy, there is no holding back on the heat: dishes such as chicken with spring onions and vinegar, and tripe and peanuts in pepper oil have a high singe factor. Reservations are required for dinner.
Other locations: 5th floor, Times Square, 93 Huaihai Zhonglu, by Liulin Lu, Xintiandi (6391 0890); 10th floor, Super Grand Mall, 168 Lujiazui Lu, Pudong (5047 1817).

Uighur Restaurant
1 Shanxi Nanlu, by Yanan Zhonglu (6255 0843). Metro Shanxi Nanlu. **Open** 11am-2am daily. **Average** RMB 50-80. **No credit cards. Map** p249 D5. **Xinjiang**
When the house band at the Uighur starts to play, nobody is allowed to remain sitting. Uniformed waiters drag diners away from their mounds of *yang rou pao fan* (saffron rice with chunks of lamb) to link yellow-stained fingers (Xinjiang is a hands-on cuisine) and join in the ring dancing. For this reason, shy visitors should sit as far away from the restaurant's stage as possible. Otherwise, expect huge mounds of fatty lamb, eaten with bread, tomatoes and grapes. It's very basic fare and the Uighur wouldn't be your first choice restaurant if you're only in town for a couple of days, but as something that is far, far removed from Shanghainese food yet still Chinese, it's certainly worth investigating. Reservations are required for dinner.

Xiao Nan Guo
2nd floor, Ruijin Guesthouse, 118 Ruijin Erlu, by Yongjia Lu (6466 2277). Metro Shanxi Nanlu. **Open** 11am-2pm, 5-9.30pm daily. **Average** RMB 125-150. **No credit cards. English menu. Map** p247 E7. **Shanghainese**
This is the flagship branch of a city-wide chain known for terrific food and efficient service. In the gorgeous garden setting of the Ruijin Guesthouse, it's an airy hangar of a dining hall – a refreshing departure from the typical cramped and smoky Shanghainese joint. Tables are correspondingly huge and designed for sharing (couples will feel very lonely here). Standout cold dishes include drunken chicken and the chopped wild herbs with diced tofu, while of the hot fare we recommend spring onion pancakes, roasted pigeon, claypot of crabmeat and roe and sautéed pea shoots. Intrepid diners can test their mettle against dishes such as turtle with sticky rice, roasted snake or marinated snake skin. Reservations are required for dinner.

Ashanti Dome: the view from table two.

Other locations: 183 Changsha Lu, by Xinzha Lu, Renmin Square (6327 7107); 1398 Nanjing Xilu, by Tongren Lu, Jingan (6289 1717); Lujiazui Food Centre, Lane 17, Yincheng Xilu Pudong (5887 7000).

Xia Wei Guan (Savoy)

Oriental Gardens, 9 Zhenning Lu, by Huashan Lu (6212 6797). Metro Jiangsu Lu. **Open** 11.30am-12.30pm daily. **Average** RMB 200-250. **Credit** AmEx, DC, MC, V. **English menu. Map** p246 B6. **Shanghainese**

A haunt of Hong Kong celebs and sundry moneyed Shanghainese, this place certainly looks the part, with a glass staircase entrance suspended over a pond. Small portions of (pricey) refined local cuisine are served in delicate china amid a polished setting of elegant teahouse tables and chairs. Choice dishes include an exceptional crabmeat tofu and what is arguably the city's best 'lion's head' meatball with crabmeat (*xie fen shi zi tou*). Other top dishes include fried beancurd skin with enoki mushrooms and sautéed spring bamboo shoot with chopped greens. Reservations are recommended.

Yin

Jinjiang Gourmet Street, 59 Maoming Nanlu, by Changle Lu (5466 5070). Metro Shanxi Nanlu. **Open** noon-3pm, 6pm-midnight Mon-Sat; noon-3pm, 6-11pm Sun. **Average** RMB 100-120. **Credit** AmEx, DC, MC, V. **English menu. Map** p247 E6. **Shanghainese**

With its charming 'Old Shanghai' decor of high ceilings, cherrywood floors and antique screens, Yin is a nostalgist's dream. But Japanese-born restaurateur Takashi is also canny enough to bring the place into the 21st century with warm lighting and splashes of

colour, courtesy of Pop artist Zeng Fanzhi. The food is superb with a menu that roams through the best of China's regional cuisine, from the far west's Xinjiang-style lamb with cumin to eastern seafood dishes such as fat Shanghainese-style shrimp. Food is served on the restaurant's own flatware, which colourfully updates traditional Asian square-cut plates and tea beakers. Before settling to dine, however, we recommend a perch at the long bar for an expertly mixed aperitif.

Yuan Yuan

201 Xingguo Lu, by Taian Lu (6433 9123). Metro Hengshan Lu. **Open** 11am-11pm daily. **Average** RMB 100-150. **Credit** AmEx, DC, MC, V. **English menu. Map** p246 A7. **Shanghainese**

A personal favourite of the late Hong Kong film star Leslie Cheung, Yuan Yuan is a two-storey casual eatery, especially popular among the well-to-do local crowd. It serves all the Shanghai classics, from jellyfish with sesame oil to spongy bean thread. Signature dishes include red-cooked pork and glutinous rice-stuffed red dates. The restaurant is also particularly well known for its seafood dishes. There's also a branch at the Maglev terminus in Pudong (*see p90* **Badly trained**).

European

Ashanti Dome

16 Gaolan Lu, by Sinan Lu (5306 6777). Metro Huangpi Nanlu. **Open** 6-12.30pm Mon-Thur, Sun; 6pm-2.30am Fri, Sat. **Average** RMB 300. **Credit** AmEx, DC, MC, V. **English menu. Map** p247 E6. **French**

A French restaurant and Spanish bar in an onion-domed Russian Orthodox church owned by a South African staffed by Chinese: how perfectly Shanghai (for more on the building, *see p78*). Ashanti is the name of a South African vineyard, while the 'Dome' part of the name refers to the deliciously kitsch vaulted ceiling over the second floor, complete with original religious iconography. If the French fare on offer isn't quite divine, it is at least solid: soups and terrines to start, fish and grilled meats in sauces to follow, crème brûlée and cakes for dessert. Ashanti cabernets and sauvignon blancs accompany. The ground floor is a tapas restaurant called Boca. Reservations are required.

Café Montmartre

55-57 Xiangyang Nanlu, by Huaihai Zhonglu (5404 7658). Metro Shanxi Nanlu. **Open** 11am-midnight daily. **Average** RMB 100-150. **Credit** AmEx, DC, MC, V. **English menu. Map** p247 D6. **French**
As authentic a French bistro as you could hope to find this side of the Swiss Alps, the Montmartre neighbours the famous Xiangyang fake market (note the handbags and pashminas stashed under everybody's tables). But cheap deals don't come any better than the set lunch here, which comprises a main course plus coffee or a glass of wine for RMB 45. The dinner menu is a checklist of textbook classics: pâté, onion soup, quiche lorraine and steak pomme frites, followed by crêpes. On sunny days savvy first-comers snap up tables on the enclosed balcony overlooking the market.

Le Garçon Chinois

Lane 9, Hengshan Lu, by Dongping Lu (6445 7970). Metro Changshu Lu or Hengshan Lu. **Open** 6.30pm-1am daily. **Average** RMB 150-180. **Credit** AmEx, DC, MC, V. **English menu. Map** p246 C7.
Spanish
Still the most romantic little eaterie in town, Le Garçon is found in an old French villa secreted down a winding, leafy alleyway off Hengshan. Tastefully decorated with chinoiserie, it boasts a delightful pocket-sized bar, invariably packed by 8pm. Turn up early for a quiet drink by the window overlooking the courtyard. The menu used to be French but in line with current trends, the flavour is now Spanish. Try the gazpacho and tuna tartare from the tapas entrées. Tender rack of lamb is possibly the highlight of the main courses. Portions are minimalist going on sparse, but beautiful to look at. Reservations are required for dinner.

Fusion

Azul/Viva

18 Dongping Lu, by Wulumuqi Nanlu (6433 1172). Metro Changshu Lu. **Open** 11am-11pm daily. **Average** RMB 150-200. **Credit** AmEx, DC, MC, V. **English menu. Map** p246 C7.
Peruvian chef Eduardo Vargas garnered a near cult following at Xintiandi tapas and cigar bar Che. Now he has his own bar-restaurant, just off the French Concession's main restaurant drag, Hengshan Lu. The drinking part of the operation is Azul, where lime margaritas and sangria are served up alongside Vargas's signature tapas (mussels in decadent cream-chilli sauce, yum). Upstairs is the restaurant, Viva, a languid affair of couches and throw cushions, much softer than the assembly of granite slab tables downstairs. You can order tapas up here too, but there's also a solid menu of new world cuisine. Dishes play on sweet and sour flavours – spicy duck breast with chilli-honey glaze, for example, or blue

Street eats

With the ongoing modernisation of Shanghai, inevitably some things are lost: old houses, tightly knit neighbourhoods and snacks that are made by hand and sold by street vendors. Time was that Shanghai had numerous purveyors of things fried, steamed, grilled and sold by the roadside. Now there are just a few food streets left in the city centre. They're pungent, exotic and inexpensive. And for the first-time visitor to Shanghai, they're also essential.

● **Yunnan Nanlu** (Map p242 G5) links the Old City and Renmin Square with a chain of small stands, stalls and eateries. Sellers at the corner with Ninghai Donglu peddle Xinjiang lamb kebabs and *nang* (round bread), while the junction with Jingling Donglu is the place for hotpot: select your meat and veg and have it boiled to order in a spicy broth.

● **Wujiang Lu** (Map p249 E4) is an appendage of main Nanjing Xilu in the Jingan district, just west of Renmin Square; it's also the rowdiest and most authentic food street in Shanghai. In fine weather crowds sit at rickety plastic sheet-covered tables spread with dishes, beer bottles and crawfish shells. Look for the vendor hand-wrapping glutinous rice dumplings (*zongzi*) in palm leaves. This is the real thing: beautifully seasoned rice, egg yolks and fatty pork.

● **Huanghe Lu** (Map p242 F4) is on the edge of Renmin Square, an area better known for high culture than cheap food. However, running north beside the Park Hotel, this is a great street for various meats on a stick and bubble teas. Walk a bit further north for fresh *la mian*, or pulled noodles, rice steamed in a bamboo tube and fish balls sprinkled with dried seaweed for RMB 4 a box.

cheese bavarois with char-grilled asparagus and nut oil dressing. Chocolate soup makes for a sinful finale. Reservations required for dinner.

Mesa

748 Julu Lu, by Fumin Lu (6289 9108). Metro Changshu Lu. **Open** 6-11pm Mon-Fri; 10am-5pm, 6-11pm Sat, Sun. **Average** RMB 250-300. **Credit** AmEx, DC, MC, V. **English menu. Map** p246 C5.
Mesa is a former factory warehouse beautifully re-appointed as a chic, airy and light-filled dining room (its original function is still apparent in the high ceilings, deco picture windows and unusual explosion-proof hanging lights that were once common in the city's factories). It's a striking space, and one that provides the setting for some of the best Western cuisine in town. Visit for classy, well-executed Mediterranean-style dishes enhanced with delicate Asian flavours such as soy, star anise and ginger-baked salmon, or soft shelled crabs with citrus and champagne salad. Save room for desserts such as spiced black rice and coconut risotto with banana jam, and homemade sorbets and ice creams. Reservations are required for dinner at weekends. Mesa's all-day weekend brunch is also excellent: *see p110* **Brunch bunch**. Next door is ace bar Manifesto (*see p124*), a sibling venture.

Japanese

Ambrosia

150 Fenyang Lu, by Yueyang Lu (6431 3935). Metro Changshu Lu. **Open** 11.30am-2.30pm, 5.30-11.30pm daily. **Average** RMB 98-200 (lunch); RMB 350-958 (dinner). **Credit** AmEx, DC, MC, V. **English menu. Map** p246 C7.
Set in sumptuous, baize-lawned grounds, the grand triple-decker villa that is home to Ambrosia was originally built by a wealthy French merchant in 1930. It's now a very impressive Japanese restaurant, where top-quality sashimi, sushi, tempura and yakiniku competes for superlatives with marble architecture and a gallery's worth of fine paintings and antiquities. Demonstrate curiosity about the surroundings and staff will present a descriptive brochure, along with a handout celebrating the restaurant's listing in *Conde Nast Traveler*'s 2003 world hot list. Reservations are required at least three days in advance.

Shintori

803 Julu Lu, by Fumin Lu (5404 5252). Metro Changshu Lu or Shanxi Nanlu. **Open** 5.30-10.30pm Mon-Fri; 11.30am-2pm, 5.30-11pm Sat, Sun. **Average** RMB 250. **Credit** AmEx, DC, MC, V. **English menu. Map** p246 C5.
Shintori gets our prize for Shanghai's best modern interior. Approach along a ghostly lit pathway amid a thicket of slender bamboo, then enter through a duo of clouded-glass, silently sliding doors. Inside is all flat grey concrete and glass with multiple galleried levels connected by ramps and platform elevators – it's a bit like the loading bay in *Alien*. Take

a seat at the cold black slab of a sushi bar or at one of the long mortuary-esque tables. Fresh sashimi is served on granite platters and delicious cold noodles come in sculpted ice bowls. The desserts are a treat to look at: mango sorbet lurches from angled wine glasses wedged in ice, while green tea tiramisu is just plain freaky thanks to its fluoru colouring. Tastes don't quite live up to the spectacular appearances, but are delicious nonetheless.

Zen

1st floor, Jinjiang Gourmet Street, 59 Maoming Nanlu, by Changle Lu (5466 5070). Metro Shanxi Nanlu. **Open** noon-3pm, 6-11pm daily. **Average** RMB 200. **Credit** AmEx, DC, MC, V. **English menu. Map** pp247 E6.
Upstairs from the Shanghainese Yin (*see p114*) is Japanese restaurant Zen. The design isn't zen at all: it's much warmer and nicer – a mix of art deco, Shanghai style and sympathetic modern additions, including some beautiful pendant light fittings. Dishes are classic Japanese – sushi, sashimi, tempura, yakatori and noodles – consumed in the company of a discerning crowd of locals, Westerners and Japanese. The service is impeccable and prices are very reasonable. Reservations are required.

South-east Asian & Indian

Indian Kitchen

572 Yongjia Lu, by Wulumuqi Nanlu (6473 1517). Metro Hengshan Lu. **Open** 11.30am-2.30pm, 5-11pm daily. **Average** RMB 80-100. **Credit** AmEx, DC, MC, V. **English menu. Map** p246 B8. **Indian**
Hard to believe that it was only as recently as the mid 1990s that Shanghai gained its first Indian restaurant (the Tandoor at the Jinjiang Hotel). There is no shortage now, but this remains our favourite. It adheres to a simple but winning concept of attractive surroundings, impeccable service and authentic Indian food, prepared by authentic Indian chefs on view for all to see in the open kitchen. The menu is all Indian classics including rich and creamy kormas, spicy curries and hot tandooris. Visit during the day for the great lunch deals of a main dish with rice, nan bread, soup and salad for around RMB 30. Reservations required for dinner.

Lan Na Thai

Building 4, Ruijin Guesthouse, 118 Ruijin Erlu, by Fuxing Zhonglu (6466 4328). Metro Shanxi Nanlu. **Open** noon-2.30pm, 5.30-10.30pm Mon-Thur, Sun; noon-2.30pm, 5.30-11pm Fri, Sat. **Average** RMB 250. **Credit** AmEx, DC, MC, V. **English menu. Map** p247 E7. **Thai**
It's decked out with elegant Ming Dynasty furniture and serene Buddhist sculptures, boasts gorgeous views of the guesthouse gardens and, since it opened in 1999, Shanghai first-timers have found the languid, colonial air of the place utterly irresistible. Long-termers get sniffy, take umbrage at the high prices and stay downstairs in the splendid Face Bar (*see p124*), but everyone has to do Lan Na at least

Mesa – a factory warehouse turned fab eatery. *See p116.*

once. The food is Thai Thai, as opposed to Chinese Thai, which is the norm around these parts. Even so, if you like your chicken larb spicy or your green curry hot, then you still need to ask for it to be prepared that way. Reservations required for dinner.

Simply Thai
5 Dongping Lu, by Hengshan Lu (6445 9551). Metro Changshu Lu or Hengshan Lu. **Open** 11am-2.30pm, 5-10.30pm daily. **Average** RMB 150. **Credit** AmEx, DC, MC, V. **English menu**. **Map** p246 C7. **Thai**
The name's apt: this is the place when you simply want Thai food and no messing about. Of the enterprise's three locations, the one on Dongping Lu is by far the most attractive. It's a cosy little two-storey house on a picturesque tree-lined street. Inside, the floors are bare concrete, the walls are avocado green and design features are limited to a couple of carved panels and a chunky back-lit display of wine bottles doubling as a service counter. The food is superb – lots of great flavours, all beautifully presented. Prices are also very reasonable (mains from around RMB 35), with a good lunchtime deal of RMB 48 for two courses and a drink. An outside patio is used for summertime dining (also a feature at the Xintiandi branch; *see below*).
Other locations: 1st floor, No.27, Lane 123, Taicang Lu, by Madang Lu & Xingye Lu, Xintiandi (6326 2088).

Xujiahui

It's not a dining destination as such, but Xujiahui's myriad shopping malls do host plenty of eateries, among which are a handful of good regional specialists: try **Fwu Luh Pavillion** for classy Yangzhou seafood or **Yunnan Gourmet**, both of which are at the Grand Gateway Mall. **Mekong River** on the fifth floor of Metro City is a good Vietnamese.

Chinese

Shanghai Lao Zhan (Old Station)
201 Caixi Beilu, by Nandan Donglu (6427 2233). Metro Xujiahui. **Open** 11.15am-1.30pm, 5-9.30pm daily. **Average** RMB 120-140. **Credit** AmEx, DC, MC, V. **English menu**. **Map** p246 A10. **Shanghainese**
Housed in an ex-convent that dates back to the 1920s, the dining rooms here are graced by classic decor of dark wood, whitewashed walls, tiled floors and ornate light fixtures. Waiters in traditionally styled jackets deliver typical Shanghainese fare, the best of which includes smoked dried fish, asparagus soup and 'eight treasure' duck. Request a table by the window for the view of a garden occupied by two

antique train carriages. One was once used by the Empress Dowager and the other by Soong Qingling (Madam Sun Yatsen).

Shanghai Uncle

211 Tianyaoqiao Lu, by Nandan Lu (6464 6430). Metro Xujiahui. **Open** 11.15am-2pm, 5.15-10pm daily. **Average** RMB 100. **Credit** AmEx, DC, MC, V. **English menu. Map** p246 A10. **Shanghainese**
Owned by Shanghai-American Li Zhongheng (son of a *New York Times* food critic), the Uncle is a favourite with locals before 8.30pm and the Hong Kong and Taiwanese set after. Its classic Shanghai dishes – illustrated on a colourful picture menu with delightful Chinglish descriptions – are heavily influenced by their regional and foreign cuisines. Book ahead for the house specialities, which include 'Uncle's crispy pork of flame' and the 'six-pounder onion duck'. The traditional Shanghainese cold dish of smoked fish is also terrific. Diners can choose from the second-floor sprawl of loud red floral chairs or one of the third-floor private eating dens, complete with TV. Reservations are required for both lunch and dinner.
Other locations: 8th floor, Time Square, 500 Zhangyang Lu, by Pudong Nanlu, Pudong (5836 7977); 222 Yanan Donglu, by Henan Zhonglu, the Bund (6339 1977).

South-east Asian

Temple Saigon

1731 Huashan Lu, by Huaihai Xilu (6281 8428). Metro Xujiahui. **Open** 11am-11pm daily. **Average** RMB 150. **Credit** AmEx, DC, MC, V. **English menu. Map** p246 A8. **Vietnamese**
An upscale joint situated in a nicely decorated villa next to Jiaotong University. It has an art deco-inspired interior imported from Saigon, with guests greeted at the entrance by a genuine cyclo (the Vietnamese bicycle taxi). The food is tailored to the Shanghainese palate, so expect lots of MSG in the mango beef, next to no chilli in the scallops and no fish sauce with the *cha gio* (deep-fried spring rolls). However, Temple Saigon does serve very affordable lunch and afternoon tea specials for RMB 48, which include a very tasty noodle soup. Reservations are required for dinner.

Pudong

In addition to the places listed below Pudong also has branches of Shanghainese restaurants **Xiao Nan Guo** (*see p113*) and **Shanghai Uncle** (*see above*) and Sichuan **Yuan Yuan**.

Chinese

Darling Harbour

3rd floor, Shiji Plaza, 855 Pudong Nanlu, by Shiji Dadao (5836 9767). **Open** 10.30am-10.30pm daily. **Average** RMB 80-100. **Credit** V. **Sichuan**

A highly successful local chain, Darling Harbour was founded by a local entrepreneur who spent time in Sichuan and subsequently decided to export its mouth-numbing cuisine to the rest of the world. The latest branch in the eastern half of the city looks like Versailles-meets-*Moulin Rouge*, dripping with chandeliers and stuffed with brocaded furniture. It can accommodate hundreds of (well-heeled) diners. Favourites include the fish-head soup, spicy beef in oil and the cold noodles, all served with heaps of sinus-clearing whole chillis and pink-hot Sichuan peppercorns. Reservations required for dinner.
Other locations: 19th-21st floors, Paramount Hotel, 1728 Nanjing Xilu, by Huashan Lu, Jingan (6248 1818); 6th floor, 755 Huaihai Zhonglu, by Rujin Erlu, French Concession (6445 9205).

Minghao Seafood Restaurant

POS Plaza, 480 Pudian Lu, by Shiji Dadao (5830 3333). Metro Dongfang Lu. **Open** 11am-2.30pm, 5-10.30pm daily. **Average** RMB 300. **Credit** AmEx, DC, MC, V. **English menu. Seafood**
An extravagant seafood palace among the skyscrapers of Pudong. The decor is ridiculously OTT, with ceilings and mouldings pressed with gold leaf and great aquatic tanks filled with marine life – nice to look at but gradually emptied during the course of an evening as the assorted sea life is fished out to be fried, baked and steamed. This is not the place to play safe with a bit of salmon or tuna fillet; many diners are here for rarer treats such as octopus, eels and even snake (fried with spicy salt; RMB 100). Other delicacies include Indonesian bird nests, shark's fin and abalone. None of this comes cheap (abalone: RMB 198-698) but what price memories?

European

Cucina at On56

56th floor, Grand Hyatt, 88 Shiji Dadao (5049 1234, ext 8908). Metro Lujiazui. **Open** 11.30am-2.30pm, 5.30-10pm Mon-Thur, Sun; 11.30am-2.30pm, 5.30-11pm Fri, Sat. **Average** RMB 300. **Credit** AmEx, DC, MC, V. **English menu. Map** p243 L4. **Italian**
Two floors above the world's highest hotel lobby (at the Grand Hyatt, *see p44*) is On56, a trio of restaurants where only sheets of glass separate diners from the wreaths of high-altitude fog that usually envelope Pudong skyscrapers. Make reservations well in advance to get a good table by the floor-to-ceiling windows. Kobachi is Japanese with sashimi, tempura and noodles, the Grill has arguably the best steak in Shanghai and Cucina does inventive modern Italian cuisine. Its offerings include delicate pastas and risottos, piquant salads and velvety desserts to finish. The wine list is about as good as it gets in Shanghai; alternatively, have a few drinks in the breathtaking On56 bar, where you can sink back into sofas and gaze all the way up to the 100th floor. Prices are not as stratospheric as the high altitude would suggest. Reservations are required. *See also p104* **Height cuisine.**

Pubs & Bars

Skyscraping cocktails or gutter-level good times.

Upstairs at Park 97.
See p128.

The Shanghainese are not fussy drinkers. They are wholly unimpressed by a noble Bordeaux and beer is nothing more than a lightweight beverage for washing down a good bowl of *jiaozi* (dumplings). In fact, there is only one drink that commands China's respect – the toe-numbing national booze, *baijiou*. And that's only because it poses a worthy challenge – the last one standing after several rounds of *baijiou* shots gains serious face in the eyes of their colleagues. This evil grain spirit tastes like a mixture of saké and Domestos and can clock in at up to 65 per cent abv. And if that's not sufficiently kamikaze, some drinkers mix it with a freshly slaughtered snake's gall bladder, which is apparently like tossing back a natural Viagra. It sure beats a splash of soda and a slice.

Quite sensibly, though, *baijiou* is not a bar staple and is far more commonly consumed with a meal in a restaurant (minus the snake offal), which is where locals traditionally do their boozing. The current scene owes a lot to

the *da bizi* or 'big noses' (Mandarin slang for Westerners) who, when they began to arrive in numbers in the 1990s, quite rightly spotted that the one thing that this mythic oriental entrepôt was missing was an Irish pub/Chicago-style sports bar.

Foreigners still make up a big part of the nightly party crowd, but increasingly the Shanghainese have both the money and the inclination for regular sessions of cocktail carousing and the odd beer-fuelled bender. Diverse punters and the absence of any solid bar-going traditions make for an anything-goes scenario. The oldest bars (which have been around for, oh, as long as ten years) include **Malone's** (*see p121*), and **Judy's Too** (*see p180*), first on the block of what's now the city's rowdiest bar strip, **Maoming Nanlu**. This infamous 200-metre stretch of neon and noise puts on a great nightly show of parading call girls, street vendors with armfuls of roses or kerbside braziers for grilling kebabs, patrolling police harassing illegal cigarette sellers and, of course, roaming crowds of semi-inebriated party freaks. Nearby **Julu Lu** offers more of the same. At the time of going to press rumours were circulating that Maoming was going to be shut down for persistent noise violations. Such threats have been made before, however, in the last couple of months several bars on the strip have, in fact, hung up their beer mats for good.

As well as the venues listed below, many of the places described in the Music and Nightlife chapters double as drinking dens.

The Bund

Back in the old days Fuzhou Lu was the city's bar and brothel street. For better or worse, not a trace remains. Nostalgists can wallow at the **Peace Hotel Bar** (*see p177*), to the tune of octagenarian jazz, but these days the smart money is at new developments such as Three on the Bund and its house bar **New Heights**.

Five

Basement, 20 Guangdong Lu, by Zhongshan Dongyilu (6329 4558). Metro Henan Lu. **Open** 10am-2am daily. **Credit** AmEx, DC, MC, V. **Map** p243 J4.
Lodged among some of the swankiest and most expensive bars and eateries in town, the remarkably casual Five brings to the Bund a welcome loosening of the collar. While the folks upstairs (at M on the

Kathleen's 5. *See p121.*

Bund and its Glamour Bar: *see below*) are sipping pricey French bubbly, the crew down in the basement are having a blast on cheap Tsingtao beer. The atmosphere is dimly lit lounge bar – open plan, red walls, comfortable deco-esque furniture – and the music on the house sound system ranges between rock, pop and hip hop. Nobody objects if you dance on the tables.

Glamour Bar

7th floor, 20 Guangdong Lu, by Zhongshan Dongyilu (6350 9988/www.m-onthebund.com). Metro Henan Lu. **Open** 5pm-midnight daily. **Credit** AmEx, DC, MC, V. **Map** p243 J4.

There are only a few places in Shanghai for which a gal can frock-up, and a night of cocktails at the Glamour Bar is one. At this, the house bar of class act diner M on the Bund (*see p99*), it's strictly no jeans, only smart-casual couture, please – all the better to blend in with your fellow corporate players lounging around a bar that was designed to look like something out of a Golden Age Hollywood gangster flick. It may be pretentious and it's certainly pricey but the drinks go down easily, mixed as they are by premier league bar staff. Glamour also regularly hosts international jazz acts (*see p176*).

New Heights

7th floor, Three on the Bund, 3 Zhongshan Dongyilu, by Guangdong Lu (6321 0909/www.threeonthebund. com). Metro Henan Lu. **Open** 10am-2am daily. **Credit** AmEx, DC, MC, V. **Map** p243 J4.

The house bar of Shanghai's most prestigious commercial complex, Three on the Bund, is tailored to the Armani-clad, foie gras-fed, spa-soothed types who strut and sashay around the floors below. It boasts top-class professional bartenders, name DJs and a terrace with intoxicating views of the night-lit Bund below. Yet customers rarely linger. Perhaps it's the sterility that comes from combining a club-style bar with an exclusive dining experience (*see p100*). The adjacent Third Degree is another lounge bar, this one slightly enlivened by a highly impressive house jazz band. The menu lists only expensive wines (from RMB 180 a glass!), champagne and spirits but ask the barman nicely and he may oblige with cocktails to order at RMB 65 a pop.

Noah's

6th floor, 37 Fuzhou Lu, by Sichuan Zhonglu (6323 7869). Metro Henan Lu. **Open** 11am-2am daily. **Credit** AmEx, DC, MC, V. **Map** p243 J4.

The views from Noah's outdoor terrace of the mighty Huangpu River and the high-rise architectural glitz of Pudong come close to rivalling those afforded by the glamour bars at M and Three on the Bund – but a beer here costs about a third of the price. That's because Noah's is part of backpacker lodge Captain's Hostel (*see p35*), where the marketing strategy can be summed up in two words: 'cheap' and 'cheerful'. It's as well to keep your gaze on the city views because the bar's marine-themed interior is painful to behold, but at RMB 15 for a Tsingtao nobody's complaining. Staff are friendly and English-speaking, and there's a bar menu of burgers and sandwiches at under RMB 50.

Renmin Square

Other than Kathleen's 5, the only dedicated drinking spot around the city's main square is the first-floor bar at the historic Park Hotel. One word: don't.

Kathleen's 5

5th floor, Shanghai Art Museum, 325 Nanjing Xilu (6327 2221). Metro Renmin Park or Square. **Open** 11.30am-11pm Mon-Thur, Sun; 11.30am-midnight Fri, Sat. **Credit** AmEx, DC, MC, V. **Map** p242 F4.
Kathleen Lau, the force behind Kathleen's 5, is a true Shanghai vet with a string of successful projects behind her – the '5' references the fact that this is no less than her fifth bar/restaurant in China. None can have been better sited: for this particular venture she has the whole roof of the Shanghai Art Museum (*see p59*) – right on Renmin Square. This is actually something of a mixed blessing as the space is dauntingly vast and can seem very lonely. The restaurant side of the operation has yet to find its feet (*see p100*) but the bar's a winner. It occupies a glass quadrangle on the open roof. Sit up at the long smoked-glass bar counter and you're looking over the barman's shoulder and across Renmin Park. With distractions like this, who needs company?

Jingan

With the concrete edifice of the Shanghai American Centre setting the corporate tone of the neighbourhood, Jingan's bars are geared towards businessmen looking for an after-work tipple. Student club **Windows Too** (*see p182*) is a cheap and hip alternative to the places listed below.

Long Bar

2nd floor, Shanghai Centre, 1376 Nanjing Xilu, by Shanxi Nanlu (6279 8268). Metro Jingan Temple. **Open** 11am-2am daily. **Credit** AmEx, DC, MC, V. **Map** p248 C4.
Nowhere near as snobby as its historic namesake, which was located at the Shanghai Club on the Bund and which served its last pink gin in 1949, alas. At the Long Bar of old a man's status determined his seat with the choicest spots reserved for the heads of the big banks. But at today's Long Bar (a narrow squeeze of a place slotted into a modern concrete structure) position means nothing. It's an egalitarian place and on Tuesday, Thursday and Friday model nights, when leggy women in bikinis parade along the bar counter, everyone present gets an eyeful. This, along with regular happy hours and a location adjacent to the Portman Ritz-Carlton, ensures that the place is one of the most popular post-work spots for unwinding foreign businessmen.

Malone's

255 Tongren Lu, by Nanjing Xilu (6247 2400/ www.malones.com.cn). Metro Jingan Temple. **Open** 11am-2am daily. **Credit** AmEx, DC, MC, V. **Map** p248 C4.
When Malone's opened in 1994 it was command central for the city's few expats who'd gather here to wolf burgers and wallow in homesickness. These days, with the city a-wash with international bars, the big M has to try a little harder. Cue the Filipino bands and Japanese School Girl theme nights at which *xiaojies* (little misses) swing their piggy tails at men who don't need a costume to look juvenile. But despite all this/because of all this, the place retains a devoted swarming of barflies, gathered for the free pool or snuggly settled on the soft-topped bar stools eyes fixed on big-screen TV sports.

Xintiandi

The Vegas version of Old Shanghai, Xintiandi's narrow *nongtang*s (lanes) provide prime retail space for inessential boutiques, as well as

The best **Bars**

Arch
Come for breakfast. Stay for lunch. Go on line. Have a sundowner. Stick around for the film or reading. Take a nightcap. Shame it doesn't do accommodation. *See p123.*

Blue Frog
Cheap booze, raucous company and ringside seating for all the action out on Maoming Nanlu. *See p124.*

Face Bar
If ever they were to film a Bacardi ad in Shanghai, this would be where. Beautiful venue, beautiful people and a great vibe come the weekend. *See p124.*

O'Malley's
An Irish bar with a difference – the difference including a fabulous villa setting and a great big beer garden. *See p125.*

People 7
The coolest bar in town – and with a sense of humour to boot. Press your nose against the back windows to see into the gents belonging to Shintori next door. *See p126.*

Yongfu Elite
Suffused with opium-age glamour, it's like drinking on the boudoir set from *The Last Emperor*. *See p128.*

Eat, Drink, Shop

plastic restaurants and bars. But among the faux and the ersatz, there are a handful of venues worth your beer money.

DR Bar

No.15, North Lane, Lane 181, Taicang Lu, by Huangpi Nanlu (6311 0358). Metro Huangpi Nanlu. **Open** 4pm-1am Mon-Thur, Sun; 4pm-2am Fri, Sat. **Credit** AmEx, DC, MC, V. **Map** p244 F6.
Not 'Doctor Bar', but DR Bar (so, alas, no chesty barmaids in white rubber nurse outfits). It stands for 'Design Resources', apparently. Appropriately enough, tables are furnished with copies of *Wallpaper** (not to be taken away). It looks like somebody spent a good deal of time immersed in these magazines because the bar is a stylish little assemblage of dark wood, black lounge sofas and subdued lighting. It's a smart date sort of venue, intended as a setting for good-looking people comfortable with cocktails (from RMB 55) and shooters, which arrive packed in ice.

KABB

House 5, North Block, Lane 161, Taicang Lu, by Huangpi Nanlu (3307 0798). Metro Huangpi Nanlu. **Open** *Bar* 5pm-midnight Mon-Thur, Sun; 5pm-2am Fri, Sat. **Credit** AmEx, DC, MC, V. **Map** p244 F6.
By day it's a diner with lunching office workers consuming gourmet sandwiches on a terrace beneath a camphor tree (*see p108*); by night it's something far more funky. Uplifting jazz (piped not live, unfortunately) provides a soundtrack for competent cocktails quaffed in spilt-wine red surrounds. Not cutting edge but certainly a cut above almost everything else in the neighbourhood, and wholly comfortable. Occasionally KABB throws a party, usually roping in one of Shanghai's better DJs.

Tou Ming Si Kao (TMSK)

House 11, North Block, Lane 181, Taicang Lu, by Huangpi Nanlu (6326 2227). Metro Huangpi Nanlu. **Open** 2pm-midnight Mon-Sun; 2pm-1am Thur-Sat. **Credit** AmEx, DC, MC, V. **Map** p244 F6.
Dreamt up by Taiwanese actress Yang Hui Shan and her husband, TMSK is two parts tack to one part delirium. The happy couple are both 'glass artists' and their bar is completely bonkers with oversized glass sculptures and a luridly multi-coloured bar that's like stained glass on acid. Mad but also quite beautiful and definitely worth a look whether you decide to stay for a drink or not. Martinis are served in glasses inspired by ancient Chinese symbols. Come after 8.30pm any night for the house band who play techno-inspired Chinese folk music while wearing cast-off outfits from *Star Trek*. Honest. We're not making this up.

French Concession

Prime bar streets are **Maoming Nanlu** and **Julu Lu**, with classier fare further west around the Hengshan/Dongping Lu area. In addition to the bars listed below, see also **Judy's Too** (*see*

p180) and jazz venues **Cotton Club** and the **House of Blues and Jazz** (for both, *see p176*). Restaurant **Le Garçon Chinois** (*see p115*) also has a fine little snug bar.

Amber

184 Maoming Nanlu, by Yongjia Lu (6466 5224). Metro Shanxi Nanlu. **Open** 7pm-2am daily. **Credit** AmEx, DC, MC, V. **Map** p247 D7.
The only smart spot on Maoming Nanlu's otherwise infamously tawdry bar strip, Amber's slick, unruffled kind of Andy Warhol-cool attracts a slightly more discerning Eurocrowd happy to neck bargain cocktails during the week and dance to French house at the weekend. As further assurance of glee, punters can count on special deals almost every day of the week: Tuesdays is a free drink on presentation of a taxi receipt; Thurdays is a free drink for the girls. There are also random free beer nights, occasional quiz nights and, last 13 February, speed dating so no one need be lonely the following day (Valentine's Day).

Arch

439 Wukang Lu, by Huaihai Zhonglu (6466 0807). Metro Hengshan Lu or Xujiahui. **Open** 10.30am-2am Mon-Fri; 8.30am-2am Sat, Sun. **No credit cards**. **Map** p246 A7.
Shanghai's bar for pointy-headed, web-savvy, Le Corbusier-loving, Cargo-panted, *Wired*-reading, would-be intellectuals. Founded by Yale-educated Taiwanese architect Leslie Chen (usually present), Arch is a diner-styled affair with a long bar counter facing banquette seating and big windows. It doubles very well as a café and by day the scene is all laptops and coffee cups (the bar has free dataports). By night, well, it's anything from cheap Belgian beer to free movie screenings or literary salons down in the basement. There's also a small library of international design mags, which are otherwise difficult and expensive to come by in these parts. For those content to keep the brain in disengage, the barman does a mean Cosmopolitan.

Blarney Stone

5A Dongping Lu, by Yueyang Lu (6415 7496). Metro Hengshan Lu. **Open** 4pm-1.30am Mon-Wed; 11am-1.30am Thur-Sun. **Credit** AmEx, DC, MC, V. **Map** p246 C7.
An unpretentious neighbourhood local, we like to think of the BS as a bar that happens to have Gaelic leanings. Yes, patrons have been known to burst into spontaneous dirges of 'Danny Boy'. And there's a live Irish band every night except Tuesday. And there are multiple Saw Doctors CDs on the jukebox. And the bear of a bartender comes from Ireland. And they serve draught Guinness, albeit a locally brewed variety. And there's that name. But please don't call it an Irish pub. It's far too good a place to be maligned by such careless pigeonholing. Pitch up, enjoy the ribaldry and if it all gets a little too lairy, retreat upstairs to play pool or chill on the rooftop terrace.

Eat, Drink, Shop

Fly the world. See new cities. Meet new people. Drink Guinness. **O'Malley's**. *See p125.*

Blue Frog

223 Maoming Nanlu, by Fuxing Lu (6445 6634/
www.kabbsh.com). Metro Shanxi Nanlu. **Open**
10.30pm-2am daily. **Credit** AmEx, DC, MC, V.
Map p247 D7.

The Frog is a (relatively) civilised place from which
to launch an evening of late-night high jinks on
Maoming Nanlu. The glass doors open directly on
to the street, making this a perfect spot to watch all
the action. For those seeking respite from the fun
and games outside, upstairs provides a quiet alternative with cosy nooks and couches. The Frog also
occasionally arranges popular booze cruises along
the Huangpu River: check the website for details.

Face Bar

Building 4, Ruijin Guesthouse, 118 Ruijin Erlu, by
Fuxing Zhonglu (6466 4328). Metro Shanxi Nanlu.
Open noon-1.30am Mon-Thur, Sun; noon-2am Fri,
Sat. **Credit** AmEx, DC, MC, V. **Map** p247 E7.

A sublime setting in the gardens of the 1920s Ruijin
Guesthouse goes some way to explaining the success of what is arguably Shanghai's most famous
bar, but that's only half the story. Inside, South-east
Asian geegaws adorn walls the colour of ripe fruit,
and red leather couches are gathered around ornamental tables in an artfully contrived neo-colonial
fashion. French windows open on to one of the city's
largest lawns, beside which patrons sit battling mosquitoes over their Mojitos. Week nights are languid
and leisurely but come weekends the place is
absolutely heaving with old-fashioned courtesy
thrown to the wind in the scrabble for bar space.
Upstairs is restaurant Lan Na Thai (*see p116*).

Goodfellas

907 Julu Lu, by Changshu Lu (6467 0775). Metro
Changshu Lu. **Open** 2am-2am daily. **No credit**
cards. Map p246 C6.

The bar that launched the infamous Julu Lu girlie
bar strip, Goodfellas looks like the bastard progeny
of a British pub and an American frat house. Lewd
graffiti is chalked all over the walls and ceiling
beams, and a poster of Batman has acquired some
memorably large reproductive tackle. The stench of
stale beer and cigarette smoke permeates the well-
worn, permanently damp wooden bar counter. It
might not sound particularly appealing but to the
lonely businessmen stuck in the Hilton just around
the corner it sure beats a night in the hotel room with
Chinese TV and a minibar.

Manifesto

748 Julu Lu, by Fumin Lu (6289 9108). Metro
Changshu Lu. **Open** 6pm-midnight Mon-Thur,
Sun; 6pm-2am Fri, Sat. **Credit** AmEx, DC, MC, V.
Map p246 C5.

While Julu Lu by Changshu Lu is known for its
parade of girlie bars, Julu Lu by Fumin Lu is a much
classier stretch of tarmac. Grouped here are the
designer diner Shintori and trendoid hangout People
7 (*see p126*) and the pairing of Med-flavoured eaterie
Mesa (*see p116*) and this, its sibling bar. The look is
a harsh – a large room sparsely filled by a large oval
bar strung with orange lamps – but the staff are
friendly and they know how to mix a drink. Not
quite a destination bar but worth dropping by if
you're in the neighbourhood and not necessarily
looking for female company.

Maoming Manhattan

207 Maoming Nanlu, by Yongjia Lu (1350 164 7257). Metro Shanxi Nanlu. **Open** 7pm-4am daily. **No credit cards**. **Map** p247 D7.

This is the kind of desperate little dive where the devil might sidle up to the bar and offer to buy a drink in exchange for the soul of anyone present – and at Maoming Manhattan someone's sure to take him up on it. On any given night witnesses to the diabolical deal would include cheeky girls in denim hot pants who spend their evenings tickling the bald spots of lecherous old men and rowdy groups involved in drinking games. Oblivious to all are the couples who regularly canoodle on bench seats divided by carved-wood separators. Matching roof beams are disguised by a covering of Polaroids depicting debauched evenings gone by.

O'Malley's

42 Taojiang Lu, by Wulumuqi Lu (6437 0667/ www.omalleysirishpub.com). Metro Changshu Lu. **Open** 11am-2am daily. **Credit** AmEx, DC, MC, V. **Map** p246 C7.

If it weren't in an old Concession villa with a private garden, O'Malley's would be just another bit of boozy Oirishry, calculatingly packaged for international consumption, complete with merchandising and imported Irish band to provide that much

Beyond the Irish bar

Western-style bar life is a new plaything in Shanghai. While licensees in much of the rest of the world have had centuries to figure out that serving booze in a room full of expensive art is probably not a good idea, the Chinese have yet to figure that one out for themselves (cf **Room with a View**, *see p163*). In the anything-goes milieu that is the Shanghai bar scene, it's not surprising there are a bunch of way-out-there watering holes. Sadly, our favourite – the pottery workshop-cum-fencing-studio-cum-bar (consider the potential for disaster!) – has vanished but, perhaps against the odds, a clutch of treasurable oddities persist.

Disc Kart Indoor Karting

326 Aomen Lu, by Jiangning Lu, Jingan (6277 5641). Metro Shanghai Railway Station. **Open** 2pm-2am daily. **Credit** AmEx, DC, MC, V. **Map** p248 C2.

Here's the deal: 4,500sq m (48,400sq ft) of tarmac, a bunch of go-karts with Honda 160cc four-strokes under the hood and a trackside pub with a view of the action. So what if staff don't know the difference between a spanner and a screwdriver? (One loosens nuts, the other's a shot of vodka with orange juice.) The fact that you have to pass through the bar to reach the cars suggests that drinking and driving isn't a big issue here, so, please, drink responsibly – wear a crash helmet.

Paramount Ballroom

218 Yuyuan Lu, by Wanghang Lu, Jingan (6249 8866). Metro Jingan Temple. **Open** 8.30pm-1am daily. **Admission** RMB 200. **Credit** AmEx, DC, MC, V. **Map** p248 B5.

Back in 1933 the Paramount was the hottest place in town to shuffle with a flapper and play a hand of poker. In 2001 Taiwanese businessman Zhao Shi Chong spent RMB 25 million to turn the place into a gaudy, neon-lit, neo-rococo abomination. But we do have him to thank for the ballroom dancing that takes place at the second-floor bar every evening. Believe it or not, ballroom dancing is a national obsession and the place gets packed at weekends with waltzing, sipping couples. If you can't bring your own partner, management will provide one for around RMB 100.

Tattoo Bar

28 Yueyang Lu, by Dongping Lu, French Concession (6210 5711). Metro Changshu Lu. **Open** 10am-2am daily. **No credit cards**. **Map** p246 C7.

It's a bar and it's a tattoo parlour. You have been warned. If you go on a bender and wake up with 'I Love Shanghai' tattooed on your butt, don't come crying to us. This hellish pairing is the brainchild of Rock (really), the tattooist from Guangzhou, who has a talent for charcoal drawings – as well as scarring people for life. The sketches of lissom sirens that line the walls are his work, but tragically the blonde furniture is all IKEA. Tatts start at RMB 200 and go up to a lifetime of regret.

Tibet Café & Bar

Lane 819, Julu Lu, by Fumin Lu, French Concession (5403 2005). Metro Changshu Lu. **Open** 10.30am-2am daily. **Credit** AmEx, DC, MC, V. **Map** p248 C5.

There is nothing karmic about this temple to Tibetan tack. It's a big, pink, art deco building chock-full of spanking new glossy Tibetan-style furniture. Show up around 7pm at the weekend for the traditional song and dance show, when you have the opportunity to knock back a Lhasa beer among blokes dressed as yak herders.

Eat, Drink, Shop

harped-on-about mythical ingredient, the craic. But on summer afternoons the garden is like a village green as forty-something patrons arrive with off-spring and lolloping dogs for lazy, hazy long-drawn out sessions. O'Malley's is also essential during rugby and soccer world cups when gatherings of fans of all nationalities trade good-natured insults in front of outdoor televisions.

People 6
150 Yueyang Lu, by Yongjia Lu (6466 0505). Metro Hengshan Lu. **Open** 11.30am-1am daily. **Credit** AmEx, DC, MC, V. **Map** p246 C8.
The first thing you need to know about People 6 is how to get in. No amount of shoving or sliding will budge the big silvery metal door. Instead, turn to the adjacent steely block and slide your hand, palm down, into the crack. Voilà, and open sesame. Inside is more shiny metal and lots of glass, including big people-watching windows (the washrooms are almost totally covered in mirrored surfaces). It's hip and smart, but also quite comfortable with lots of big white sofas and armchairs. The drinks list is enticing and includes an array of reasonably priced saké cocktails (RMB 35-50).

People 7
805 Julu Lu, by Fumin Lu (5404 0707). Metro Changshu Lu. **Open** 11.30am-1am daily. **Credit** AmEx, DC, MC, V. **Map** p246 C6.
If People 6 is hip, People 7 is hipper. If the secret door release gimmick at People 6 is baffling but fun, then this is doubly so at People 7, where there are two sliding doors (slip your hand into the central of the nine round holes, twice). The interior is a wow – a shell of a two-storey building with the raw concrete beams and walls exposed in their seemingly unfinished state and a corrugated steel ceiling. The bar counter is one immensely long, eerily glowing light-box. It's one part Kosovo, one part Tokyo. The drink to go for is the 'tube wine' (RMB 160), a fruit bowl heaped with ice embedded with 20-plus test-tube shots of booze. Don't be foolish – it's meant to share. The toilets are also deliberately designed to perplex alcohol-addled minds: the doors are hinged in the opposite fashion to which they appear and there's no light switch – just close the door behind you and *voilà*! What a lark.

Red
284 Anfu Lu, by Wulumuqi Zhonglu (5403 7997/ www.redbites.com). Metro Changshu Lu. **Open** 5pm-2am daily. **Credit** MC, V. **Map** p246 B6.
Not so much location, location, location as the setting, the setting, the setting. Red boasts the charms of a gorgeous two-storey 1920s Concession-era villa complete with a beautifully kept lawn and lush gardens – quite magical at night strung with (red) lanterns. Downstairs is devoted to eating – though with often disppointing results – while upstairs is an elegant lounge with a large balcony overlooking the grounds. An extensive drinks list majors in predominantly new world wines, with a fair selection

by the glass at RMB 38-58, plus cocktails. The atmosphere is relaxed, the service attentive and the soundtrack is smooth jazz.

Sasha's
House 11, 9 Dongping Lu, by Hengshan Lu (6474 6167). Metro Changshu Lu. **Open** 10am-1am Mon-Thur, Sun; 10am-2am Fri, Sat. **Credit** AmEx, DC, MC, V. **Map** p246 C7.
Sasha's combines the laid-back nonchalance of a Maoming Nanlu bar with the classy stylings that come with the setting of an old Concession-era villa – one that's said to have once belonged to Chiang Kaishek and his wife, no less (although this is unconfirmed history that, according to the blurb on the menu, is still under investigation). Thankfully, the lurid red paint job inflicted on the exterior is an anomaly, and the interior is feet-up comfortable. There's a nice long bar counter with stools for singletons, sofas for groups and a pool table for the competitive. The beer includes John Smith's and Guinness and there's decent pub grub. The large garden patio is a big plus on summer nights.

Shanghai Sally's
4 Xiangshan Lu, by Sinan Lu (5382 0738). Metro Shanxi Nanlu. **Open** 4pm-2am daily. **Credit** AmEx, DC, MC, V. **Map** p247 E7.
As one of the handful of boozy old warhorses that have been around since the mid '90s, Shanghai Sally's is an ageing mama-san with a hoarse cackle from too many ciggies and make-up applied with a trowel. But while she may be grey and saggy, she still has a penchant for living life large. Week nights are busy with darts and pool tournaments (8.30pm Tue-Thur) and salsa classes, while at weekends there's live Chinese hip hop.

The Seven
1110 Huaihai Zhonglu, by Donghu Lu (6415 7777). Metro Shanxi Nanlu. **Open** 11am-midnight daily. **Credit** AmEx, DC, MC, V. **Map** p246 C6.
This is building number seven (hence the name) of the Donghu Hotel complex, built in 1921 and formerly belonging to the legendary gangster 'Big-Eared' Du Yuesheng. Post-1949 it was home to state leaders, senior army officers and red capitalists. These days it's a seriously gorgeous venue for what's likely to be a majorly disappointing drink – the handful of cocktails that make up the menu are ineptly made. Stick with a glass of wine or something relatively unfuck-upable, such as a gin and tonic, and take it out on to the veranda overlooking the beautiful lawn and gardens.

Time Passage
183 Lane 1038, Huashan Lu, by Fuxing Xilu (6240 2588). Metro Jiangsu Lu. **Open** 5pm-2am Mon-Fri; 2pm-2am Sat, Sun. **No credit cards. Map** p246 A6.
A small bar hidden down a nondescript alley next to a tennis court, Time Passage is divinely unpretentious. It's a real neighbourhood bar – a category that's highly uncommon in Shanghai – dark, pokey and popular with students. Staff are friendly, the

YY's (Yin Yang). *See p128.*

beers are cheap and the choice of music is unobjectionable going on great. A Chinese band covers jazz classics and evergreen favourites from 10pm on Fridays and Saturdays (*see p176*).

Upstairs at Park 97

2nd floor, 2 Gaolan Lu, within Fuxing Park (5383 2328). Metro Shanxi Nanlu. **Open** 8pm-2am Mon-Thur, Sun; 8pm-4am Fri, Sat. **Credit** AmEx, DC, MC, V. **Map** p247 E6.

During the week Upstairs is an elegant lounge bar with bum-friendly sofas and a covetable terrace overlooking the green spread of Fuxing Park. Come weekend, however, it's absolute hell on earth. As the current 'in' place for the beautiful new rich it is quite literally besieged each Friday and Saturday night. The Prada hordes jam the staircase that leads up from California Club (*see p179*) below, prevented from going any further by the sheer number of bodies already up there (did somebody say 'fire regulations'?). For those who make it, drink of choice is champagne, quaffed in great quantities to a soundtrack of live salsa and R&B. It ain't our idea of fun but it obviously appeals to plenty.

Yongfu Elite

200 Yongfu Lu, by Fuxing Xilu (5466 2727). Metro Changshu Lu. **Open** 11.30am-midnight daily. **Credit** AmEx, DC, MC, V. **Map** p246 B7.

Yongfu Elite has the honour of being housed in a building once occupied by the British Consulate. But that's probably the least remarkable thing about the place. Since the civil servants left in 1998, the villa, twin pavilions and gardens have been renovated and decorated in the most extraordinary fashion. Interiors feature European vintage like green Gucci leather sofas, and Chinese vintage like Ming Dynasty furnishings, deco chandeliers and drapes decorated with peacock feathers. The garden sports a massive Buddha, a carved wooden temple gateway and an original Beijing Opera outdoor theatre. It took two and a half years to bring it all together, creating what may well be the most fabulous hangout in all Asia. Cocktails start at RMB 50 (plus obligatory service) but then you do get to swan around feeling like Dietrich (and that's just the boys).

YY's (Yin Yang)

125 Nanchang Lu, by Maoming Nanlu (6466 4098). Metro Shanxi Lu. **Open** 2pm-4am daily. **Credit** AmEx, DC, MC, V. **Map** p247 E6.

Around the end of the 1990s, YY's was *the* place. Under the stewardship of owner Kenny it was the haunt of subculturals, artists and radicals – characters like Mian Mian (author of banned sex 'n' drugs novel *Candy*) and Wei Hui (author of *Shanghai Baby*, who was once gloriously condemned by Chinese state media as 'decadent, debauched and a slave of foreign culture'). It's no longer quite so essential – and the downstairs nightclub has become a boutique – but the sparse and well-worn ground-floor bar still serves as a sort of common room for the city's young chain-smoking alternative set.

Hongqiao

Hongqiao is an absolute party desert. Shanghai drinkers cringe at the name.

The Door

4th floor, 1468 Hongqiao Lu, by Yanan Xilu (6295 3737). **Open** 6pm-2am daily. **Credit** AmEx, DC, MC, V.

Visitors to the Door have got to watch their alcohol intake. You don't want to lose it here and bump into something because chances are it'll probably be a Ming Dynasty antique. The setting is an imposing 1920s faux-Tudor mansion. Inside old sideboards, screens, ceramics and several stores' worth of Chinese antiquities fill the cavernous space to arguably unfortunate result – the place feels more like a Christie's showroom than a classy bar. Still, it's an undeniably extravagant venue and worth flagging a taxi for.

Tang Hui

13 Xingfu Lu, by Fahuazhen Lu (6283 6162). Metro Xujiahui. **Open** 7pm-midnight daily. **No credit cards. Map** p246 A7.

The musicians, poets, idlers and intellectuals have finally been granted another haven away from the housey beats, multiple mirrors and velour-glam of the rest of the city's nightspots. Tang Hui's ace design references the Tang Dynasty, an aesthetic that's currently enjoying a rebirth in the city – intricate wooden carvings, doors and knockers, opium beds dressed in delicate pink silk gauze. It all sounds terribly fancy but it's not. Stand and down pints (Carlsberg RMB 40) or kick off your shoes and lounge on a bed sipping green tea. Turn up with your acoustic, say hi to guitar-playing owner Zhang Du and sit in on one of the regular jam sessions.

Pudong

Vertigo sufferers might try **BATS** (at the Shangrila Hotel) and the **Dublin Exchange** (at the HSBC Building), which offers the friendliest pint this side of the Huangpu.

Cloud 9

87th floor, Grand Hyatt, Jinmao Tower, 88 Shiji Dadao (5049 1234). Metro Lujiazui. **Open** 6pm-midnight Mon-Fri; noon-midnight Sat, Sun. **Credit** AmEx, DC, MC, V. **Map** p243 L4.

At 420m (1,386ft) above sea level, Cloud 9 is the highest bar on earth (so says *Guinness World Records 2004*). Be warned, though, the heavenly views that this height suggests are mainly of adjacent building sites with the rest of the city obscured by clouds. It's pretty spectacular all the same – and the cool, dark and steely interior is a sight in itself. Prices match the altitude, with an imposed minimum spend of RMB 120 per person. If you don't want to blow all that on booze, there are some delicious alcohol-free alternatives including freshly made fruit punches, and delicious desserts.

Shops & Services

Shang*buy*!

Shopping is the city's favourite pastime. Most visitors catch the bug: casual browsers quickly capitulate to become fervent buyers. Locals increasingly favour malls (*see p130*) but visitors will find more joy among the myriad boutiques of the French Concession, the booty-filled holes-in-the-wall of the Old City and the all-senses-assaults that are the city's numerous and varied open-air markets (*see p130*). Pirate goods aside – shelve your morals for the best buys in town; *see p133* **Faking it** – prime legit purchases include tailor-made clothing (get copies of your favourite outfit knocked up in a few days for next to nothing; *see p135* **Suits *you!***); tea (*see p142*); antique furniture and repros (even after paying for shipping, the cash savings are still immense compared to Europe or North America; *see p132*); Cultural Revolution kitsch (*see p136* **Mem-Mao-ries are made of this**); ultra-comfortable straw houseshoes (a steal at RMB 10); and, for those with the figure to fit, slinky, silky, split-thigh *qipaos*, beloved of drag queens everywhere; *see p146* **Thigh fashion**.

Outside of high-end stores, prices are cheap and often negotiable. Cash is king (although credit cards are accepted in all the swankiest places), but be sure to try before you buy as there are no refunds and rarely will goods be exchanged, with or without a receipt.

SHOPPING AREAS

The **French Concession** is prime shopping turf. The area on and off **Huaihai Zhonglu**, between Shanxi Nanlu and Chongqing Nanlu, is packed with clothing boutiques and tailors, while **Fuxing Xilu** houses a number of popular home decor and gift shops. To the south-east is **Taikang Lu** (*see p81* **Half-arted street**), a centre for arts, crafts and fashion accessories.

Upmarket apparel and more home decor shops fill the cobblestoned alleys and plazas of **Xintiandi**, while a short stroll east is **Dongtai Lu**'s famed antique market. The stretch of **Huaihai Zhonglu** immediately north of Xintiandi houses the best electronics market in the city, as well as half a dozen or more Western-style malls and department stores.

The area around **Renmin Square** has a mix of everything, from state-owned stores to modern malls. The most modern malls, however, are on **Nanjing Xilu** in the district of **Jingan**, where free spenders can lose it big time cavorting with the likes of Gucci, Prada and Shiseido.

Numbers add up at **Plaza 66**. *See p130*.

Anchored by the Yu Gardens and surrounding bazaar, the **Old City** is good for knick-knacks, jade and jewellery and items for which dubious claims of antiquity are made. To the south is the custom-tailoring heaven of the fabric market on **Dongjiadu Lu**.

One-stop shopping

Shanghai Friendship Store

65 Yanan Donglu, by Jiangxi Lu, the Bund (6337 3555). Metro Henan Zhonglu. **Open** 9.30am-9.30pm daily. **Credit** AmEx, DC, MC, V. **Map** p243 J4. Established in 1958 in the darkest red-dyed days of international isolation, the Friendship Store was historically the only store authorised to receive foreign guests, the only place that the rare visitor could spend his or her specially issued Foreign Exchange Certificates. Local Chinese were rebuffed at the door. These days it's the official China gift shop peddling everything from miniature terracotta warriors to impressively sized dildos. Jewellery, cosmetics, books, luggage and 'sex health' implements fill the ground floor, with silk and cashmere on the second. On the third are carpets, jade and colourful kites. Prices are a little more than you'll pay elsewhere but quality is guaranteed. Best buys are silk robes and pyjamas, and 100% cashmere sweaters. Rumours that the store was slated for demolition were yet to be confirmed, so phone ahead to check.

Malls

The Shanghainese are currently obsessed with these big, shiny, air-conditioned boxes of commerce. At the time of writing, the city boasts no fewer than 40 malls with many more on the drawing board. Nanjing Xilu in Jingan is home to the big three (CITIC Square, Plaza 66 and Westgate) with more along Huaihai Zhonglu in the French Concession and in the western district of Xujiahui, where four malls square up to each other at the junction of Hengshan Lu and Zhaojiabang Lu.

CITIC Square
1168 Nanjing Xilu, by Jiangning Lu, Jingan (6218 0180/www.citicpacific.com). Metro Shimen Yilu. **Open** 10am-10pm daily. **Map** p249 D4.
A six-floor marketplace filled with international brands. There's an Esprit Salon (*see p145*) on the third floor, sports gear on the fourth and the small but excellent foreign language bookshop CNPIEC (*see p136*) on the fifth. In addition to miscellaneous Chinese eateries, plus Starbucks and McDonald's, CITIC also boasts expat haunt Wagas (*see p103*).

Grand Gateway
1 Hongqiao Lu, by Huashan Lu, Xujiahui (6407 0115/ www.grand-gateway.com). Metro Xujiahui. **Open** 10am-10pm daily. **Map** p246 A9.
Although only a handful of metro stops away, Grand Gateway is more affordable than the big downtown malls. It boasts a few higher-end stores including Guess and Hong Kong's G2000 and Giordano. Upper floors host Chinese eateries, KFC and Pizza Hut, plus a cinema that screens English-language films.

Maison Mode (Mei Mei)
1312 Huaihai Zhonglu, by Changshu Lu, French Concession (6431 0100/www.maisonmode.com). Metro Changshu Lu. **Open** 10am-9.30pm daily. **Map** p246 C7.
A place to drop some serious cash, Mei Mei harbours high-class labels such as Hugo Boss, Dunhill, Ferragamo, Gucci and Anne Klein, as well as choice upmarket local outfits.

Plaza 66
1266 Nanjing Xilu, by Shanxi Beilu, Jingan (6279 0910/www.plaza66.com). Metro Shimen Yilu. **Open** 10am-10pm daily. **Map** p249 D4.
There are few faster ways to blow your holiday budget than taking your plastic for a spin here. Stores include the likes of Fendi, Louis Vuitton, Moschino and Prada. High-quality dining options include dim sum at Zen (no relation to the Zen in Xintiandi), and conveyor-belt soup noodles at Red Door, aka Xiamien Guan (*see p103*).

Raffles City
268 Xizang Zhonglu, by Fuzhou Lu, Renmin Square (6340 3600). Metro Renmin Park or Square. **Open** 10am-10pm daily. **Map** p242 G4.
Opened by Singapore's CapitaLand in early 2004, this is the city's newest mall (for now). There are seven floors of local and international shops; foreign fashion brands include Guess, Denmark's ONLY, Japan's Uniqlo and the UK's Peace Angel. Global cuisines are also well represented, from Taiwanese and Brazilian to Singapore's Bread Talk and popular Japanese chain Ajisen Ramen.

Westgate Mall
1038 Nanjing Xilu, by Jiangning Lu, Jingan (6218 7878). Metro Shimen Yilu. **Open** 10am-10pm daily. **Map** p249 D4.
Incorporating a wide fashion spectrum from mainstream to high-end, Westgate is notably more egalitarian than its swankier neighbours, CITIC Square and Plaza 66. Burberry and plush Japanese department store Isetan share space with more affordable shops such as MNG (Mango), Naf Naf and Sisley. There's a cinema on the fifth floor that plays both Chinese and English features.

Markets

Stockpiling everything from fashion and fabric to antiques and live animals, the city's markets are a haggler's paradise. Food and flowers excluded, the starting price is generally three times the local, and ultimately acceptable, price.

Even if you're not self-catering, it's worth checking out one of the city's wet markets to see how many locals still do their grocery shopping. Fresh vegetables and live animals are trucked in daily. Soft shell turtles and freshwater eels swim in tubs next to pens of clucking chickens and tables of garden-fresh aubergine and coriander. With the busiest traffic in the morning, the vendors practically give away the remaining items by dusk.

A good wet market is located at the southeast corner of **Xiangyang Market** (*see p132*) with others on **Wulumuqi Lu**, near Wuyuan Lu (indoor warehouse), on **Ruijin Erlu** near the Taikang Lu Art Street, on **Yanqing Lu** near Xinle Lu, and on **Wukang Lu** near Anfu Lu.

Dongjiadu Lu Fabric Market
Dongjiadu Lu, by Zhongshan Nanlu, Old City. **Open** 8am-5pm daily. **Map** p245 K8.
The cheapest and biggest place in Shanghai to buy fabric, this massive alfresco warehouse is home to over 100 different stalls carrying domestic and imported, natural and synthetic fibres. Most places

Dongjiadu Lu Fabric Market. *See p130.*

Jinwen Flower Market. *See p132.*

Xiangyang Market. *See p132.*

Xiangyang Market. *See p132.*

Eat, Drink, Shop

Hu & Hu Antiques. *See p133.*

provide custom tailoring according to the samples on display, but quality really varies. Watch out for vendors who try to pass polyester off as silk or a blend as pure cashmere. For fair-priced genuine and imitation brocade try stall No.118: RMB 25 per metre for silk; RMB 10 per metre for polyester.

Dongtai Lu Antique Market
Dongtai Lu & Liuhekou Lu, by Xizang Nanlu, Xintiandi. Metro Huangpi Nanlu. **Open** 9am-6pm daily. **Map** p244 G6.
Only a fraction of what you see could qualify as an antique but it's still a great place to pick up Mao memorabilia, fake propaganda posters, imitation porcelain, little Buddhas, snuff bottles and other interesting curios. Reputable dealer Chine Antiques (*see p133*) has an outlet at 38 Liuhekou Lu.

Gubei Flower & Bird Market
Gubei Nanlu, by Guyang Lu, Hongqiao/Gubei. **Open** 8am-6pm daily.
Much more than just orchids and swallows (as if that wasn't exotic enough), stalls here also peddle everything from antiques and rattan to silk gifts and accessories. Along the closest track parallel to Gubei Nanlu are crockery dealers selling discounted local and import wares. Along the northern outskirts of the market are golf shops selling price-slashed Callaways and Nikes, while the western side features Hong Gu Wan Pedestrian Walk, better known as Pearl Street. The market is slated for a move in 2004.

Hong Kong Shopping Centre
Corner of Renmin Dadao & Xizang Zhonglu, Renmin Square. Metro Renmin Park or Square. **Open** 10am-9pm daily. **Map** p242 G4.
Beneath the grass and concrete parades of Renmin Square is a whole warren of passageways packed with fashion and accessory stores including a great many mainstream labels from Baleno and Giordano to Esprit and ONLY. There's also an infinity of cosmetics, bag and shoe stores. Best buys are the colourful wigs, hair extensions and glittery hair clips just off the row of cheap manicure stalls. To locals this market goes by the name of Dimei or D-Mall.

Jinwen Flower Market
225 Shanxi Nanlu, by Yongjia Lu, French Concession (6467 6500). Metro Shanxi Nanlu. **Open** 8am-8pm daily. **Map** p247 D7.
A huge multi-storey warehouse with a basement and ground floor blooming with fresh flowers from simple stems and elaborate bouquets to potted orchids and large house plants. The upper floor sells artificial flowers and heavily discounted holiday decorations during the Christmas season.

Xiangyang Market
Xiangyang Nanlu, between Huaihai Zhonglu & Nanchang Lu, French Concession (6466 3790). Metro Shanxi Nanlu. **Open** 9am-8.30pm daily. **Map** p247 D6.
No Shanghai visit is complete until you've bargained your way through the city's busiest outdoor market. Stalls hawk everything from athletic apparel to table settings and DVDs. Generally a quarter of the asking price, designer knock-offs are incredibly cheap – but so is the quality. Best buys are North Face jackets, Puma trainers, designer handbags and fake pashminas. Xiangyang is also great for cheesy gifts like Mao watches. The market is slated for a move to Pudong or Hongqiao in 2004 or early 2005.

Yu Bazaar (Yuyuan Shangsha)
Corner of Fuyou Lu & Jiujiachang Lu, Old City. **Open** 8.30am-8.30pm daily. **Map** p243 J5.
If you can bear the crowds, the inflated prices and the cloying stench of tofu, then this is a great place to stock up on Chinese souvenirs. Stalls overflow with embroidered robes, custom chops, Tai Lake pearls, ceramic tea sets, imitation Cultural Revolution posters, rattan, wooden fans and painted scrolls. Shops along Fangbang Lu offer much of the same. Persistent souls have been known to unearth the odd treasure at the Fuyou Antiques Bazaar (No.459) and this is also the location of multi-storey jewellery enterprises Lao Miao and First Asia.

Antiques

Shanghai is best known for the restoration of old furniture, as well as high-quality repros. Along **Hongqiao Lu** and **Wuzhong Lu** in the far western Hongqiao/Gubei district are a number of reputable dealers with immense warehouses of furniture both old and new. For antiques of a smaller, more portable nature, it's worth scouring the junky stalls and shops of **Dongtai Lu Antique Market** (*see p132*).

Note that foreigners are not allowed to take anything out of the country that's more than 200 years old. Make sure that your piece carries the official seal that marks it as OK for export.

Chine Antiques

1660 Hongqiao Lu, by Shuicheng Lu, Hongqiao/ Gubei (6270 1023). **Open** 9am-5pm daily. **No credit cards.**

In business for more than 15 years, this small store in the Liu Haisu Art Museum specialises in high-quality, antique furnishings. Products are at least 100 to 150 years old and are gathered mostly from the Beijing, Tianjin, and Zhejiang and Jiangsu provinces. Items include screens, cabinets and wedding baskets. Chine also has a store in New York. **Other locations**: 38 Liuhekou Lu, Dongtai Lu Market, Xintiandi (6387 4100).

Hu & Hu Antiques

1685 Wuzhong Lu, by Laohongjing Lu, Hongqiao/ Gubei (6405 1212/www.hu-hu.com). **Open** 9am-6pm daily. **Credit** AmEx, DC, MC, V.

Since 1998, sisters-in-law Lin and Marybelle Hu have been combing the countryside for stylish bits of antiquity to fill their large showroom and warehouse. Finds include a wide selection of furniture, from Anhui wedding beds to Shandong wine cabinets. Pieces are tastefully restored according to customer specifications.

Shanghai Antique &

218-240 Guangdong Lu, by Jiu the Bund (6321 4697). Metro I. 9am-5pm daily. **Credit** AmEx, L p243 J4.

Dimly lit and library-hushed, this ___ store a few blocks from the Bund certai ___ reels like the real deal. It's been around for more than 100 years and all the stock is appraised by experts and carries an official seal of authenticity. Visit for furniture, ceramics, jade and other antique collectibles, as well as a smaller selection of repro items. Foreign exchange and global delivery are available.

Arts & handicrafts

China is famed for its silk, embroidery and ceramic production, but also worth a look are folk paintings, batik, carpets and rattan. Beware of the goods at the Yu Bazaar and Xiangyang Market, which are largely cheap and mass produced. *See also pp142-4* **Gifts & interiors**.

Chinese Handprinted Blue Nankeen Exhibition Hall

No.24, Lane 637, Changle Lu, by Changshu Lu, French Concession (5403 7947). Metro Changshu Lu. **Open** 9am-5pm daily. **Credit** MC, V. **Map** p246 C6.

Established by Japanese artist Kubo Mase, this museum-cum-shop has been selling fine blue and white cotton products for over 20 years. Originating in the Jiangsu, Zhejiang and Guizhou provinces, the

Faking it

Fake goods are everywhere in Asia, but China's pirate industries really do stand in a league of their own. It's reckoned that more than 80 per cent of the branded goods on sale in Shanghai are forgeries or imitations – as well as everything else from college diplomas to car tax stickers. As the Chinese themselves joke, in Shanghai 'everything is fake except your mother'.

The combination of digital technology and censorship laws has spawned a massive and largely tolerated counterfeit music and movie industry. While highly controversial and morally dubious, the enormously cheap pirated (*daoban*) CDs and DVDs are a temptation most can't resist: *see p158* **Not the reel thing**. Apart from DVDs, the best buys in Shanghai are 'seconds' or surplus designer clothing and handbags sold 'out the back door' to retailers. Have a good look around the stalls at the **Xiangyang Market** (*see p132*) or the **Ni Hong Children's Plaza**

(*see p156*) or check out the many export clothing shops dotted around the French Concession. Another big hit are imitation golf clubs, with high-quality copies of top brands such as Callaway and Nike copies manufactured from Guangzhou to Taipei.

Cheap thrills aside, buyer beware: pirated goods are not confined to obvious categories like watches or DVDs, or obvious places like street markets. Almost everything you buy outside of Shanghai's legitimate department stores and supermarkets will be fake. Lurking behind familiar brands can be shampoo as strong as floor cleaner, or razor blades that blunt after one shave. Smokers should know that Marlboro has never manufactured a single cigarette in China, and all but a trickle of tobacco imports are fakes. A phoney Rolex may be a fun gift, but fake antibiotics are a different matter. For imported equipment, stick to licensed dealers in major stores, and always get a receipt (*fapiao*).

handmade blue calico, akin to batik, carries traditional Chinese patterns. The delicate designs adorn everything from clothing to curtains and are currently the mobile phone case covering of choice.

Eddy Tam's Gallery

20 Maoming Nanlu, by Xinle Lu, French Concession (6253 6715). Metro Shanxi Nanlu. **Open** 9am-9pm daily. **Credit** AmEx, DC, MC, V. **Map** p247 D6.
Specialising in the acquisition and custom framing of Chinese art, Eddy Tam's is the pick of the numerous galleries along this stretch of Maoming Nanlu. It carries lots of handpainted Jinshan stencils (brightly coloured folk images) and is also the exclusive agent for local artist Xie Weimin, whose oeuvre includes watercolours of Shanghai buildings.

Harvest Studio

Room 118, Building 3, Lane 210, Taikang Lu, by Sinan Lu, French Concession (6473 4566). Metro Shanxi Nanlu. **Open** 9am-6pm daily. **Credit** AmEx, DC, MC, V. **Map** p247 F8.

This t
ghetto
The Mi
China. V
passed d
embroide.
and silk a
The colour
accessories

Shangha

*Shanghai Ar
Square (6327
or Square.* Op   ... AmEx, DC, MC, V. **Map** p2
A large space with everything from painted scrolls and calligraphy sets to embroidered slippers and assorted silk apparel. The lower level has an impressive assortment of ceramics from Jingdezhen, including reproductions of items in the museum's Zande Lou Ceramics Gallery. There are also attractive jade pendants, agate teapots and blue calico.

Suits *you*!

Like most parts of Asia, Shanghai is a steal for custom-made clothes. The city's tailors are genius at making copies and it really is worth packing a few cherished items from your wardrobe at home to get them reproduced over here, probably for a fraction of the price you paid for the original.

As the client, you select the fabric, and the best place for this is the **Dongjiadu Lu Fabric Market** (*see p130*). It's a good idea to try and stick as close to the original material as possible, and remember that shrinkable fibres such as cotton and corduroy should be pre-washed – the tailor should do this before they're cut and sewn. Lining is essential for most business and formal wear and it's worth paying a little extra to get breathable silk instead of polyester. Details like zips and buttons are best brought from home. It usually takes anything from two or three days to two weeks for garments to be made up. Plan on at least two fittings and always have someone other than the tailor on hand for a second opinion.

There are plenty of tailors at Dongjiadu Lu Market. Otherwise, for custom-made *qipaos* or other traditional Chinese fashions, try **Silk King**. Despite its tacky appearance, this state-owned operation does high-quality custom-tailored garments at reasonable prices. English-speaking staff can help you choose from the hundreds of local silk, cashmere and wool bolts on display. As well

as *qipaos*, the King's expert tailors can stitch anything from business suits to slinky pyjamas. *Qipaos* start at RMB 1,000, including fabric.

For gents **Dave's Tailors** in the French Concession (not to be confused with Dave's Tailors next to the Portman Ritz-Carlton) does excellent work. The handmade suits are fabulous and the shop has a good selection of fine wools and cashmeres. Expect to pay from RMB 3,000. There's also **WW Chan & Sons**, a Hong Kong tailoring firm that has been specialising in men's suits for over 50 years. Superior-quality Italian and English fabrics are finished with handstitched linings and button holes.

Dave's Tailors
Unit 6, Lane 288, Wuyuan Lu, by Wukang Lu, French Concession (5404 0001). Metro Changshu Lu. **Open** 10am-8pm daily. **Credit** AmEx, DC, MC, V. **Map** p246 B6.

Silk King
819 Nanjing Xilu, by Shimen Yilu, Jingan (6215 3114/www.silkking.com). Metro Shimen Yilu. **Open** 9.30am-10pm daily. **Credit** AmEx, DC, MC, V. **Map** p249 E4.

WW Chan & Sons
129 Maoming Nanlu, by Huaihai Zhonglu, French Concession (5404 1469). Metro Shanxi Nanlu. **Open** 10am-10pm daily. **Credit** AmEx, DC, MC, V. **Map** p247 D6.

Mao-ries are made of this

Mao Zedong, Marxist dictator, ...ator of mass crimes against ...manity, ravisher of teenage dancing girls. He's about as loveable as Stalin, Pol Pot or Hitler. But boy is his merchandise seductive.

There's nothing like a little memorabilia to ensure a lasting legacy. Except that when it comes to Mao memorabilia, it's nothing like a little. There's loads of it. Mao may have labelled icon worship as counter-revolutionary but he made an exception for the cornucopia of wares emblazoned with his own domed image.

Since the great helmsman's death in 1976 many Chinese have held on to his stuff because they believe it brings luck and protection. But nowadays, Mao-morabilia is a big hit with Western collectors too. Not only is it a bit of pocket-sized history, it also looks cool. Mao alarm clocks with ramrod straight, clenched fist workers as the hour and minute hands are as groovy as paisley bell bottoms.

Just about every antique or souvenir shop in Shanghai stocks Mao. At the **Dongtai Lu Market** (see p132) and along Yu Yuan's **Fangbang Nanlu**, numerous stalls sell doodads like badges, key rings, watches and musical cigarette lighters, not to mention the infamous Little Red Book. Seal Military is one of the better stores, with a stock of old military motorcycle helmets, T-shirts and

entire Red Guard uniforms. For posters try the **Propaganda Poster Art Centre** (see p84) or the **Unique Hill Studio**; both are expensive but you can at least be sure that you are getting the genuine article. (The bulk of Shanghai's Mao memorabilia is mass produced on the outskirts of town. How to tell the real thing? During Mao's time goods were of the cheapest materials people could find, like scrap metal, so the shoddier something looks the more likely it is to be original.)

Seal Military

361 Fangbang Nanlu, by Jiujiaochang Lu, Old City (6330 2492). **Open** 9am-7.30pm daily. **No credit cards. Map** p245 J6.

Unique Hill Studio

Room 301, Tianlong Apartments, 907 Tianyueqiao Lu, by Zhongshan Nanerlu, French Concession (5410 4815). **Open** 9am-6pm Mon-Fri; 1-6pm Sat. **No credit cards. Map** p246 A10.

Books, movies & music

Most high-end hotels carry a basic selection of international press; the best is offered at the newsstand at the **Ritz-Carlton** (see p39). **Fuzhou Lu**, which runs between Renmin Square and the Bund, has traditionally been the booksellers' street, but there's not a whole lot of joy for English-language readers. By far the best selection of books about Shanghai, and China in general, is found at the **Shanghai Museum** bookshop (see p59). Movies (DVDs) and music (CDs) are almost always found in pirate territory; see p133 **Faking it**.

Book City

401 Fuzhou Lu, by Fujian Zhonglu, Renmin Square (6328 2891). Metro Renmin Square. **Open** 9am-8pm daily. **Credit** AmEx, DC, MC, V. **Map** p243 H4.
A favourite with expats, Book City's substantial inventory ranges from popular novels and the

classics to Chinese-language learning materials and some Western CDs and DVDs. A selection of second-hand books is also available.

China National Publications Import-Export Corporation (CNPIEC)

5th floor, CITIC Square, 1168 Nanjing Xilu, by Jiangning Lu, Jingan (5292). Metro Shimen Yilu. **Open** 10am-10pm daily. **Credit** AmEx, DC, MC, V. **Map** p249 D4.
This minuscule foreign-language bookstore located on the fifth floor of the CITIC Square mall (see p130) majors in mostly non-fiction English titles. It also stocks a selection of international publications, including *The Economist, Newsweek,* the *Wall Street Journal* and *Wallpaper**.

Foreign Languages Bookstore

390 Fuzhou Lu, by Fujian Zhonglu, Renmin Square (6322 3200/www.sbt.com.cn). Metro Henan Lu. **Open** 9.30am-6pm Mon-Wed, Sun; 9.30am-7pm Fri, Sat. **Credit** V. **Map** p242 H4.

Visit for maps and books about Shanghai, in addition to Chinese-language learning materials (find them on the first floor, aka the ground floor for British shoppers). English-language fiction, with a focus on the classics, is up on the fourth floor.

Electronics

While still not as cheap as Hong Kong, prices for electronics have fallen dramatically in recent years thanks to the proliferation of quality local brands. You can score good deals on homegrown DVD and MP3 players, portable CD players and digital cameras. But if you're looking to buy an international brand, stiff import taxes keep prices high. In addition to the places below, try the electronics market at Fuxing Zhonglu and Xiangyang Nanlu.

Cybermart
282 Huaihai Zhonglu, by Huangpi Nanlu, Xintiandi (6390 8008/www.cybermart.com.cn). Metro Huangpi Nanlu. **Open** 10am-8pm daily. **Credit** V. **Map** p244 F6.
Impossible to miss with its deafening music booming from the massive speakers outside, Cybermart is the best place for high-quality electronic and digital devices. Computers, printers, memory sticks and digital music players occupy the first floor, while mobile phones, blank CDs, webcams and computer components for tecchie DIYers are on the second and third. The place is ISO 9001-certified signifying high quality overall.

Photography

Film processing is cheap in China; a good bet is **Guanlong** (*see below*) or **Kodak**, which has branches at Xintiandi and on Huaihai Zhonglu near the Shanghai Library.

Guanlong Photographic Equipment Company
180 Nanjing Donglu, by Jiangxi Zhonglu, the Bund (6323 8681). Metro Henan Lu. **Open** 9am-9pm daily. **Credit** AmEx, DC, MC, V. **Map** p243 J4.
A shutterbug paradise, this massive electronics store has everything from high-end digital and point-and-shoot cameras to MP3 players and camcorders. Prices aren't cheap but you're paying for reputable brands such as Sony and Nikon. On-site photo processing is available, as are other professional photographic services.

Fashion

Shanghai stores do carry international designer labels but high import taxes mean that you'll end up paying more than back home. Instead, the best deals are made on the designer surplus and seconds found in boutiques in the French Concession – most notably on **Maoming Nanlu**

(Nos.90-94 are especially good), **Ruijin Lu** between Nanchang Lu and Julu Lu and on **Changle Lu** between Ruijin Yilu and Maoming Nanlu (try Grace's Detail at No.169). Cheaper still are the blatant knock-offs at the 'fake' **Xiangyang Market** (*see p132*).

Lu Kun Fashion of Mirror Studio
2nd floor, 60 Anlan Lu, by Xizang Nanlu, Old City (6378 2120). **Open** 9am-6pm daily. **No credit cards. Map** p244 G7.
In a class of his own (although his work has been compared to Dolce & Gabbana and Lanvin), tailor/designer Lu Kun specialises in made-to-order high fashion. Customers view studio samples or come armed with their own ideas. For women's blouses expect to pay in the order of RMB 600-900; jackets start at around RMB 1,000, while the average dress is in the region of RMB 1,600. Typical turnaround from order to delivery is two weeks.

Shanghai Tang
59 Maoming Nanlu, by Changle Lu, French Concession (5466 3006/www.shanghaitang.com). Metro Shanxi Nanlu. **Open** 10am-10pm daily. **Credit** AmEx, DC, MC, V. **Map** p247 E6.
The famous Hong Kong brand (with outlets in New York, London, Paris and Bangkok) excels in trad China with a kitsch twist. The shop itself is a sultry space of dark wood, bright chinoiserie and delicate wafts of ginger flower essence. Wares range from leather coats to silk-covered diaries, but the most popular buys are the signature reversible 'double fish' motif velvet Tang jackets and custom-made *qipaos* from the Imperial Tailor department. The labels may read 'Made by Chinese' but be warned, prices are wholly Fifth Avenue.

Shirt Flag
718 Changle Lu, by Fumin Lu, French Concession (5403 9373). Metro Changshu Lu. **Open** 11am-9.30pm daily. **No credit cards. Map** p246 C6.
Casual wear for national socialists: designer Shan Qi Zhi does Revolutionary T-shirts adorned with hammer and sickles and skateboards and computers rendered in Maoist style. Each design comes in four different colours and all are a mere RMB 70.

Three Retail
1st & 2nd floors, Three on the Bund, 3 Zhongshan Dongyilu, by Guangdong Lu, the Bund (6323 3355 ext 2/www.threeonthebund.com). Metro Henan Lu. **Open** 11am-10pm daily. **Credit** AmEx, DC, MC, V. **Map** p243 J4.
Three Retail's loft space is home to cherry-picked collections of such exclusive labels as Yohji Yamamoto, Ann Demeulemeester and Alain Mikli. The open-plan space is arranged with free-standing racks and open shelves, and instead of bland changing rooms there are floor-to-ceiling rattan dressing niches with sliding panels. If you feel the urge to do some serious financial damage, head downstairs to the ground floor where you can pay through the nose at Giorgio Armani's flagship China store.

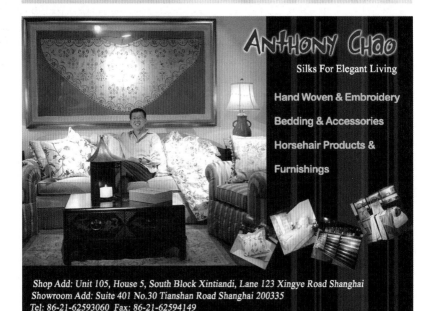

Fashion accessories & services

For the cheap stuff, head to **Xiangyang Market** (*see p132*), which is teeming with knock-off designer bags, watches, trainers and trinkets. Otherwise, **Xintiandi** and **Taikang Lu** (*see p81* **Half-arted street**) are home to a number of expat and local designers creating high-quality handbags, jewellery, shoes and other accessories for a more discerning crowd.

Bags & scarves

Jooi Design
Studio 201-203, Lane 210, Taikang Lu, by Sinan Lu, French Concession (6473 6193/www.jooi.com). Metro Shanxi Nanlu. **Open** 10am-6pm daily. **Credit** AmEx, DC, MC, V. **Map** p247 F8.
Danish design company Jooi adapts traditional Chinese techniques and detailing to modern sensibilities. Bestsellers include silk evening bags and scarves with hand-embroidered butterflies, blossoms and filigree coins. Lifestyle and home decor products are also popular – place settings, cushion covers, silk robes and hand-crocheted silk blankets.

Xavier
Unit 2, 181 Taicang Lu, by Madang Lu, Xintiandi (6328 7111). Metro Huangpi Nanlu. **Open** 10.30am-11pm daily. **Credit** AmEx, DC, MC, V. **Map** p244 F6.
Drawing inspiration from ancient Chinese design and the glamour of '30s Shanghai, Australian designer and all-round eccentric Xavier peddles a flamboyant collection of flashy hats, showy jewellery and his signature feathered handbags. All products are 'proudly made in China' and will soon be available in France, Bangkok and Moscow.

Jewellery

The Old City and the pedestrianised section of Nanjing Donglu, inland of the Bund, are home to several multi-storey, state-run jewellery operations, but the counters in such places are typically tended by off-puttingly surly staff. If you want to brave the indifference, try **Lao Miao** (462 Nanjing Donglu, by Shanxi Lu) and **Chow Tai Fook** (300 Huaihai Zhonglu, by Madang Lu), both of which offer heaps of precious metals, diamonds, jade and pearls.

Amy's Pearls & Jewellery
77 Xiangyang Nanlu, by Huaihai Zhonglu, French Concession (5403 9673). Metro Shanxi Nanlu. **Open** 9am-8.30pm daily. **Credit** AmEx, DC, MC, V. **Map** p247 D6.
Graced by pictures of the foreign dignitaries and celebrities who've shopped here, this is Shanghai's foremost pearl dealer. Choose from natural pink, white and lilac or, for more adventurous tastes, dyed green, yellow and black Zhejiang freshwater strands. South Sea salties and semi-precious stones are also available. Prices include custom stringing and staff speak fluent English.

Fanghua Pearls
Units 102-103, No.11, Lane 1398, Gubei Nanlu, by Guyang Lu, Gubei (6209 4152/www.fanghua.com). **Open** 9am-8pm daily. **Credit** AmEx, DC, MC, V.
Fanghua's brightly lit and tasteful displays of fresh and saltwater pearls are in welcome contrast to those in the assorted dives along Hongqiao's famed Pearl Street (otherwise known as the Hong Gu Wan Pedestrian Walk). Purchase by the strand for custom threading, or choose from the in-house design collection. Items such as the exotic Tahitian black chokers may bust the ceiling on your budget but there are plenty of affordable semi-precious alternatives. The staff are supremely knowledgeable and English-speaking.

Kenjad
Suite 11C, Concord World Building, 2066 Nanjing Xilu, Jingan (1380 176 8527). Metro Jingan Temple. **Open** by appointment only. **No credit cards.** **Map** p248 C5.
Raphaelle Muller's funky and colourful jewellery reflects her international upbringing in Thailand, Mexico, Egypt and France. Earrings, bracelets, necklaces and belts are made from pearls, semi-precious stones, metals, resin and optical fibres. Select pieces are sold in Isetan at the Westgate Mall (*see p130*) and at the boutique at the Portman Ritz-Carlton (*see p39*), but the majority of clients find the boutique by word of mouth.

Marion Carsten Silver Jewellery
Suite 115, 200 Taikang Lu, by Ruijin Erlu, French Concession (6415 3098). Metro Shanxi Nanlu. **Open** 11am-5pm Tue-Sat. **Credit** AmEx, DC, MC, V. **Map** p247 E8.
German expat Marion Carsten spent four years studying goldsmithery in Dusseldorf. Her chokers and matching bracelets are hand-assembled and finished, using inventive combinations of silver, suede, leather and pearl. The signature piece of the collection is a signet ring employing the Chinese *shou*, symbol of longevity.

Q&W Design
Unit 3, No.25, North Block, 181 Taicang Lu, by Xingye Lu, Xintiandi (6326 2140). Metro Huangpi Nanlu. **Open** 10.30am-10.30pm daily. **Credit** AmEx, DC, MC, V. **Map** p247 F6.
Shanghainese designer Qionger Jiang says that she aims to 'bridge the abyss separating the commonplace and the extraordinary'. Quite. What that means in practice is bold, striking necklaces and earrings fashioned out of such mundane elements as stainless steel, screw nuts and even washers. The Q&W collection also includes more traditional shiny metal earrings and vibrantly coloured necklaces adorned with oversized pendants.

Eat, Drink, Shop

Shops by area

The Bund

Blue Shanghai White (Gifts & interiors, *p142*); **Guanlong Photographic Equipment Company** (Electronics, *p137*); **Shanghai Antique & Curio Store** (Antiques, *p133*); **Shanghai Friendship Store** (One-stop shopping, *p129*); **Suzhou Cobblers** (Shoes, *p141*); **Three Retail** (Fashion, *p137*).

Renmin Square

Book City (Books, movies & music, *p136*); **Hong Kong Shopping Centre** (Markets, *p132*); **Raffles City** (Malls, *p130*); **Shanghai Art Museum Store** (Arts & handicrafts, *p135*); **Foreign Languages Bookstore** (Books, movies & music, *p136*); **Shanghai No.1 Foodstore** (Food & drink, *p142*).

Jingan

China National Publications Import-Export Corporation (CNPIEC) (Books, movies & music, *p136*); **CITIC Square** (Malls, *p130*); **Esprit Salon** (Hairdressing, *p145*); **Kenjad** (Jewellery, *p139*); **Nanjing Cosmetology & Haircut Co Ltd** (Hairdressing, *p145*); **Plaza 66** (Malls, *p130*); **Westgate Mall** (Malls, *p130*).

Jooi Design. *See p139.*

Lee's Decor. *See p144.*

Shoes

Small sizes and poor-quality leather mean most visitors are disappointed with local footwear brands. The alternative is to pay top dollar for real designer kicks at **Three Retail** (*see p137*) or **IT**, an industrial-style space in Xintiandi's South Block, stocking labels such as Costume Nationale, Marc Jacobs and Bikkembergs. Otherwise, heavily discounted imports can be found in French Concession boutiques on and off Huaihai Zhonglu east of Shanxi Nanlu.

Hot Wave

108 Shanxi Nanlu, by Changle Lu, French Concession (5403 6909). Metro Shanxi Nanlu. **Open** 10am-10pm daily. **No credit cards. Map** p247 D6.
A wide assortment of discounted men's and ladies' footwear from such international favourites as Nine West, Timberland and Liz Claiborne. The crowded store also stocks casual wear from Miss Sixty, Tommy Hilfiger and Morgan and boasts a decent selection of outdoor and camping gear.
Other locations: 390 Shanxi Nanlu, by Nanchang Lu, French Concession (6472 0376).

Eat, Drink, Shop

Old City

Dongjiadu Lu Fabric Market (Markets, *p130*);
Lu Kun Fashion of Mirror Studio (Fashion,
p137); **Tong Hang Chun Traditional Chinese
Medicine Store** (Health stores & pharmacies,
p145); **Yu Bazaar** (Markets, *p132*).

Xintiandi

Cheese & Fizz Gourmet Shop (Food & drink,
p142); **Cybermart** (Electronics, *p137*);
Dongtai Lu Antique Market (Markets, *p132*);
Fulintang Xinyidai (Health stores &
pharmacies, *p145*); **I WAS** (Gifts & interiors,

p142); **Q&W Design** (Jewellery, *p139*);
Simply Life (Gifts & interiors, *p144*);
Xavier (Bags & scarves, *p139*).

French Concession

Amy's Pearls & Jewellery (Jewellery,
p139); **Annabel Lee** (Gifts & interiors,
p142); **Carpenter Tan** (Cosmetics, *p144*);
**Chinese Handprinted Blue Nankeen
Exhibition Hall** (Arts & handicrafts, *p133*);
Eddy Tam's Gallery (Arts & handicrafts,
p135); **Harvest Studio** (Arts & handicrafts,
p135); **Hot Wave** (Shoes, *p140*); **Hot Wind
Shoe Shop** (Shoes, *p141*); **Huangshan Tea
Company** (Food & drink, *p142*); **Jinwen
Flower Market** (Markets, *p132*); **Jooi Design**
(Bags & scarves, *p139*); **Lee's Decor** (Gifts
& interiors, *p144*); **Madame Mao's Dowry**
(Gifts & interiors, *p144*); **Magazine** (Gifts
& interiors, *p144*); **Maison Mode** (Malls,
p130); **Marion Carsten Silver Jewellery**
(Jewellery, *p139*); **Paddy Field** (Gifts &
interiors, *p144*); **Shanghai Tang** (Fashion,
p137); **Shanghai Trio** (Gifts & interiors,
p144); **Shirt Flag** (Fashion, *p137*);
Watson's (Health stores & pharmacies,
p145); **Xiangyang Market** (Markets, *p132*);
Ye Huo (Sports & outdoor gear, *p146*).

Xujiahui & Hongqiao/Gubei

Bauernstube (Food & drink, *p142*); **Chine
Antiques** (Antiques, *p133*); **Fanghua Pearls**
(Jewellery, *p139*); **Grand Gateway** (Malls,
p130); **Gubei Flower & Bird Market** (Markets,
p132); **Hu & Hu Antiques** (Antiques, *p133*);
Pines, the Market Place (Food & drink, *p142*).

Pudong

Jun Peng Lamps (Gifts & interiors, *p144*).

Jun Peng Lamps.
See p144.

Eat, Drink, Shop

Hot Wind Shoe Shop
*131 Ruijin Yilu, by Changle Lu, French Concession,
(5386 0418). Metro Shanxi Nanlu.* **Open**
10am-10pm daily. **Credit** AmEx, DC, MC, V.
Map p247 E6.
Local product dominates the shoe section, but there
are also trousers and tops that are 'inventory, display
or b-type items' for the export market; familiar
brands include BCBG, Calvin Klein, Catherine
Malandrino and Moschino. The store also carries a
range of camping gear including sleeping bags, gas
stoves and walkie talkies.

Suzhou Cobblers
*Room 101, 17 Fuzhou Lu, by Zhongshan Dongyilu,
the Bund (6321 7087/www.suzhou-cobblers.com).
Metro Henan Lu.* **Open** 10am-6pm daily. **No credit
cards. Map** p243 J4.
Suzhou Cobblers is an emporium of fine handmade
silk slippers, which can be worn both at home and
around town. Mary Janes and mules feature Suzhou
embroidery, including 'double fish', floral and
vegetal designs. Particularly popular is the funky
leather slide with a red plastic star. As seen at New
York's Anthropologie.

Food & drink

Shanghai No.1 Foodstore (*see below*) and **Shanghai No.2 Foodstuff Shop** (955-965 Huaihai Zhonglu) are as much sightseeing experiences as shops – the same goes for the city's many **wet markets** (*see p130*). For Western-style foodstuffs try **City Shopping**, which has a branch at the Shanghai Centre (Map p248 C4), or French hypermarché **Carrefour**, which has its flagship store in Gubei (269 Shuicheng Nanlu, by Yanan Xilu).

Bauernstube

Sheraton Grand Tai Ping Yang Hotel, 5 Zunyi Nanlu, by Xing Yilu, Hongqiao/Gubei (6275 8888). **Open** 10am-8pm Mon-Fri, Sun; 9.30am-8.15pm Sat. **Credit** AmEx, MC, V.

For indulgent self-catering, this store one escalator up from the Sheraton lobby boasts a wide assortment of imported meats, seafood and cheeses. International delicacies include Angus beef, Norwegian salmon and cheeses from Germany, Italy, France and Switzerland. Local meats and seafood are also stocked, as are handmade sausages from cervelat to chorizo. Adjoining Alpen Rose has fresh baked goods and superb own-made ice-cream.

Cheese & Fizz Gourmet Shop

Unit 105, North Block, 119 Madang Lu, by Taicang Lu, Xintiandi (6336 5823). Metro Huangpi Nanlu. **Open** 9.30am-12.30am daily. **Credit** AmEx, DC, MC, V. **Map** p244 F6.

Imported and pricey delicacies range from over three dozen French cow, goat and ewe-milk cheeses to Italian marinated artichoke hearts, olives and biscuits. French/Chinese duo Clarence and Glendy also sell freshly baked quiches, rustic pâté and crusty baguettes for eat-in and takeaway.

Huangshan Tea Company

605 Huaihai Zhonglu, by Gusi Nanlu, French Concession (5306 2974). Metro Huangpi Nanlu. **Open** 9am-10pm daily. **Credit** AmEx, DC, MC, V. **Map** p244 F6.

Specialist in high-grade Chinese teas by weight. The store also carries an assortment of classic teapots, made in the town of Yixing 193km (120 miles) northwest of Shanghai. Supposedly, after a few year's use you can brew tea just by pouring water into the pot, such is their ability to absorb flavour. **Other locations**: Westgate Mall, 1038 Nanjing Xilu, by Jiangning Lu, Jingan.

Pines, the Market Place

18 Jianhe Lu, by Hongqiao Lu, Hongqiao/Gubei (6262 9055). **Open** 8am-8.30pm daily. **Credit** MC, V.

A two-storey speciality supermarket with an enormous array of international food and beverages, from Alaskan king crab claws and Australian beef to American cold cuts and French wines. There are plenty of South-east Asian goods too, including fresh herbs from Thailand and Singaporean fish balls and cooking pastes. There's an on-site Australian butcher and an in-house sommelier. Home delivery is available.

Shanghai No.1 Foodstore

720 Nanjing Donglu, by Guizhou Lu, Renmin Square (6322 2777). Metro Renmin Park or Square. **Open** 9.30am-10pm daily. **No credit cards**. **Map** p242 G4.

Operating since 1954, this massive food store on the pedestrian stretch of Nanjing Donglu west of the square sells domestic and imported products. The ground-floor sprawl stocks everything from fresh-baked goods and dried fungus to salted fish and Dove chocolate bars. Pay-by-weight nuts and preserved fruits are particularly popular. Tobacco and spirits are available, in addition to supplies of Eastern and Western health remedies.

Gifts & interiors

The gift shop at the **Portman Ritz-Carlton** (*see p39*) and **Mitsukoshi** at the Okura Garden Hotel (*see p42*) stock good selections of popular local products including designs by Annabel Lee, Shanghai Trio and Simply Life. Otherwise, the place to browse is the French Concession, particularly along **Fuxing Xilu, Dongping Lu** and around the area of **Taikang Lu** (*see p81* **Half-arted street**).

Annabel Lee

225 Shanxi Nanlu, by Yongjia Lu, French Concession (6445 8218). Metro Shanxi Nanlu. **Open** 10am-7.30pm daily. **Credit** DC, MC, V. **Map** p247 D7.

Local designer and owner Feng Bo has spent a lot of time in Japan, and it shows in her minimalist approach. Her simple but elegant designs include fine linen place settings, raw silk travel pockets and business card holders, graceful candles and sleek silk pyjamas with jade buttons. **Other locations**: Unit 3, North Block, Lane 181, Taicang Lu, Xintiandi (6320 0045).

Blue Shanghai White

Unit 103, 17 Fuzhou Lu, by Hankou Lu, the Bund (6323 0856). Metro Henan Lu. **Open** 10am-6pm daily. **No credit cards**. **Map** p243 J4.

This is the sales space for Shanghai native Wang Hai Chen's distinctive furnishings, which combine blue-and-white porcelain with hand-polished antique pear wood. Fine celadon tea cups with hand-woven tassles are popular, as is the crockery with painted images of *shikumen*, the celebrated but vanishing architecture of Old Shanghai.

I WAS

203 Danshui Lu, by Zizhong Lu, Xintiandi (6284 3496). Metro Huangpi Nanlu. **Open** 11am-8.30pm Mon-Fri; 10am-9pm Sat. **Credit** AmEx, DC, MC, V. **Map** p244 F7.

Many shoppers make the short walk from Xintiandi to I WAS for charming and unusual home furnishings. Most of the stock is designed by Anglo-French

Eat, Drink, Shop

Xiangyang wet market. *See p132.*

Natasha and her Beijingese partner Edward, and their range includes Dehua ceramics and camphor wood vases. Other lines include photographic greeting cards, embroidery from minority regions of China, colourful Taiwanese glass pendants and red lacquerware imported from Vietnam.

Jun Peng Lamps

571 Jujiaqiao Lu, by Jinqiao Lu, Pudong (5034 0919). Metro Dongfang Lu. **Open** 8am-5pm daily. **No credit cards.**
This small store specialises in custom-designed Chinese lamps. It's a bit of a hike from the centre – over in Pudong and, even then, a ten-minute taxi ride from the Grand Hyatt – but then its prices are half those in town. Choose from over 100 silk and cotton fabrics and myriad styles, from free-standing to ceiling fixtures. Custom orders take around two weeks.

Lee's Decor

1586 Huaihai Zhonglu, by Gaoan Lu, French Concession (6431 3654). Metro Hengshan Lu. **Open** 10.30am-8pm daily. **Credit** AmEx, DC, MC, V. **Map** p246 B7.
Tina Lee's store showcases Chinese design in the form of slinky, vividly coloured furnishings and accessories. All items are made from traditional textiles such as linen and Hangzhou silk; these include lotus-shaped lamps and sleek business card holders, picture frames and all manner and size of boxes, photo albums and embroidered cushion covers.

Madame Mao's Dowry

70 Fuxing Xilu, by Yongfu Lu, French Concession (6437 1255). Metro Changshu Lu. **Open** 10am-6pm daily. **Credit** AmEx, DC, MC, V. **Map** p246 B7.
Its English and Chinese owners conceived this as the store in which Madame Mao – head of art and culture during the Cultural Revolution – might have shopped with her daughters. Two floors are filled with vintage posters, paintings and industrial propaganda, as well as antique furniture and lifestyle products. Old and new are combined to create pieces such as the 'golden brick' table, which incorporates a piece of floor slab from an imperial palace.

Magazine

410 Wukang Lu, by Huaihai Zhonglu, French Concession (6431 9971/www.magazine.sh.cn). Metro Changshu Lu. **Open** 11am-8pm daily. **Credit** DC, MC, V. **Map** p246 A8.
A complete lifestyle store-cum-café showcasing a collection of furniture and fashion sourced from the Philippines. The 400sq m (4,300sq ft) industrial space hosts the best the Pinoys have to offer, with fine furniture from Cebu-based Kenneth Cobonpue and Pampango designer Claude Tayag in addition to other home accessories made from odd materials such as bamboo, banana bark and seashells.

Paddy Field

30 Hunan Lu, by Huaihai Zhonglu, French Concession (6437 5567). Metro Hengshan Lu. **Open** 11am-8pm daily. **Credit** AmEx, DC, MC, V. **Map** p246 B7.

Gurgling fountains and fragrant woody scents provide a tranquil setting for furniture and home furnishings from Indonesia, Thailand and Myanmar. Bigger pieces include Thai teakwood dining sets and Indonesian leather sofas, complemented by more portable items such as shell plates and sandstone candleholders. Global delivery can be arranged.

Shanghai Trio

House 6, 37 Fuxing Xilu, by Wulumuqi Nanlu, French Concession (6433 8901). Metro Changshu Lu. **Open** 9am-6pm Mon-Fri. **Credit** AmEx, DC, MC, V. **Map** p246 B7.
Located in a charming old residence, this showroom is a sublime setting for the innovative creations of owner/designer Virginie Fournier. Favourites include vibrantly coloured silk pouches and small silk cases shaped like rice baskets. These – and other products such as duvets, cushion covers and baby clothes – are fashioned from all-natural Chinese cashmere, linen, silk and cotton.
Other locations: Lane 181, Taicang Road, by Huangpi Nanlu, Xintiandi (6433 8901).

Simply Life

South Block, Building 5, Lane 123, Xingye Lu, by Madang Lu, Xintiandi (6387 5100/www.simplylife-sh.com). Metro Huangpi Nanlu. **Open** noon-11.45pm daily. **Credit** AmEx, DC, MC, V. **Map** p244 F6.
A city-wide chain that's a one-stop shop for quality and pricey Chinese-style home decor and gift products. Choice items include house-brand silk boxes, place settings, embroidered pillows, appliqué greeting cards and glazed ceramic crockery sets and vases. The flagship store in Xintiandi also stocks local fashion brand INSH, as well as such high-end imports as Alessi and Bodum.
Other locations: 9 Dongping Lu, by Hengshan Lu, French Concession (3406 0509).

Health & beauty

City Shopping at the Shanghai Centre (Map p248 C4) and Carrefour (*see p142*) stock Western beauty and personal care brands. Otherwise, try the department stores in the various malls (*see p130*).

Cosmetics

Carpenter Tan

75 Xiangyang Nanlu, by Huaihai Zhonglu, French Concession (1331 188 6907/www.crpttan.com). Metro Shanxi Nanlu. **Open** 10am-8pm daily. **No credit cards. Map** p247 D6.
Aka Combs 'r' Us. From humble origins, this head-grooming franchise now boasts over 300 stores throughout China. By stimulating blood flow to the scalp, combing (so it's claimed) promotes quicker hair growth and prevention of dandruff. The kaleidoscope of choice here includes combs made from peach wood (*tao mu*) and poplar (*huang yang mu*), plus intensely fragrant sandalwood (*tan xiang mu*).

Hairdressing

Esprit Salon

301B CITIC Square, 1168 Nanjing Xilu, by Jiangning Lu, Jingan (5292 8800). Metro Shimen Yilu. **Open** 10am-10pm daily. **Credit** AmEx, DC, MC, V. **Map** p249 D4.

Favoured by in-the-know expats for its affordable yet cutting-edge hairstyles. All the stylists have trained at Esprit in Hong Kong and most can speak English. Discontented customers can return to the salon within seven days for the same service free of charge. Women's haircuts start from RMB 400, but although that seems steep, the salon often runs promotional deals for up to 50% off.
Other locations: Super Brand Mall, 168 Lujiazui Xilu, by Yincheng Xilu, Pudong (5049 3988).

Nanjing Cosmetology & Haircut Co Ltd

784 Nanjing Xilu, by Shimen Yilu, Jingan (6253 2958). Metro Shimen Yilu. **Open** 9am-9pm daily. **No credit cards. Map** p249 E4.

In business for more than 70 years, Nanjing is considered by locals as the best in men's and women's hairdressing. The place reeks of history, with traditional barber stations on the ground floor, and ladies' cuts and colouring up a sweeping balustraded staircase on the second. Apart from the RMB 50 cut/wash/shave for men, prices are steep – a hair-wash/massage (*tou bu a muo*) will set you back RMB 75, but the package includes a 15-minute special head and upper body massage. The list of services is available in English.

Health stores & pharmacies

For opticians *see p222.*

Fulintang Xinyidai

Unit 1A, South Block, 123 Xingye Lu, by Madang Lu, Xintiandi (6384 5987/www.fulintang.com). Metro Huangpi Nanlu. **Open** 10.30am-midnight daily. **Credit** AmEx, DC, MC, V. **Map** p244 F6.

Although it's been around since the days of the Qing Dynasty, this venerable institution has adopted a modern approach to Chinese herbal medicine. Healthy ingredients are administered in convenient snacks and floral teas; go for liver-relieving osmanthus tea, for example, or soup packs and Chinese mushrooms coated with sweet sesame.

Tong Hang Chun Traditional Chinese Medicine Store

20 Yuyuan Xinlu, by Jiuxiao Lu, Old City (6355 0308). **Open** 8.30am-9pm daily. **No credit cards.**

Established in 1783, Tong Hang Chun is the city's oldest medicine store. Large glass jars containing sea horses, antlers and placentas share space with modern-day over-the-counter medications. With everything labelled in Chinese and no English-speaking staff, you're best bringing someone who can translate or just browsing through the bear bile powder and gnarly ginseng.

Watson's

787-789 Huaihai Zhonglu, by Ruijin Yilu, French Concession (6431 8650). Metro Shanxi Nanlu. **Open** 9.30am-10.30pm daily. **Credit** AmEx, DC, MC, V. **Map** p247 E6.

Say cheese at **Shanghai No.1 Foodstore**. *See p142.*

Eat, Drink, Shop

Born in Hong Kong, this Western-style chain drugstore is a one-stop for toiletry and personal care needs. In addition to deodorants, razors and the like, it also carries affordable make-up brands such as Maybelline, L'Oréal and Revlon, Chinese and Western health remedies and teas, basic first aid supplies and the entire Scholl footcare line. **Other locations**: 218B Westgate Mall, 1038 Nanjing Xilu, by Jiangning Lu, Jingan.

Sports & outdoor gear

Many malls reserve an entire floor for sporting gear, notably **CITIC Square**, **Raffles City** and **Westgate** (*see p130*). **Hot Wind** (*see p141*) and **Hot Wave** (*see p140*) are good for outdoor and camping gear. Stalls at **Xiangyang Market** (*see p132*) sell knock-off Adidas, Nike and North Face, and even discounted golf clubs.

Ye Huo

296 Changle Lu, by Ruijin Yilu, French Concession (5386 0591/www.yehou.com). Metro Shanxi Nanlu. **Open** 10.30am-10pm daily. **No credit cards.** **Map** p247 E6.

A camping store that stocks all the goods necessary for a weekend with Mother Nature. Quality local brands – of which the best are Backpackers, Zealwood and Zebra – are cheap, and flawed or last-season foreign brands are also reasonably priced, but no bargains otherwise. English-speaking staff can suggest the best places in China to pitch your tent.

Thigh fashion

In old films, cigarette posters and even the contemporary imagination, Shanghai's sinful heyday is evoked by nothing so much as the *qipao*. Better known to the West by its Cantonese name of *cheongsam*, the *qipao* is the infamously tight women's dress, the slinky number with the slit up to there.

Qipaos look highly sultry in images of old, yet when encountered these days they can seem very unflattering. Designers and fashion writers complain that Chinese women today, with their ultra-slim beauty ethos, cannot wear *qipaos* attractively. But part of the problem lies in the design itself. Mainland Chinese women rediscovered the *qipao* in the 1990s and borrowed from the West to redesign it, adding massive 1980s power-suit shoulder pads. Collars are low in deference to bad posture. In a self-conscious attempt to be 'Chinese', the fabric of choice is stiff silk brocade, which means the garment doesn't hug the curves as it was originally designed to. Figures are further disguised by the additional design feature of front pockets, which give the wearer an artificial belly bulge.

The 1930s-style *qipao*, in contrast, flatters any figure, Asian or Western; if well made, it actually better suits the voluptuous. In its classic form it was light and supple and curve-clinging. Collars were high, between one and a half inches to as high as the wearer's neck allowed, kept closed with two or three frogs up the neck. These high collars tucked in extra chinnage and ensured good posture, forcing shoulders back and breasts out front. Sleeves were seamless, made from the same piece of cloth as the dress's body, effecting a round, natural shoulder. The flap over the chest was dramatically square, not rounded as today, and the front fell straight down from the breasts, sans paunch pouch. The best way to get a classic *qipao* today is to take an Old Shanghai photo or postcard and to stress no shoulder pads or front pockets. While upscale *qipao* shops can demand upwards of several thousands of *yuan*, private tailors will charge only RMB 300 to RMB 400, excluding cloth but including fittings and adjustments – see 135 **Suits you!**. A more budget option can be found in Xiangyang Market, where many stalls sell surprisingly tasteful and flattering mass-produced cotton/lycra *qipaos*, stretchy enough to accommodate wider Western derrières, for RMB 30 to RMB 50.

Arts & Entertainment

Festivals & Events

Dragon boats, grave sweeping, lantern-lit nights... And now Formula 1.

Qing Ming Festival. See p149.

The Shanghai events calendar is by turns enchanting and maddening. Traditional fixtures such as the Lantern Festival, which sees the Yu Gardens glowing beautifully by lantern light, are accessible and appeal to all ages. Other festivals such as Qing Ming (the 'grave-sweeping' festival) are a more private sort of affair but there is nevertheless great interest in watching the locals pouring into the city's graveyards to pay their respects to the dead.

However, Shanghai festivals are nothing if not haphazard. A combination of inexperience in event planning, an excess of governmental red tape and insufficient funding means that often plans are not confirmed until the eleventh hour. It's not untypical to only hear about an event or festival after it has happened.

As with many of the city's ills, this one can largely be blamed on the repressions endured during Communist rule. Under that regime, the upholding of Chinese traditions was discouraged as superstitious and wasteful. So, while the Hungry Ghost was kept alive in places like Taiwan, Hong Kong, Singapore and Chinatowns around the world, in the People's Republic it was allowed to fade away. As a consequence, many Shanghainese remain ignorant on the basic beliefs behind these traditions.

Instead, as the new Shanghai increasingly covets 'world city' status, a new raft of annual happenings is being taken on board. Events like the International Fashion Culture Festival, the Shanghai Beer Festival and Formula 1 have nothing to do with traditional culture and everything to do with raising the city's international profile.

Note that traditional Chinese holidays follow a lunar calendar, meaning that dates change every year. The exact dates are only confirmed by the State Council in Beijing just a few weeks before the festival; therefore dates for lunar festivals given in this guide are for 2005 and, even then, are only approximate.

Tickets & information

Tracking down up-to-date and accurate information on coming events is a challenge. The best sources are the *Shanghai Daily* and *Shanghai Star* newspapers. Monthly English-

▶ For dates of **national public holidays**, see p229.

language magazines such as *that's Shanghai* (www.thatsmagazines.com), *City Weekend* (www.cityweekend.com.cn) and *Shanghai Talk* are also good sources. Concierge staff at high-end hotels usually keep some sort of what's on list, and they also speak English. The state-run tourist information centres (*see p228*), with their surly, unhelpful staff, are there only as a last and probably fruitless resort.

Purchasing tickets may require sleuthing around. To book in advance, try the box offices at theatres around town; the **Shanghai Grand Theatre** (*see p185*) is one of the largest and some of the staff speak English.

Spring

Shanghai International Fashion Culture Festival

Various venues (information 6439 1818/ www.fashionshanghai.com). **Date** mid Mar.

Shanghai's answer to the European fashion weeks – glamouratti and fashionistas strut around town in full regalia, on their way to the fashion shows and model competitions held at a variety of venues all over town. Xintiandi and the Westgate Mall (*see p130*) are among the top places to catch the action.

Birthday of the Queen of Heaven

Longhua Temple, 2853 Longhua Lu, by Longhua Park, Xuhui (6456 6085). **Date** 23 Mar. **Admission** free. **Map** p240 C4.

The birthday of Matsu, the Queen of Heaven, is fêted with the arrival of merchants from the Fujian province. They bring traditional offerings such as joss paper money and incense to be burnt in her honour, and pray for safety and wealth. Devotees often stage special theatrical performances.

Qing Ming Festival

Various temple & graveyard venues (information 6439 1818). **Date** 4 or 5 Apr.

Qing Ming, aka grave-sweeping day, is one of the oldest and most important Chinese festivals. It's the day on which relatives visit the tombs of their ancestors, lay flowers and do a bit of spring cleaning. The occasion is also celebrated with picnics, kite-flying and outdoor games. Although not an official holiday, hospitals and stock exchanges are noticeably quieter because with so many spirits wandering the earth, the day is considered inauspicious for medical procedures or business dealings. Traffic jams can result in acute gridlock on the city's outer roads.

Birthday of Sakyamuni Buddha

Jingan Temple, 1686 Nanjing Lu, by Wanghang Lu, Jingan (6256 6366). Metro Jingan Temple. **Date** 8 Apr. **Admission** RMB 15. **Map** p248 B5.

Public displays of faith are rare in Shanghai, but the birthday of Sakyamuni Buddha is an exception. Monks at Jingan Temple chant prayers and perform a ritual cleaning of their Buddhas.

Longhua Temple Fair

Longhua Temple, 2853 Longhua Lu, by Longhua Park, Xuhui (6456 6085). **Date** 1st 10 days in Apr. **Admission** RMB 15. **Map** p240 C4.

The Temple Fair dates back to the Ming Dynasty and is the largest of its kind in Shanghai. Rites are performed for Maitreya (the Buddhist messiah) and a grand Buddhist ceremony is held. The fair includes music, opera and vegetarian food stalls.

Nanhui Peach Blossom Festival

Huinan Town, Nanhui County (5801 2020). No.2 bus from Shanghai Stadium. **Date** 10 days in mid Apr. **Admission** RMB 30.

The Nanhui district is filled with hundreds of hectares of peach trees, which come into full bloom in April. Thousands of people flock to enjoy the pink blossoms and take in the folk dancing and singing that are part of the festivities. Shanghai's posh city folk also like to marvel at the quaint rural peasants tending to the trees and engaging in manual labour. To get to Nanhui take the Line 2 tourist bus from the station at 2 Zhongshan Nanlu.

International Tea Culture Festival

Various venues, Zhabei district (information 6439 1818). Metro Shanghai Railway Station. **Date** mid-late Apr. **Admission** varies.

Tea fanatics from around the world pour into Shanghai to attend tea ceremonies, seminars, tastings and exhibits. To escape the city there are also tours of nearby tea fields, while folk performances are held at the stage around the Zhabei train station.

International Tea Culture Festival.

International Flower Festival

*Changfeng Park, 451 Daduhe Lu, Changfeng
(information 6286 0458).* **Date** Apr (biennial).
Map p240 B2.

For the festival Changfeng Park is carpeted with
exotic spring flowers and rare herbs including
peonies and tulips. There's also folk dancing and
singing at the park's aquarium.

Summer

May Day

Various venues (information 6439 1818). **Date** 1st
wk in May.

In years past, the May Day holiday celebrated the
heroic achievements of workers and farmers with
military parades and government rallies. Today
revellers roam up and down Nanjing Lu or Huaihai
Lu waving giant inflatable plastic toys in anticipation
of the evening's firework show. The holiday lasts
for a week and is the peak of the Chinese tourist
season – expect a crush at airports and train and bus
stations. Some shops and services may also close.

BMW Asia Open

*Thomson Shanghai Golf Club, 1 Longdong Dadao,
by Luoshan Lu, Pudong (5855 5858).* **Dates** 13-16
May. **Admission** tbc.

Golf is becoming increasingly popular in China, and
this tournament hopes to establish itself as the pre-
eminent event of its kind on the mainland. A honey
pot of $1.5 million prize money attracts the big
hitters, plus some top-flight homegrown talents such
as Zhang Lian Wei.

Shanghai International Music Festival

Various venues (information 6386 8686). **Date** May.
The music in question is a mixed bag of classical,
jazz, pop, world beat and folk music. Previous
performers have included popular Celtic band
Molly's Revenge and bluegrass wunderkids the
Puny Pickers (no, we've never heard of them either).
The Shanghai Grand Theatre on Renmin Square
stages the top shows. For those unable to get
advance tickets, scalpers usually stand outside
theatres a few hours before the shows.

Children's Day

Various venues (6439 1818). **Date** 1 June.
The products of China's stringent one-child policy
have their own holiday. Schools are decorated and
parties thrown, while amusement parks, children's
palaces, cinemas and museums offer free admission
or discounts to the wee'uns.

Dragon Boat Festival

Suzhou Creek (information 6439 1818). **Date** 11 June
in 2005.
The festival celebrates the venerated Chinese poet,
Qu Yuan, who drowned himself in 278 BC in protest
against corruption in the imperial court. Legend has
it that a fisherman tried to save him by throwing

International Flower Festival

bamboo stuffed with cooked rice into the water to
prevent the fish from eating his body. These rice
snacks, known as *zongzi*, are still served as a
reminder of Qu Yuan's noble sacrifice. The event is
also celebrated with exhilarating dragon boat races
held on the Huangpu River.

Shanghai International Film Festival (SIFF)

*Various venues (information 6253 7115/
www.siff.com).* **Date** mid June.
The festival focuses on the latest Chinese movies but
spices things up with an eclectic mix of foreign
flicks. Be warned that foreign films may be dubbed
into Chinese and Chinese films may not have English
subtitles. Ticket purchasing can be a challenge due
to the popularity of première events, which are often
sold out well in advance. *See also p159.*

Founding of the Chinese Communist Party

*Museum of the First National Congress of the
Chinese Communist Party, 374 Huangpi Nanlu,
by Xingye Lu, Xintiandi (5383 2171). Metro
Huangpi Lu.* **Date** 1 July. **Map** p244 F6.
On this day every year government newspapers run
front-page editorials extolling the supreme glory of
the People's Party. Old stagers organise ceremonies
around the city, including notably at the Museum
of the First National Congress (*see p74*). One for
the political perverts.

Zhongyuan Festival

*Jade Buddha Temple, 170 Anyuan Lu, by Shanxi
Beilu, Jingan (6266 3668).* **Dates** 15 & 30 July.
Admission free. **Map** p248 C2.
Zhongyuan is a celebration of the redemption of the
dead. It is an opportunity for the living to make offer-

ings to the spirits in the hope of easing the suffering of their loved ones in the afterlife. Expect ancient Buddhist rites performed amid shimmering lotus lanterns and flaming bundles of incense.

Shanghai Beer Festival

The Bund (information 6439 1818). Metro Henan Lu. **Date** last wk in July. **Admission** free. **Map** p243 J4.

The best festival to beat the sweltering Shanghai summer – beer tents sponsored by various foreign and local breweries are set up along the city's most famous promenade. Worth attending if only for the sight of Chinese wearing lederhosen.

Seven Sisters' Festival

Various locations (information 6439 1818). **Date** 11 Aug in 2005.

Seven Sisters is the Chinese equivalent of Valentine's Day. Legend has it that two lovers were forcibly separated and can only reunite on this bittersweet day. Although the tradition has faded in recent years, lovers still exchange gifts and go out for romantic dinners. Summer fruits are served to celebrate the reunion of the unfortunate couple.

Hungry Ghost Festival

Various temples (information 6439 1818). **Date** 19 Aug in 2005.

The Hungry Ghost Festival is the day when dead souls from hell are supposedly released to wander the earth, taking the forms of living creatures from animals to beautiful women. They are thought to cause insanity or illness and should be avoided – steer clear of walking close to walls, where lost souls apparently loiter. Staying out late at night is also discouraged: ghosts, like barflys, enjoy the night. If a ghost is spotted it should be ignored in the hope

that it will leave. Families hold sumptuous banquets, offer paper gifts and burn incense to appease the dead. Believers crowd local Taoist and Buddhist temples to pray for their relatives.

Autumn

Mid Autumn Festival

Various venues (6439 1818). **Date** 18 Sept in 2005.

In Chinese, Zhongqiu Jie, aka the Moon Festival. It's a time for family gatherings, moon-gazing and eating the ubiquitous moon cakes. These creations are usually stuffed with red bean paste and egg yolk, or fruit and preserves. Some speciality stores create modern versions with chocolate or ice-cream. To understand the origins of the festival, children are told the story of a fairy who lives alone on the moon with her jade rabbit. A celestial general pays her an autumn visit and she dances to entertain him. Shadows visible on the moon on the day of the festival are thought to be their silhouettes.

Formula 1

Shanghai International Circuit, Anting, Jiading (9682 6999/www.icsh.sh.cn). **Admission** tbc. **Date** 26 Sept.

Formula 1 is the latest and most high profile addition to the city's international sporting calendar. September 2004 sees the Grand Prix debut of the city's newly-constructed racetrack, which is a 40-minute drive north-west of the city centre. *See p193* **On track for success**.

Heineken Open

Xianxia Tennis Centre, 1885 Hongqiao Lu, by Hongxu Lu, Hongqiao (6261 5984). **Date** mid-late Sept. **Admission** RMB 300-2,000.

Arts & Entertainment

The week-long Heineken Open has in the past attracted the biggest and best players in tennis – Andre Agassi and Michael Chang among them. Over the course of the year the Xianxia also plays host to other international tennis tournaments including the Masters Cup and Polo Open.

Shanghai Sweet-Scented Osmanthus Festival

Guilin Park, Caobao Lu, by Guilin Lu, Caohejing (6439 1818). **Date** late Sept-early Oct.

Around the time of the annual Mid Autumn Festival (*see p151*), thousands of trees in Guilin Park in the south-west of the city burst into bloom releasing a heady, blissful fragrance. The festival, which began in 1989, celebrates the occurrence with outdoor film screenings, magic and acrobatic shows, martial arts demonstrations, fashion shows and even a healthy baby competition.

Shanghai Tourism Festival

Various venues (6439 1818). **Date** mid Oct-early Nov.

A steady fixture since its launch in 1989, the tourism festival incorporates a fair diversity of goings on including a colourful float parade, model shows, firework extravaganzas, music, street parties, parachute displays, tea ceremonies and whatever else the tourism bureau can come up with as a means of promoting Shanghai's image.

Shanghai Biennale

Shanghai Art Museum, 325 Nanjing Xilu, Renmin Square (6327 4030). Metro Renmin Park or Square. **Date** Oct-Nov, even years. **Admission** RMB 15. **Map** p242 F4.

The Biennale offers the opportunity to size up where the arts in China are at – out on the edge if past shows are anything to go by (*see p163*). In addition to the Chinese, there is a sizeable contingent of participating foreign artists. In addition to the main event at the art museum there are also a host of other, often more experimental, even controversial, exhibits at other smaller galleries.

Winter

Shanghai International Arts Festival

Various venues (6439 1818). **Date** Nov.

This international arts fest has emerged as the highlight of the cultural calendar. For one whole month the city comes alive with artistic, theatrical and musical activity. Institutions such as the Shanghai Museum and Shanghai Art Museum put on blockbuster shows, while the Grand Theatre and others field some top-notch productions.

Toray Cup

The Bund (6467 4118). Metro Henan Lu. **Date** Nov. **Map** p243 J4.

Shanghai's street marathon takes over the city for a day one weekend each November. The event includes a less intense 21km half-marathon – plus a 4km fun run – for those not up to the full 42km long-haul. Expect congested traffic as many roads, including the Bund, are closed in order to accommodate the stampede of 10,000 racers.

Shanghai Asian Music Festival

Various venues (6439 1818). **Date** early Dec.

Aspiring Faye Wongs or Andy Laus bring their hopes of discovery to this festival, which features wannabe pop singers from across Asia competing in talent competitions. In addition, folk musos perform traditional songs and host seminars and workshops on topics ranging from music in the internet era to piracy in Asia.

Longhua Bell Festival

Longhua Temple, 2853 Longhua Lu, by Longhua Park, Xuhui (6456 6085). **Date** 31 Dec. **Admission** RMB 15. **Map** p240 C4.

The origins of this festival are slightly hazy – it appears to be a Buddhist thing but is set on the Gregorian calendar. The events take place over the course of the evening and include lion dragon dances, ritual bell ringing, of course, and monks displaying their new cassocks.

Chinese New Year

Various locations. **Date** 9 Feb in 2005.

In Chinese it's Yuandan, or Chun Jie (Spring Festival). Families celebrate new beginnings and tidy up any unfinished business during this, the biggest fixture on the Chinese calendar. Officially, it lasts three days but often the festivities stretch to around two weeks. On the first day, families gather in homes or restaurants to eat special meals symbolising good fortune, prosperity and health. Typical dishes include dumplings (eaten for luck), blood clams (representing wealth) and fish balls (a symbol of family harmony). Fireworks are set off to scare away evil spirits. Visitors who want to experience the pyrotechnic blowout should try to get a window seat in a tall building or hotel. Another good way to participate is to book a table at an upscale Chinese restaurant, where families feast noisily on traditional foods and exchange cash-laden red envelopes (bookings should be made at least a few weeks in advance). There are also dragon and lion dancers and special services held at the Jingan and Longhua temples.

Lantern Festival

Yu Gardens, 115 Yuyuan Lu, Old City (6328 0602). **Date** 23 Feb in 2005. **Admission** RMB 10. **Map** p243 J5.

In Chinese it's Yuan Xiao, and it marks the end of the season. It is customary to display a red lantern outside the home so that the Taoist Lord of Heaven can visit and bestow luck and happiness on the morally deserving. People wander the streets carrying lanterns, but the largest and most impressive display is at the Yu Gardens, which looks very beautiful but gets just as crowded. Lots of *yuanxiao* and *tangyuan* – sweet dumplings – are consumed.

Children

There's plenty to entertain Little Emperors (and Little Empresses).

Shanghai Zoo.
See p155.

If you believe the ambitious city planners, by 2010 Shanghai will have its own Universal Studios theme park, undercover ski runs and several ice rinks. There's talk of a Disneyland too. Until then, however, the city is ill equipped when it comes to keeping the kids distracted. The weather is a major problem. At various times of the year this can range from torrential rain to blistering sun and unbearable humidity. At such times options are confined to shopping (snap up some bargain kids' booty), museums (and not many of them) or possibly a movie (though, again, cinemas screening English-language fare are few: *see p157*). If you have such a thing, it's a good idea to bring along a laptop or portable DVD player; children's films and cartoons on DVD are easy and cheap finds in Shanghai (*see p133* **Faking it**).

Practicalities

It is a good idea to give your children a copy of the hotel address written in Chinese characters, and the hotel phone number, just in case you get separated while out. Also, while public toilets are reasonably clean, many will be without toilet paper, so carry some of your own, plus wetwipes for cleaning hands.

Where to stay

Shanghai hotels are geared primarily towards business travellers and tailor their facilities accordingly. With advance notice, most high-end hotels can at least provide cots, high chairs and babysitting (RMB 30-50 per hour). Hotel swimming pools, though, may refuse to admit children, especially if there is no shallow end.

The Shanghai Centre, where the **Portman Ritz-Carlton** (*see p39*) is located, has a kids' playroom (for ages six months to six years), open to hotel guests for a daily fee of RMB 50. The hotel's pool can also be used by children with parental supervision. The **Hilton** (250 Huashan Lu, French Concession, 6248 0000) has a pool that kids can use, again under parental supervision. The **Novotel Atlantis** (728 Pudong Dadao, by Fushan Lu, Pudong, 5036

Ocean Aquarium.
See p155.

6666) also has a pool accessible to children, and on Sunday it hosts a kid-friendly brunch with half-price grub for six- to 12-year-olds (free for under-sixes), plus there's a kids' play area complete with play-gym and electronic games.

For anyone staying a week or more, a better bet may be a serviced apartment. Try the **Shanghai Centre Serviced Apartments** (6279 8502), which are at the heart of downtown surrounded by shops and restaurants. The **Shanghai Racquet Club** (555 Jinfeng Lu, Minghang, 2201 0000) also has a few short-stay apartments available over the summer to non-members. These come with pools, an artificial mini-beach and tennis courts. It is essential to book well in advance; note that the club is a 40 to 50 minute shuttle-bus trip from the city centre.

Sightseeing

For kid-friendly activities, the Bund and Pudong riverfront beat other areas of town sticky hands down. There's the riverboat tour (*see p47*) and the sound and light show of the **Tourist Tunnel** (*see p88*) under the Huangpu River. Once over on the far side of the water there's the **Oriental Pearl Tower** (*see p89*) with its fantastic views and, between it and the river, the **Natural Wild Insect Kingdom** (*see p155*), while just to the north is the **Ocean Aquarium** (*see p155*).

Other museums that might entertain include the interactive **Science and Technology Museum** (*see p90*), which is also in Pudong, and boasts sound and light displays, an indoor rainforest and an amusement area. It also has two IMAX cinemas with documentaries on topics such as dinosaurs and sea life.

On Renmin Square, the **Urban Planning Centre** (*see p59*) contains a reconstruction of an Old Shanghai street and a huge scale model of what city planners envisage for their buzzing metropolis by 2020.

Attractions

Aquaria 21

Gate 4, 21 Changfeng Park, 451 Daduhe Lu, by Jingshajiang Lu, Putou (5281 8888). Metro Zhongshan Park. **Open** 8.30am-6pm daily. **Admission** RMB 110; RMB 80 children; free children under 1m. **No credit cards. Map** p240 B3.

About half an hour north-west of the city centre, this impressive underground theme park has over 10,000 sq m (107,500 sq ft) of tanks filled with sharks, fish and penguins, plus a new 2,000-seat stadium with Beluga whales and fur seals. The foyer is designed like an airport, with a 25-seat cinema that simulates a flight to South America. Visitors go on a journey through Inca temples, waterfalls and the Amazon jungle before reaching fresh- and saltwater tanks. The exhibit is good for all ages, and children over ten can scuba dive (under supervision) with some of the marine life, including sharks. The complex is housed inside/under Changfeng Park, which itself has amusement rides and a large boating lake. Highly recommended.

Natural Wild Insect Kingdom

1 Fenghe Lu, Lujiazui, Pudong (5840 5921). Metro Lujiazui. **Open** 9am-5pm Mon-Fri; 9am-5.30pm Sat, Sun. **Admission** RMB 35; RMB 20 children; free children under 0.8m. **No credit cards. Map** p243 K3.
Boasting over 200 different kinds of insects from as far afield as Africa and Latin America, this place has endless appeal for young bug-catchers. The alarming and deadly stuff is dead and pinned down in display cases, but visitors are allowed to handle small beetles and other insects. You can even buy real live creepy crawlies from the shop.

Ocean Aquarium

158 Yincheng Beilu, by Dongyuan Lu, Pudong Park (5877 9988). Metro Lujiazui. **Open** 9am-9pm daily. **Admission** RMB 110; RMB 70 children; free children under 0.8m. **Credit** AmEx, DC, MC, V. **Map** p243 L3.
An impressive joint Chinese-Singaporean venture, the Ocean Aquarium is one of the largest attractions of its kind in Asia. The highlight is the 155m (509ft) underwater clear viewing tunnel offering 270-degree views of sharks, turtles and exotic fish – of which there are some 13,000 representing 300 species.

Shanghai Zoo

2381 Hongqiao Lu, by Hami Lu, Hongqiao (6268 7775). Bus 925 from Renmin Square or No.4 Tour Bus Line from Shanghai Stadium. **Open** Oct-Mar 7am-5pm daily; *Apr-Sept* 6.30am-5.30pm daily. **Admission** RMB 30; RMB 24 children; free children under 1.2m. **No credit cards. Map** p240 A3.
Not a model institution by any means, but this is at least better than most zoos in China. The giant pandas invariably disappoint, spending most of their days sleeping, but other animals including giraffes, seals and monkeys are usually a hit. One virtue of the place is the extensive green spaces (it used to be a golf club for the British), making it ideal for picnics. There is also an amusement park with bumper cars and a Ferris wheel, and an indoor playground for small children. It takes about 25-30 minutes to get here by taxi from the city centre.

Gardens, parks & playgrounds

Although it is an unremittingly urban space, children might enjoy **Renmin Square** for its kite flyers. There are also, predictably enough, kite sellers. At the **Yu Gardens** (*see p68*) kids might enjoy partaking in a traditional tea ceremony at the teahouse on the lake; they'll certainly love climbing the ladder-like steps to the upper levels to look at the view.

More conventional (indoor) playgrounds are found at the **Yao Han Department Store** (501 Zhangyang Lu, by Pudong Nanlu, Pudong, 6210 5886) and at the **Xiangyang kids' play area** (cnr Nanjing Xilu & Maoming Lu, Jingan, open 10am-5pm, RMB 10).

Century Park

1001 Jinxiu Lu, by Shiji Dadao, Pudong (5833 5621). Metro Century Park. **Open** 5.30am-6pm daily. **Admission** RMB 10; free children under 1.2m. **No credit cards. Map** p241 F3.
Kids can amuse themselves with bicycles, tandems and covered pedal cars for hire (all at RMB 20-40), or bring your own rollerblades. Century also incorporates a wildlife park, picnic grounds, a miniature golf course and waterways with pedal boats at RMB 30 per hour. For more on the park, *see p90.*

Fuxing Park

Gaolan Lu, by Sinan Lu, French Concession (5386 0662). Metro Huangpi Nanlu. **Open** 6am-6pm daily. **Admission** RMB 2; free children under 1.2m. **No credit cards. Map** p247 E7.
This survivor of old Frenchtown has a rose garden, amusement rides, bumper cars and remote-control boats to steer on a large pond. While the attractions aren't exactly cutting edge, the park is convenient to reach from the centre of town.

Zhongshan Park

780 Changning Lu, by Yuyuan Lu, Hongqiao (6210 5806). Metro Zhongshan Park. **Open** 5am-6pm daily. **Admission** RMB 2; free children under 1.2m. **No credit cards. Map** p240 B3.
Inside Zhongshan is one of Shanghai's biggest amusement parks, with everything from merry go rounds and bouncy castles to dodgem cars and paintball. Animal fans will like the large fish tanks and peacocks. The park has a huge indoor kids' playground, Fun Dazzle (open 9am-5pm), with tunnels and mazes, slippery slides and swings.

Eating & drinking

Small, grumbling stomachs shouldn't be hard to appease in Shanghai. For fast-food fixes, there are plenty of McDonald's, KFCs and Starbucks, plus local noodle and dumpling joints.

If you are visiting the kiddie-friendly sights in Pudong, there is a Häagen-Dazs (first floor, Yao Han Department Store, 501 Zhangyang Lu, by Pudong Nanlu) for ice-creams and the Paulaner Brauhaus (next to the Shangrila Hotel, on Binjiang Dadao, 6888 3935) for casual German food and beer – both places have great views and are kid-friendly.

Many upscale restaurants and hotels relax at the weekend for family-friendly brunches, with some of the hotels even adding supervised kids' play clubs and kids' menus. Worth trying are the **Four Seasons** (*see p39*), the **Portman**

Arts & Entertainment

Ritz-Carlton (*see p39*) and the **Westin** (*see p34*). Brunch at the panoramic **M on the Bund** (*see p99*) includes a kids' menu, and **Mesa** (*see p116*) is an

At other times, **O'Malleys** (*see p125*) is an Irish pub with a huge sunny garden and baby-changing facilities in the (clean) toilets. **Park 97**, inside Fuxing Park, offers Italian and Japanese eats, plus a Western-style brunch on the weekend. A few tables outside overlook the park where the kids can gambol while the adults linger over coffee. The open-air mall that is **Xintiandi** is usually a big hit with youngsters for its myriad fast-food outlets (including McDonald's and noodle joints), cafés (Starbucks) and ice-cream (VenIce and Häagen Dazs).

To put together a picnic, the bakery at the **Hilton** (250 Huashan Lu, French Concession) has ready-made gourmet sandwiches, quiches and other bakery items, as does the bakery at the **Westin** (*see p34*). A good and cheap supermarket is **Parkson Supermarket** in the basement of Parkson department store (on the corner of Huaihai Zhonglu and Shanxi Nanlu) – this is also a decent place to pick up baby supplies. **City Shopping**, at the Shanghai Centre on Nanjing Xilu, is not so cheap but it does have lots of great stuff.

Shopping

Shopping for children in Shanghai can net some real bargains. Most of the world's biggest children's brands for clothes and shoes, plus some toys, are made in factories outside Shanghai. As a result, you will find samples, overruns, fakes and plenty of the real thing in the wealth of small shops around the French Concession (try Changle Lu for a concentration of kids' clothes stores) and in the markets. English-language children's books can be picked up at the **Foreign Languages Bookstore** (*see p136*) on Fuzhou Lu.

Decathlon
393 Yinxiao Lu, by Longyang Lu, Pudong (5045 3888). Metro Longyang Lu. **Open** 9am-8pm Mon-Thur, Sun; 9am-9pm Fri, Sat. **Credit** MC, V.
This large sports goods warehouse store is a 20-minute metro or taxi ride from the city centre but worth the trip for stocking up on things like cheap trainers, sportswear (for both children and adults), racquets, camping and hiking gear. Almost every sport you can think of – from golf to horse-riding and swimming – is covered.

Isetan
6th floor, Westgate Mall, 1038 Nanjing Xilu, by Jiangning Lu, Jingan (6272 1111 ext 424). Metro Shimen Yilu. **Open** 10am-9pm daily. **Credit** AmEx, DC, MC, V. **Map** p249 D4.

An upscale Japanese department store within the Westgate Mall (*see p130*). Isetan fills six floors with upmarket clothes and accessories; the top floor is given over to children's clothes and toys including some good-value Chinese brands.

Ni Hong Children's Plaza
10 Puan Lu, by Yanan Donglu, Xintiandi (5383 6218/ www.shnhgc.com). Metro Huangpi Nanlu. **Open** 9.30am-8pm daily. **No credit cards. Map** p242 G5.
This underground market is the best place to go for cheap, quality kids' gear. The entrance is down some stairs near the corner of Jinling Lu and Puan Lu, near the bus station. Dozens of shops sell brand-name clothes and shoes for all sizes. Bargain down the price and go for an extra discount if you are buying multiple items from the one store.

Oriental Plaza
8 Caoxi Beilu, by Zhaojiabang Lu, Xujiahui (6487 0000/www.orient-shop.com). Metro Xujiahui. **Open** 10am-10pm daily. **Credit** AmEx, MC, V. **Map** p246 A9.
This local department store, depsite being one of the oldest in town, has the best selection of foreign-brand toys and baby supplies.

Xiangyang Market
999 Huaihai Zhonglu, by Xiangyang Nanlu, French Concession (5403 5437). Metro Shanxi Nanlu. **Open** 9am-8.30pm daily. **Map** p247 D6.
A notorious fake market with many stalls devoted to kids' clothes, shoes, toys and video games. In 2004 the market was rumoured to be under threat of closure, so phone ahead before leaving. *See p132.*

Services

Childminding
Temporary childcare can be difficult to arrange at short notice – check with your hotel before you book. The plusher hotels will generally have some babysitting services in-house.

Health
Shanghai has two special children's hospitals, both good. Generally, some English-speaking staff will be on hand. For more general information on healthcare, *see p219.*

Children's Hospital of Fudan University
Opposite Zhongshan Hospital, 183 Fenglin Lu, by Qingzhen Lu, French Concession (5452 4666). Metro Hengshan Lu. **Credit** MC, V. **Map** p246 C9.

Shanghai Children's Medical Center
3rd floor, 1678 Dongfang Lu, by Pujian Lu, Pudong (5839 5238/5873 2020 ext 6172). Metro Dongfang Lu. **Credit** MC, V.

Film

DVD pirates threaten cinemas, but the Shanghai film industry is full steam ahead.

Once upon a time they called it Shollywood. By the 1930s Shanghai had a studio system, scores of cinemas and even its own tragic starlets. But the glory days were short-lived. After the Communist takeover in 1949, film was refashioned as revolutionary propaganda and glamour went out of style. For 30 years, the industry was tightly controlled, with scripts pumped out by government bureaux determined to promote the latest initiatives of Chairman Mao and his cronies. The end of the Cultural Revolution (1966-76) saw the rebirth of popular cinema, however, and the masses flocked back to the movie houses.

With its prestigious Film Academy (whose alumni include virtually every successful native actor, director and cinematographer since 1980), Beijing perceives itself as the natural home of modern Chinese cinema. In 1986, when Bernardo Bertolucci dropped by to shoot *The Last Emperor* in the Forbidden City, the capital's cinematic dominance seemed to be confirmed. But that same year, a man named Spielberg started production on *Empire of the Sun*, sections of which were shot on the Bund, and Shanghai came into its own once again.

Some of the best-known 'Shanghai' films, in fact, never came here at all. For 1932's *Shanghai Express*, Marlene Dietrich barely ventured beyond California, and although Madonna and Sean Penn headed east in 1986 for *Shanghai Surprise*, they got no further than Hong Kong.

Spielberg inspired a trickle of intrepid producers to give Shanghai a go in the 1990s, and in 2002 director John Dahl (*Joyride*) plumped for the Shanghai Film Studio backlot to shoot a large chunk of his World War II epic *The Great Raid*. With its Hollywood-sized budget, stellar cast (including Joseph Fiennes and Connie Nielsen) and enormous crew, the film injected much needed morale (and money) into the local industry. Perhaps most importantly, the Miramax-backed flick was not set in China at all; Shanghai was a stand-in for 1940s Manila, in the Philippines. 'We made the right choice,' said producer Marty Katz at the time. 'Shanghai just had the right look.'

Now that the city is established as a decent – and relatively cheap – production base with the potential to stand in for pretty much anywhere bar the Arctic, more films have headed this way.

Lou Ye's moody **Suzhou River**.

Hip British director Michael Winterbottom (*24 Hour Party People*) chose Shanghai as the setting for *Code 46*, a futuristic love story starring Tim Robbins and Samantha Morton. Hong Kong's Wong Kar-Wai recently shot large sections of his much delayed *2046* here. At the time of writing, Milla Jovovich was in town filming Kurt Wimmer's *Ultraviolet*. And more are on the way.

Local filmmakers are also starting to take to Shanghai. In 1995 director Zhang Yimou put the city back on the map with his 1930s gangster flick *Shanghai Triad*, starring Gong Li. For a few years after that, you couldn't turn a corner without bumping into film sets peopled by men in trilbies and women in *qipaos* and feather boas. In 2002 Lou Ye's *Suzhou River* brought present-day Shanghai back into fashion. An edgy tale of love gone wrong set on the banks of the city's main waterway, the film beckoned in a new filmic voice for Shanghai. Underground filmmakers – who work under the keen radar of the official censors – are starting to reclaim Shanghai as their own; stories about sex, drugs and disillusionment are back with a vengeance.

Not the reel thing

'DVD! VCD! CD!' It's a Shanghai mantra, shouted by the hundreds of vendors who hawk pirated films and music on the city streets. Pirated entertainment is rife across China, and Shanghai is no exception. Even the more conservative estimates suggest that 90 per cent of the films watched here are illegal copies.

And it's no surprise, if you think about it. With foreign movie imports restricted to 20 a year, how else does a discerning movie lover keep up with the latest releases? A cinema ticket costs around two days of the average salary, while DVDs sell for just RMB 8 a pop (about 55 pence). And although they sell cheaply, DVDs bring phenomenal injections of cash into the national economy.

On virtually every block in Shanghai, you will find legitimate shops peddling a mix of officially released and pirated DVDs, along with their fading cousins, VCDs. Quite how they avoid the much publicised regular government crackdowns on copyright theft is anybody's guess. (If you do see a policeman in one of these shops, he's probably just browsing for some off-duty entertainment.)

Contrary to the general belief in Hollywood, most Asian pirated films are not shot on camcorders during cinema screenings. Though poor-quality 'cinema copies' (*dianyin ban*) do crop up now and then, the majority of pirated DVDs these days look and sound like the real thing (they are known as 'laser disk copies' or *dadie ban*) and were clearly nicked at source. Hollywood, take note.

Duff disks that just won't play in any DVD machine are, however, common. And, if you are tempted by the mind-bogglingly vast array

of pirated films on offer (everything from Golden-era Hollywood to Dogme, Manga and the hottest hits of the day), beware. It's not always what it says on the tin. An early copy of *The Matrix: Reloaded*, on the streets before the film was even released in the US, turned out to be *Johnny Mnemonic*. Film fans were even more surprised in early 2004 when *Lord of the Rings: 4* turned up. Gullible purchasers found themselves watching a low-budget 1980s fantasy flick.

For an illicit industry, however, film piracy has a rather refined sense of customer service. Most shops will refund or replace disks that won't play, and if your copy of *Brief Encounter* turns out to be *Close Encounters of the Third Kind*, you can usually swap it for something else or get your money back.

In 2004 Shanghai is set for another big film industry milestone with the opening of the Shanghai Film Academy. In the 1930s Shanghai's film schools were famous, but the last of them closed during the Cultural Revolution, leaving Beijing to dominate film studies for the next three decades. A local film school will be a big boost to a city whose film studio still kicks out more than 20 films a year.

Cinemas

With fewer than 3,000 screens nationwide, China suffers from a serious lack of cinemas. Shanghai is doing its best to compensate, with a multitude of new multiplexes – most of them

located in shopping malls – desperately trying to wean the masses off pirate DVDs (*see above* **Not the reel thing**). With film exhibition now open to foreign investment, Warner Bros, UME, Kodak and Golden Harvest all operate swanky new city-centre cinemas.

Film buffs are likely to be disappointed with the limited fare, however. China's movie laws restrict foreign film imports to 20 a year, and most of those are Hollywood blockbusters. Beijing's Film Bureau has a strict 'No Sex Please, We're Chinese' policy, so films featuring dangly bits are likely to suffer the censor's scissors. Anything that shows China in a bad light (*Tomb Raider 2*, for example, with its Chinese triads) is likely to be banned altogether.

Arts & Entertainment

Despite the quota, foreign productions dominate at the box office, taking 60 per cent or more of total revenue each year.

Dubbing is the norm for foreign films, though the cinemas listed below regularly play original language versions. It pays to call ahead and check which print will be playing at what time. Most Chinese films are not subtitled in English.

Multiplexes have brought with them international multiplex prices. Expect to pay RMB 50 and upwards for a ticket, more during opening week and at the weekend. Online and phone bookings are usually possible – though service in most places is in Chinese only.

For more adventurous programming, you'll have to look beyond the licensed cinema chains. The **Canadian Consulate** (6279 8400) and **German Consulate** (6391 2068 ext 602) both organise regular screenings of films from, unsurprisingly, Canada and Germany. **Ciné-Club de l'Alliance** (6357 5388) does the same for Francophiles. For underground local (often subtitled) and international cinema, check out **ddmwarehouse** (*see p161*). **Maria's Choice** (1380 163 6497, www.topica.com/lists/MariasChoice) is a film club that meets monthly to watch indie films (directors sometimes attend) at different locations around town including ddmwarehouse and Kodak CinemaWorld (*see below*).

Kodak CinemaWorld
5th floor, Metro City, 1111 Zhaojiabang Lu, by Caoxi Beilu, Xujiahui (6426 8181 ext 168/ http://cinemaworld.kodak.com/english.htm). Metro Xujiahui. **Tickets** RMB 50-60. **No credit cards.** **Map** p246 A9.

One of Shanghai's better-established multiplexes, Kodak does its best to play a decent mix of local and international fare, as well as hosting special film events including Maria's Choice (*see above*). English-language films are played almost exclusively in their original version. The cinema's website is in English and it provides profiles of upcoming international releases, as well as listing showtimes.

Paradise Theatre (Yongle Gong)
308 Anfu Lu, by Wukang Lu, French Concession (6742 2606). Metro Changshu Lu. **Tickets** RMB 40. **No credit cards.** **Map** p246 C6.

The Paradise is a taste of what cinemas used to be like in Shanghai. A decade ago this was the only venue in town playing undubbed foreign films. Those days are long gone, and the drab-looking entrance, dingy railway waiting-room lobby and cramped screening halls don't bear comparison to the city's newer, shinier multiplex arrivals. But nestled above beautiful tree-lined Anfu Lu, the cinema still has its plus sides: it gets most of the big-hitting foreign movies on or fairly close to their Chinese release date, it's hardly ever sold out and it features some wonderful retro tiling.

Paradise Warner Cinema City
6th floor, Grand Gateway, 1 Hongqiao Lu, by Huashan Lu, Xujiahui (6407 6622/www.paradise warner.com/index-en.htm). Metro Xujiahui. **Tickets** RMB 50-60. **No credit cards.** **Map** p246 A8.

Warner Bros' first foray into China looks and feels like a top-notch multiplex. Nestled on the sixth floor of a mall, it's rapidly gaining in popularity, with even late-night screenings often close to full. All the trimmings are here: thick carpets, lots of screens, popcorn by the bucketful and foreign films screened alternately in English and dubbed Mandarin. Paradise was also the first cinema in China to install a digital projector. Its website details films and showtimes, although the info is not always up to date.

Shanghai Film Art Centre
160 Xinhua Lu, by Huahai Xilu, Changning (6280 4088). Metro Xujiahui. **Tickets** RMB 50-60. **No credit cards.** **Map** p246 A8.

About as close to an arts cinema as you'll get in this city, the Film Art Centre is home to most of the major screenings during the Shanghai International Film Festival (*see below*); it gets its fair share of VIPs if you fancy some celeb-spotting in June. Film buffs should enjoy its retro-stylish lobby, featuring a shop that stocks Chinese-language film books as well as, bizarrely, irons. All the latest films, local and foreign.

UME International Cineplex
5th floor, No.6 Lane 123, Xingye Lu, by Madang Lu, Xintiandi (6384 1122 ext 807). Metro Huangpi Nanlu. **Tickets** RMB 50-60. **No credit cards.** **Map** p244 F6.

One of Shanghai's newest multiplexes, UME is also located in one of its trendiest areas, Xintiandi, fitting in perfectly among the hip boutiques and nightclubs. With a mix of moneyed local and international customers, the cinema plays foreign films in their original versions, plus most current Chinese films.

Festivals

If you are in town in June, it's definitely worth checking out the **Shanghai International Film Festival** or SIFF. In business since 1993 this is China's only globally recognised movie fest, and it usually attracts a few stars. It's worth noting that films shown during SIFF are outside the official import quota and largely uncut by the censors, so this is your big chance to glut yourself on the sins of the silver screen. Don't waste it! *See also p150.*

Shanghai International Film Festival (SIFF)
Information: 11th floor, STV Mansions, 298 Weihai Lu, Jingan (6253 7115/www.siff.com). Metro Shimen Yilu. **Date** mid June.

▶ For other **films with a Shanghai connection**, see *p231*.

Galleries

Demand for contemporary Chinese art is increasing, but not necessarily among the Chinese.

Stoned socialists at **ShanghArt Warehouse**. *See p162.*

Shanghai might be China's former and future economic hub but, when compared with Beijing, it's traditionally seen as a cultural dwarf. That has started to change. A series of recent events has given this centre of commerce a little added artistic credibility. Buoyed by the wave of expats and returnees flooding the city in the '90s, in 1994 Swiss entrepreneur Lorentz Helbling opened ShanghArt – the first privately owned contemporary art gallery in Shanghai. In 1996 Shanghai inaugurated its Art Biennale. Since then, new galleries have been popping up all over town, including several heavy-hitters such as BizArt, Art Scene China and, most recently, the Shanghai Gallery of Art (SGA), whose opening in March 2004 attracted massed media, event sponsors and just about anyone who was anyone in Shanghai society.

Critics are quick to point out that it is precisely high-end galleries like the SGA that are the problem with Shanghai, where art equals commerce. But at the same time, there is a less glamorous 'underground' scene that

has emerged among the spalled concrete and rusting iron of an industrial wasteland along Suzhou Creek (*see p162* **Alt art**). Even these galleries, however, still rely heavily on foreign patronage. Conceptual gallery Eastlink, for instance, reports that 80 to 85 per cent of Chinese art is bought by Westerners, 15 to 20 per cent by foreign Chinese and only one per cent by local Chinese. Happily, foreign interest extends beyond Shanghai's expat community. Chinese artists are increasingly cropping up overseas. In 2003 Shanghai artist Zhou Tiehai contributed a controversial portrait of Rudy Giuliani with elephant dung to a show at the Whitney Museum in New York, while the same year there was a show of China's avant garde at the Pompidou Centre in Paris.

For more traditional permanent collections of art visit the **Shanghai Art Museum** (*see p59*) on Renmin Square and the **Doland Modern Art Museum** (*see p92*) in Hongkou. For details of what's on where check the listings in the monthly magazine *that's Shanghai*.

Galleries

Art Scene China

No.8, Lane 37, Fuxing Xilu, by Wulumuqi Lu, French Concession (6437 0631/www.artscenechina.com). Metro Changshu Lu. **Open** 10.30am-7.30pm daily. **Map** p246 B7.

What began as a website in 1997 became a bricks-and-mortar gallery in Hong Kong, relocating to Shanghai in 2002. Housed in a beautiful 1930s villa, the gallery hosts regular exhibitions by the 25 or more Chinese artists it represents. Their work is almost uniformly figurative and safe – which is not to say unappealing – ensuring that openings are hugely popular with the expat crowd. The excellent website features artists' portfolios and critical essays. ASC also has a warehouse gallery in the Moganshan Lu art area (*see p162* **Alt art**).

Aura Gallery

5th floor, 713 Dongdaming Lu, by Gaoyang Lu, Hongkou (6595 0901/www.aura-art.com). Metro Renmin Guangchnag. **Open** 10am-5pm Tue-Sun. **Map** p243 L2.

Founded in 2000 by art buff William Zhang, Aura majors in young artists born in the 1960s and '70s (the YCAs, as it were). Their work varies widely in medium and subject, from Han Lei's dreamlike art inspired by Chinese calligraphy to Han Chongwu's black-and-white photo documentation of religious statuary found in the provinces. The gallery itself is housed in 700sq m (7,500sq ft) of warehouse space on the banks of the Huangpu River; it's a five-minute taxi ride from the Peace Hotel.

ddmwarehouse

3rd floor, 713 Dongdaming Lu, by Gaoyang Lu, Hongkou (3501 3212/www.ddmwarehouse.com). Metro Renmin Guangchnag. **Open** 9.30am-6pm Tue-Sat; by appointment only Mon, Sun. **Map** p243 L2.

Two floors below Aura (*see above*), ddm hosts exhibitions of contemporary paintings, photography, video art and sculpture. This is supplemented with an often innovative programme of cultural events, such as documentary film screenings and concerts of electronic music. The gallery lacks polish and some exhibitions are lacklustre, but for certain art lovers this only adds to the 'underground' appeal.

Deke Erh Centre

Building 2B, Lane 210, Taikang Lu, by Ruijin Erlu, French Concession (6415 0675/www.han-yuan.com). Metro Shanxi Nanlu. **Open** 9.30am-5.30pm daily. **Map** p247 E8.

Deke Erh is a photographer, traveller and collector, and a one-man cultural movement. His projects include the Deke Erh Folk Art Museum, the Old China Hand Press – publishers of glossy photobooks on Shanghai's architectural heritage – and the Old China Hand Reading Room, a café-cum-bookstore (*see p80*). In the words of his webpages: 'Being an intellectual, Deke Erh's creativity never ceases'. This, his gallery, occupies a former warehouse and

is part of the Taikang Lu Art Factory development (*see p181*). The main space is dedicated to romanticised oils with Tibetan motifs but it also serves as a venue for photo exhibitions, occasional jazz and classic recitals, drama performances and opera.

Gang of One Gallery

3rd floor, Training Centre, Lane 461, Tianshan Lu, by Shuicheng Nanlu, Gubei (6259 9716/gangfeng@yeah.net). Metro Zhongshan Park. **Open** by appointment only.

This tiny gallery sits at the end of a small lane in a residential area (last house on the right, third floor). It's devoted to an ongoing exhibition featuring Gang Feng Wang's photos of life in the urban neighbourhoods of Shanghai, as well as images of everyday life in rural villages. Wang is a former farmer, violin player and factory worker and his work possesses a simple beauty. Call in advance or email.

Haishangshan Art Centre

618 Wuzhong Lu, by Hongxu Lu, Hongqiao (6406 4626). Metro Zhongshan Park. **Open** 10am-6pm daily.

The Haishangshan is Taiwanese-run but the artists exhibited here include both internationals and local Chinese. Past shows have included installations by Qin Chong inspired by water, fire and air, and installations by Qin Feng combining performance art with calligraphy. It's a generous display space of 600sq m (6,400sq ft), with bedrooms and studio space on the second-floor 'art hotel' for visiting creatives.

ShanghArt Gallery. See p163.

Liu Haisu Art Centre

1660 Hongqiao Lu, by Shuicheng Lu, Hongqiao (6270 1018). Metro Zhongshan Park. **Open** 9am-4pm daily.

This strikingly futuristic, state-owned art centre is better known for its collections of Chinese antiques, public reading room and Haisu bookstore, but several times a year curator/collector Mr Liu Haisu gives over one of the halls to a hanging of contemporary art. In 2004 this included a show called 'Unrelated to Reality', featuring the work of 15 mixed media Chinese artists. Shows tend to run for not more than one week; keep an eye on the local free press for details.

Peninsula Gallery

2nd floor, Building 5, Peninsula Garden, Lane 1518, Xikang Lu, by Yichang Lu, Jingan (6276 3721). Metro Jingan Temple. **Open** 9am-5pm Mon-Fri. **Map** p248 B1.

Hidden away on the ground floor of a real estate company, the Peninsula is funded and managed by a collective of ten Shanghai artists. At its regular exhibits of local and overseas artists, the quality of work varies wildly. Much of the time expect unimaginative decorative watercolours of Chinese village life; on occasion the place throws up surprises such as a show by Japanese artist Yayoi Kusama, famed for her prolific period in 1960s New York.

Alt art

New York has its Meatpacking District and London has Hoxton: Shanghai has Moganshan Lu. In a grim industrial park beside fetid Suzhou Creek, Moganshan's chill warehouses offer a solution to the high rents and cramped spaces faced by artists elsewhere in the city. So it's here, in a series of cheap, vast and far-from-pretty workspaces that Shanghai's underground art scene thrives.

The artists moved in towards the end of the 1990s and around 20 now have studios in the area. They've gradually been joined by a handful of major galleries (some of which are listed below). These art spaces host many of the edgiest and most interesting art events in the city including, memorably, the Biennale satellite show at the Eastlink in 2000 entitled 'Fuck Off'.

A round of the galleries is best ended with a stop at artist Xue Song's hole-in-the-wall bar the Boiler Room, next to the ShanghART Warehouse and a favourite post-opening hangout. The slogan above the door reads, 'Gaogao xinxin shanban, pingping anan huijia' or 'Go to work happy, return home safely'.

The easiest way to get to Moganshan Lu, which is just north of the Jade Buddha Temple, is by taxi. Given the constant rumours of redevelopment in the area and corresponding threat of the bulldozers moving in, phone in advance to check these places are still open.

Art Scene Warehouse

2nd floor, Building 4, 50 Moganshan Lu, by Aomen Lu, Jingan (6277 2499/www.artscene warehouse.com). Metro Shanghai Train Station. **Open** 11am-8pm daily. **Map** p248 C2.

A huge 2,000sq m (21,500 sq ft) space used to showcase many of Art Scene China's roster of artists (*see also p161*).

ArtSea Studio & Gallery

2nd floor, Building 9, 50 Moganshan Lu, by Xisuzhou Lu, Jingan (6227 8380). Metro Shanghai Train Station. **Open** 10.30am-6pm Tue-Sun. **Map** p248 C2.

Dvir Bar Gal, an Israeli photojournalist based in Shanghai, founded this place to show contemporary art and photography.

BizArt

4th floor, Building 7, 50 Moganshan Lu, by Aomen Lu, Jingan (6277 5358/www.biz-art.com). Metro Shanghai Train Station. **Open** 10am-6pm daily. **Map** p248 C2.

Launched in 1998 by three Europeans, BizArt represents some 40 artists (with a strong showing in multimedia) and stages regular exhibitions, as well as art exchanges, live music, theatre and film screenings.

Eastlink

5th floor, Building 6, 50 Moganshan Lu, by Aomen Lu, Jingan (6276 9932). Metro Shanghai Train Station. **Open** 10.30am-5.30pm Tue-Sun. **Map** p248 C2.

Founded by a local returnee, who lived 12 years in Sydney, Eastlink is maybe the most avant garde of the city's galleries. During the Shanghai Biennale in 2000 'Fuck Off' featured animal carcasses, self-mutilation and a photograph of an artist eating a human foetus – until it was closed by the police.

ShanghART Warehouse

50 Moganshan Lu, by Aomen Lu, Jingan (6359 3923). Metro Shanghai Train Station. **Open** by appointment only. **Map** p248 C2.

Lorentz Helbling, owner of ShanghART, uses his warehouse space for storing as well as exhibiting various works and big installation pieces. Call beforehand to set up a tour.

Room With a View

12th floor, 479 Nanjing Donglu, by Fujian Lu, the Bund (6352 0256/www.topart.cn). Metro Henan Lu. **Open** 3.30-10pm daily. **Map** p242 H4.

RWV is a bar (a weird combination of frosted glass, black leather, and corrugated iron) with a small exhibition space attached. The place is renowned for its 'events', which in the past have included a 'leather and fur' party and a 'handsome man meet beautiful girl' party. Otherwise, art exhibitions lean toward political Pop art, installations and photography. There are also regular documentary film screenings.

Shanghai College of Fine Arts

99 Shangda Lu, by Hutai Lu, Baoshan (6613 3637). Metro Shanghai Railway Station. **Open** 8.30am-4.30pm Mon-Fri (during term time).

A spacious gallery attached to Shanghai's most important arts school. It occasionally features works by students, as well as foreign artists. Also in the vicinity and worth a look is Mi Qiu's Studio (2nd floor, 311 Shenhua Lu, 6251 6589); Mi Qiu is a tutor at the fine arts college and he frequently hosts exhibitions.

Shanghai Gallery of Art

3rd floor, Three on the Bund, 3 Zhongshan Dongyilu, by Guandong Lu, the Bund (6323 3355/ www.threeonthebund.com). Metro Henan Lu. **Open** 11am-11pm Tue-Sun. **Map** p243 J4.

The city's ritziest gallery, the SGA is part of the Three on the Bund complex and so shares lodgings with the likes of Armani and celeb chef eaterie Jean-Georges. It boasts 1000 sq m (10,750sq ft) of floor space and a staggering ziggurat-like atrium designed by Brit architect Michael Graves. The policy seems to be to roll out the 'greatest hits' of contemporary Chinese art, which covers anything from paintings and sculpture to video installations and digital media. Exhibitions change regularly; the calendar is listed in English on the website.

ShanghArt Gallery

2A Gaolan Lu, by Huaihai Lu, in Fuxing Park, French Concession (6359 3923/www.shanghart.com). Metro Shanxi Nanlu. **Open** 10am-7pm daily. **Map** p247 E6.

ShanghArt has enjoyed a well-deserved monopoly of the city's art scene since its opening in 1994. It shares premises with the entertainment complex Park 97 in Fuxing Park. Despite being fairly modest in size, the gallery hosts reliably impressive shows of interesting artists, all of whom are profiled on its excellent website, along with some 3,000 images of their work. There's also a ShanghArt Warehouse on Moganshan Lu, *see p162*.

Festivals

Shanghai Art Fair

Shanghai Mart, 2299 Yanan Donglu, by Loushangquan Lu (6225 4977). **Date** Nov.

This is the biggest art fair in Asia, typically featuring some 600 exhibiting galleries from China and the rest of the world. The art for sale runs the gamut

Shanghai Art Museum. *See p160.*

from traditional to contemporary, and there are also decorative arts and framings. Visit for Salvador Dali lithographs and Picasso prints, but also for displays from Art Scene China and ShanghArt. Part of the Shanghai International Arts Festival, *see p152*.

Shanghai Biennale

Shanghai Art Museum, 325 Nanjing Xilu, Renmin Square (6327 4030). Metro Renmin Park or Square. **Date** Oct-Nov, even years. **Admission** RMB 15. **Map** p243 F4.

The Shanghai Biennale launched in 1996. However, it wasn't until 2000 that international artists were invited. In 2002 the theme was 'Urban Creation', addressing ideas of space, architecture and urban life. The show-stopper was Lin Tianmiao and Wang Gongxin's creepily beautiful costumes fashioned from human hair accompanied by videos of models wearing them. In the 2004 edition (29 Sept-28 Nov) the theme is 'Techniques of the Visible', focusing on modern technology in contemporary art.

Shanghai Spring Art Salon

Intex Centre, 88 Loushangquan Lu, by Xingyi Lu, Hongqiao (6217 2011/www.cnarts.net/artsalon). Bus 72, 737, 831, 911. **Date** Sept. **Admission** RMB 25.

Launched in 2003, the Spring Art Salon is a five-day event that in its first year brought together works by nearly 200 Chinese and German artists under the banner 'Kann man Seele sehen' ('Is the soul visible'). Despite that bit of portentousness, the event is unashamedly populist with crowd-pulling names and even a kids' salon, which in 2003 had 24 life-sized ceramic bears painted by local artists.

Arts & Entertainment

Gay & Lesbian

419ers and for-lifers: there ain't no closet big enough to contain Shanghai's LesBiGays.

Vogue in Kevin's. See p167.

Although Shanghai's gays and lesbians are virtually invisible in public, spend any time in China and you realise that same-sex affection and relations are neither new nor revolutionary. In the country's long and colourful history, more than a few major episodes are shaded pink. It's recorded, for example, that the male lover of the Han emperor Ai Di dressed in silk and feathers to please. In fact, according to scholar Pan Guangdan, nearly every emperor in the Han Dynasty had one or more male sex partners. Explicit prints and paintings depicting fruity male-on-male goings on survive from almost every period of history, and in the 19th century Chinese sexual behaviour shocked early European settlers.

Homosexuality went underground after the formation of the People's Republic. The practice was condemned as contributing to the 'moldering [sic] lifestyle of capitalism' and the communist regime actively persecuted gays, especially during the Cultural Revolution.

It wasn't until 2001 that the new Chinese Classification and Diagnostic Criteria of Mental Disorders removed homosexuality from its list of mental illnesses (sodomy was decriminalised

in 1997). There is now no explicit law against homosexuality or same-sex acts between consenting adults. Then again, there are no laws protecting gays from discrimination. Nor are there any gay rights organisations in China.

But if conservative authorities still refuse to promote either gay issues or gay rights in China, Shanghai just gets on with having a gay old time regardless. While there are no Pride marches and visitors will be hard pressed to spot any rainbow flags, momentum is building. Gay figures hold high-profile positions, run brand-name businesses and restaurant chains. Truth is, such are the low levels of gay consciousness among the populace at large, it would rarely cross the mind of a local that someone might be gay, no matter how obvious the signs might be. Businesses that do flaunt their gay identity – mainly bars and clubs – are monitored and prone to occasional closures 'for renovations' while sorting out spurious police attention. Outside of gay yuppie circles, many are still wary of expressing their sexuality. This is true in particular of the poorer gays who flock to the city from the hinterlands without much education, seeking low-wage work.

They can be seen sitting around Renmin Square or encountered at some of the seedier joints flogging their particular brand of impoverished sex appeal.

SUDS AND SOUP

In addition to the listed bars and clubs there are other venues that draw a significant gay crowd. The city's bathhouses for example, which, though they are actually used for bathing, are also typically segregated. Such an all-male, near nude and literally steamy scenario makes for a charged atmosphere. Fumblings and sexual play are no-nos but there's no bar on looking. In a similar vein, there are certain gyms that are notably cruisey, including **Ambassy Club** (1500 Huaihai Zhonglu, 4437 9800), **MegaFit** (398 Huaihai Zhonglu, 5383 2252) and **Total Fitness** (*see p194*).

Given that Lady Shanghai is more a culinary queen than a boozer, much gay socialising goes on over food. There are a handful of dining spots that fall under the heading gay-friendly including **Arch** (*see p123*), **KABB** (*see p108*), **M on the Bund** (*see p99*), **Simply Thai** (*see p117*) and **Wagas** (*see p103*). Some of these places are gay-owned, some just have cute staff – either way, you'll find a significant gay clientele at them all.

INFORMATION

Heavy press censorship means that there are no real local gay publications. In 2004 a glossy mag called *Menbox*, peddling softcore pics reprinted from other publications, chanced it at the newsstands and has managed several issues to date.

Otherwise, look to the web. International site gay forum **www.gay.com** has worldwide location profiles and includes a Shanghai chat room frequented by Chinese and the city's gay expats. Gay dating site **www.gaydar.co.uk** allows members to seek fellow members listed as local to China or those travelling in the area. Adult-rated **www.gaychina.com** is a bulletin-board site with several forums for personals, photos and general postings. Most information is in Chinese but you could try translating with an online service such as www.babelfish.com. Expect plenty of ads from college students offering 'companionship' in exchange for financial aid. Aiming to be South-east Asia's largest portal for its gay community, **www.fridae.com** has member profiles in English for those looking to connect before or during a visit to Shanghai. Also recommended is **www.utopia-asia.com**, which is one of the most current and useful gay Asia resources; from the navigator bar choose China, then Shanghai for the latest online news and gossip.

Bars & clubs

Gay Shanghai has a limited but growing variety of nightspots. With the odd exception the scene is too young to have developed cliques, and crowds are pleasingly diverse: local Chinese, returnees, Western and Asian expats plus, of course, money boys (rent boys). It's a tight-knit crowd and newcomers will receive plenty of curious attention.

Bo Bo

670 Sichuan Zhonglu, by Nansuzhou Lu, the Bund (6350 9447/www.chinag.org). Metro Henan Lu. **Open** 7pm-2am daily. **Admission** free. **No credit cards. Map** p243 J3.

Who'd have thought it? A bear bar in China! A quick taxi ride to the neighbourhood of Suzhou Creek transports the intrepid to an oddly familiar world of flannel shirts and Patsy Cline. The ground floor is where the crowd gathers to mingle and natter, while the bar-less upstairs room is quieter and more intimate (OK, it's usually dead). Regulars include both expats and Chinese men, not just from Shanghai but from further afield as well (weeknights are heavily Chinese, while weekends see more foreigners). Belly up to the bar and discover your inner panda.

Dream Star Bar

307 Shanxi Nanlu, by Jianguo Xilu, French Concession (6471 2887). Metro Shanxi Nanlu. **Open** 7.30-midnight Mon-Thur, Sun; 7.30pm-6am Fri, Sat. **Admission** free. **No credit cards. Map** p247 D8.

Hard to imagine but Shanghai has its very own gay and lesbian pool party scene. The action takes place in the basement recreation centre of a large apartment complex, with decks and speakers set up beside a large swimming pool. Guests can strip down and make a splash before putting themselves into a fast spin on the makeshift dancefloor. There's a bar for après-swim quenchers and sofas for snuggling up to that special someone you picked up ten minutes ago. Ladies, take note: this is one of the premier lesbian meets in town.

Eddy's

1877 Huaihai Zhonglu, by Tianping Lu, French Concession (6282 0521/www.eddys-bar.com). Metro Hengshan Lu. **Open** 8pm-2am daily. **Admission** free. **No credit cards. Map** p246 A8.

The longest serving gay venue in town, Eddy's will have been around ten years in April 2005. In that time it has changed premises no less than six times. From just being a small gathering place for friends of a certain mindset and inclination, Eddy's is now a super stylish bar with a sophisticated, not to mention expensive-looking, Chinoise interior of bold colouring and dramatic lighting. The crowd is an international mix and Eddy himself is a fixture at the bar. The cocktails (from RMB 30) are excellent and this remains one of the best places from which to launch a night on the town.

Focus Coffee Bar

7th floor, Super Brand Mall, 168 Lujiazui Lu,
Pudong (5047 1396). Metro Lujiazui. **Open** 10am-
1am daily. **Admission** free. **No credit cards.**
Map p243 K4.

Weekend evenings at the Focus see maybe the
largest regular gathering of girlz in Shanghai. Come
for natter, drinks, the small dancefloor and the hope
of smouldering eye contact. It's just a shame about
the location – in a massive, modern shopping mall
over on the wrong side of the river. Still, romance
blooms in the most unlikely places. Note that this is
not a lesbians only venue; boyz hang out here too.

Home & Bar

18 Gaolan Lu, by Sinan Lu, French Concession,
(5382 0373/www.barhome.com). Metro Shanxi
Nanlu. **Open** 8.30pm-2am Mon-Thur, Sun; 8.30pm-
3am Fri, Sat. **Admission** RMB 20 Fri, Sat. **Credit**
MC, V. **Map** p247 E6.

Shanghai's best and brightest star gay bar attracts
a suitably attractive and amped-up crowd. Look for
the glowing blue H on doors set back off the street
just next to the old Russian Orthodox church, in the
neighbourhood of Fuxing Park. Inside, a simple formula of a clean modern look (with plush red couches), switched-on service (from staff dressed in
orange) and a proper DJ ensures that every weekend
is gay pride. In the warmer months, patrons spill out
on to the grass in the large back garden.

Hunter Bar

86 Nanyang Lu, by Xikang Lu, Jingan (6258 1438).
Metro Jingan Temple or Shimen Yilu. **Open** 8.30pm-
2am daily. **Admission** free. **No credit cards.**
Map p249 D4.

It may be lodged behind the glass-and-steel malls of
central Nanjing Lu, but the Hunter is a far cry from
your average urban gay bar. It feels more like a blue
collar veterans' club – tiled floor, simple wooden furniture, basic bar counter with neon beer signs – more
suited to rounds of dominoes than playing nooky.
Whatever, it's friendly enough and typically filled
with a predominantly Chinese crowd. To find the
place, slip into the lane at 86 Nanyang Lu, just
behind Plaza 66, then make a left beside the Pretty
Woman hairdresser's.

KM

513 Haifeng Lu, by Xikang Lu, Jingan (6256 4209).
Open 8pm-2am daily. **Admission** free. **No credit
cards. Map** p248 C2.

The original Shanghai gay bar is a small, couch-
filled, dimly lit den of intimacy and cosiness, and
makes a nice change from the pheromone-charged
disco queenery that constitutes the gay traffic on the
French Concession circuit. KM has a reputation as
a haunt of MBs (local shortspeak for 'money boy' or
rent boy), as well as the men with cash to part for
their company. Surprisingly, this is not the usual
story of rich foreigners paying for sex with poor

Speaking in tongzhi

You could compare the situation of gays in
modern Shanghai to that of gays in the West
in the 1960s. Homosexuality just wasn't
talked about and closets remained well and
truly closed. What gay scene there was was
well and truly underground and, in order to
keep it that way, the active community – in
Britain at least – developed its own exclusive

slang, known as Polari. In modern-day
Shanghai, such coding goes hand in hand
with the trend for shorthand that comes of
posting in chatrooms and texting on mobiles.
The result is something called *tonghzi*. You're
most likely to encounter the following phrases
online but give them a try around town and
you're sure to raise a grin.

Chinese	Translation	Meaning
tongzhi	comrade	gay
bo li	glass	gay
diao yu	going fishing	cruising
yu chang	fishing hole	cruising grounds
mu	feminine	effeminate
ta shi mai de	he's for sale	prostitute
MB	money boy	prostitute
xiao lang gou	little hunting dog	prostitute
ya	duck	prostitute
419	for one night	one-night stand
yi ye guanxi	one-night relation	one-night stand
yao/ling	1 and 0	top and bottom
yi dui yi pengyou	one to one friend	monogamous partner
xiong	bear	bear
taozi	cover	condom

locals – this is Chinese on Chinese action, and there's little English spoken among the patrons. Still, any foreigners who take the trouble to travel up here (the bar is far north of Nanjing Lu on a small side street up near the Jade Buddha Temple) are always made to feel welcome.

Vogue in Kevin's
946 Changle Lu, by Wulumuqi Lu, French Concession (6248 8985). Metro Changshu Lu. **Open** 8pm-2am daily. **Admission** free. **No credit cards. Map** p246 B6.

Odd of name, VinK's bar is both a favoured launch pad for setting a merry evening afloat and a crash mat for a heavy landing at the end of same. Its newly remodelled interior has gained some comfortable sofas and low tables with room to stretch out but it remains dominated by a gargantuan central bar – totally un-feng shui. Despite being the de facto nerve centre of gay Shanghai, it's not the easiest of places to find: look for the sign at the top of Lane 946, which is opposite a large apartment complex, then brave the gloom to locate a large tiled courtyard. The cluster of tight-topped Colt boys networking their evening on mobiles tells you you've arrived.

Saunas & massage

Lianbang
228 Zhizaoju Lu, by Xietu Lu, Xintiandi (6313 0567). **Open** 24hrs daily. **Admission** RMB 40. **No credit cards. Map** p244 G9.

China has a tradition of public bathhouses but Lianbang goes well beyond the naked camaraderie of the average local scrubbing spot. It's hidden down an alley that serves as the entrance to a neighbouring hotel. Look for a doorway with a red-jacketed attendant, pay the admission, switch your shoes for slippers, then steel yourself for the most thorough staring down you've probably ever experienced. Inside are three floors of dingy corridors and rooms filled with languid pyjama-clad locals of all ages lounging, smoking, napping, or getting it on. Forge ahead if you like being the centre of attention (the sauna attracts few foreigners, so your every move will be scrutinised), but be mindful that you need to keep your jammies on once out of the bath.

Sal Massage
155B Wuyi Lu, by Yanan Xilu, French Concession (6212 7838). Metro Jiangsu Lu. **Open** 2pm-2am daily. **Treatments** *oil massage* RMB 260/hr. **No credit cards. Map** p246 A6.

Shanghai's only gay massage parlour promises over 20 handsome young guys with strong firm hands. The business sits within the mainstream Jiajun Massage Centre, but mention 'men' and you will be ushered through into a lounge bar area where the country music on the stereo is suggestive of a Nevada brothel. Only massage is on the menu but given the noises we've heard emanating from the quintet of treatment rooms plenty of extra services must be available on request.

Eddy's. *See p165.*

Body

to 200 days under the knife.

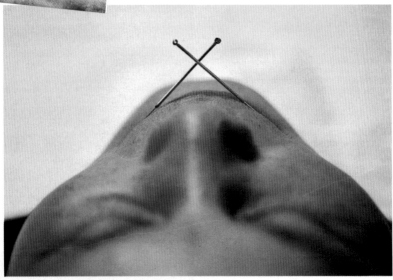

Lip service at the **VIP Clinic of Shanghai Qigong Institute**. *See p170.*

In recent years, Shanghai has been sprouting massage centres and spas at a phenomenal rate. Or at least a rate in line with the clip of the city's booming economy. These places provide treatments to relax and rejuvenate, and to help recovery from urban ills such as pollution (and too much partying). From the now ubiquitous, cheap and frill-free neighbourhood foot massage parlours to the five-star pampering of the luxury spas, there are treatments to fit all preferences and budgets.

Not that any of this is particularly new. Medicinal massage (or *tuina*, meaning 'push' or 'grasp') has at least a 2,000-year history in China, used in traditional medical practice for a range of ailments from chronic pain to allergies. It's reported that around 500 BC a doctor named Bian Que was already employing *tuina* in the effective treatment of his patients. Tuina works by addressing the *qi*, or internal energy, of the patient to balance their overall state of health. The work is done entirely with the practitioner's hands, helping to increase and regulate the beneficial flow of *qi* through the patient's meridian (energy) system.

The first of Shanghai's new wave of massage centres opened around four to five years ago, kicking off with the curious but ingenious concept of blind massage (*see p169* **Invisible touch**), and an influx of foot reflexology studios. Foot reflexology involves massaging specific regions of the feet that are believed to correspond to particular organs or body systems. So stimulating a particular area of the foot is supposed to relieve energy blockages that cause pain or disease in the associated part of the body. In the best foot massage parlours, the practitioners are older masseurs with wizened and knowledgeable hands. But be warned, if you visit one of these small, neighbourhood joints and have a low pain threshold, you should make it abundantly clear.

The latest boom in the massage market is the chic, professionally managed parlour, which caters to a mostly expat crowd. Rather than medical therapy, such places mostly provide massage for relaxation and fun. Prices are high compared to the blind massage places, but they still represent a bargain compared to what you could expect to pay for similar treatment in

Europe or America. Chinese massage is done on a massage table, focusing on rubbing and rolling hands over muscles from neck to toes; sometimes the head and face are massaged as well. Japanese *shiatsu* is usually done on a floor mat with the emphasis on finger, palm and elbow pushing and pressure.

Meanwhile, tuina is still actively practised in clinics and hospitals. Many places in Shanghai offer this kind of traditional treatment, as well as acupressure, acupuncture, *qigong* (an ancient practice using movement, meditation and breathwork to increase the flow of *qi* in the body, meant to strengthen the immune system) and other Chinese therapies.

Chinese medicine

Traditional Chinese medicine (TCM) is rooted in ideas of balance and harmony. In Chinese cosmology, creation is thought to be born from the marriage of two polar principles: yin and yang. Yang represents active, hot and bright;

yin represents things th[...]
dim. The relationship betw[...]
is fundamental to the tradition[...]
outlook, and is seen to affect all a[...]
from personal health to the state of t[...]

In TCM, yang represents the energy a[...]
movement of the body, while yin is the fles[...]
blood and bone. Harmony of this union means[...]
good health, while disharmony leads to disease; thus the strategy of TCM is to redress any imbalances. Diagnosis starts by assessing the pulse, face, tongue and body, and also takes the patient's medical history, living habits and emotional wellbeing into consideration.

Many Chinese believe that the strength of Western medicine is in its trauma care and therapies for acute problems, while TCM excels in treating chronic problems and applying preventive medicine. Western expats living in Shanghai seem to concur and many visit TCM doctors and acupuncture practitioners for help with asthma, persistent migraines, nicotine addiction and even losing weight.

Invisible touch

One of the perks of being in Shanghai is that almost every street has a massage centre, open until late, where you can get an hour-long traditional foot and body rub for about the price of a coffee at Starbucks. What's most intriguing about the experience is that your masseur will more than likely be blind.

Massage is one of the few professions open to the blind in China and businesses employing the visually impaired get tax breaks. As a result you pay a lot less than you would at any 'sighted' establishment. Good, thorough pressure point massages are not impeded by lack of sight either.

But the parameters of vision are often stretched. Some 'blind' therapists have an uncanny knack of recognising that you're foreign before you've spoken. The only visual impairment seems to be tinted sunglasses.

Levels of cleanliness and service vary too. The standard blindman massage hall has dimmed lights and rows of massage tables with recliners for the footwork. Sometimes there will be a curtain for privacy, but usually not. The therapist will put a clean sheet over your (clothed) body, and if the massage includes your face, they should wash their hands first. For a standard foot massage your feet will be soaked in hot water, dried, wrapped in towels, then massaged. Close your eyes, and enjoy.

Ease Massage Centre
89 Fahuazhen Lu, by Xinfu Lu, Xujiahui (6281 1081). Metro Xujiahui. **Open** noon-midnight daily. **Treatments** *body & foot massage* RMB 95/100mins; *body massage* RMB 35/50mins. **No credit cards**. **Map** p246 A7.

Funing Blind Massage Centre
597 Fuxing Zhonglu, by Maoming Nanlu, French Concession (6437 8378). Metro Shanxi Nanlu. **Open** noon-2am daily. **Treatments** *body or foot massage* RMB 60/hr. **No credit cards**. **Map** p247 D7.

Jingbin Blindman Massage
West Building, Jingan Hotel, 370 Huashan Lu, by Wulumuqi Beilu, French Concession (6248 1888 ext 6660). Metro Changshu Lu. **Open** 10am-2am daily. **Treatments** *body or foot massage* RMB 68/hr. **No credit cards**. **Map** p248 B5.

No.1 Comfort Club
277 Xingguo Lu, by Huaihai Nanlu, French Concession (6431 8281). Metro Changshu Lu. **Open** noon-2am daily. **Treatments** *Chinese body or foot massage* RMB 68/hr; *oil massage* RMB 108/hr; *shiatsu massage* RMB 120/90mins. **No credit cards**. **Map** p246 A7.

French
…lu.
…rds.

…erted into a
… that caters
…hinese mas-
…eatments are
…peciality is a
…atment using
dissolvable …   …ed in the body
and absorbed over two-week… . Yikes. This is
also the only official *qigong* institute in China.

Xiangshan Hospital

*11 Xiangshan Lu, by Sinan Lu, French Concession
(5306 0037). Metro Shanxi Nanlu.* **Open** 7.30-11am,
1-4.30pm Mon-Fri; 7.30-11am Sat. **No credit cards.**
Map p247 E7.

Xiangshan specialises in weight-loss programmes,
bone and spine injuries and stomach illnesses. It
treats these and other ailments with *tuina*, acupuncture, moxibustion (applying heat from burning
herbs) and Chinese medicines. Take a number, pay
a paltry sum and receive a consultation with a
knowledgeable TCM doctor (RMB 35). Then take
your prescription to the appropriate building to be
prodded or pricked or have your medicine measured
out in herbs, spices, dried roots and seeds. Speak
Chinese or bring someone who does.

Massage

Beyond the street-corner 'blindman massage'
parlours (*see p169* **Invisible touch**) is a tier
of mid-market body-rub joints. Perfumed oases
of incense candles, Asian-inspired design and
chill-out music, they generally offer a menu of
Chinese-style massages, Japanese shiatsu and
aromatherapy oil treatments.

Dragonfly

*206 Xinle Lu, by Donghu Lu, French Concession
(5403 9982/www.dragonfly.net.cn). Metro Shanxi
Nanlu.* **Open** 11am-2am daily. **Treatments** *aroma
oil massage* RMB 200/hr; *Chinese body massage* RMB
120/50mins; *shiatsu massage* RMB 120/hr. **Credit**
AmEx, MC, V. **Map** p246 C6.

Dragonfly is all dark wood and heavenly smells –
oh, and fantastic massage too, administered by
friendly and experienced therapists. While the
Donghu branch is highly popular, especially on
weekend nights, we like the Xinle branch, just down
the street, which offers more privacy in its treatment
rooms and has a 'love nest' on the fifth floor for couples, offering massage in a tranquil room with gorgeous Chinese-inspired decor and two antique beds.
The same branch has a first-class nail spa.
Other locations: 20 Donghu Lu, by Huaihai Zhonglu,
French Concession (5405 0008); Kerry Centre, 1515
Nanjing Xilu, by Tongren Lu, Jingan (6279 4625).

Everlasting

*380 Shanxi Beilu, by Beijing Lu, Jingan (6218
30799). Metro Haigang.* **Open** 9.30am-9.30pm
daily. **Treatments** *aroma oil massage* RMB 480/hr;
shiatsu massage RMB 280-350/hr. **Credit** AmEx,
DC, MC, V. **Map** p249 D4.

The grand stone façade of Everlasting's building
and its friendly reception leads first-time visitors to
expect something more than the basic set-up of the
treatment room, but there should be no complaints
about the quality of the massage. Specialities include
rose oil body massage, hot stone therapy and facial
treatments (not offered at every branch).
Other locations: 225 Shanxi Nanlu, by Yongjia
Lu, French Concession (6415 1169); 175 Xiangyang
Nanlu, by Nanchang Lu, French Concession (6415
9494); 2nd floor, Peace Square, 18 Shuicheng Lu,
by Hongqiao Lu, Gubei (6208 2370).

Green

*58 Taicang Lu, by Songshan Lu, Xintiandi (5386
0222). Metro Huangpi Nanlu.* **Open** 10.30am-2pm
daily. **Treatments** *Chinese body massage* RMB 198/
2 hrs; *natural vegetable oil massage* RMB 138/hr;
shiatsu massage RMB 98/45mins. **Credit** MC, V.
Map p244 F6.

Green was one of Shanghai's first posh massage parlours, attracting a clientele that remains around 90%
expat. It has a soothing interior and boasts some of
the most consistent, no-nonsense masseurs in town.
Arrange yourself on a Chinese-style massage bed,
or *tatami*, and submit to a traditional Chinese massage, Japanese finger massage or foot massage.

Magpie

*685 Julu Lu, by Shanxi Nanlu, French Concession
(5403 3867). Metro Shanxi Nanlu.* **Open** noon-2am
daily. **Treatments** *aroma oil massage* RMB 188/hr;
Chinese body massage RMB 128/hr; *shiatsu massage*
128/hr. **Credit** AmEx, DC, MC, V. **Map** p249 D5.

In contrast to most other massage parlours, Magpie
is kitsch – stuffed with antique Chinese furniture
amassed by its owner. Rooms are large and can hold
several massage beds, so there's not much in the
way of privacy. Still, the place offers a divine oil
massage: the secret is in the combination of oil and
the application of a steam machine. The lymph gland
massage is thought to work against body toxins.

Ming

*298 Wulumuqi Nanlu, by Jianguo Xilu, French
Concession (5465 2501). Metro Hengshan Lu.*
Open 11am-2am daily. **Treatments** *body massage*
RMB 108/hr; *foot massage* RMB 88/hr; *natural oil
massage* RMB 248/hr. **Credit** AmEx, DC, MC, V.
Map p246 C8.

The design is striking: enter across a small bridge
over running water into five small treatment rooms,
each with a Japanese look of white walls, pale wood
floors and black beams. On a more tactile level, the
towels provided here are, hands down, the softest in
town. Slip into pyjamas (provided) to receive treatment from highly professional masseurs. Between
11am and 4pm daily women receive a 20% discount.

Yining Oriental Oasis

*438 Xiangyang Nanlu, by Jinguo Xilu, French
Concession (5465 8808/www.shanghaimassage.com).
Metro Shanxi Nanlu.* **Open** 11am-2am daily.
Treatments *body massage* RMB 138/45mins;
foot massage RMB 118/hr; *oil massage* RMB 298/hr.
Credit AmEx, DC, MC, V. **Map** p247 D8.

Housed in a lovely old building, Yining is a quality
operation and one that places an emphasis on the
therapeutic side of Chinese massage. Treatments
include the usual foot and body massages and aromatherapy baths, but there are also one-on-one yoga
sessions, tai chi and martial arts classes. Rates are
very affordable; sessions are by appointment only.

Dragonfly.
See p170.

Banyan Tree.
See p172.

Evian Spa.
See p173.

Spas

At the high end of the pampering spectrum are Shanghai's clutch of lux spas, which feature international-standard attention to detail and some truly stunning interiors.

Banyan Tree

Level 3, Westin, 88 Henan Zhonglu, by Guangdong Lu, the Bund (6335 1888/www.banyantreespa.com/shanghai). Metro Henan Lu. **Open** 10am-11pm daily. **Treatments** *facial* RMB 450; *massage* RMB 450-720; *pedicure* RMB 350; *complete packages* RMB 1,100-2,100. **Credit** AmEx, DC, MC, V. **Map** p242 H4.

Originating in Phuket, the Banyan Tree spas are an Asian success story founded on opulent treatment rooms equipped to the hilt. Rooms are gorgeously decorated in themes of earth, gold, water, wood and fire, which correspond with treatments including aromatherapy, facials and Balinese, Hawaiian, Swedish and Thai massage (many of Banyan's experienced therapists are from Thailand). Come to be pampered like royalty, but expect royal prices.

David's Camp Men's SPA & Skin Care Centre

2nd floor, 200 Yanan Xilu, by Wulumuqi Beilu, French Concession (6247 3602). Metro Jingan Temple. **Open** noon-midnight daily. **Treatments** *facials* RMB 190-680; *shiatsu* RMB 98-280; *packages* RMB 450-1,200. **Credit** AmEx, DC, MC, V. **Map** p248 B5.

Expensive treatments for *Vogue Hommes* types in a modern Asian setting. Visit for Japanese shiatsu (the most popular treatment) and thorough facials with quality Swiss products. Chinese staff have limited English, but deliver treatments with a delicate touch. Single and double rooms are available, and all guests have access to showers and a sauna.

Nip, tuck and suck

Shanghai folk have always loved to look good, from their silk *qipao*s and brocade jackets to their carefully coiffed locks. Fifty years of Communist-imposed drabness did nothing to dim the passion for beauty, only now it's not just the clothes and hair that are being cut to suit. Flesh goes under the knife too.

Over the past few years cosmetic surgery has not only gained acceptance but also glamour. Tales of surgical enhancements and transformations have become a fixture of the media. In April 2004 an already good-looking guy named Zhang Yinghua was selected to become 'the city's first artifical handsome man' in a well-publicised competition organised by a local plastic surgery outfit. Zhang Di (Shanghai) and Hao Lulu (Beijing) are his female counterparts, 'man-made beauties', or *renzao meinu*, whose surgeries were sponsored by local beauty parlours. Hao Lulu underwent 200 days of plastic surgery on her entire body including face, neck, breasts, abdomen, bottom and thighs.

But this growing phenomenon of 'man-made beauties' is throwing up increasingly bizarre cases. In May 2004 a man in north-eastern China divorced his wife after discovering that she had undergone surgery in South Korea to acquire her good looks. He found out the truth in the most unlikely way – their newborn child was 'spectacularly ugly', according to state media reports.

If Zhang Di and Hao Lulu (who said 'I think society today needs more beautiful people') are happy with the results, the clinics are ecstatic. The cut-and-suck industry is booming, so much so that the plastic surgery department of the Chinese Academy of Medical Sciences has been obliged to set up a 24-hour hotline.

The most popular surgery is double-eyelid reconstruction, which makes Asian eyes look more Western; it takes all of ten minutes and costs around RMB 1,000 (US$ 120). A nose job starts at around RMB 5,000 (US$ 600).

Tempted? Shanghai's Fuhua Plastic and Aesthetic Hospital is an immaculate facility equipped with the latest international equipment. It offers every kind of cosmetic enhancement from face-lifts to breast implants and liposuction, and all at around a tenth of the price in Western countries. Fuhua also does LASEC corrective eye treatment, cutting-edge laser skincare, permanent hair removal and first-rate dental services, from cleaning to tooth whitening.

A word of warning. Competition between rival cosmetic surgery centres is pushing the industry towards increasingly outrageous stunts. In May 2004 state broadcaster CCTV aired the story of Ge Ying who beat 119 other contestants to be 'remade' into the number one beauty in her native Nanjing. She had 15,000ml of fat drawn from her body during an operation that lasted over six hours. That was about 20 per cent of her body weight and three times the acceptable limit.

Fuhua Plastic & Aesthetic Hospital

818 Jiangning Lu, by Haifang Lu, Jingan (6266 3333). Map p248 C2.

Breeze Yoga.

Evian Spa

2nd floor, Three on the Bund, 3 Zhongshan Dongyilu, by Guangdong Lu, the Bund (6321 6622/ www.threeonthebund.com). Metro Henan Lu. **Open** 10am-10pm daily. **Treatments** *facials* from RMB 520; *manicures* from RMB 150; *massages* from RMB 680/hr; *pedicures* from RMB 200. **Credit** AmEx, DC, MC, V. **Map** p243 J4.

Evian is heaven with oriental angels. White on white with water channels splishing along slate-paved corridors, steps that incorporate polished rocks, and walls with the textures of stone, wood, leaves and metal – it's cool, serene and utterly gorgeous. Massages and body treatments, as well as superb manicures, waxing and skincare with top imported products, are administered in individual rooms decorated with themes such as Chinese ink painting and bamboo. Other highlights include a hydrotherapy jacuzzi with underwater coloured lights in the setting of a shimmering mother-of-pearl room – it's like bathing in a hot spring under the aurora borealis.

Mandara Spa

6th floor, JW Marriott, Tomorrow Square, 399 Nanjing Xilu, Renmin Square (5359 4969 ext 6798/ www.mandaraspa.com). Metro Renmin Park or Square. **Open** 10am-10pm daily. **Treatments** *facial* RMB 480; *manicure* RMB 180; *massages* from RMB 680/90mins; *pedicure* RMB 220. **Credit** AmEx, DC, MC, V. **Map** p242 F4.

First Chinese branch of the successful Thai spa chain. Experienced massage therapists offer treatments in Thai and Chinese themed-rooms equipped for one or two clients. Although in the middle of a stark glass and marble hotel and shopping centre, once inside, the spa's all dark-wood timber-rich interiors, abundant flowers and aromatherapy odours really do make you feel you've been transported to somewhere wholly exotic. Huge terrazzo bathtubs, soothing music and steam showers and toilets make for a thorough pampering experience.

Yoga

Nothing at all to do with China – yoga has its roots in India, of course – but since the country opened up to the world at large, all those celebrity-endorsed, international health fads have gained their fair share of followers here too. In addition to the two specialist centres listed below, yoga classes are also offered at many gyms: *see p194.*

Breeze Yoga & Health Centre

380 Zhuguang Lu, by Huqingpinggong Lu, Hongqiao (5988 5908/www.breezeyoga.com). **Open** 9am-9pm daily. **Fees** RMB 140/class. **No credit cards**.

Breeze's two branches together offer a full weekly schedule of hatha, ashtanga, power and prenatal yoga, plus Pilates. Children and teens are welcomed and benefit from discounted classes. The Hongqiao branch, which is within walking distance from the Gubei Carrefour, is a clean and cosy, if smallish, studio at the back of the Xijiao Sports Centre, a massive complex that also includes indoor and outdoor tennis courts, squash courts and a swimming pool. **Other locations:** 1949 Hongqiao Lu, by Hongshi Lu, Gubei (6295 9068).

Y Plus Yoga Centre

299 Fuxing Xilu, by Huashan Lu, French Concession (6433 4330/www.yplus.cn). Metro Changshu Lu. **Open** 10am-9pm Mon-Fri; 10am-7pm Sat, Sun. **Fees** RMB 150/class. **Credit** AmEx, DC, MC, V. **Map** p246 A6.

The first fully dedicated professional yoga studio to open in Shanghai, three-storey Y Plus has a cadre of experienced instructors (mostly American), who teach in beautiful studios filled with natural light. Classes are also sometimes held on the rooftop terrace. Bikram, ashtanga and trendy 'hot' and 'flow' yoga are all offered, as well as Pilates.

Music

Expats settle for Pinoy and jazzy noodlings, while the Chinese go for Shampoo…
And everybody's waiting for Britney.

Shanghai rocks, only – as with many other facets of the local arts scene – it's just not apparent on the surface. It doesn't help that most visible live music is performed by the multifarious Filipino covers bands, with their pretty, scantily clad female singers squeaking out bland renditions of tired AOR. It's enough to drive any music lover to drink – except that almost every bar in town has its Pinoy (Filipino) band, so no solace there. Fortunately, there is more to the scene than sequined tube tops and 'The Ketchup Song'.

Although less high profile, Shanghai rock, pop, metal and hip hop have been blooming since around 2000, when the city government removed a ban on using the word 'rock' and showing long-haired men in the media. The city has a decent stable of bands, although only a few have the pulling power to draw crowds, journalists and fans who will earnestly debate their idols' wardrobes and sex lives online.

Independent Shanghai music is split into two amicable camps, one mainstream pop-rock, the other underground and more alternative. The first group is mostly influenced by British groups like Blur, Suede, the Clash, the Cure and U2, although they are also fiercely adoring of older Chinese and Taiwanese music. The resulting sound has been dubbed 'Shampoo'. The more prominent Shampoo groups include the heavy but melodic **Crystal Butterfly**, the ethereally gothic **Cold Fairyland**, the cheerfully poppy **Honeys** and **Midnight Bus**, newcomers from Xian with a recently released album and an aggressive performance schedule. The underground camp ranges in style from grunge to punk to death metal to folk and electronica and is represented by bands such as Shanghai's oldest extant band, **Prague Spring**, the death metal merchants **Capitol Crime** and **Topfloor Circus**, visual artists with an eclectically folksy musical repertoire.

But these scenes operate mostly outside of the city's more mainstream nightlife and so rarely register on foreigners' radars. Concerts typically take place at college auditoriums or in parks at government-sponsored music festivals. Only foreigners who read the Chinese-language press, or visit Chinese-language music chat rooms, will be aware of them, and more than a smattering of Caucasian faces at a concert is

Ark Live House. See p175.

rare. There are only a handful of conventional regular live music venues that non-Chinese attend in any numbers, chief of which is state-of-the-art **Ark Live House** (*see p175*).

Hip hop is gaining in popularity with young Shanghainese, although it's not quite hip hop as it's known in the West. The genre arrived in Shanghai via Taiwan, Japan and, in particular, Korea, mutating along the way into something that's called 'chopstick hip hop'. It's mostly about fashion, with the kids in their basketball jerseys and Converses totally into the attitude, dance and lifestyle without really developing any distinct, indigenous hip hop music of their own. Notable among the few Shanghainese hip hop bands are **Pun Pun**, who muse on life, love, work and identity (politics are left to the more cutting-edge Beijing artists). A separate scene of MCs, foreign and Chinese, exists on the nightlife circuit rapping at various nightclubs, particularly Pegasus Club (see p181).

LABELS AND DISKS

Record stores are dominated by Hong Kong and Taiwan hits, including popular favourites like top Chinese band Yu Quan and Taiwanese boy band F4. Distribution woes largely keep local independent music out of most stores. In fact, Shanghai currently has only one major independent rock record label, Fanyin (although some Shanghai bands are signed with Beijing labels). Chain store Maya stocks some Chinese rock labels, particularly at its larger outlets like the one in Xujiahui. WALL, on Changle Lu in the French Concession, also offers a selection of records and demos by Shanghai artists. Bands also often make their records or demos available at their gigs.

The multinational recording giants have a presence in Shanghai, but thus far have shown little interest in supporting local talent. Instead, they're here to promote their international stables of artists. They do occasionally, however, lure international stars to the city on their Asian tour schedules including, perhaps, Britney Spears in 2005 (although authorities are reportedly concerned with the state of undress during her stage shows). Big concerts are heavily publicised, and tickets are available from the venues – usually the Shanghai Stadium or Hongkou Stadium.

Major venues

Shanghai hosts an increasingly regular stream of famous Asian and Western performers who pack out one of the city's three large stadia. The largest, **Shanghai Stadium**, has featured performers like mandopop stars Faye Wang and Zheng Jun (the Rolling Stones cancelled in 2003). It consists of the *tiyuchang*, an 80,000-seat outdoor stadium built in 1997, and the *tiyuguan*, a smaller indoor arena; both are typically called Shanghai Stadium in English. Mariah Carey and veteran rockers Deep Purple are among the acts to have play recently at the **Hongkou Stadium**, which was rebuilt in its current 35,000-seat incarnation in 1999. Concerts are also sometimes held at the **Changning Stadium** – which is also known as the Shanghai International Stadium. Confusing, no?

Changning Stadium

777 Wuyi Lu, by Zhongshan Xilu, Jingan (6228 9488). Metro Zhongshan Park. **Map** p240 B3.

Hongkou Stadium

715 Dongtiyuhui Lu, by Zhongshan Beierlu, Hongkou (6540 0009). Metro Hongkou Stadium. **Map** p241 D1.

Shanghai Stadium

1111 Caoxi Beilu, by Zhongshan Nanerlu, Xujiahui (6438 5200/www.shanghai-stadium.online.sh.cn). Metro Shanghai Stadium. **Map** p240 B4.

Pop & rock

Ark Live House

181 Taicang Lu, North Block, Lane 15, Xintiandi (6326 8008/www.ark-lh.com). Metro Huangpui Nanlu. **Open** 5.30pm-1am daily. **Admission** RMB 30 Fri, Sat. **Credit** AmEx, DC, MC, V. **Map** p244 F6.
Opened in 2001 and named after Japanese super-group (believe us, they're big over this way) L'arc en Ciel, Ark is Shanghai's premier destination for non-covers live music. It boasts one of the best sound systems in China (so say the musicians) and an eclectic line-up of nightly performances. Most of Ark's foreign acts are Japanese metal, punk and pop bands, joined by the occasional Western group. Along with the imports, Ark regularly showcases Chinese talent; both established and new Shanghai groups play regularly, and at least one Beijing or Guangzhou group passes through each month. Sporadic weekend afternoon concerts pull in mad throngs of student fans.

Malone's

255 Tongren Lu, by Nanjing Xilu, Jingan (6247 2400/www.malones.com.cn). Metro Jingan Temple. **Open** 11am-2am daily. **Admission** free. **Credit** AmEx, DC, MC, V. **Map** p248 C4.
One of Shanghai's oldest extant Western bars, Malone's (see p121) goes live nightly with a competent covers band fronted by the pretty female singer prerequisite to Shanghai bar bands. The repertoire is classic pop-rock mixed with a bit of contemporary stuff. What differentiates Malone's from the other expat watering holes with covers bands is that it hires mainly local, not Filipino, performers. Many of Shanghai's best-known bands have had rent-paying Malone's gigs early on in their careers. So, while it might be 'big big girl in a big big world' tonight, you could be watching next year's big big stars.

M-Box

3rd floor, Peregrine Plaza, 1325 Huaihai Zhonglu, by Baoqing Lu, French Concession (6445 1777). Metro Changshu Lu. **Open** 6pm-2am daily. **Admission** free. **Credit** AmEx, DC, MC, V. **Map** p246 C7.
Malone's little sister, M-Box, was opened in 2001 and perpetuates the policy of booking Shanghainese bands for its nightly performances. The difference is the clientele, which is largely Hong Kong and Taiwanese, not Western. As a result the music is

Arts & Entertainment

Asian pop – Chinese-language with some Japanese. mandopop and cantopop focus more on vocals than instrumentals, and M-Box accommodates with a coterie of female vocalists who, while still pretty, are also talented singers and flash dancers.

SUS2

57 Guoding Lu, by Huangxing Lu, Yangpu (5506 0118/www.sus2music.com). Metro Renmin Park. **Open** 1pm-midnight daily. **Admission** RMB 10. **No credit cards**.

Sure, the sound system crackles and breaks down every half hour, and the place takes an hour to get to from the city centre, but then that's as it should be given that SUS2 is Shanghai's rawest, most authentic rock dive. Primarily a music school and instrument shop in a bungalow hidden behind a scrap iron yard, SUS2's occasional concerts attract crowds of dyed and pierced youth from nearby Fudan and Tongji Universities. SUS2's mission is to support new, mostly student, local bands, but established groups sometimes come to jam, as do some of the visiting acts flown in by Ark. Concerts occur irregularly (usually the first two Saturdays of the month) and are only publicised on SUS2's Chinese-language webpage.

Time Passage

183 Lane 1038, Huashan Lu, by Fuxing Xilu, French Concession (6240 2588). Metro Jiangsu Lu. **Open** 5pm-2am Mon-Fri; 2pm-2am Sat, Sun. **Admission** free. **No credit cards**. **Map** p246 A6.

The grungy but cosy Time Passage is a favoured downtown watering hole of Shanghai's boho types (*see p126*), both local and foreign. On weekends, aspiring local musicians, usually a duo with guitars, belt out unplugged covers of Western rock standards. Many of Shanghai's professional rockers, and visiting musicians from around China, hang out at Time Passage, and sometimes, after a few rounds of beer and under pressure from owner Ai Jun, they take the floor for an impromptu jam session.

Jazz

Shanghai's jazz scene is almost an exact negative of the rock scene: it is bar centered, expatriate dominated and rarely original. Pretty much every four- or five-star hotel has a resident jazz act, and there is a healthy number of independent venues. Shanghainese jazz groups, or even individual performers, are thin on the ground. The few notable exceptions like the band Five Guys on a Train and flamboyant gay singer Coco (a semi-celeb in this defiantly straight city) stick strictly to old standards.

But the imported bands performing in the city's jazz bars are at least tight and professional, injecting verve into their covers, often wrapping up with an energised jam. Upper-income young Shanghainese are developing an appetite for jazz, in no small part because of its perceived associations with a sophisticated Western way of living. The cultural bureau has responded by organising a number of jazz festivals, all theoretically annual but none yet reliably so, but jazz acts are also included in most general festivals. Between these and independently organised events, a number of international jazz figures have visited Shanghai, including Wynton Marsalis.

CJW

1st floor, 2 Lane 123, Xingye Lu, by Madang Lu, Xintiandi (6385 6677). Metro Huangpi Nanlu. **Open** 1pm-2am daily. **Admission** free. **Credit** AmEx, DC, MC, V. **Map** p244 F6.

Standing for cigars, jazz and wine (not necessarily in that order), this Taiwanese-owned relative newcomer approaches jazz as an upmarket lifestyle accessory. With locations in two of the city's poshest developments, Xintiandi and the Bund Centre, it appeals to mostly Hong Kong and Taiwanese expatriates with performances by very competent foreign bands, changed every few months.
Other locations: 50th floor, Bund Centre, 222 Yanan Donglu, by Henan Zhonglu, the Bund (6339 1477).

Cotton Club

8 Fuxing Xilu, by Huaihai Zhonglu, French Concession (6437 7110). **Open** 9.30pm-12.30am daily. **Admission** free. **Credit** AmEx, DC, MC, V. **Map** p246 B7.

No relation to the New York original, Shanghai's oldest outlet of jazz and blues is the closest thing in town to a sure bet for smooth sounds. A good crowd of both Westerners and Chinese packs the small, smoky club for nightly sets. Compared to most clubs, which rotate bands every few months, consistency is key at the Cotton Club. The house band consists mostly of foreigners, some of whom have been playing there for a decade. A handful of semi-regulars join in and jam a couple of nights a week.

Glamour Bar

7th floor, 20 Guangdong Lu, by Zhongshan Dongyilu, the Bund (6350 9988/www.m-onthebund.com). Metro Henan Lu. **Open** 5pm-midnight daily. **Admission** varies. **Credit** AmEx, DC, MC, V. **Map** p243 J4.

The Glamour Bar at M on the Bund, Shanghai's first and still leading upmarket eaterie (*see p99*), usually has weekend gigs. It presents top-quality international acts in a broad range of styles, from modern jazz to world music to classical to cabaret. Contact the bar directly for upcoming events, and be sure to make a reservation as space runs out quickly. The ticket price, which varies depending with who's on, usually includes a few drinks. *See also p120*.

House of Blues & Jazz

158 Maoming Nanlu, by Fuxing Zhonglu, French Concession (6437 5280). Metro Shanxi Nanlu. **Open** 7pm-2am Tue-Sun. **Admission** free. **Credit** AmEx, DC, MC, V. **Map** p247 D7.

Cotton Club. *See p176.*

Brainchild of radio and TV personality Lin Dongfu, the House has existed in various incarnations around Shanghai since the mid 1990s. The current format has proved the most successful. Being a bit of an Old Shanghai buff, Dongfu has outfitted the club in deco, with an impressive collection of antique furniture and lamps. The music is more modern, a mixture of blues and jazz fusion delivered by a roster of highly competent foreign bands.

JZ Club
1111 Huaihai Zhonglu, by Fenyang Lu, French Concession (6415 5255). Metro Changshu Lu. **Open** 9.30pm-2am daily. **Admission** free. **Credit** AmEx, DC, MC, V. **Map** p247 D6.
Opened in late 2003 by a local jazz enthusiast who studied music overseas, JZ has already established itself as one of Shanghai's leading jazz dives. Its unpretentious but stylish atmosphere and inclusion of young, Chinese musicians makes it more accessible to young Shanghainese jazz aficionados than most of its competitors. JZ is not the place to hear your Billie Holiday covers: the three nightly sets primarily consist of contemporary and fusion jazz, often evolving into a rousing jam session. Watch your head stepping into the upstairs washroom.

Paramount Ballroom
218 Yuyuan Lu, by Wanghang Lu, Jingan (6249 8866). Metro Jingan Temple. **Open** 8.30pm-1am daily. **Admission** RMB 200. **Credit** AmEx, DC, MC, V. **Map** p248 B5.
Back in the '30s the dizzyingly deco Paramount was Shanghai's chicest dance hall. It reopened in 2001, complete with live music. On a stage overlooking the main second-floor dance hall, pretty girls with big band backing belt out swinging nostalgic renditions of pop songs, mostly pre-1950s but with a few reinvented revolutionary songs, old Deng Lijun and modern tunes. Imagine the *Titanic* theme meets Lawrence Welk. The more mellow fourth-floor dance hall features a singer and a smaller band focusing more exclusively on jazz.

Peace Hotel Bar
20 Nanjing Donglu, by Zhongshan Dongyilu, the Bund (6321 6888/www.shanghaipeacehotel.com). Metro Henan Lu. **Open** 8pm-2am daily. **Admission** RMB 50. **Credit** AmEx, DC, MC, V. **Map** p243 J4.
The most famous, or infamous, jazz venue in Shanghai is the bar of the historic Peace Hotel (*see p32*). Since reopening in the 1980s, it has created a vision of Old Shanghai with six old-timers playing retro jazz and big band favourites. The cover charge is steep, especially on weekends, and the atmosphere is decidedly unhip, with a crowd that's made up exclusively of tourists.

Portman Ritz-Carlton Bar
1376 Nanjing Xilu, by Tongren Lu, Jingan (6279 8268). Metro Jingan Temple. **Open** 9.30pm-2am daily. **Admission** free. **Credit** AmEx, DC, MC, V. **Map** p248 C4.
Most of Shanghai's five-star hotels include jazz in their entertainment offerings, but the bar at the Portman Ritz-Carlton (*see p39*) stands out. Its bar is streamlined and elegant, with low-slung and comfortable chairs. The music is provided by foreign pros, who are invariably American. The names and faces rotate every few months.

Arts & Entertainment

Try to set the night on fire at **Rojam**. *See p182.*

Let's get the nay-sayers out of the way first. International scenesters have been known to comment that while Shanghai clubs may look the part, everything from the decor to the music uninspiringly apes Europe or Hong Kong. Expat clubbers point out that the average DJ in Shanghai is a foreign hack who couldn't get a gig back home. Oh, and the locals are so musically naïve they wouldn't know Lisa Lashes's house from Faye Wong's mandopop. All true to some extent, but aural snobbery aside, Shanghai still offers plenty of late-night action with all the hedonism that made this the sin city of the 1920s.

That infamous melange of sing-song girls, horny sailors and pockmarked gangsters was snuffed out under Communism, but when President Deng Xiaoping opened the city up to economic reform in 1992 the corks began popping again – with a partying vanguard of foreign businessmen in hotel bars and Australian Embassy staff out on the raz on a Friday night. Decadent mass dance orgies and gleeful drug abuse were still some way off.

Further relaxation of government restrictions on nightlife in the late '90s coincided with the arrival of Chinese returnees from the West and curious foreign language students. Shanghai had its first club-savvy crowd, and venues such as glorified disco Real Love began to appear.

In other words, Shanghai clubbing is barely out of nappies. Walking, let alone shaking ass, is proving problematic. Continued government censorship prevents aspiring local DJs from accessing the very heart of their trade – vinyl. Records are exotic fruit, something that locals can only lay their hands on abroad. Periodically, and unpredictably, a 2am curfew is imposed on late-night venues, while inviting celebrity DJs from overseas is a bureaucratic headache, not to mention prohibitively expensive. And outdoor raves or music festivals? Get outta here.

But thanks to the bloody determination of the party organisers and a new generation of teens who are flirting with music subcultures such as chopstick hip hop (*see p174*), the scene is alive, kicking and maturing at a frantic pace. Every weekend, the French Concession throbs with Shanghainese wide boys, girlies in counterfeit couture and drug dealers making a fast buck off Ecstasy-seekers (local clubbers have dubbed Ecstasy *yaotouwan*, or 'head-shaking pill'). And somehow, on occasion, local promoters do get it together to host the international big names; Fatboy Slim, John Digweed and Paul Oakenfold have all played Shanghai in recent times. It may not be Ibiza but it's head-shaking stuff all the same and it's getting better all the time.

PRACTICALITIES

Most of the action happens at the weekend. But even then many clubs are hit-and-miss, relying on gimmicky theme nights, drink specials and guest DJs to keep Shanghai's fickle crowds happy. Pick up the city's free listings mags to get tips on what's going on, notably *that's Shanghai*, *City Weekend* and *Shanghai Talk*, all of which are distributed at hotels, bars and restaurants.

Cabaret

La Maison

Lane 181 Taicang Lu, North Block Xintiandi (5306 1856). Metro Huangpi Nanlu. **Open** 11.30am-2.30pm, 6pm-midnight daily. Show time 9pm daily. **Credit** AmEx, DC, MC, V. **Map** p244 F6.
A bit of Moulin Rouge in Shanghai, La Maison hosts cabaret shows with a lot of feathers, legs and cleavage. Unfortunately, the price you pay for the show is that you are required to eat; the food is a poor attempt at French cuisine. Neither is it cheap with main courses stating at around RMB 130.

Clubs

Babyface

180 Maoming Nanlu, by Yongjia Lu, French Concession (6445 2330). Metro Shanxi Nanlu. **Open** 9pm-2am daily. **Admission** RMB 40 Fri, Sat. **No credit cards**. **Map** p247 D7.
Babyface is a bit like the Shanghai princesses who swan around its bar in tinted sunglasses casting disdainful looks at enterprising males: sexy, but with a sting. The small, red space with beaded curtains may look warm, but that doesn't mean it's friendly. In fact, after 1am squabbles frequently break out over possession of the very few (and very small) tables. Still, it's worth staking out your territory and facing down all upstarts for DJ Gilles Bihi-Zenou, one of the most popular decksmen in town and the guy responsible for bringing Paul Oakenfold to town. The venue was slated for closure in 2004.

Buddha Bar

172-174 Maoming Nanlu, by Yongjia Lu, French Concession (6415 2688). Metro Shanxi Nanlu. **Open** 8pm-3am Mon-Thur, Sun; 8pm-6am Fri, Sat. **Admission** RMB 30 Fri, Sat. **Credit** AmEx, DC, MC, V. **Map** p247 D7.
Crimson neon Sanskrit characters appear to bleed off the walls, while up on an unfeasibly raised dancefloor clubbers cavort around a glowing Buddha. Even the shortest of the ravers can press their palms against the ceiling, while taller *laowai* (foreigners) stoop to dance. All around, those who are too stoned to negotiate the stairs to the dance dias slump in red couches amid wafts of incense. Buddha Bar is one of the few places in town where ravers are comfortable using all kinds of chemicals. It's also famous for juking the curfew – even when the local constabulary has the rest of Maoming Nanlu calling time at 2am, Buddha Bar usually manages to carry on regardless. But its lucky number may not run forever: at the time of press, the venue was under threat of closing down for good.

California Club

Park 97, 2 Gaolan Lu, within Fuxing Park, French Concession (5383 2328). Metro Shanxi Nanlu. **Open** 9pm-2am Mon-Thur, Sun; 9pm-4am Fri, Sat. **Admission** free. **Credit** AmEx, DC, MC, V. **Map** p247 E6.
A hedonistic entertainment complex, Park 97 has two floors of restaurants and bars (including hotspot of the moment Upstairs, *see p128*), and is hugely popular with expats, locals and HK sophisticates. At the California Club, the bar is typically draped with gorgeous professional girlfriends who specialise in foreign males, while the dancefloor will be packed with Shanghai's nouveaux riches. The venue regularly hosts international DJs as well as local talents, so expect to be serenaded by anything from deep house to breakbeat, funk and R&B. By 2am, Park 97 becomes one large party space, with clubbers spilling out into the open air of Fuxing Park.

Guandii

2 Gaolan Lu, by Chengdu Lu, within Fuxing Park, French Concession (5383 6020). Metro Huangpi Nanlu or Shanxi Nanlu. **Open** 8.30pm-2am Mon-Thur, Sun; 8.30pm-4am Fri, Sat. **Admission** RMB 30-40 Fri, Sat. **Credit** AmEx, DC, MC, V. **Map** p247 E6.
Guandii began life mopping up the overspill from neighbouring Park 97 and its California Club (*see above*), but these days it has become a destination in its own right. It pulls a devoted crowd of ABCs (American-born Chinese) and Taiwanese sophistikids to its spacious dancefloor tripped out in laser lighting and shaken up by fat-bass speakers. In a smaller adjacent space Guandii's resident DJ Deep spins a mix of hip hop and R&B classics. Every Friday night the club ships up talent from the south for its Hong Kong DJ night, while summer nights see some of the action shift to outdoor chill-out seating overlooking Fuxing Park.

Doing it their way

To the club-scene alliteration of dancing, drinking and drugging, Shanghai adds drunken drawling – otherwise known as karaoke.

Enjoying a little privacy with friends and associates is a luxury in the hyper-densely populated People's Republic, so when Japanese-style karaoke bars first switched on the vocal-free backing tracks in the 1980s, they proved an instant hit. The notion of a soundproofed room with vinyl couches, no windows and a miked-up box of toons proved highly appealing to all sorts, from giggly teens looking for laughs and gossip to criminals looking for privacy in which to effect their dubious business dealings.

As a consequence, the city is lousy with karaoke joints. Many are abysmal and plenty are little short of brothels, but the best are a uniquely Chinese add-on to the clubbing scene where dancefloors are supplemented by warrens of karaoke boxes. Punters use them like chill-out rooms, or as somewhere to drop a pill with a few friends. At the same time, stylish karaoke complexes have been set up within stumbling distance of the hippest clubs – glitzy, Taiwanese-owned Partyworld is a popular example just across the park from California Club and Guandii.

Generally, the karaoke machines are filled with lamentable mandopop or cantopop tunes. In fact, such is the popularity of karaoke that the local pop industry is awash with tunes created specifically to be sung across Asia by millions of kara-cuties – girls with terrible voices who look so good that all males present cheer wildly regardless.

Most karaoke boxes also have an English-language song list of camped-up numbers like 'It's Raining Men'. If *Lost In Translation* had been set in Shanghai, there's no way Bill Murray would have wound up singing anything as fine as Roxy Music's 'More Than This'.

But when lubed up on *baijiou* (stomach-stripping Chinese liquor), it hardly matters what's playing anyway. The following are a few of the more respectable karaoke venues.

D8

7th floor, Lansheng Building, 8 Huaihai Zhonglu, by Xizang Nanlu, Old City (6319 0837). Metro Huangpi Nanlu. **Open** 8pm-2.30am daily. **Admission** Min spend on food & drink RMB 980 in room for 6. **Credit** AmEx, DC, MC, V. **Map** p244 G6.

Gold Glorious

4th & 5th floors, Golden Bell Plaza, 98 Huaihai Zhonglu, by Longmen Lu, French Concession (5385 8608). Metro Huangpi Nanlu. **Open** 8pm-2am daily. **Admission** Min spend on food & drink RMB 980 in room for 6. **Credit** AmEx, DC, MC, V. **Map** p244 G6.

Partyworld (Cashbox)

109 Yandang Lu, within Fuxing Park, French Concession (6374 1111). Metro Huangpi Nanlu. **Open** 7am-2am daily. **Admission** RMB 39/hr in room for 4. **Credit** MC, V. **Map** p247 E6.

Pu-J's Podium

Level 3, Jinmao Building, 88 Shiji Dadao, Pudong (5049 1234 ext 8732). Metro Lujiazui. **Open** 7pm-1am Mon-Thur; 7pm-2am Fri, Sat. **Admission** Min spend on food & drink RMB 1,200 in room for 4. **Credit** AmEx, DC, MC, V. **Map** p243 L4.

Rojam

4th floor, Hong Kong Plaza, 283 Huaihai Zhonglu, French Concession (6390 7181). Metro Huangpi Nanlu. **Open** 8.30pm-2am daily. **Admission** Min spend on food & drink RMB 360 (RMB 540 Fri, Sat) in room for 6. **Credit** V. **Map** p244 F6.

Judy's Too

176 Maoming Nanlu, by Yongjia Lu, French Concession (6473 1417/www.judysco.com). Metro Shanxi Nanlu. **Open** 8pm-2am Mon-Wed, Sun; 8pm-5am Thur-Sat. **Admission** RMB 50 Fri, Sat incl 1 drink. **Credit** AmEx, DC, MC, V. **Map** p247 D7.

If Shanghai's expat wives had their way Judy's would be painted with a scarlet 'A'. Scrubby, small and a bit of a dive it may be, but it's also one of Shanghai's oldest clubs (opened 1992) and much beloved by a genuinely mixed crowd. Businessmen

trolling for lycra-clad ladies of the night dance with foreign students looking for no more than cheap drinks. Girls gyrate on the bar, shaking their boob tubes to the likes of 'Lady Marmalade'. Inebriated patrons are encouraged to join in, and they do. Thursday night hosts sweaty '80s party 'Footloose'. The venue was due to move to Tongren Lu in 2004.

The Loft

323 Fuxing Zhonglu, by Huangpi Lu, French Concession (5386 6268). Metro Huangpi Lu. **Open** 6pm-2am daily. **Admission** free. **Credit** DC, MC, V. **Map** p244 F7.

On the top floor of entertainment centre Club Fusion (a cut-rate Park 97), the Loft is one of Asia's super-clubs (as in it's very big). It has hosted some of Shanghai's most prestigious club events, including the 2003 China DMC DJ championships, the Ministry of Sound tour and a gig by American DJ Roger Sanchez. But when not hosting big bashes, it struggles to attract crowds large enough to fill the place. A pity, because the club otherwise has everything going for it – labyrinthine space, plenty of intimate nooks and one huge dancefloor equipped with cutting-edge sound and lighting.

Mural

697 Yongjia Lu, by Hengshan Lu, French Concession (6433 5023/www.muralbar.com). Metro Hengshan Lu. **Open** 6pm-2am Mon-Thur, Sun; 9.30pm-3am Fri; 6pm-3am Sat. **Admission** RMB 100 Fri, free drinks 10pm-2am. **Credit** AmEx, DC, MC, V. **Map** p246 B8.
Mural's cave-like interior of mud-brown walls, amorphous shapes, cross-legged idols and faded frescoes looks like something uncovered by Indiana Jones after cleverly negotiating a trap-filled tunnel of scything blades. Most people's greatest discovery here, however, is Friday night's all-you-can-drink special – yours for RMB 100. It's a highly successful gimmick that guarantees the place is packed with so many students and scrooges that you almost wonder why the club bothered with the theme park interior – nobody can see it through all the bodies. Regular guest DJ Daddy Vegas works his way through a mighty fine collection of rare funk 45s, but sadly the crowd here is far more interested in getting their money's worth of booze.

Pegasus Club

2nd floor, Golden Bell Plaza, 98 Huaihai Zhonglu, by Longmen Lu, French Concession (5385 8189/ www.judysco.com). Metro Huangpi Nanlu. **Open** 9pm-2am Mon-Thur, Sun; 9pm-4am Fri, Sat. **Admission** free. **Credit** AmEx, DC, MC, V. **Map** p244 G6.
Pegasus's Thursday night hip hop parties hosted by DJ V-Nutz (China's 2002 DMC Champion) are legendary around these parts. Otherwise, the club is a bit hit-and-miss. It underwent a facelift in 2003 – moving the bar and adding a few white, Kubrick-esque couches – and has yet to regain its favoured status among Shanghai's clubbers. Manager Paul Grey remains a solid supporter of local hip hop, and occasionally books quality international talents.

Real Love

10 Hengshan Lu, by Gaoan Lu, French Concession (6474 6830). Metro Hengshan Lu. **Open** 8pm-2am daily. **Admission** RMB 30 for men Mon-Wed incl 1 drink; RMB 30 Thur, Sun; RMB 40 Fri, Sat. **Credit** AmEx, DC, MC, V. **Map** p246 B8.
A neon heart monitor pulses along one wall, plastic grapevines hang from the ceiling, neo-rococo vases fill wall recesses and the house furniture is of the moulded garden variety. Tasteful? We think not. But Real Love still draws a large crowd of not so club-savvy locals and students, attracted by cheap drinks and the venue's reputation as a prime pick-up joint. As far as the music goes, expect old-school techno tunes and limp electronica. Five years ago all Shanghai clubs looked like this and sometimes, when you don't fancy making the effort and paying RMB 50 for a drink, it's nice to be able to go back.

Waving, not dancing at **Pegasus Club**.

Goddesses and mortals at **Mural**. *See p181*.

Rojam

4th floor, Hong Kong Plaza, 283 Huaihai Zhonglu, by Songshan Lu, French Concession (6390 7181/ www.rojam.com). Metro Huangpi Nanlu. **Open** 8.30pm-2am daily. **Admission** RMB 50 for men Mon, Wed incl 1 drink; RMB 40 Tue, Thur, Sun; RMB 50 Fri, Sat. **Credit** V. **Map** p244 F6.

Two bodacious Russian babes in go-go boots are raised high above the dancefloor. Their supporting platforms are hidden by the massed bodies so that they appear to be suspended in mid air. But despite being finer than Beluga caviar, hardly anyone pays attention, dwarfed as the girls are by the colossal main dancefloor-cum-bar area. Heaving crowds are strafed by a strobing light show and bombarded by atom-splitting hardcore. There's some respite in two chill-out/VIP areas, karaoke rooms out the back and a laid-back top floor. The venue has hosted the likes of John Digweed and diva DJ Lisa Lashes, but lately the Japanese owners have been content to fly in Japanese acts from their own record label (called, surprisingly enough, Rojam).

Windows Too

J104 Jingan Si Plaza, 1699 Nanjing Xilu, by Huashan Lu, Jingan (3214 0351). Metro Jingan Temple. **Open** 6.30pm-2.30am daily. **Admission** RMB 30 Fri, Sat incl 1 drink. **No credit cards. Map** p248 B5.

Ancient beings over, ooh, around 24 years old may want to give this place a miss. But for newly post-pubescents this is party central: RMB 10 drinks and hormones whipped into a frenzy by the likes of Salt 'n' Peppa's 'Push It'. Resident DJ Ellie spins hip hop and R&B, with a little Bob Marley thrown in to please the regular crowd of Africans. Come the wee small hours this place – which is basically a dive bar with dancefloor in a shopping mall – is as hot and heavy as a school prom with spiked punch. The same people also own Windows Roadside on Maoming Nanlu, which generates a similar atmosphere.

Comedy

In addition to the CCC, listed below, another Irish pub, **O'Malley's** (*see p125*), has been providing a stage for acts brought in by the international franchise that is the Punchline Comedy Club (www.punchlinecomedy.com); phone to see if anything is happening.

China Comedy Club

Malone's, 255 Tongren Lu, by Nanjing Xilu (6247 2400/www.chinacomedyclub.com). Metro Jingan Temple. **Shows** phone for dates and times. **Admission** RMB 200. **Credit** AmEx, DC, MC, V. **Map** p248 C4.

For a couple of nights each month the CCC takes over the third floor of American bar Malone's (*see p121*) and gives the stage to visiting top English (or at least English-speaking) comedians. Past performers have included Phil Nichol, Jarred Christmas and Rob Rouse. Shows kick off at 9pm and you should book well in advance as they often sell out.

Performing Arts

The musicals are old but the money they make is new.

Shanghai is a show-me-the-money kind of town, and, of late, its performing arts industry has been seeing a lot of dollar signs. Commercial spectacles such as *David Copperfield* and *Riverdance* have arrived and there's a sizeable 1980s-born, foreign-friendly generation eager to welcome them.

That's not to discount the more serious theatre groups active in Shanghai, nor the grey-haired audiences who favour the traditional Beijing, Yue, Kun and Yang opera scene (*see p185* **Chinese opera**). But in recent years the popularity of English-language musicals has been hard to ignore. In spring 2003 more than 80,000 attended an Australian-South African production of Andrew Lloyd Webber's *Cats*, despite a recent outbreak of SARS. It banked nearly $30 million. *Phantom of the Opera* arrives in 2004, and it's predicted that it will draw even bigger crowds.

Never less than absurdly ambitious, Shanghai plans to have its own equivalent of Broadway by 2010, stretching along Huashan Lu and Anfu Lu in the French Concession. There are already nine theatres in the neighbourhood, but the plan calls for more neon, more names in lights and more theatres. In fact, there are around 100 theatre builds or restorations planned around the city, including grand-scale projects such as an Oriental Arts Centre and World Expo Theatre. The latter provides the clue as to the reason for all this investment in culture, namely the desire to impress at the World Expo 2010.

With Western-style theatre looming larger and wealthier, the local and experimental scene looks ever more puny. Only a few of its players have any kind of profile; chief among them is Shanghai-based modern dancer Jin Xing (*see p186* **A good move**). The most prominent homegrown talents are usually of the acrobatic variety – those who can juggle porcelain, balance bicycles and form human pyramids.

TICKETS AND INFORMATION

The easiest way to get tickets is simply to buy them at the venue just before the show starts (note that for big hits such as the musicals at the Shanghai Grand Theatre, advance booking is essential). Tickets for most performances can also usually be bought through **China Ticket Star** (800 820 7910/www.ticket365.com.cn); its website is Chinese-language, but it shows pictures of what's on at each venue. Another source of tickets is the **Shanghai Cultural Information and Booking Centre** (6217 2426/www.culture.sh.cn). Try **Jinjiang Tours** (6329 1025) for the acrobat shows.

For information about what's on, check listings in the local free press, particularly *that's Shanghai*.

Major venues

Lyceum Theatre

57 Maoming Nanlu, by Changle Lu, French Concession (6256 5544). Metro Shanxi Lu. **Open** *Box office* 9am-7pm daily. **Tickets** RMB 100-580. **No credit cards. Map** p247 E6.
The Lyceum was built in 1931. Several redecorations later it still boasts stunning art deco architecture. International shows have included ballet troupes from Vancouver and violin quartets from Vienna. The theatre also stages local versions of children's plays like *The Emperor's New Clothes*, as well as more traditional fare such as Beijing and Yue opera.

Majestic Theatre

66 Jiangning Lu, by Nanjing Xilu, Jingan (6217 2426). Metro Shimen Yilu. **Open** *Box office* 9am-7.30pm daily. **Tickets** RMB 20-4,000. **No credit cards. Map** p249 D4.
When it went up in 1941, the dome-shaped Majestic was considered one of the best theatres in Asia and hosted peformances with Beijing opera superstars. Nowadays the focus is on local productions such as the Shanghai Youth Dance Troupe's award-winning take on *Farewell My Concubine*. Contemporary choreography, folk music and Hu opera also feature.

Shanghai Centre Theatre

1376 Nanjing Xilu, by Xikang Lu, Jingan (general 6279 8663/acrobatics 6279 8948). Metro Jingan Temple. **Open** *Box office* 9am-7pm daily. **Tickets** RMB 100-200. **No credit cards. Map** p248 C4.
Part of the same complex as the Portman Ritz-Carlton hotel, the Shanghai Centre hosts drama, opera, ballet and concerts, as well as film festivals and conferences. Past performers have included cellist Yo Yo-Ma, pianist Ivo Pogorelich, the Vienna Boy's Chorus, the Hong Kong Ballet and Harry Connick Jr and the Chieftains. The regular default performance (7.30pm nightly) is a popular acrobatic show.

Shanghai Circus World

2266 Gonghe Xinlu, by Guangzhong Lu, Zhabei (5665 3646/www.circus-world.com). **Open** *Box office* 9am-7.30pm daily. **Tickets** RMB 50-280. **No credit cards. Map** p240 C1.

Arts & Entertainment

Shanghai Grand Theatre. *See p185.*

At Shanghai Circus World, which looks like a giant golden golf ball half embedded in the ground, audiences are treated to *A Grand Evening of Acrobatic and Circus Performances*: expect conjuring, juggling, balancing acts and trained dogs, horses, lions, tigers and orangutans (the latter, according to the website, being a 'clever pet with strong desire of showing himself'). In addition, there's a regular acrobatic show performed by the Shanghai Acrobatic Troupe at 7.30pm Friday and Saturday.

Shanghai Grand Stage

1111 Caoxi Beilu, Shanghai Stadium, Xujiahui (6438 5200). Metro Shanghai Stadium. **Open** *Box office* 8.30am-5pm daily. **Tickets** RMB 80-1,680. **No credit cards**. **Map** p240 B4.

The indoor stage of Shanghai Stadium is neither friendly nor cosy, but this is usually where the shows that are too big for the likes of the Shanghai Centre end up. The fare here has included star turns from American magician David Copperfield and singer Sarah Brightman.

Shanghai Grand Theatre

300 Renmin Dadao, by Huangpi Beilu, Renmin Square (6386 8686 ext 2116/www.shgtheatre.com). Metro Renmin Park or Square. **Open** *Box office* 9am-7.30pm daily. **Tickets** RMB 80-6,000. **Credit** AmEx, DC, MC, V. **Map** p242 F4.

The city's premier venue for opera, classical music, ballet and drama. The most popular billings include musicals such as *Les Misérables, Cats, Sound of Music* and, coming soon, *Phantom of the Opera*. Performed in English, they are entirely imported, with foreign actors and producers. The theatre has also staged operas like *La Traviata* and solo performances with José Carreras. *Swan Lake* is performed every six months or so by the Kirov Ballet or other, lesser known companies. The Shanghai Broadcasting Symphony Orchestra gives regular concerts, and visitors such as the British Royal Philharmonic Orchestra also occasionally drop by.

Yifu Theatre

701 Fuzhou Lu, by Yunnan Nanlu, Renmin Square (6351 4668). Metro Renmin Park or Square. **Open** *Box office* 10am-7.30pm daily. **Tickets** RMB 30-500. **No credit cards**. **Map** p242 G4.

Around since 1921 but massively revamped in the early 1990s, the Yifu is the main venue for grand Chinese operas, particularly the Beijing variety – as indicated by the massive Beijing opera mask that dominates the theatre's entrance. Regular productions include such classics as *Dream of the Red Mansions*, and revolutionary fare like *Taking the Bandit's Stronghold*. Regular weekly performances take place at 7.30pm Tuesday and 1.30pm Sunday.

Chinese opera

Chinese opera is wrought from monotone music, simple props and minimalist staging. To express an action such as opening a door or riding a horse, only dance-like movements are used. It's fascinating to watch but often impossible to understand, as costumes, make-up and movements can carry specific motifs, and also denote a character's age, status and personality. The plot fodder is more familiar: heroes battle foes, good faces evil and lovers escape from unjust parents. To get a basic grasp of the story, you need to be aware of the four standard roles: *sheng* (male role), *dan* (female role), *jing* (painted face) and *chou* (clown).

Adding to the confusion are the many varieties of Chinese opera – estimates for the number of different types range from 300 into the thousands. Generally, these forms are discernible by their use of local dialects and distinct 'melodies'. Beijing opera (also called Peking opera) is considered to be the most refined. Weaving together elements of mime, dance, swordplay, song and acrobatics, it is a combination of operatics, drama and sketches. Add in stylised high-pitch voices accompanied by loud gongs, crashing cymbals, pounding drums and droning stringed instruments and you have a performance art that is compelling to some, sheer torture for others.

Huju, or Shenju, is the Shanghainese opera, but the style from nearby Shaoxing (also called Yue) is better known and more melodic, usually focusing on love stories. The older Kunju opera, established in the 16th century, originates from the Kunshan region of the Jiangsu province. Some Chinese ethnic minority groups also have their own local form of opera.

During Mao's Cultural Revolution, Beijing opera suffered as only eight 'model plays' were permitted, each themed around Communist activities during the anti-Japanese war or the civil war with the Nationalists, as well as the class struggles after the founding of the People's Republic. Traditional Beijing opera was allowed to be shown again in 1978, but it has lost much of its audience since then. Despite initiatives such as the Plum Blossom competition, which strive to bring Beijing opera to a younger crowd, the faithful fans are nearly always from an ageing generation.

Arts & Entertainment

A good move

A mother of three, a successful choreographer and an ex-colonel educated by the People's Liberation Army, Jin Xing is also the first official Chinese transsexual artist of modern times. After decades in the arts business, she is widely regarded as China's top avant-garde dancer. None of which has excited popular comment as much as the issue of why a few years ago she left Beijing, a city famed for its experimental arts and thriving cultural scene, and moved to Shanghai.

Ambition seems to have played a big part. Shanghai, it seems, has greater commercial potential. With the support of the government (transsexuality is no longer a dangerous taboo in China) allowing her Jinxing Modern Dance Company to stage shows in the Shanghai Grand Theatre, she has managed to marry her modern approach with popular success.

Xing so far has used Shanghai as a source of inspiration for her work, piquing the curiosity – already raised by her gender – of her new audience. In the show *Shanghai Tango*, the 'female' city of Shanghai meets true tango passion. In a collaboration between Xing and avant-garde pianist Joanna McGregor, *Cross Borders*, she draws on everyday Shanghai life with humour and clever observation, using revolutionary opera to inform the choreography. She is, by all reports, a brilliant dancer (as a young talent she was sent in 1987 to study in New York

with the likes of Martha Graham, Merce Cunningham and Jose Limon). Her innovations have attracted international attention, and there are plans to tour *Shanghai Tango* around the world.

Jin Xing is an unorthodox Chinese success story, and in that sense, she should be at home in Shanghai.

Other venues & companies

The quality of Shanghai's smaller venues is variable and might not be as dazzling as the write-ups in the English free press promise.

BizArt

4th floor, Building 7, 50 Moganshan Lu, by Aomen Lu, Jingan (6277 5358/www.biz-art.com). Metro Zhongtan Lu. **Open** 9am-6.30pm daily. **Tickets** varies. **No credit cards. Map** p240 C2.

A gallery majoring in installation art (*see p162*), BizArt also occasionally hosts theatre evenings. In 2004 the gallery was involved in a joint project with the experimental Lubricat Theatre Company.

Shanghai Art Theatre (Yihai Theatre)

466 Jiangning Lu, by Wuding Lu, Jingan (6256 8282). Metro Shimen Yilu, then taxi or 15 mins walk. **Open** 10am-8pm daily. **Tickets** RMB 30-280. **No credit cards. Map** p249 D3.

The Art Theatre is used mainly for classical music but it's also occasionally employed for productions of Yue and Yang opera and contemporary dance (Britain's Rambert Dance Company has performed here), as well as slightly more esoteric fare: at the time of writing the show is an educational drama about traffic rules called *Safety First*, which is set to run until 2006.

Shanghai Theatre Academy
630 Huashan Lu, by Zhengning Lu, French Concession (6248 8103). Metro Jingan Temple. **Open** *Box office* 8am-8pm daily. **Tickets** RMB 20-80. **No credit cards. Map** p246 B6.
Budding thesps from the Academy periodically stage interesting drama and dance at the school's theatre. Visiting troupes also turn up on occasion – in early 2004 the Academy was the venue for an intriguing ballet production of *The Last Emperor* that meshed traditional Chinese dance with waltz and jazz.

Yunfeng Theatre
1700 Beijing Xilu, by Jiaozhou Lu, Jingan (6258 2258). Metro Jingan Temple. **Open** *Box office* 10am-5pm daily. **Tickets** RMB 150-200. **No credit cards. Map** p248 B4.
A bit of a tourist trap, the Yunfeng offers a diet of acrobatics (including a popular motorcycle number) and regular porcelain juggling, with shows kicking off at 7.30pm nightly. From time to time the theatre breaks rank with shows such as March 2004's *Shadow of the Fencing Wall*, a drama exploring feminist questions in modern China.

Classical music

Apart from the extensive repertoire of the **Shanghai Grand Theatre** (*see p185*), classical music gets a sparse airing. Some of the hotels have regular recitals: at the **Jingan Hotel** (*see p42*) members of the Shanghai Symphony Orchestra play chamber music each Sunday from 8pm onwards (RMB 20). The **Jinjiang Hotel** (*see p41*) also has Sunday concerts, starting at 2pm (RMB 50). Students of the **Conservatory of Music** (20 Fenyang Lu, 6431 0334) regularly hold lunchtime concerts at their auditorium, as well as at 7.15pm on Sundays. The **Glamour Bar** (*see p120*) has chamber music provided by members of the Shanghai Broadcasting Symphony Orchestra every last Sunday of the month. Tickets are RMB 50; call 6350 9988 for bookings.

Shanghai Broadcasting Symphony Orchestra
Office: 1498 Wuding Lu (6252 3277/fax 6252 3267).
Despite its youth (established in 1996), the SBSO has already notched up collaborations with artists including Placido Domingo, Luciano Pavarotti, Isaac Stern and Barbara Hendricks. SBSO is the orchestra in residence at the Shanghai Grand Theatre.

Dance

See also p186 **A good move.**

Shanghai Oriental Youth Dance Company
Office: 1674 Hongqiao Lu, by Shuicheng Lu, Hongqiao (6270 6586/fax 6270 6586).
The city's most innovative dance company, although to call it 'experimental' would be an exaggeration. Successful shows to date include *Farewell My Concubine* and *Wild Zebra*. The 30-strong troupe has an average age of 20.

Shanghai Song & Dance Ensemble
Office: 1650 Hongqiao Lu (6219 5181/ fax 6275 9642).
The city's most high profile troupe focuses on ethnic dance, and large-scale opera and ballet. The ensemble was established in the late 1970s and the principal dancer and choreographer is 27-year-old Huang Doudou, who is responsible for a clutch of well-received shows including *China Go*.

English-language theatre

English-language theatre is on the increase, both as performed by local groups and by foreign drama troupes on tour. Musicals at the **Shanghai Grand Theatre** (*see p185*) are performed in English. For cabaret and English-language comedy, *see pp178-182* **Nightlife**.

Shanghai Dramatic Arts Centre
288 Anfu Lu, by Wukang Lu, French Concession (6473 4567). Metro Changshu Lu. **Open** *Box office* 9.30am-6.30pm daily. **Admission** RMB 80-800. **No credit cards. Map** p246 B6.
Shanghai's only consistent forum for international drama, established in 1995, also stages Chinese drama in English. Classics such as *Waiting for Godot* are bolstered by more modern fare like *The First Intimate Touch* and *www.com* – both stories of couples going online to find love. In 2003 the venue premièred the taboo-breaking AIDS melodrama *The Dying Kiss*. This is also where Eve Ensler's rabble-rousing *Vagina Monologues* was intended to run in late 2004, before it was stopped by the authorities.

Festivals & events

Shanghai's governing bodies are festival-happy, which generally means that cultural activity hits the city in the form of all-in-one events rather than as part of ongoing schedules. Some of the biggest annual arts fests include the **Lotus Award** (February), a competition between ten different song and dance shows; the **Shanghai International Spring Music Festival** (May), a cornucopia of international and local musicians playing everything from classical to jazz; the **Shanghai International Tourist Festival** (September), which features some open-air concerts; and the **Shanghai International Ballet Competition** (June/July), which brings together competitors from all over the world.
The most important festival, however, is the **Shanghai International Arts Festival** which, every autumn, floods the city with theatre, ballet and music events (*see also p152*).

Arts & Entertainment

Sport & Fitness

Sport in Shanghai is no longer an also-ran.

Gearing up for the new fitness fad on Renmin Square.

Sport culture in Shanghai, as in the rest of China, is still getting into shape. The plucky Han Dynasty days of 'kickball' – kicking around a pig's bladder stuffed with animal fur – have yet to be recaptured. This is hardly surprising given that China only resumed competing in global sporting events with the 1984 Olympics, and its football league didn't become professional until 1994. Prior to this, China was both banned from, and chose to boycott, world sports.

The situation has moved on. Yao Ming (*see p190* **Hoop and glory**), the golden boy from the Shanghai Sharks, is now huge in American basketball. International big-name sponsors are now eyeing China's honey-pot market and, as a consequence, Shanghai now has a piece of the BMW Asia Open, the Tennis Masters Cup and the International Formula 1 scene (*see p193* **On track for success**). Not to mention the fall-out from the Beijing 2008 Olympics.

Down at grass-roots level the situation is less dazzling. Schools and universities have nothing like the sporting programmes offered in the West, while governmental support is confined to the big fish. On the plus side, the number of domestic sports channels increased from zero in 1993 to a whopping 42 by 2003. The interest is obviously there, it's now just a matter of making the transition from the sofa to the sports ground.

Spectator sports

Sports fans are largely content to follow the action from the city's sports bars, notably **Malone's** (*see p121*), **O'Malley's** (*see p125*), and the **Long Bar** (*see p121*). To follow local sports check **www.s2mgroup.com.cn**, which carries an events calendar plus news.

Basketball

Yao Ming (*see p190* **Hoop and glory**) put the Shanghai Sharks in the big sea, but his departure to the Houston Rockets has left the team gasping for air in the mediocre China Basketball Association. Games are held at Luwan Stadium, which can get icy cold, and with no concessions in its empty corridors it lacks a certain something (including crowds). But for basketball die-hards, it can still be fun.

Luwan Stadium

128 Zhaojiabang Lu, by Ruijin Erlu, French Concession (6467 5358). Metro Shanxi Nanlu. **Tickets** RMB 40. **Map** p247 D8.

Football

Despite the odd Chinese footballer enjoying success in Europe, it would seem that turning out to watch Shanghai International or Shanghai Shenhua play at their respective Hongkou and Shanghai stadiums is as gripping as watching Accrington Stanley FC try-outs. How else to explain the paltry 5,000 who turned out in May 2004 to watch Shenhua beat Italian giants AC Milan 2-0 in an exhibition game? However, both teams regularly achieve top placings in the Chinese Super League. Catch them on their home turf most Sunday evenings from 7.40pm; tickets are RMB 50 and can be bought just before the match at the stadium. Shanghai Stadium, with a capacity of 80,000, is about twice the size of Hongkou Stadium.

Hongkou Stadium

715 Dongtiyuhui Lu, by Zhongshan Beierlu, Hongkou (6540 0009). Metro Hongkou Stadium. **Map** p241 D1.

Shanghai Stadium

1111 Caoxi Beilu, by Zhongshan Nanerlu, Xuhui (6438 5200/www.shanghai-stadium.online.sh.cn). Metro Shanghai Stadium. **Map** p240 B4.

Motor sports

The new Shanghai International Circuit is the pride of auto fans nationwide. Its shape emulates the Chinese character *shang*, meaning 'to grow', and symbolises money, money and more money (*see p193* **On track for success**). If you miss the annual F1 race, there's still the Motor GP (bikes), Formula 3, BMW, Renault and Formula 3000 events.

Shanghai International Circuit

Anting, Jiading (9682 6999/www.icsh.sh.cn). Shuttle bus from Shanghai Stadium. **Open** 9.30am-3.30pm daily. **Admission** RMB 400-500. **No credit cards**.

Participation sports

Some of the free city magazines, especially *that's Shanghai*, showcase a huge variety of sports from scuba-diving in the local aquarium to kite-surfing down the Huangpu River.

Basketball

Most universities have games in the evening; to join, you'll need to blag your way in as a student. For casual games try Xujiahui Park (between Zhoujiabang Lu and Hengshan Lu, 7.30am-9pm daily, with a break for lunch). Teams here are mixed and the play remains friendly. Participation is free and there is no official organiser – you just have to turn up.

Gang of Basketball Fans

Dynamic Recreation Club, 1011 Zhongshan Xilu, by Hongqiao Lu (contact David Shen 1381 635 5670/ davidshen99@canada.com). Metro Hongqiao Lu. **Meetings** (males only) 7-9pm Thur. **Admission** RMB 30.

The name says it all.

Girls Basketball

Shanghai Stadium, 1111 Caoxi Beilu, Xuhui (contact Virginia 1381 720 3586). Metro Shanghai Stadium. **Meetings** 6.30-9.30pm Wed; 7-10pm Sat; 7-10am Sun. **Admission** free. **Map** p240 B4.

The only strictly female practice in town.

Promax International Basketball League

404 Yuyuan Lu, by Wulumuqi Beilu, Jingan (contact Carlo 1381 832 4605/basiagroup@yahoo.com). Metro Jingan Temple. **Meetings** 12.30-4pm Sat, Sun. **Admission** RMB 3,500/team. **Map** p248 B5.

The best bet for organised and competitive play.

Dragon boat racing

This is a traditional Chinese form of rowing in long, narrow boats that sit around 20. Rowers are kept to their stroke by the beat of a drum. It's very demanding, but if you're going to row in China, this is how.

Shanglong Dragon Boat Club

Contact Cathy 1366 144 7145. **Meetings** 8am Sun at Gubei Starbucks, 20 Shuicheng Nanlu, for onward travel to Dianshan Lake (45mins away). **Admission** RMB 40-70, depending on numbers.

This club, formed in 1999, has been dubbed the 'United Nations Dragon Boat Team' due to its mix of over 20 different nationalities. Practice sessions involve more than one boat so beginners are welcome. Remember to bring gloves (preferable) and a change of clothes (obligatory – everything gets wet).

Football

Shanghai's international league is the most competitive amateur league in China. Ten teams organised by nationality compete weekly. They are sponsored by different bars around the city, who offer pitch rent, team strip, transport and a good chance of a free beer at the end of the match. There is also the possibility of competing in Asian tournaments – hot team of the moment are the Shanghai Shooters, sponsored by long-serving expats' bar Malone's and 2004 winners of the Thailand and Manila championship titles.

Arts & Entertainment

rnational
jue

untry Club, 3958 Zhaokun Lu,
ngjiang (5766 1666 or contact
182 7960/www.eteams.com/sifl).
Meeting ι Sat. **Admission** free.
Matches take place at the club's two pitches.

Golf

Check the local magazines for golf leagues.
Sasha's (*see p126*) runs a corporate league
the last Wednesday of the month. RMB 540
covers transport, lunch and all fees – a bargain.
For information contact Sunny: 1370 179 3840.

Shanghai Binhai Golf Club

Binhai Resort, Baiyulan Dadao, Pudong (5805 8888/
www.binhaigolf.com). **Membership** RMB 3,380/yr.
Non-members approx RMB 500 Mon-Fri; RMB 900
Sat, Sun.
Designed by five-times British Open Champion
Peter Thomson, a course packed with bunkers.

Shanghai Lujiazui Golf Club

501 Yindheng Zhonglu, Pudong (5878 3844/
www.lujiazui-club.com). Metro Lu Jia Zui. **Admission**
RMB 20 with box of 30 balls Mon-Fri; RMB 120/hr
with unlimited balls Sat, Sun.
A driving range in the Lujiazui business district, with
98 bays and a distance of 250 yards to the net.

Tianma Country Club

3958 Zhaokun Lu, Tianma Town, Songjiang
(5766 1666). **Membership** US$50,000/lifetime.
Non-members RMB 730 Tue-Fri.

A popular course that scores lots of plus points
for its fairly challenging layout and impressive
mountainous backdrop.

Horse-riding

Most horses at the schools are of the retired
racehorse variety, except those at the spanking
new and professional Meadow Brook.

Huijhang Riding Ranch

517 Xinhua Lu, Pudong (5084 8898). **Open** 8.30am-
9pm daily. **Rates** RMB 160-200/hr Mon-Fri; RMB
200-250/hr Sat, Sun. **No credit cards.**
This ranch has three practice areas and a VIP track
with jumps. However, neither the well-maintained
facilities nor the friendly instructors and good ratio
of grooms to horses is enough to detract from the
forlorn state of the horses.

Jialiang Equestrian Club

1858 Sanlu Lu, Pudong (3411 0089/www.horse
china.com). **Open** 8.30am-5.30pm daily. **Rates**
RMB 190/45mins Mon-Fri; RMB 230/45mins Sat,
Sun. **Credit** AmEx, MC, V.
Set amid rolling fields and boasting 30 well-groomed
horses, this is a winning location, only 20 minutes
from the town centre.

Meadow Brook

3088 Shenzhuan Highway, Qingpu (6983 0055/
www.meadowbrookshanghai.com). **Open** 9am-7pm
Tue-Fri; 8am-7pm Sat, Sun. **Rates** *without instructor*
RMB 210/45mins Mon-Fri; RMB 260/45mins Sat, Sun.
Local instructor RMB 130-170/lesson. *Foreign*
instructor RMB 250-350/lesson. **No credit cards.**

Hoop and glory

At 2.25 metres (seven feet six inches) and
140 kilograms (310 pounds), Yao Ming is big.
So big that when riding in a car or standing in
an elevator he takes on mismatched, *Alice
in Wonderland* dimensions. Yao is also a
huge success story – a Shanghainese
basketball ace who bounded out of China to
the top of the US league, earning senseless
amounts of cash along the way.

It wasn't easy. Only a few years ago he
was still trying to gain permission from the
Chinese authorities to break free from his
hometown team, the Shanghai Sharks,
to play with the big guns in the US. As he
pointed out in a 2001 interview given in
Beijing, 'In China, basically, I don't have
any opponents.' Yao eventually got his wish
and more, becoming the first foreign rookie
number one draft pick in NBA history. And
boy, is he popular. Ticket sales for his

matches have reached record levels, thanks
in no small part to a particularly fanatic
American-Asian fan base.

His score card hasn't been bad either.
As centre for the Houston Rockets, Yao made
the NBA's All-Stars team for both his first
seasons, averaging 17.7 points and nine
rebounds per game this season. Although
the sports pages sometimes criticise Yao
for being too 'nice' and not greedy enough on
court, he's been held up as an answer to the
Lakers' legendary centre Shaquille O'Neill.
His income has also rocketed ($14.6 million
in 2003) thanks to endorsement deals with
McDonald's, Reebok, Pepsi, Visa and Apple
Computers. Yao's outsized income and
status as one of the world's most recognised
players put him at the head of *Forbes*
magazine's 2004 list of Chinese celebrities.
Not bad for a 23-year-old boy from Shanghai.

Basketball pin-up **Yao Ming** observes
a young wannabe. *See p190.*

Those cats were fast as lightning.

The newest addition to Shanghai's riding schools, Meadow Brook is also one of the best. Its main selling point is that it boasts fresh horses – not a retired racehorse in sight. Beginners enjoy sand tracks, more advanced riders can take on grass courses. The school is a one-hour trip out of the city.

Racquet sports

Tennis and squash courts increase in number with each new upmarket residence or hotel. Court rental should cost around RMB 50/hour. For a game of badminton, try the Shanghai Stadium (see p189).

JC Mandarin

1225 Nanjing Xilu, by Shanxi Nanlu (6279 1888). Metro Jingan Temple or Shimen Yilu. **Open** 7am-10pm daily. **Rates** *tennis* RMB 40/hr; *squash* RMB 75/hr. **Credit** AmEx, MC, V. **Map** p249 D4.
Blissfully central, and its squash courts are said to be the best in town – however, the sports wing was under renovation at the time of writing.

Rugby

Shanghai Rugby & Football Club

Biyun Lu, by Lanan Lu, Pudong (5030 3886/ www.shanghaifootballclub.com). **Open** 9.30am-4.30pm Sat, Sun. **Admission** free.
A proper centre for sport and expats, equipped with large playing fields and a clubhouse for refreshments. Check the website for details of multiple team sports and tournaments.

Sailing

Shanghai Boat & Yacht Club

Shanghai Aquatic Sports Centre, Puqingping Hwy, Qingpu (www.shanghaibyc.org). **Membership** RMB 2,000/yr, plus joining fee RMB 500.
This club has recently moved to the well-equipped Government Water Activity Centre in the Qingpu district, 32km (20 miles) west of the centre. Meet at Sasha's (see p126) between 9am and 10am Sunday for onward travel to the centre. Help is offered to beginners, although this is not an instructing club.

Skiing

Shanghai Yinqixing Indoor Skiing

1835 Zixing Lu, by Gudai Lu, Minhang (6478 8666/ www.skiing.com.cn). Free shuttle bus from Xinzhuang metro station every 30mins. **Open** 9.30am-11pm Mon-Thur; 9.30am-1am Fri, Sat. **Admission** RMB 118/hr; RMB 98/hr 7pm-1am Fri, Sat. **Credit** AmEx, MC, V.
The second biggest indoor slope in the world holds more novelty value than serious skiing action. It's doubly curious when you consider that most Shanghainese have never seen snow.

Swimming

Hotels and fancy apartment complexes usually have pools and most allow visitors in for around RMB 40 a pop. It is always obligatory to wear a swimming hat, which can be bought at most pools.

Dino Beach

78 Xinzhen Lu, Minhang (6478 3333). Metro Xinzhuang, then bus 763 for 4 stops. **Open** *25 June-mid Sept* 9am-9pm daily. **Admission** RMB 100/day; RMB 50/day children. **No credit cards**.

A poular water amusement park with an artificial beach and the world's biggest wave pool.

Jingan Sports Centre

151 Kangding Lu, by Jiangning Lu, Jingan (6772 6137). Metro Shimen Yilu. **Open** 7am-9.30pm daily. **Admission** RMB 15-30. **No credit cards**. **Map** p249 D3.

Three indoor pools of which two are roped off with lanes for serious swimmers. There's also a super-vised kiddies' area.

Mandarin City

788 Hongxu Lu, by Shuicheng Lu, Changning (6405 0404 ext 8612). Bus 69, get off at Guyang Lu stop. **Open** 7am-1.30pm Mon-Wed, Fri-Sun; 7.30am-1.30pm Thur. **Admission** RMB 50/day; RMB 30 for kids.

Located inside a residential compound, this is an open-air pool with snack bar.

Martial arts

Would-be Bruce Lees looking to learn their craft in Shanghai can sign up for karate, tae kwon do, viet vo dao and judo; check the local magazines and gyms (*see p194*) for further details of courses and classes.

Kung fu

Most schools teach modern kung fu, which only covers the basics of the original form. Learning traditional kung fu takes lifetime commitment and most 'real' Masters have been practising since childhood. The instructors listed below teach the traditional form and expect extreme dedication from their pupils. Foreigners are humoured because they pay money.

Long Wu International Kung Fu Centre

215 Shanxi Nanlu, by Fuxing Zhonglu, French Concession (5465 0042). Metro Shanxi Nanlu. **Times** 7-9pm daily. **Rates** RMB 400/5 lessons. **No credit cards**. **Map** p247 D7.

Teachers include Kai Uwe Pel, who practises the authentic Praying Mantis of the Shaolin style. Yes, he's German, but word in the kung fu world is that he is a very good instructor. Modern wushu style is also available and some English is spoken.

Wang Xiao Peng

Kerry Centre Gym, 2nd floor, Kerry Centre, 1515 Nanjing Xilu, by Tongren Lu, Jingan (6279 4625). Metro Jingan Temple. **Times** varies, call for details. **Rates** *membership* RMB 13,000/yr. **Credit** AmEx, MC, V. **Map** p248 C5.

Wang (aka Darren) is a sixth-generation member of the Heart and Soul 6 Harmony Boxing Kung Fu family. He teaches tai chi and kung fu motivational

On track for success

Money and motor sports have long been bedfellows. But as Formula 1 makes advances towards the Middle East and China, it's big money that's being sought. Malaysia has a new circuit, as does Bahrain and, most recently, Shanghai. All three courses were designed by Hermann Tilke, and all three are breathtaking. Tilke, a 50-year-old German architect-engineer, began his career drafting plans for tennis centres; he is now the pre-eminent name in racetrack design, favoured for his technically punishing but visually striking creations. This latest project in Shanghai was bankrolled to the tune of RMB 2 billion, and it carries the bulk of China's hopes for achieving a significant footing on the international sports circuit.

The course opened in early June 2004, ahead of its first major roadtest: the inaugural Chinese Grand Prix on 26 September. Through the PR blitz of models and fanfares, a general consensus seemed to emerge that the track is something of a toughie. There are 14 turns,

some at eight per cent grades. 'What the hell was the guy who designed this smoking?' asked one buff on an online motor sports forum. The difficulty is deliberate – Tilke himself said he aimed to create 'closely fought, spectacular races'.

Typical of Shanghai's dramatic turnarounds, Tilke's concrete and steel vision rose out of flat swampy farmland in the Jiading suburb, traditional home of the city's car industry. It now stands as an unmissable landmark, a distinctly futuristic affair pronged by two long hairpin bends and protected by huge Chinese umbrella-esque sunshades. Silverstone looks like a supermarket car park in comparison. The circuit's strange shape is not entirely born of Tilke's imagination: in keeping with the Chinese love of symbols, it is a rough approximation of the Chinese character *shang*, which means to grow or flower. An apt association for Shanghai and a neat way to underline that this is a Chinese imprint on an international market.

Arts & Entertainment

The serenity and poise of **tai chi**.

training for corporate executives. If the harmony of business and kung fu principles doesn't turn you off, you can also find Wang instructing classes at the Hilton Hotel Spa. This is a good option for those who don't speak Chinese and aren't short of cash.

Tai chi

Early-morning tai chi practice remains one of the most magical aspects of Shanghai. Groups start at 4.30am in winter and 5am in summer and continue until around 9.30am. You should ask the Master's permission to join and offer payment, although usually it is free. If he sees you are committed, he will guide you, but it may be months before this happens. **Fuxing Park**, **Renmin Park** and **Liuxun Park** (next to Hongkou Stadium) are the most popular parks.

Fitness

For yoga studios and classes, *see p173*.

Dance

Jazz du Funk
555 Yanan Zhonglu, by Shanxi Lu, French Concession (6466 8755/www.jazzdufunk.com). Metro Shanxi Nanlu. **Rates** (20 wks) RMB 1,300-3,300. **No credit cards. Map** p249 D5.

Beginner, intermediate and advanced belly dancing, hip hop, tango, jazz, street jazz, jazz ballet, ballet and salsa. Dancewear available.

Shanghai Swings
2nd floor, Shanghai Community Centre, 400 Hongqiao Lu, by Yishan Lu, Xujiahui (contact Jimbo 1316 625 5905/www.chinaswings.com). Metro Xujiahui. **Classes** (beginners) 4-7.30pm, (advanced) 6-7.30pm Sun. **Rates** RMB 300/4 classes. **No credit cards.**

Swing classes are taught in English and Mandarin. On Wednesday nights there is an informal 'bop' at Jazz Seeker (1 Wulumuqi Nanlu, by Taojiang Lu), with a basic lesson starting at 8pm, followed by a band (9-11pm); entrance is RMB 35.

Gyms

Prices teeter around RMB 1,500 per month for the luxury of a swimming pool, otherwise, standard gym facilities cost around RMB 600 per month. Check with hotel concierges and *that's Shanghai* for full listings. Customer service, however, is something that no amount of money will buy. Staff are often too busy with their own workouts to bother with customers.

Fitness First
Plaza 66, 1266 Nanjing Xilu, by Tongren Lu, Jingan (6288 0152). Metro Jingan Temple. **Open** 6.30am-11pm Mon-Fri; 7am-10pm Sat, Sun. **Membership** RMB 1,600/3 mths (minimum). **Credit** AmEx, DC, MC, V. **Map** p249 D4.

Down in the basement of the plush shopping centre, FF is spacious with rows of high-tech equipment, nationally certified trainers and a particularly well-organised free weights area. There's also a solarium.

Kerry Centre Gym
2nd floor, Kerry Centre, 1515 Nanjing Xilu, by Tongren Lu, Jingan (6279 4625). Metro Jingan Temple. **Open** 6am-11pm daily. **Membership** RMB 13,000/yr. **Credit** AmEx, DC, MC, V. **Map** p248 C5.

Small and perfectly formed. Membership is limited so the place never gets crowded. The facilities include a swimming pool, jacuzzi, steam room, sauna, solarium and outdoor tennis courts.

Physical
5th floor, Metro City, 1111 Zhaojiabang Lu, by Hengshan Lu, Xujiahui (6426 8282). Metro Xujiahui. **Open** 7am-10pm daily. **Membership** RMB 650/mth. **Credit** AmEx, MC, V. **Map** p246 A9.

A large basic gym with swimming pool, sauna and aerobics studio in the middle of shopping-mall land.

Total Fitness
5th floor, 819 Nanjing Xilu, by Shimen Yilu, Jingan (6255 3535/www.totalfitness.com.cn). Metro Shimen Yilu. **Membership** RMB 600/mth; day pass RMB 140. **Credit** AmEx, DC, MC, V. **Map** p249 E4.

No swimming pool, but there is exercise machinery aplenty, a sauna and a solarium. Plus, for those who care, this is the only gym to boast a boxing ring.

Trips Out of Town

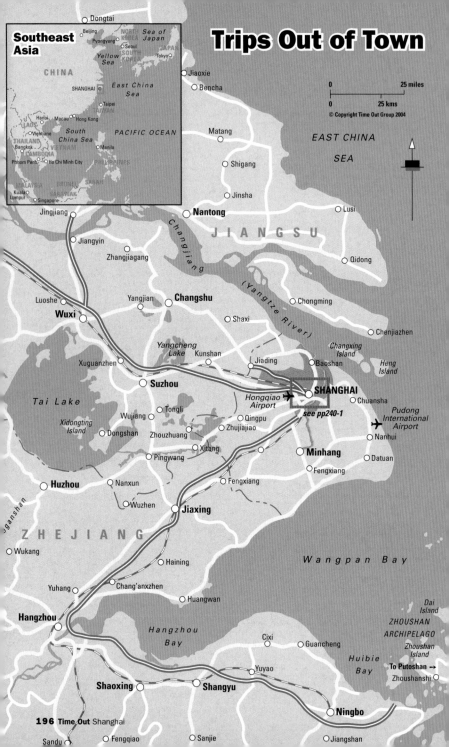

Trips Out of Town

Southeast Asia

East China Sea

0   25 miles
0   25 kms
© Copyright Time Out Group 2004

EAST CHINA SEA

Dongtai

Jiaoxie

Bencha

Matang

Shigang

Jinsha

Lusi

Nantong

JIANGSU

Qidong

Jingjiang

Changjiang

Jiangyin

Zhangjiagang

Chongming

(Yangtze River)

Chenjiazhen

Luoshe

Yangjian

Changshu

Wuxi

Shaxi

Yangcheng Lake

Kunshan

Jiading

Changxing Island

Heng Island

Baoshan

Xuguanzhen

Suzhou

Hongqiao Airport

SHANGHAI

Chuansha

Pudong International Airport

Tai Lake

Wujiang

Tongli

Qingpu

see pp240-1

Xidongting Island

Dongshan

Zhouzhuang

Zhujiajiao

Nanhui

Xitang

Minhang

Datuan

Pingwang

Fengxiang

Fengxiang

Huzhou

Nanxun

Wuzhen

Wangpan Bay

Z H E J I A N G

Jiaxing

Wukang

Dai Island

Haining

ZHOUSHAN ARCHIPELAGO

Chang'anxzhen

Yuhang

Huangwan

Zhoushan Island

Hangzhou

Hangzhou Bay

Cixi

Guancheng

Huibie Bay

To Putoshan →

Zhoushanshi

Yuyao

Shaoxing

Shangyu

Ningbo

Sandu

Fengqiao

Sanjie

Jiangshan

Getting Started

No matter where you travel around Shanghai you're never far from a madding crowd.

Slipping away from Shanghai for peace or adventure leads you into one of two provinces, Zhejiang or Jiangsu. Situated to the west of the city, both regions are gradually being threatened by encroaching urbanism and it's necessary to travel quite far afield to find tranquility and unspoilt ruralism. What these territories have traditionally prospered from is water – it's everywhere. Canals, rivers and lakes dominate the scenery and, to a large extent, the tourist industry.

The ancient 'canal towns' that once served as cargo waterways now trade on their picture postcard looks, and are more successful (and more crowded) than ever. The old cultural capital of Jiangsu, Suzhou, has attempted to clean up its polluted canals, but it remains most famous for its beautiful Zen gardens. The capital of Zhejiang, Hangzhou, also has a watery asset in Lake Xihu.

Zhejiang in general is more lush than Jiangsu, and boasts some beautiful green mountains. It also encompasses the Zhoushan archipelago, including the pretty Buddhist island of Putuoshan, which is beginning to be opened up to travellers through improved transport links.

Hangzhou, the nearby village of Moganshan, and Putuoshan island are all best visited over a couple of days – indeed, for the latter two, if you tried to make it there and back within one day you'd only be leaving yourself a couple of hours to look around. By contrast, a paucity of accommodation and their relative close proximity to Shanghai makes the canal towns best done as daytrips.

Leaving the chaos and dazzle of Shanghai for the surrounding towns can result in a city come-down. Asides from Hangzhou, out in the sticks settlements are shabbier, fewer people speak English and spitting is a more prevalent pastime. But the balance is restored by some stunning coastal and mountain vistas and friendly country folk. Some areas – especially the canal towns – are verging on tourist traps but it usually takes no more than a short stroll off the main drag to find life being lived untouched: monks chanting on islets at sunset, bamboo farmers taking breaks on mountainsides and red courtyard roses being tended in canal towns.

Welcome to **Zhouzhuang**. See p200.

TOURIST INFORMATION

There are few official tourist information centres outside Shanghai and information is patchy. Some places have a China International Travel Service (CITS) but you will probably be better gathering any information you need before you leave Shanghai. Alternatively, you can look up many destinations on the web at either www.travelchinaguide.com or www.chinatravel.com. For discounted hotel rooms in any destination, try the Chinese online giants – www.elong.com or www.ctrip.com.

BASICS

All hotel prices given are the rack rate. Discounts of up to 40 per cent can normally be negotiated outside of peak season, and especially on winter weekdays. During the spring, May and October holidays prices may well rise higher than the rack rate.

Getting around

By bus

Local buses run to all the destinations covered in this chapter, apart from Putuoshan and Zhujiajiao. The easiest option is to catch one of the sightseeing buses that run from **Shanghai Stadium** (1111 Caoxi Beilu, by Zhongshan Nanerlu, Xujiahui, metro Shanghai Stadium, map p240 B4). These buses are largely used by domestic daytrippers. They typically leave from 8am onwards and return before dark.

For information (in Chinese) call 6426 5555. There are also terminals at **Hongkou Stadium** (5696 3248) and **Yangpu Stadium** (6580 3210).

By rail

Travel by train often results in a better view and is usually more sociable. As everyone is born equal in Communist China there are no first- or second-class sections; the Chinese equivalents are 'soft seat' and 'hard seat'. The former is a comfortable way to travel, the latter more of an experience. Trains run to Hangzhou, Suzhou and Wuzhen.

Tickets can be bought on the day at the train station and there is an 'English-speaking' window for those lacking the necessary language skills. The spring, May and October holidays are a crowded time to travel and you need some determined elbow-work to get a ticket. For railway station details, see p214. Alternatively, tickets can be bought from the **China Youth Travel Service** (see p215).

By car

Most of the places listed in this chapter (apart from Putuoshan) are extremely accessible by car. It is especially good to have a car in the surrounds of Hangzhou and Moganshan, as it gives you the freedom to stop off and explore the lovely surrounding countryside. Cars are less practical in the canal towns and also unnecessary in Suzhou, where most sights are in the town. Unless you start heading off down country lanes, roads are usually in extremely good condition and many new highways have been built. For more information on driving and car hire, see p216.

By boat

Ferries can be taken to Putuoshan and other domestic destinations. Tickets can be bought from either the **CITS** (2 Jinling Donglu, 6323 8749), the **ferry booking office** (1 Jinling Donglu) or **Shiliupu wharf** (111 Zhongshan Dong Erlu), where most domestic ferries depart. There are also a number of travel agencies just along from the ferry office on Zhongshan Dongerlu. As obvious as it sounds, don't buy the tickets from the men outside the ferry offices as nobody will give you a refund when it turns out the tickets are fake. Safety is dubious on most of the ferries but you're probably still safer afloat than on Shanghai's roads.

By bike

All the places listed in this chapter are accessible by bike. While you don't need to be Lance Armstrong to manage these rides, the best places to cycle to are probably those where you can get a train half the way, for example Suzhou and Hangzhou.

Wolf's bike shop (contact Lao Wang 1380 195 3000, wolfs@263.net) both repairs and rents bikes, and organises weekly trips out of the city (these are a good option as main roads are avoided and there's no chance of getting lost). The shop can also provide details of routes.

The best Destinations

For a stroll in the country
Moganshan has endless swathes of green bamboo forest. See p206.

For gazing at the moon
Hangzhou is renowned for its beautiful clear evenings – go for autumn nights, when the moon is full. See p203.

For having your prayers answered
Thousands of pilgrims flock to **Putuoshan** every year to ask for blessing from the Buddhist goddess Guanyin. See p210.

For horticulture and philosophy
The beautifully groomed, feng shui'd gardens at **Suzhou** make the Chelsea Flower Show look scrubby. See p209.

For water running through it
Canal town **Xitang** has kept a low profile and lots of charm. See p200.

For diversity
Tongli combines canal-town prettiness with a UNESCO-rated garden – and a sex museum. See p199.

Trips Out of Town

The Canal Towns

Like a daytripper to water...

Reflective but far from quiet **Zhouzhuang**. *See p200*.

The canal towns all line the banks of the Grand Canal system, which was first burrowed across the Yantze River delta during the era of the Tang Dynasty (AD 618-907). The canals were a vital link connecting southern China with the Imperial court in the north. This network of waterways is considered one of China's greatest feats of engineering, ranking alongside the Great Wall. Despite the first clod of earth being spaded well over a thousand years ago, the system is still very much a work in progress with the Chinese having just completed a mind-bogglingly enormous dam on the upper reaches of the Yangtze.

The region of the river delta is currently the scene of an entertaining battle between the so-called canal towns. Through the medium of advertising they bicker over who has the oldest 'world-renowned' buildings and the most famous canals, and which town's restaurants do the most delicious pork leg (a local favourite).

Whatever their relative merits, the formula in each town is basically the same: a chunk of prime real estate is pedestrianised to create a fiction of ye olde China, often with gondoliers in

costume, to which a front entrance hurdle is erected for the purpose of collecting an entrance fee (typically around RMB 60). Admission gets visitors on to all the rides – or rather into all the old houses and museums. But despite being trussed-up tourist spectacles, some of these towns are worth a daytrip; beyond the hype and the packaging they do offer fascinating insights into Confucian gentrification and the obsession with aesthetics that prevailed during the towns' heydays.

There are many more more canal towns than we describe in this guide but the following are the most accessible and boast some of the best scenery. For anyone whose time is limited, don't worry: visit one and you've seen them all.

Tongli

Tongli is a good two-and-a-half hours distant from Shanghai but it's only 18 kilometres (11 miles) from Suzhou (*see pp207-209*), and the two are usually combined in one trip. Tongli is remarkably pretty and has managed to get one up on all its rival canal towns by securing

Laundry hour...

a coveted UNESCO World Heritage listing for its **Tuisi Garden**. Built by retired government official Ren Lansheng between 1885 and 1887, this is considered to be one of the finest gardens in the region, and the equal of anything to be seen in famed garden city Suzhou. Other than 49 stone bridges (you'd think they would build one more to make it a round half-century) the town had few other genuine tourist attractions until quite recently, but that has changed with the high-profile arrival of the sex museum – *see p202* **Sex (but not in the city)**.

Wuzhen

Wuzhen is a slickly-packaged town, where tourists are led by the nose down alleys lined with museums and little shops selling all sorts from locally made rattan baskets to cloth shoes. Despite deft presentation and marketing, the town is less attractive to the Shanghai tourist crowds simply because it's so far away from the big city – which is good news to the more independent traveller because amid the souvenir dross there are some truly worthwhile sights. The best of these is the **Shadow Puppet Play House**, where intricately sewn leather puppets are used to cast shadows in the telling of ancient legends. This is one of the few

places where you can still see this dying art being performed. Also worth a look is the **rice wine distillery**, if only for the tasting session at the end. Wuzhen is known for its rice wine, called *sanbai* (thrice white wine), which is nasty stuff similar to Japanese saké.

Xitang

Xitang has only recently jumped on the 'canal town' band wagon, possibly because it has few famous sights to tempt the local tourists and it's relatively off the beaten path. Bad news for municipal revenues maybe, but good news for visitors who'll find one of the prettier, less heavily-trodden towns on the delta, complete with friendly, laid-back residents who are as yet uncorrupted by the tour bus dollar (or *yuan*).

Xitang's handful of formal attractions run to a few small museums, including the **Pearl Button Museum**, where you can watch – what else? – buttons being hand made. It sounds dull but it's a surprisingly interesting cottage craft and far more entertaining than anything on offer at the **Museum of Fans**, which is a little further up the cobbled lane.

Unlike other canal towns, many of Xitang's narrow alleys are roofed – every homeowner is responsible for maintaining the section of roof in front of their house. The 1,300-metre (4,290-foot) main alley is stunning at dusk when as locals hang red lanterns along its length.

Zhouzhuang

Zhouzhuang is currently winning the canal town popularity race and all because of a painting. Several years ago, Chen Yifei, a reasonably well known New York-based Chinese artist, completed a watercolour of Zhouzhuang, which was subsequently presented to Deng Xiaoping. Not only was the town thrust into the spotlight by this brush with a national leader, it was then capped with the official governmental title of 'Number One Tourist Destination'. So now Chinese tourists are flocking to visit and the authorities are spending a fortune sprucing the place up.

Zhouzhuang is an undeniably picturesque concentration of some of the best-preserved Ming and Qing Dynasty canal homes – more than 60 per cent of buildings in the town centre dates from these eras. Several sites have been set aside as tourist attractions including the **Hall of Shen's Residence**, which is a rambling residence of 100 rooms surrounding a central courtyard and, just down the lane, the **Hall of Zhang's Residence**, which features the less-than-charming-smelling Roujiang River running through one of its 70 rooms.

Zhujiajiao

Zhujiajiao is close to Shanghai but that
accessibilty is a double-edged sword. While you
can easily bus here in under an hour, so can 16
million-plus residents of Shanghai. It doesn't
help that the place is so small. The hordes of
tourists usually head for the **Setting Fish
Free Bridge**, from which you can do just that
– toss a goldfish into the canal. Legend has it
that there was once a Buddhist temple by the
bridge where devotees could buy a captive fish
and set it free as a form of worship. These days
it's more of a death sentence considering the
state of the filthy canals.

Where to stay

Like any tourist attraction that suffers the
plague of daytrippers, the canal towns are at
their most peaceful at night. But not all the
towns have hotels – at least not anywhere
near the centre – and the only option may be
to brave some dodgy local hostel. In fact, the
situation is so bad that most tourist agencies
discourage tourists from staying in the canal
towns, claiming the accommodation is not
suitable for foreign guests. **Jinjiang Tours** in
Shanghai (191 Changle Lu, French Concession,
6289 7830) is one of the few agencies that can
help with accommodation in the canal towns.

Otherwise, in Wuzhen, try the **Midi
Grand Hotel** (Ziye Lu, 0573 872 6688, R.
480) or the **Hanlin Hotel** (27 Bang Hai Shan
0573 871 8799, RMB 580). The **Yuejiao Hotel**
in Xitang (8 Hongfu Lu, 0573 456 4344, RMB
130) has clean, old-style standard rooms. In
Zhouzhuang try the **Yun Ting Villa** (99
Quanwang Lu, 512 5721 9999, RMB 380).

Because the towns are busiest on the weekend,
many hotels offer discounts during the week.
Another option is to stay in Suzhou (*see pp207-
209*) and make daytrips from there.

Getting there

By bus

Shanghai City Sightseeing Buses (Shanghai
Stadium, Gate 5, 666 Tianyao Qiao Lu, 6426 5555)
leave daily for all of the canal towns. Zhouzhuang
buses depart at 7am, 8.30am, 9am, 9.45am and return
at 2.30pm or 4pm. Wuzhen buses depart at 8.45am
and return at 4.30pm. Xitang tours leave at 8.35am
and include a morning at nearby town Jiaxing.
Zhujiajiao tours depart every half hour from 7.30am
to 11am and return half-hourly until 4pm. Tongli
buses depart at 9am and return at 4.30pm. Prices
range from RMB 70 to RMB 120 depending on
whether lunch and guides are included in the fare.

By train

Visiting the canal towns by train is more complicated
than doing it by bus. The best option is to take a
train to either Jiaxing or Suzhou (*see p209*) and travel

... and rush hour at **Tongli**. *See p199*.

om there. Almost every ...g those to Hangzhou, ...services to Jiaxing ...oon from the Shanghai ...ng train station there are ...5) and Wuzhen (RMB 12),

Gui...

China Internatio...... ravel Service (CITS, Room 610, 1277 Beijing Xilu, 6289 8279) can tailor individual tours with a car and driver or group tours in a minivan. CITS tours are the most comfortable and flexible option but they are also the priciest at RMB 1,120 for an individual tour and up to RMB 380 per person for a group of ten people or more. Prices vary depending on the destination, group size and the inclusion of lunch, town entrance fees and English-speaking guide in the package.

Tourist information

The canal towns' entrance ticket booths double as tourist information centres but the service is very limited, particularly if you don't happen to speak Mandarin. However, tickets are accompanied by an invaluable English-language map of the town. If this map is not provided with your ticket, ask for it. Each town has a tourist website that gives an overall feel for the place before you go:

Tongli www.china-tongli.com
Wuzhen www.wuzhen.com.cn/wuzhen.eng/
Xitang www.xitang.com.cn
Zhouzhuang www.zhouzhuang.net
Zhujiajiao www.zhujiajiao.com

Sex (but not in the city)

Originally located in a prime tourist spot off Shanghai's Nanjing Donglu, China's sole sex museum was forced to move two years after opening when the local government decreed that no external signage was allowed because it would contravene a Chinese law that forbids the advertising of sexual products.

The museum moved to a new location where septuagenarian director and Professor of Sexology, Liu Dalin was permitted to hang a sign but it was so far off the beaten track that nobody ever visited. And then Tongli stepped in to the rescue, offering a free home for the museum in a spacious old Qing Dynasty girls' school. Where once rows of chaste little maidens recited from the Red Book are now 4,000-plus items of erotica representing over 5,000 years of Chinese sexual history including double-headed lesbian dildos, brush-paintings of outdoor orgies and a set of enamel tiles depicting a naked couple frolicking with assorted bemused animals. That's not to mention the rings worn by high-class hookers to symbolise oral services; the statues of double-bodied Mizong Buddhas engaged in intercourse; and wooden chairs specially fitted with elongated arms and wooden pillows to support wide-flung legs and lift the buttocks.

It's not all titters and sniggers. As women were tokens of wealth they were often treated as mere chattels. Cue saddles with wooden erections used to 'ruin' adulterous women, and binding equipment made to constrict the growth of a girl's feet – not only did Chinese men find the deformity attractive, it made the women physically incapable of running away.

Chinese Ancient Sex Culture Museum

Wu Jiang, Tongli, Jiangsu (0512 6332 2973/ 0512 6332 2972). **Open** 7.45am-5.30pm daily. **Admission** *over-18s only* RMB 15-20.

Chinese Ancient Sex Culture Museum

Hangzhou & Moganshan

Misty forests, orange moons and secluded temples – but modernisation is creeping up fast.

Xihu, the lake at Hangzhou.

Hangzhou

On arrival, the much-hyped beauty of Hangzhou ('tourist capital of China') is not immediately apparent, and visitors may wonder why Marco Polo – who stopped here in the 13th century – described it as one of the world's most splendid cities. The main sprawl is commercial, industrial and ruthlessly expanding, but Xihu (West Lake) is why travellers flock here. Stretching three kilometres (two miles), the lake is surrounded by hills and lush green forests, scattered with pagodas and temples. For thousands of years the views have inspired Chinese poets and writers; now they appeal to newly-weds posing in bridal finery against the backdrop of so many ancient Chinese love stories. Hangzhou has long been on the Chinese tourist trail but it has felt, at times, a little shabby around the edges. Now, with major investment funding a facelift, it is being turned into a truly cosmopolitan 'weekender' destination.

HISTORY

The setting of the modern town of Hangzhou was formed in the first century BC when river currents flowing into the sea threw up enough silt to form a lake. The Grand Canal was then built at the end of the sixth century AD, making Hangzhou the centre of trade between the north and the south. In the Tang era the city continued to thrive, and during the Song Dynasty – when the Tartars invaded the north – the imperial family relocated to Hangzhou (from 1138 to 1279), making it the country's imperial city. When the Song Dynasty was overthrown by the Mongols, Hangzhou remained an important commercial centre, revered for the beauty of its gardens. Ming rulers later deepened the Grand Canal, increasing trade opportunities by allowing goods-laden boats to sail up to Beijing. Two Qing emperors also favoured Hangzhou as a place of rest, and added to its architecture. The Taiping Rebellion in the mid 19th century (*see p12*) destroyed much of the city but foreign concessions created towards the end of that century along with improving communications soon put the place back on the map.

Sightseeing

The train (which is how most visitors arrive: *see p196*) terminates at the swanky new station on the eastern edge of town. From here it's about a 1.5-kilometre (one-mile) walk to the centre; head north then take a left along Jiefang Lu. First stop for most is **Xihu**, the lake. To escape the shores, there are two causeways – the Baidi, running across the north side, and the Sudi, running across the south. It's on these paths in the early evening, meandering through the willows with fish leaping out between the

Nightfall at **Xihu**. See p203.

lily-pads and an orange moon rising above the water, that the enchanting power of the lake begins to make itself felt – despite the crowds. Baidi runs on to **Gushan** (Solitary Hill), the lake's biggest island. Formed by a volcanic explosion, it now has a more sedentary character, including a hillside park dotted with small wooden studios where you can watch members of the Xiling Seal Engravers' Society at work.

It's possible to rent boats (prices vary, peaking at sunset) to be paddled out into the lake from the south end of the Baidi, or join the outings aboard a mock dragon boat for an hour-long tour of the lake's islands (RMB 45, tickets can be bought at pine stands around the lake).

For lake views head off Beishan Lu, up one of many hidden footpaths, through the moist woodlands to **Qixiashan** (which means 'the Mountain Where Rosy Clouds Linger'). The stone path meanders past hawkers (woodland dwellers living in tumble-down cottages), **Baoshuta** (a 1933 recontruction of a Song Dynasty tower) and, more interestingly, the **Baopu Daoist Compound** – home to an elegant group of both male and female followers of the Taoist religion who can often be heard, or seen, performing many of their traditional ceremonies, especially in the late afternoon.

In the city itself, the main street of interest to travellers is the **Qinghefang Lu** tourist street: a tastefully reconstructed historical street with views of the lake's misty blue mountains in the background. The shops and cafés sell Chinese medicine, folk art, the area's renowned Lonjing tea, woodcarvings and stinky tofu. To escape the smell, there are two nearby sights of

interest, both lodged in restored Qing Dynasty houses: the **Guanfu Classic Art Museum** (131 Hefang Jie Lu, 0571 8781 8181, RMB 18) is a fine furniture museum, tracing the social history of furniture in China from straw mats to opium beds, while the **Hu Qing Yu Museum of Traditional Chinese Medicine** (95 Dajingxiang Lu, off Hefang Jie Lu, 0571 8702 7507 ext 8620, RMB 10) is exactly what it says on the plaque.

Excursions

West of the city is **Feilai Feng** (meaning 'the Hill that Flew Here'; RMB 15). People visit to see the Buddhist sculptures. In the area is the **Lingyin Si** (RMB 12), one of the biggest temple complexes in China and one of the few that managed to survive the Cultural Revolution intact. It's fully functioning with daily services. Further afield is the village of **Longjing**, set amid emerald-green tea plantations. Just south is the **Hupaomeng Quan** park, where a natural spring issues forth the only water serious tea-suppers would consider using to boil their brew. If you want to test that your water is the real thing, Hupao spring water is supposed to have a surface tension so strong that a cup can be filled three milimetres too high, and it still won't spill.

Those who like to watch others get wet can head up to the **Liuheta** (RMB 10) situated on a stunning site over the Qiantang River. It was originally built to appease the Dragon King, who was thought to be responsible for the floods that would routinely wreck farmers' crops. Now, ironically, it has become the favoured spot from which to watch the – as yet unsurfed – tidal bore that thrusts up the river every autumn equinox.

Where to eat & drink

To entice more foreigners to visit Hangzhou, RMB 1 billion has been invested in the first phase of **Xihutiandi** ('West Lake Heaven and Earth'), Hangzhou's version of Shanghai's sleek Xintiandi entertainment complex. Here you'll find **Va Bene** (House 8, 147 Nanshan Lu, 0571 8702 6333, mains RMB 108-188), an upmarket Italian restaurant serving dishes such as lamb cutlets marinated with Italian herbs and fillet of sea bass dressed with basil sauce and Ligurian olives. Nearby **Zen** (House E, 147 Nanshan Lu, 0571 8702 7711, mains RMB 60-80) specialises in South-east Asian cuisine: recommendations include the deep-fried shrimp and scallop spring rolls or braised cod with potato gratin and crispy shallots. Upstairs is a cool smoked-glass den, **Zenzibar**.

When the Chinese visit they stop off at one of three historical restaurants: **Wang Runxing** (101-103 Hefang Lu, 0571 8780 0111), famous for its tofu with fish head – not to everyone's liking but a truly traditional Hangzhou dish nonetheless; **Zhuang Yuan Guan** (85 Hefang Jie Lu, 0571 8707 6583), renowned for its high-quality fish dishes; or **Louwailou** ('Pavilion upon Pavilion' as it's translated on the signs, Solitary Hill, 0571 702 9023) for good views over the lake and unusual delights such as Beggar's Kitchen (a whole chicken cooked inside a ball of mud).

For local snacks and home-made specialities, **Wushan Lu** allows eating to be interspersed with browsing at the night market, which sells a fantastic array of goods from *qipao*s and attractive wooden sandals to kitsch Maoist memorabilia and 'antiques'.

For nightlife, **Kana Bar** (152 Nanshan Lu) is one of Hangzhou's original foreign-run bars, renowned for its cocktails and live music. For cheap alcohol, thumping tunes and a young crowd, the collection of bars opposite the Art Institute on Nanshan Lu is where it's at. These include **Absolute House** (101 Nanshan Lu) hosting local and foreign DJs in a hip, red-lit concrete den and the **Bather Club** (4 Luyang Lu, by Nanshan Lu) throwing out a mixture of progressive house, hip hop and Latino. On the same street are a hotchpotch of nondescript

student dives, not worth taking a chance on. Elsewhere, there's **LA Club** (6th floor, 169 Qingchun Lu, 0571 8703 0077) where turntable luminaries such as DJ Lavelle from Unkle and DJ Howie B have both played.

Where to stay

Shangri-La (78 Beishan Lu, 0571 8797 7951, www.shangri-la.com, doubles from $200) is a safe bet for those who want to go five-star – but make sure to stay in the west wing. Not far away, in a 1920s building with an ugly but unobtrusive add-on, is **New Hotel** (58 Beishan Lu, 0571 8798 7101, doubles with lake views from RMB 480, rates negotiable). For cheap and friendly, plus a site next to the lake with a pleasant outdoor eating area, herad for the **Hangzhou International Youth Hostel** (101 Nanshan Lu, 0571 8791 8948, www.hzhostel.com, dorm rooms from RMB 40, doubles with views RMB 280).

Getting around

The bus network covers most destinations but taxi rides within Hangzhou should not cost much more than RMB 10. Otherwise, most places around the lake can be reached on foot. Touring by bicycle is not a bad idea: these can be hired from several hotels including **Radisson Plaza** (333 Tiyuchang Lu, 0571 8518 8888, RMB 20/hr).

Incense-lighting at **Lingyin Si**. *See p204.*

Trips Out of Town

Lingyin Si. *See p204.*

Getting there

Hangzhou is 170 kilometres (105 miles) south-west of Shanghai. At least five trains per day leave for Hangzhou from Shanghai Railway Station (RMB 48, soft-seat), with the first departure at 7.29am. The journey takes between two and three hours. By bus, take a **Shanghai City Sightseeing Bus** (line 20, RMB 208, weekends only, 8.05am) from Shanghai Stadium (Shanghai Stadium, 666 Tianyao Qiao Lu, 6426 5555).

Moganshan

The village of Moganshan, up on the cool, green hills of north Zhejiang, originally came to life as a heat retreat for the inhabitants of opium-fuelled Shanghai. In the early 1900s a group of foreigners somehow found their way up these slopes and claimed the peak as their exclusive summer playground. They would have ridden up on sedan chairs carried by porters, as there were no roads at the time. Others followed, including missionaries, criminal gang leaders such as the infamous Du Yuesheng and, later, Chiang Kaishek and Chairman Mao. The original international inhabitants built European-style villas and ran the village much like the city concessions they were escaping from, forming their own governing committee to decide who was allowed to join their elite community. Eventually, communism sucked the colour out of the enclave and the village returned to being a simple rural community. But now it seems as though the party may be starting again, with a handful of city folk renting and slowly restoring some of the village's ageing villas. Cocktails on the terrace at six, anyone?

Sightseeing

On entering Moganshan visitors pay RMB 65 (plus RMB 10 per car) to gain access to 'the sights', which don't add up to much. There are a couple of waterfalls, the house where Chiang Kaishek lived – now nothing more than an empty shell – and the place where Chairman Mao stayed, a similarly dull museum. You can play at being decadent with a tattered sedan chair ride, offered by villagers for a fee. The real joy, however, is in wandering off the tourist path and up towards the back of the village. Here you'll find an old school, still in use, a church and chapel built by the community's original missionaries, and an ageing municipal, spring-fed swimming pool. There is also a market in the middle of the village, selling wild tea and mushrooms picked in the forests.

Other distractions include a meander to an outlying pagoda; simply follow the road from the village out in a north-westerly direction, past some villas until the road forks to the right, then follow the path that forks off to the left. Maps are available in the village but they're not much help as they're all in Chinese. However, a walk off the mountain in any direction will take you through the bamboo forests into the valley below, where you'll encounter plenty of farmers and, eventually, an isolated Buddhist temple.

Where to eat & drink

Eating and drinking can be done at any of the small, simple restaurants on the (nameless) main street. Local specialities are bamboo shoots, plus wild celery and wild partridge. For fine dining the best bet is to head for either of the Radisson hotels (*see below*).

Where to stay

Radisson hotels have recently taken over two villas on the mountain: the coldly luxuriant country pad once belonging to **Du Yuesheng** (0572 303 3601, rooms from RMB 1,100 or RMB 10,000 for the whole villa) and the **Priest Villa** (0572 303 3601, rooms from RMB 800 or RMB 11,000 for the whole villa), where a priest once stayed when attempting to convert the villagers.

Getting there

Moganshan is 60km (37 miles) north-west of Hangzhou, from where it's a one-and-a-half-hour taxi journey (RMB 200). Alternatively, catch a bus (RMB 12) from Hangzhou North Station (758 Moganshan Lu, 0571 8809 7761) to Wukang, at the foot of the mountain. From Wukang catch a minibus to the top.

Suzhou

Yesterday's 'Venice of the East' is today's 'little Singapore'.

Suzhou Canal.

Back when Shanghai was nothing but a quaint little fishing village, its near-neighbour Suzhou was the most desirable address in the Middle Kingdom. Suzhou's real estate skyrocketed around AD 600 when, after centuries of construction, the emperor's engineers finally finished the north-south axis of the Yangtze River delta's Grand Canal system. Rural Suzhou found itself smack at the centre of the country's busiest trade network and received a timely rescue from an eternity wallowing on a boggy fluvial plain. It quickly grew into a commercial hub criss-crossed with canals and populated by merchants, retiring court officials, artisans and, as legend has it, the country's pluckiest courtesans, who set the fashions of the day.

These new, well-heeled residents introduced highfalutin' ideals of imperial court life. They planted beautiful private gardens around lavish homes (see p209 **The gardens of Suzhou**), kick-started a local silk industry and spent their spare time eulogising the weeping willow-lined canals. Suzhou's greatest coup came when Marco Polo passed through town and dubbed it the 'Venice of the East', a sobriquet that has since become clichéd and which appears everywhere from restaurants to the train station.

Suzhou's day as a cultural capital are well and truly over. These days its alternative name is 'little Singapore' on account of the billion-dollar Singaporean-owned industrial estates mushrooming on the city's outskirts. All this industry is taking its toll on the environment, polluting the air and the canals. In an attempt to clean up its act, the local government recently gave downtown streets and bridges a makeover, fished the worst of the garbage out of the water and white-washed the old town's homes. They did a reasonably good job.

Sightseeing

The main thing to do in Suzhou is to get on the water. The canals form a four-sided circuit around the city centre and are best experienced on a **boat tour**. These depart from a landing stage directly across the road from the train station on Guangji Lu (which is at the north end of town). Break the tour at the southern corner of the circuit at **Pan Men** (2 Dongda Lu, 521 826 7737, 8am-5pm, RMB 30), which is the only gate remaining from the old city walls. The Pan Men complex also includes the **Ruiguang Pagoda** and picturesque **Wumen Bridge**.

The city's main street is **Renmin Lu**, just a few strides east of the train station. At its northern end, not far from the train station, is the **Suzhou Silk Museum** (661 Renmin Lu, 0521 6727 6538, RMB 7). The staff may be nodding off in a corner but the exhibits give an excellent impression of the city's 4,000-year-old silk industry with displays of antique silk embroidery and looms. It also boasts a fully operational reproduction of a 13th-century silk farm – live worms and all. Silk clothing and embroidery are sold at the museum but the best place to buy these is several blocks south at the **Suzhou Embroidery Factory** (262 Jingde Lu, 521 522 2403, free).

Just across the road from the silk museum you can't miss the **North Temple** (Beisi Ta; 660 Renmin Lu, by Dongbei Jie, RMB 30), a nine-storey Buddhist pagoda that has been destroyed and rebuilt many times during its 750-year history. It is possible to climb to the top for a sweeping view of the city.

Although some distance out of town, it's worth making the effort to visit the **Yunyan Pagoda** (Yunyan Ta; 8 Huqiushan, 521 826 7737, RMB 30) on artifical Tiger Hill. This 1,500-year-old tower is slowly tilting and needs concrete struts to keep it up. Locals flock to it because it is said to be the resting place of the fabled Emperor Wu, who apparently shares his burial chamber with 3,000 swords all guarded by a white tiger. Tiger Hill is four kilometres (2.5 miles) north-west of the city centre and the easiest way to get there is to take a taxi.

Where to eat & drink

Songhelou Caiguan (141 Guanqian Jie, by Renmin Lu, 0521 6727 7006) is said to be the oldest restaurant in town and remains hugely popular; go for marinated duck or 'squirrel-shaped Mandarin fish'. Not far away, the **Huangtianyuan Pastry Shop** (Guanqian Jie, 0521 6770 4427) set up business in 1821. The pastries for which it is famous use a lot of bean curd filling. **Caizhizhai Food** (91 Guanqian Lu, 0521 6515 7826) has also been in business since the 19th century; sweets and sesame cakes are its speciality. Suzhou is not the place for Western food but if you must have it, head straight for the Sheraton (*see below*).

Where to stay

The **Sheraton** (388 Xinshi Lu, 0521 6510 3388, www.sheraton-suzhou.com, RMB 1,000-1,650) is the city's best five-star option. It's housed in a spanking new replica of a traditional Chinese house and garden. Until the Sheraton arrived, the **Bamboo Grove Hotel** (168 Zhuihui Lu, 0521 6520 5601, www.bg-hotel.com, RMB 995-1,160) was about the smartest lodging in town. It's still pretty nice: three inter-connected, low-rise buildings overlook an inner garden courtyard. The **Nanyuan Guesthouse** (249 Shiquan Jie, 0521 6519 7661, RMB 480), which is inside a walled garden compound near the Humble Administrator's Garden, has secluded grounds and worn but clean facilities.

Getting there

Suzhou is 100 kilometres (62 miles) west of Shanghai. To get here by train catch one of the Nanjing express services that depart about every hour from the Shanghai Railway Station. A one-way ticket costs RMB 25 and the journey takes around 70 minutes. Coaches (RMB 26-30) leave hourly from 7.15am onwards departing Xujiahui bus station; the journey takes 90 minutes. Weekend sightseeing buses depart at 8am from Shanghai Stadium. A return trip from Shanghai to Suzhou by taxi should cost around RMB 500; ask your hotel to make the arrangements.

North Temple.
See p207.

The gardens of Suzhou

Besides canals, Suzhou's main crowd-puller is its gardens. These are not the kind of gardens that attract retirees with a rose fetish but *feng shui*'d masterpieces that demonstrate staggering attention to detail. Every pebble or clump of bamboo is carefully arranged into what is ultimately a living, three-dimensional version of a Chinese landscape painting. There is a philosophy underlying each garden and they are meant to be experienced as a series of visual vignettes linked by meandering paths.

The zen-like names given to the gardens (the 'Garden for Lingering') are testament to the Chinese flair for lyrical hyperbole and not a true indication of most visitors' experience. More accurate names might be the 'Garden of Jabbering Tour Groups' or the 'Garden of One Thousand Camera Flashes'.

For anyone strapped for time – or whose interest is unlikely to hold out for long – we recommend the **Garden of the Master of Nets**, the **Humble Administrator's Garden** or the **Garden for Lingering**. For more information, visit the Suzhou Municipal Administrative Bureau of Gardens' website at www.szgarden.sz.js.cn.

Blue Wave Pavilion

Shiquan Jie, by Renmin Lu. **Open** 7.30am-5.30pm daily. **Admission** RMB 30.
This is one of the older gardens and was originally built for a prince around AD 950. The design is less formal than that of other Suzhou gardens with wilderness areas and winding, pond-lined corridors replacing the usual fussy pavilions. Its carved lattice windows are considered to be among the finest in Suzhou and it's also home to some rare species of bamboo.

Garden for Lingering

80 Liuyuan Lu (521 533 7940). **Open** 8.30am-5pm daily. **Admission** RMB 30.
One of the largest of the gardens, with an impressive collection of *penjing* (bonsai) and a wilderness area. Its pull for fans of traditional horticulture is the Crown of Clouds Peak, which is a six-metre (18-foot) chunk of rock from the nearby Taihu Lake. In an attempt to give a sense of the garden being lived in rather than simply looked at, women decked out in full Ming Dynasty regalia play instruments and sing in the pavilions and walled recesses.

Garden of the Master of Nets

11 Kuotao Xiang, down an alley off Shiquan Jie (521 522 3550). **Open** 8am-4.30pm daily. **Admission** RMB 30.
The Shirley Temple of the gardens – everybody's favourite because it's tiny and charming. It is also home to a group of wood-block painters who sell their work in one of the pavilions. Each night the garden hosts a popular traditional dance and music performance that moves from pavilion to pavilion (RMB 60).

Humble Administrator's Garden

178 Dongbei Jie (521 826 7737). **Open** 8.15am-4.15pm daily. **Admission** RMB 30.
Ming Dynasty official Wang Xianchen built this garden around 1513 when he retired from court life. It is said that he was inspired by the Chinese saying, 'To cultivate his garden and to sell his vegetable crop is the occupation of a humble man'. Its most talked-about feature is its use of water, with inter-connected, bamboo-covered islands and waterfront pavilions. It is considered one of the most beautiful gardens, second only to the Garden of the Master of Nets.

Lion Grove Garden

23 Yuanlin Lu, by Lindun Lu (521 727 2428). **Open** 7.30am-5pm daily. **Admission** RMB 30.
The Buddhist monk Tianru built this garden in memory of his master Zhong Feng in 1342. It changed hands a number of times and suffered many centuries of neglect. It gets its current name from its labyrinthine limestone rockery, for which stones from Taihu Lake were arranged into the shape of lions playing, roaring, fighting and sleeping.

Trips Out of Town

Putuoshan

An island close to Nirvana.

Putuoshan waters.

Putuoshan appears out of the sea like a microcosm of fantasy China: rugged grey cliffs capped by lush greenery scattered with temples and teahouses. It's one of China's four holy Buddhist mountains, dedicated to the Buddhist goddess of mercy Guanyin, and it sits amid the more than 1,000 (mostly smaller) islands that make up the Zhoushan Archipelago in the East China Sea. Go in summer, especially at a weekend, and you'll find yourself dodging tour groups and city escapees heading to the island's beaches. Go off-season and you'll have much of the mountain to yourself. Either way you won't escape the pilgrims: over one million of them visit the island each year, creating an intense atmosphere of spiritual fervour – despite the stalls selling flashing Buddhas and take-me-home gold Guanyins.

HISTORY
The history of Putuoshan is inextricably linked with the Boddhisattva Guanyin. Originally a man, (s)he had a sex change just before coming to the island and is now particularly popular with women, who are drawn by her compassion and supposed ability to bless the devoted with male children. She arrived in Putuoshan, so the story goes, in AD 916 when a Japanese monk was taking a statue of her back from the Chinese mainland. He got as far as the island when a fierce storm blew up. At that point Guanyin appeared to him in a vision and promised she would see him home safely if he left the statue on the island. He did, and she hasn't left since.

Her name was originally Guanshiyin, from the Indian origins of Mayahana Buddism. It translates literally as 'seeing the voice of the world' and is taken to mean 'the one who hears the cries of human suffering'. She has become the most popular figure in Chinese Buddhism and has been hearing the cries on Putuoshan for hundreds of years.

Trouble hit the isalnd in the 16th and 17th centuries when Japanese pirates and Dutch traders began stopping off in Putuoshan to ravage and pillage, but patronage by the wealthy Chinese elite allowed it to flourish. At one point there were three main temples, 88 nunneries and 128 thatched cottages on the island. Much of this was destroyed during the Cultural Revolution and the island now has only three main temples and a few dozen nunneries. Plus a naval base: no pictures please.

Sightseeing

The main area of worship is around **Puji Temple**. Walk through old narrow streets to Haiyan Pool (or 'Setting Free Pool', so-called because of the practice of visiting Buddhist pilgrims who release turtles into the pool to gain merit) and the temple beyond. Here crowds of pilgrims move like ghostly apparitions through the clouds of incense to kneel in front of Guanyin, or burn offerings to the gods and goddesses. At almost any time of day, but especially at dawn, there's a murmuring soundtrack provided by chanting monks or nuns chanting over the bustle. Nearby are stalls selling Buddhist garb and unusual souvenirs in the form of packets of assorted dried fish.

Two kilometres (1.2 miles) to the north of Puji Temple is **Fayu Temple**, which is situated uphill from One Thousand Step Beach (not to be confused with One Hundred Step Beach, which is a short distance east of Puji). It is quieter here and the monks are more intrigued by foreign visitors.

The third-largest temple is **Huiji Temple** on Fodor Hill, which is north again, about a kilometre (half a mile). Follow the 1,000 steps back up the hill to witness female pilgrims prostrating themselves on each step. Along the way are small shrines, together with carved calligraphy and lotus leaves believed to cleanse visitors of their worldly sins. Those who know they're beyond hope can take the cable car.

Also worth visiting is the **small chapel** on an islet situated just off to the right after you exit the harbour on arrival. It's the perfect place to watch the sunset in the harbour, as you listen to the monks chanting in time to the clipped percussion of a huge conch shell. Elsewhere on the island is the unmissable (purely because it's so large) modern **bronze statue of Guanyin** who looks out to sea cradling a huge ship's wheel to demonstrate her allegiance to the area's fishermen. Her four, grizzly-faced protectors are the Buddhist guardians of the world, each leading an army of supernatural creatures to keep evil at bay. Scattered around the island are also a number of rocks, which have proved a huge draw to Chinese tourists who pose beside them for snapshots. They are not of interest to everyone, although the Two Stone Tortoises climbing up the hill near Meiling Peak provide quirky entertainment. The story goes that they were sent over from another palace to listen to Guanyin's teachings and became so enraptured they forgot to head home and instead turned to stone.

At the end of the island furthest from the harbour is **Fan Yin Dong**, the Sanskrit 'Sound Cave' where a small temple sits wedged in a gully between two cliff-faces. Look down to see the sea crashing up on the rocks below or behind to see the cave. For more watery experiences try the **Cave of Tidal Sounds**, where Guanyin has appeared to visitors throughout the ages. These visions eventually led to a cult of suicides after a monk burnt his fingers like candles in an offering to the goddess, who then appeared before him. Following his example dozens of believers in the Ming Dynasty flocked to the site and threw themselves on to the rocks below in the hope of entering Nirvana. An island official eventually felt forced to put up a sign on a rock, still visible, forbidding suicides or finger-burning.

Hedonists can instead get their fix at either **Hundred Step Beach** or **Thousand Step Beach**. Lying alongside each other separated by a pavilion, both charge to enter and tend to get crowded in summertime, although they are far emptier – and free of charge – in the evenings and off-season (from mid October).

Where to eat & drink

Although Putuoshan's seafood offerings are much hyped, it's worth remembering that this isn't a place where you'll find lobster salads and lemon sole. Putuoshan serves very simple, fresh seafood cooked Chinese-style – bones and all.

Island fisherman.

Guanyin's birthday

Buddhist pilgrims from around the world flock to Putuoshan Island to celebrate the birthday (19 June) of its goddess in residence, Guanyin. Also known as Avalokitesarva, the Goddess of Mercy, she assists the poor, weak and sick. She also bails out troubled fishermen in local island waters. The grandest ceremonies are held at Puji Temple and all festivities are free. Due to the festival's popularity, advance ferry reservations are highly recommended. The day is also celebrated in Shanghai temples.

The hotel food on Putuoshan has a bad reputation. Far better are the restaurants (whitewashed, nameless buildings that are simply the front of people's houses) on the road from the harbour or further along the sea road, where fresh fish in all sorts of sauces and seasonal greens are served up on roughshod outdoor tables. Try the firm fresh prawns. Non-fish fans can eat simple vegetable dishes or eggs and tomato. Most of these places are of a similar quality, and serve exactly the same dishes.

The restaurants up from the beaches offer more variety and meat, as do those near the naval base. Alternatively, the **Putuoshan Teahouse** (6 Xianghua Jie, 0580 609 1208) on the side of Hauiyuan Lake has a large variety of dishes including many traditional vegetarian Buddhist options and, of course, the Putuo tea that the island is renowned for.

Where to stay

Hotel options are not great, although there is the odd monastery conversion. Some visitors stay with locals, but this is technically illegal. Prices vary enormously from season to season. During high season it's almost madness not to book ahead but at other times you can simply turn up and take your pick from the hotel touts in the harbour arrivals hallway; they all offer double rooms at about RMB 200. Bargaining is expected and most hotels will be largely empty. Good bets include the **Putuoshan Hotel** (93 Meicen Lu, 0580 609 2828, doubles from RMB 430-1,291), a four-star venue near the beaches and Puji Temple, although not exactly bursting with character. For something more isolated, try **Putuo Shanzhuang** (Miaozhuangyan Lu, 0580 609 1666, doubles from RMB 250) or **Xilai Yuan** (west of Puji Temple, 0580 609 1119, doubles from RMB 260), the latter is a small converted monastery.

Getting around

The most pleasant way to get around Putuoshan is on foot, clambering over the seaside rocks or wandering through the Purple Bamboo Forest and up and down mountains, peeking into monasteries and islanders' courtyards, or watching fishermen return with their catch. Alternatively, you can zip around the island in a minibuses; routes cover the whole of the island and the vehicles depart from just outside the entrance to the Puji Temple area.

Getting there

By air

Flights from Shanghai's Hongqiao Airport to Putuoshan Airport (which is actually on the nearby Zhujiajian Island) are operated by China Eastern Airlines (021 6247 5953, www.ce-air.com). From the airport, take a taxi to Wugongzhi Dock before zipping across the sea on a five-minute speedboat trip to Putuoshan.

By sea

Slow ferries leave from Wusong Dock (timetables 021 5657 5500, 251 Songbao Lu), situated where the Huangpu River flows into the sea. (The easiest way to get to the dock is by taxi but you can also take bus Nos.51, 116, 522 or 728.) The slow ferries leave Shanghai at 8pm daily and arrive in Putuoshan at 7.30am the next morning; they return from Putuoshan at 4.30pm daily and arrive in Shanghai at 6am the next morning. One-way tickets are RMB 340 (first class); RMB 270 (second class); RMB 167 (third class) and RMB 112 (fourth class).

Fast ferries leave from Luchaogang Dock (timetables 021 5828 2201) in the Nanhui district (to the south of Shanghai). A bus service runs to the dock (8am, 2pm daily) from 1588 Waima Lu (near Nanpu Bridge, just out of central Shanghai). The ferry crossing takes four to four-and-a-half hours. Tickets are RMB 225/195 (first class/second class). The price includes both the bus and the ferry part of the journey. There is a return ferry from Putoshan at 4.30pm daily.

Both fast and slow ferry tickets are available from 1 Jinling Donglu (no phone). Go in person to buy the tickets, preferably a few days in advance. Alternatively, you can buy them from CITS (2 Jinling Donglu, 6323 8749).

Tourist information

Entrance to Putuoshan Island is currently RMB 60 per person (paid on arrival), with each additional site charging an entrance fee of RMB 5, or a fraction more.

Trips Out of Town

Directory

Features

By air

Shanghai has two airports: Pudong and Hongqiao. All international and some domestic flights go through the newly built Pudong, while Hongqiao handles domestic flights only. Shuttle buses (6834 6189) run between the two every 20 to 30 minutes (Hongqiao 6am-9pm; Pudong 7.20am-last flight; RMB 30).

Pudong International Airport

3848 4500-2/www.shairport.com/en/ contact.jsp

Pudong International Airport is 30km (18 miles) from the city proper, and 40km (25 miles) from Hongqiao Airport. A **taxi** to downtown Shanghai will cost around RMB 160 and take approximately one hour. To downtown Pudong it's around RMB 130 and will also take about an hour. Avoid the touts inside the airport as they charge four times the rate.

The new, bullet-quick **Maglev train** (*see also p90* **Badly trained**) connects the airport to the Longyang Lu metro station on the outskirts of Pudong. The journey only takes seven minutes, but on arrival you are still a 25-minute or more taxi ride from downtown Shanghai, while taking the metro from Longyang Lu is inconvenient if you have heavy luggage. Tickets are available at the entrance gates to the Maglev (single/return RMB 50/80; VIP single/return RMB 100/160). The service runs every 15 mins from 8.28am to 5.30pm.

Public **airport shuttle buses** (6834 6189) depart from outside the baggage claim to different locations around the city. Useful lines include Bus No.5, which departs to Shanghai Railway Station every 20 minutes (7.20am-11pm, RMB 18) and stops at Renmin Square. Bus No.2 goes to Jingan Temple and leaves every 15 minutes (7.20am-last flight, RMB 19). The shuttle buses are much cheaper (RMB 18-30) than taxis. Many hotels also offer shuttle bus services.

Left luggage facilities are situated in the domestic arrivals hall (6834 6324), domestic departures hall (6834 5021), international arrivals hall (6834 6078) and international departures hall (6834 5035). Rates are RMB 30 for three hours or RMB 100 per day. The service is open from 6am until the last flight arrives.

Lost property is located between the 8th and 9th door of the domestic arrivals hall (6834 6324).

There is a reliable HSBC **ATM** in near the visa section in international arrivals.

China Telecom has a **cyber café/business centre** (6834 6519, open 7am-11.30pm) in the international terminal. Business-class passengers may access the net via the computers provided in the lounges.

Hongqiao Airport

6268 8918-2/www.shairport.com/en/ contact.jsp

Hongqiao is the closest airport to downtown Shanghai, with most central destinations ten to 15km (six to nine miles) away. A **taxi** to central Shanghai should cost no more than RMB 45 and will take around half an hour. Hongqiao also has a large fleet of **public buses** (5114 6532), which depart from in front of the arrivals hall. Useful lines include the Special Line, a direct service to Jingan Temple, which leaves every 15 to 20 minutes (6am-8pm, RMB 4). Bus No.938 leaves for Pudong every ten to 15 minutes (6am-9.30pm, RMB 2-4). Bus No.925A departs for Renmin Square every ten to 15 minutes (6am-9pm, RMB 2-4).

The **left luggage** facility is located in the domestic arrivals hall (6268 8899). Rates are RMB 30 for three hours or RMB 100 per day.

ATMs are located within the arrivals hall near the customs office and in the departure hall near the airport tax booth; the Bank of China ATM is the most reliable.

For domestic travellers, Shanghai Airlines offers a convenient **downtown check-in** facility (1600 Nanjing Xilu, 3214 4600), although it only operates if your scheduled departure time is after 11am. Check your luggage in two and a half hours before departure, get your boarding pass, then hop on the direct airport bus (RMB 20), which departs from a station downstairs.

AIRLINES

Major airlines currently flying to Shanghai include:

Air Canada *Room 3901, United Plaza, 1468 Nanjing Xilu, Jingan (6279 2999/www.aircanada.ca).*

Air China *600 Huashan Lu, by Wulumuqi Beilu, French Concession (5239 7227/www.airchina.com.cn).*

Northwest Airlines *Room 2810, Plaza 66, 1266 Nanjing Xilu, by Xikang Lu, Jingan (6884 6884/ www.nwa.com).*

Shanghai Airlines *212 Jiangning Lu, by Beijing Xilu, Jingan (6255 0550/www.shanghai-air.com).*

United Airlines *Room 204, West Tower, Shanghai Centre, 1376 Nanjing Xilu, by Tongren Lu, Jingan (6279 8009/www.united.com).*

Virgin Atlantic Airways *Suite 221, 12 Zhongshan Dongyilu, by Fuzhou Lu, the Bund (5353 4600/ www.virgin.com/atlantic).*

By rail

Trains for Beijing, Hong Kong and Suzhou leave from the **Shanghai Railway Station**, in the north of the city. Trains for Hangzhou leave from **Shanghai South Railway Station**. Rail services are generally used for short-distance travel within China. For more information on travel by train, go to www.rail.sh.cn.

Shanghai Railway Station

385 Meiyuan Lu, Zhabei (6317 9090/6354 5358). Metro Shanghai Railway Station. **Map** *p249 D1.* The northern terminus for Metro Line 1. Beware of pickpockets.

Shanghai South Railway Station

200 Zhaofeng Lu, Xinlonghua (6317 9090/6404 1317). Metro Shanghai South Railway Station. **Map** *p240 B5.* Note that the Shanghai South Railway Station stop on Metro Line 1 does not connect directly with the station; just follow the crowd or ask for directions.

Directory

Passengers get on

The city's traffic jams are notorious but at least travelling by taxi provides amusing distraction in the form of the notices to passengers that are posted on the back of the driver's seat. They all seem to be the work of one syntactically challenged, pedantic killjoy. It's maybe a little unfair to single out just one company for this – but we will anyway. The following all appear in cabs operated by the Dazhong Taxi Co. We wouldn't travel with anyone else.

Passenger Notice
Rule No.1: Don't connive at the driver's violation of the passenger transport of traffic amanagement regulations.
Rule No.2: Passengers are not allowed to carry with them any contraband goods, smoke, spit, or to dump inside taxis. Psychos or drunkards without guardians are prohibited to take taxis. Be sure to check your belongings when you get off.

Standard Service Process
A. Pasengers get on – ask for the destination – choose the roads – open the taxi meter.
B. Reach the destination – pause – quote – print.
C. Settle the taxi fare – declare the amount received from the passenger – give back change – give receipt.
D. Passengers get off – remind – check – say goodbye.

By sea

Located at the mouth of the Huangpu River, Shanghai is in an excellent position for cruising down the coastline of China and beyond.

Most domestic ships and ferries dock at the **Shilipu Passenger Terminal** (111 Zhongshan Dongerlu, 6326 0050), one mile south of the Bund. Ships from Hong Kong and overseas dock at the **International Passenger Terminal** (1 Waihongqiao Lu, 6326 0269), which is about a mile north-east of the Bund.

TICKETS
Tickets can be booked directly at the ferry offices or through one of the following agencies:

China Youth Travel Service/ STA Travel *2 Hengshan Lu, by Dongping Lu, French Concession (6445 5396).* **Map** p 246 C7.
China International Travel Service (CITS) *2 Jinling Donglu, by Zhongshan Dongyilu, the Bund (6323 8770).* **Map** p243 J5.

Public transport

Shanghai's public transport system is near unfathomable without some degree of fluency in Chinese. While buses are plentiful the lack of English signage – not to mention the overcrowding – makes using them a headache. The metro is perhaps the single exception: it's efficient and has some English signposting, but, again it suffers from too many bodies in too confined a space. It's best used for longer journeys, for example out to Pudong. Generally speaking, for convenience and minimal stress taxis are the best option.

Fares & tickets

Visitors who are planning to use public transport fairly frequently over a week or more can buy a **stored-value card**, or *jiaotong*. The cards can be purchased at metro stations and are valid for the metro, buses and even taxis. The cards cost RMB 100, but the stored value is RMB 70 – RMB 30 is taken as a deposit, to be refunded when the card is returned. The card deducts a fee when scanned by the reader above the metro turnstile. There are scanner machines on buses and taxi dashboards. There is no expiry date for credit on the cards.

Note that on Shanghai's public transport discount tickets for children, students and the elderly are only valid for Chinese nationals.

Metro

Metro stations are easily identifiable by their red on white 'M' signs. Although not always easy to spot, stations do have signage in English; station announcements are also bilingual.

There are three metro lines. **Line 1** runs south from the Shanghai Railway Station down through Renmin Square, the French Concession and Xujiahui to Xinzhuang in the southern suburbs. **Line 2** runs west from Zhangjiang, which is out beyond Pudong, via the Bund area, Renmin Square (where it connects with Line 1) and Jingan to terminate at Zhongshan Park (an extension out to Hongqiao Airport is due to be completed in late 2004). The third line is the elevated **Pearl Line** which loops out around the city centre; it's of little use to most visitors except for the extension north of Shanghai Railway Station, which runs up via East Baoxing Lu (for Duolun Lu) and Hongkou Stadium.

The metro runs from 6am to midnight and trains are very frequent. Ticket machines or staff at the metro stations sell single-journey metro tickets costing RMB 2-5 depending on the distance travelled. Keep your ticket until you exit.

Buses

There are over 1,000 bus lines in Shanghai. Buses 1 to 199 operate from 5am to 11pm. Buses within the 200 and 400 series are peak-hour buses. The 300 series are night buses.

Prepare to hit a major language barrier when using the buses – the destinations are listed only in Chinese characters and there is no English-language telephone line. Chinese-speakers can contact the **Shanghai Urban Transportation Bureau** (6321 1200).

Don't expect peaceful rides, either – the buses are always crowded, unbearably so during rush hour. Air-conditioning seems optional. There is also the added stress of potential pickpocketing. Buy tickets from the on-board conductor (RMB 1-2) or use a stored-value *jiaotong* card (*see p215*).

Taxis

Travelling by taxi is not an extravagance. Fares are cheap, and taxis are plentiful; the only noticeable shortages are during rush hour or on rainy days. If you're having trouble finding a taxi, head to a five-star hotel where you'll find plenty waiting at the forecourt taxi rank.

Taxis are metered and in our experience drivers are scrupulously honest about observing them. **Fares** are RMB 10 for the first two kilometres (1.2 miles) and then RMB 2 for every additional kilometre. Fares rise steeply after 11pm.

Tipping is not expected. Cash or stored-value *jiaotong* cards (*see p215*) are accepted forms of payment.

Most drivers have limited English so it's essential to have your destination written in Chinese – most hotels supply cards with the addresses of major sites in both English and Chinese. Failing that ask the concierge to write it out for you. Keep hold of business cards for places to which you might return.

The driver will supply you with a **receipt** (*fapiao*). This shows the taxi number and the company telephone number – useful if you discover you've left something in the cab. The number for complaints is 6323 2150.

Taxi companies
Bashi Taxi *6431 2788.*
Dazhong Taxi *800 620 1688.*
Jinjiang Taxi *6464 7777.*
Qian Wei Red Flag *5683 2029.*
Qiangsheng *6258 0000.*

Cycling

Cycling is a good (and popular) way to get around the city. Inexperienced cyclists should, however, be cautious of Shanghai's aggressive drivers and its dangerously ill-kept roads. Bikes should be registered at a police station, but bike shops can also offer this service. The **Captain's Hostel** (*see p35*) offers bike rentals and tours.

Giant Bicycle Store
743 Jianguo Xilu, by Hengshan Lu, Xujiahui (6437 5041). Metro Hengshan Lu. **Open** 9am-8pm daily. **No credit cards. Map** p246 B8. Everything from top-of-the-line mountain and racing bikes to inexpensive city peddlers.

Driving

Tourists are not forbidden from Shanghai's roads, but there is plenty of red tape deterring them from doing so.

Licences

Most expats apply for Chinese licences at the **Shanghai Vehicle Management Bureau** (1101 Zhongshan Beiyilu, 6516 8168). To do this you will need your passport, residence permit, health certificate and a driving licence held for over three years, plus an official translation of the driving licence. You will also have to undergo a short written driving test and a medical examination. The total cost of the application is RMB 210. Drivers with less than three years' experience are required to take a road test.

Travellers who do not have a tourist visa and intend to rent a car can get a temporary driving licence at the Pudong Airport **Public Security Bureau** (open 9am-4pm Mon-Thur), a short drive from the main terminal. For this you need the aforementioned papers, plus an international driving licence. Again, you will undergo a written test and a medical. The length of licence issued depends on your residence permit.

If you do not have a foreign driving license, you will be required to attend driving lessons for 70 hours at the **Shanghai Traffic Rules Education** school (2175 Pudong Dadao, 5885 6222).

Vehicle hire

Those visiting Shanghai on tourist L-visas are unable to drive rental cars but they may hire a car with a driver. An average daily rental cost is about RMB 600-800.

Car rental companies
Dazhong *98 Guohuo Lu, by Zhongshan Nanlu, Old City (6318 5666).* **Map** p245 J9.
Hertz Car Rental *Suite 306, Chengfeng Centre, 1088 Yanan Xilu, Hongqiao (6252 2200).* Also at Pudong International Airport.
Shanghai Anji Car Rental *1387 Changning Lu, by Zhongshan Beilu, Changning (6268 0862).* **Map** p240 B3. Avis partner in China.

Walking

Distances are such that the city centre is easily navigated on foot but beware – pavements double as express lanes for bicycles and scooters. At least they are well maintained.

Resources A-Z

Addresses

All street signs in Shanghai are written in both Chinese and Pinyin (the romanised version of Chinese). Lu means street. The prefix *bei* is north; *dong* is east; *nan* means south; *xi* is west; . When getting around it is common to give the cross street of the address, for example Nanjing Xilu, by Jiangning Beilu.

Age restrictions

The age of consent for sex is 14. There is no age of consent for homosexuals as gay sex is not officially recognised. Under-18s are still considered minors. There is no legal drinking age but smoking is illegal for under-18s.

Attitude & etiquette

See p218 **Attitude problems**.

Business

As a starting point visit the Shanghai government's business website: **www.investment.gov.cn**

Business cards

Business cards are always offered or accepted with both hands. Cards can be printed locally at **Copy General** (Kerry Centre, 1515 Nanjing Xilu, by Tongren Lu, Jingan, 6279 1694). *See also p218* **Attitude problems**.

Chambers of Commerce

American Chamber of Commerce *Portman Ritz-Carlton, 1376 Nanjing Xilu, Jingan (6279 7119/www.amcham-shanghai.org).* Map p248 C4.
Australian Chamber of Commerce *1440 Yanan Zhonglu, Jingan (6248 8301/www.austcham shanghai.com).* Map p248 B5.
British Chamber of Commerce *17th floor, Westgate Tower, 1038 Nanjing Xilu, Jingan (6218 5022/ www.sha.britcham.org).* Map p249 D4.
Canada China Business Council *Hong Kong Plaza, 283 Huaihai Zhonglu, by Songshan Lu, French Concession (6390 6001/ www.ccbc.com).* Map p244 F6.

Convention centres

International conventions and conferences are flocking to Shanghai. The following are the major venues.

Shanghai Everbright Convention & Exhibition Centre *66 Caobao Lu, by Caoxi Lu, Xujiahui (6484 2500/www.secec.com).* Map p240 B4.
Shanghai International Convention Centre *2727 Riverside Avenue, by Lujiazui Lu, Pudong (5037 0000/www.shicc.net).* Map p243 K4.
Shanghai Mart *2299 Yanan Xilu, by Gubei Lu, Hongqiao (6236 6888/ www.shanghaimart.com.cn).* Map p240 A3
Shanghai New International Expo Centre *2345 Longyang Lu, by Hunangong Lu, Pudong (2890 6666/www.smiec.net).* Map p241 F4.

Couriers

DHL *Sinotrans, Shanghai International Trade Centre, 2200 Yanan Lu, by Loushanguan Lu, Hongqiao (6275 3543/www.dhl.com).* **Open** 8.30am-6pm Mon-Fri; 8.30am-4pm Sat. **No credit cards.** Map p240 B3.
Federal Express *10th floor, Aetna Building, 107 Zunyi Lu, by Xianxia Lu, Hongqiao (6275 0808/ www.fedex.com).* **Open** 8.30am-6pm Mon-Fri; 8.30am-3pm Sat. **No credit cards.** Map p240 B3.
UPS *Room 1318, Central Plaza, 318 Huaihai Zhonglu, French Concession (6391 5555/www.ups.com).* Metro Huangpi Nanlu. **Open** 8.30am-6.30pm Mon-Fri; 9am-2pm Sat. **No credit cards.** Map p244 F6.

Office hire & business centres

Most major four- and five-star hotels (*see pp32-44* **Where to Stay**) offer complete business service but expect to pay premium rates.

Executive Centre

3501 CITIC Square, 1168 Nanjing Xilu, by Shanxi Beilu, Jingan (5292 5223/www.executivecentre.com). Map p249 D4. Full service office rental with complete secretarial support.

Translators

Shanghai Interpreters Association *Room 702, 66 Nanjing Donglu, by Henan Zhonglu, the Bund (6323 3608). Metro Henan Lu.* **Open** 9.30am-4pm Mon-Fri. **No credit cards.** Map p242 H4.

Travel advice

For up-to-date information for travelling to a specific country – including the latest news on safety and security, health issues, local laws and customs – contact your home country government's department of foreign affairs. Most have websites packed with useful advice for would-be travellers.

Australia
www.dfat.gov.au/travel

Canada
www.voyage.gc.ca

New Zealand
www.mft.govt.nz/travel

Republic of Ireland
www.irlgov.ie/iveagh

UK
www.fco.gov.uk/travel

USA
http://www.state.gov/travel

Directory

Attitude problems

The intricacies of Chinese etiquette mean that it's all too easy for beginners to feel lost or embarrassed. The pitfalls are many.

Face off

You've just enjoyed a feast in a restaurant with your local host and the bill has arrived. Your host reaches for his credit card. 'No,' you say, 'I'll pay.' A to-and-froing ensues and to end the discussion, you grab the bill and pay, believing your generosity will be appreciated. Wrong. You've just committed a serious faux pas. Your host has lost 'face' (also known as *guanxi*) and that's just about the cardinal sin in Shanghai.

Face is a peculiar Chinese concept and its importance can never be underestimated. Some folk go to great lengths to acquire it by displays of wealth or generosity.

Complimenting someone on their appearance or business acumen – especially in front of their pals or colleagues – is a sure-fire winner. Confrontation and criticism are guaranteed face-destroyers. When in doubt, be lavish with those compliments.

Greetings

Chinese people have a family name, followed by a first name – Chen Wu, for example. To address someone, use their family name together with their professional title or 'Mr', 'Madam' or 'Miss', plus the family name – eg Mr Chen. Only family members or close friends use first names. Always acknowledge the most senior person first.

The Chinese will nod or bow slightly as an initial greeting. Handshakes are also popular, but wait for your Chinese counterpart to initiate the gesture.

Public behaviour

Avoid expansive gestures or unusual facial expressions. The Chinese do not use their hands when speaking, and will become annoyed with a speaker who does.

The Chinese, especially those who are older and in positions of authority, dislike being touched by strangers. Conversely, the Chinese generally stand closer to each other than Europeans and North Americans.

Do not put your hands in your mouth – it's considered vulgar. Hence nail-biting, flossing and similar practices are also no-nos. Members of the same sex often hold hands in public.

Conversation

Negative replies are considered impolite. Instead of saying 'no', answer 'Maybe', 'I'll think about it', or 'We'll see.'

Questions about your age, income and marital status are common. If you don't want to reveal this information, remain unspecific.

In Chinese culture, the question 'Have you eaten?' is the equivalent to 'How are you?' in Western culture; it's a superficial inquiry that does not require a literal answer.

Do not be surprised if there are periods of silence during business or dinner. It is a sign of politeness and of thought. Do not try to fill the silence with words.

Gestures

Shanghainese body language has several gestures that appear strange. These include touching one's own face several times quickly in a similar manner to scratching, but with the forefinger straight. This means 'Shame on you!'. It is a semi-joking gesture.

Touching or pointing to the tip of one's own nose with raised forefinger means 'It's me,' or 'I'm the one'.

Using both hands in offering something to a visitor or another person equals respect. For example, when one's tea cup is being refilled by the host or hostess, putting one or both hands upright, palm open, beside the cup means 'Thank you'.

Gifts

Official policy in Chinese business culture forbids giving gifts; the practice is seen as akin to bribery. Consequently, your gift may be declined. In many organisations, however, attitudes towards gifts are beginning to relax. Discretion is still important, and if you wish to give a gift to an individual, you must do it privately, in the context of friendship, not business. The Chinese will decline a gift three times before finally accepting, so as not to appear greedy.

Numbers

Eight is considered one of the luckiest numbers in Chinese culture. If you receive eight of any item, consider it a gesture of good will. But avoid four of any item – in Cantonese, the word 'four' sounds similar to 'death'. Scissors, knives, or other sharp objects can be interpreted as the severing of a friendship or other bond.

Speed Shanghai *Ziyuan Mansion, Guangyaun Lu, by Huashan Lu, Xujiahui (6447 4184/www.speed-asia.com). Metro Xujiahui.* **Open** 8.30am-5.30pm Mon-Sat. **No credit cards. Map** p246 A8.

Consumer

Buyer beware. Returning faulty products is a trial, even with a receipt or guarantee. Consumers can file an online complaint with the **Shanghai Bureau of Quality and Technical Supervison** (go to www.sbts.sh.cn) but it's in Chinese only.

Customs

Visitors can bring in 400 cigarettes and two 0.75-litre bottles of alcohol, plus one each of the following items: camera, portable tape-recorder, portable cine-camera, portable video-camera and portable computer. There are no restrictions on the amount of foreign currency.

It's forbidden to take out of China any antiques over 200 years old. Check with the shop when you make your purchase and keep the receipt and the shop's business card to present to customs if necessary.

Disabled

Shanghai poses problems for disabled travellers. Wheelchair access is provided at the airports, metro and train stations, and at a handful of the international five-star hotels, but nowhere else. Pavements on major streets have raised strips for the visually impaired to follow. However, the frequency and quality of special needs facilities should improve in short time given that Shanghai will be hosting the Special Olympics in 2007.

Shanghai Disabled Persons' Federation *189 Longyang Lu, Pudong (5873 3212/fax 3889 0002/ shdisabled@online.sh.cn).*

Drugs

Street drugs are becoming more readily available, especially in nightclubs, but the punishments for drug use remain harsh. Consulates can offer only the most limited of legal assistance to those caught with illegal drugs.

Electricity

China runs on 220 volts. The most common plug type is the dual prong. 110-volt appliances may be redundant as some adaptors have been known to overheat.

Embassies & consulates

All foreign embassies are located in Beijing, but many countries also maintain a consulate in Shanghai.

Australian Consulate *22nd floor, CITIC Square, 1168 Nanjing Xilu, by Shanxi Beilu, Jingan (5292 5500/ www.aus-in-shanghai. com).* **Open** 8.30am-5pm Mon-Fri. **Map** p249 D4.
British Consulate *Room 301, Shanghai Centre, 1376 Nanjing Xilu, by Tongren Lu, Jingan (6279 7650/ www.britishconsulate.sh. cn).* **Open** 8.30am-4.30pm Mon-Fri. **Map** p248 C4.
Canadian Consulate *Room 668, Shanghai Centre, 1376 Nanjing Xilu, by Tongren Lu, Jingan (6279 8400/ www.shanghai.gc.ca).* **Open** 8.30am-5pm Mon-Fri. **Map** p248 C4.
Irish Consulate *Room 700A, Shanghai Centre, 1376 Nanjing Xilu, by Tongren Lu, Jingan (6279 8729).* **Open** 9.30am-5.30pm Mon-Fri. **Map** p248 C4.
New Zealand Consulate *15th floor, Qihua Tower, 1375 Huaihai Zhonglu, by Fuxing Lu, French Concession (6471 1108/www.nz embassy.com).* **Open** 8.30am-5.30pm Mon-Fri. **Map** p246 C7.
South African Consulate *Room 2706, 222 Yanan Xilu, by Loushanguan Lu, Hongqiao (5359 4977/sacgpolitical@yahoo.com).* **Open** 8am-4.30pm daily. **Map** p240 B3.
US Consulate *1469 Huaihai Zhonglu, by Wulumuqi Nanlu, French Concession (6433 6880/ www.usembassy-china.org.cn/ shanghai/).* **Open** 8am-5pm Mon-Fri. **Map** p246 B7.

Emergencies

For more useful numbers, *see below* **Health**; *p222* **Helplines**; and *p224* **Police**.

Useful numbers

Ambulance *120.*
Directory assistance *114.*
English-speaking police *6357 6666.*
English-speaking tourist information *6439 8947.*
Fire services *119.*
IDD code enquiry *106.*
Operator-assisted Yellow Pages *96886.*
Police *110.*
Time *117.*
Weather forecast *121.*

Gay & lesbian

See pp164-7 **Gay & Lesbian**.

Health

China does not have reciprocal healthcare agreements with other countries, so it is advisable to take out private insurance. However, some clinics do accept private international insurance such as BUPA or TIECARE. Check with your insurance provider before departure.

Vaccinations against Hepatitis A and B, polio, tetanus, flu, chickenpox, typhoid, tetanus-diphtheria, Japanese encephalitis (if travel plans include rural areas) and rabies are the most commonly recommended. Some travellers may complain of stomach upsets due to the change in diet. Tap water should be avoided but the bottled water sold everywhere is fine.

Hospitals

Shanghai has some good public hospitals and private international clinics. The main public hospitals (*yiyuan*) will treat visitors on an outpatient or emergency basis, often in a special foreigner ward. For international and local clinics you will need to bring your

Directory

passport and cash for the consultation fees, which vary wildly (RMB 100-500).

Be aware that Chinese hospitals often prescribe antibiotics and drips regardless of whether the cause of illness merits such action. The tendency to over-prescribe is exacerbated because hospitals in China also act as general pharmacies, and upwards of 60 per cent of their income is made from drug sales. Make sure you're clear about the necessity of any medication prescribed.

The following hospitals provide comprehensive medical care. Levels of hygiene are well maintained and staff are knowledgeable but comfort and privacy may be found lacking. Both Chinese- and Western-style treatment is available at these hospitals.

In an emergency dial 120.

Huashan Hospital Foreigners' Clinic
19th floor, 12 Wulumuqi Zhonglu, by Huashan Lu, French Concession (6248 9999 ext 1900). Metro Changshu Lu or Jingan Temple. **Open** *Clinic* 8am-5pm Mon-Fri. *Emergencies* 24hrs. **Credit** AmEx, DC, MC, V. **Map** p246 B6.
Part of one of Shanghai's largest hospitals, with modern facilities. Staff outside the Foreigners' Clinic will only have limited English.

Ruijin Hospital
197 Ruijin Erlu, by Yongjia Lu, French Concession (6437 0045 ext 668101). Metro Shanxi Nanlu. **Open** 24hrs daily. **Credit** AmEx, DC, MC, V. **Map** p247 E7/8.
A complete range of medical facilities is available. Some English spoken.

Private clinics/ doctors

International Medical Care Centre of Shanghai
People's Hospital No.1, Wujing Lu, by Wusong Lu, Hongkou (6324 3852). **Open** 24hrs daily. **Credit** AmEx, DC, MC, V. **Map** p243 J1.
A private health centre attached to a teaching hospital north of Suzhou Creek offering all medical services,

including dentistry. The standard of care in the Medical Centre is higher than in other departments.

Shanghai East International Medical Centre
551 Pudong Nanlu, by Pudong Dadao, Pudong (5879 9999/www.seimc.com. cn). Metro Dongchang Lu. **Open** *Clinic* 8am-9pm Mon-Fri; 9am-2pm Sat; 9am-1pm Sun. *Emergencies* 24hrs daily. **Credit** AmEx, DC, MC, V. **Map** p241 E3.
Joint-venture clinic run by Shanghai East Hospital and a California-based healthcare group. Full-time expat doctors and English-speaking nurses provide experienced, world-class family healthcare.

World Link
Suite 203, Shanghai Centre, 1376 Nanjing Xilu, by Tongren Lu, Jingan (6279 7688/www.worldlink-shanghai. com). Metro Jingan Temple. **Open** 9am-7pm Mon-Fri; 9am-4pm Sat; 9am-3pm Sun. **Credit** AmEx, DC, MC, V. **Map** p248 C4.
One of several World Link clinics in Shanghai. Doctors are from the US, UK, Canada and Japan. Medical assistance is available in English, Japanese and Chinese. The clinics offer a complete range of services from walk-in medical treatment for minor ailments to internal medicine. Dental treatment is also available.

Contraception & abortion

Due to its one-child policy China has some of the most affordable, modern and accessible contraceptive and abortion facilities in the world. Contraceptives are available over the counter at pharmacies throughout the city. Abortions are available at the hospitals listed above. For help contact the **American Sino OB-GYN Clinic** (6249 3246).

Dentists

The following services are all English-speaking.

Arrail Dental
Unit 204, Lippo Plaza, 222 Huaihai Zhonglu, Xintiandi (5396 6538/ www.arrail-dental.com). Metro Huangpi Nanlu. **Open** 9.30am-8pm Mon-Thur; 9.30am-6.30pm Fri-Sun. **Credit** AmEx, DC, MC, V. **Map** p244 F6.

Dental treatment by American-trained staff, with strict CDC/ADA's infection control protocol. Popular with US Consulate staff.

DDS Dental Care
2nd floor, 1 Taojiang Lu, by Wulumuqi Nanlu, French Concession (6466 0928). Metro Changshu Lu. **Open** 9am-5pm Mon-Sat. **Credit** AmEx, DC, MC, V. **Map** p246 C7.
Affordable and complete dental treatment. Western-trained Chinese staff speak English.

Dr Harriet Jin's Dental Surgery
Room 1904, Hui Yin Plaza, 2088 Huashan Lu, by Hengshan Lu, Xujiahui (6448 0882). Metro Xujiahui. **Open** 9am-6pm Mon-Fri; 9am-1pm Sat. **Credit** AmEx, DC, MC, V. **Map** p246 A9.
A small clinic with a big following among expats – Dr Jin used to work in the UK.

Opticians

For a reasonable price, most optical shops will grind your lenses within a few hours according to a prescription or on-site eye exam. Opticians can be found on Nanjing Xilu in Jingan and Huaihai Nanlu in the French Concession.

Pharmacies & prescriptions

All medications are available over the counter, although as of July 2004 antibiotics will require a doctor's prescription. It is always advisable to purchase medicine at larger pharmacies to avoid the risk of counterfeit medications.

Huaihai Pharmacist *528 Huaihai Zhonglu, by Chongqing Nanlu, French Concession (6372 2101). Metro Huangpi Nanlu.* **Open** 24hrs daily. **Credit** MC, V. **Map** p247 F6.

Huashi Pharmacist *910 Hengshan Lu, by Tianping Lu, French Concession (6407 8985). Metro Xujiahui.* **Open** 24hrs. **Credit** AmEx, MC, V. **Map** p246 A9.

No.1 Pharmacy *616 Nanjing Donglu, by Zhejiang Lu, Renmin Square (6322 4567). Metro Henan Lu.* **Open** 9am-10pm daily. **Credit** AmEx, DC, MC, V. **Map** p242 G4.

Directory

STDs, HIV & AIDS

Treatment is available at the hospitals listed above. For discreet service go to **World Link** (*see p221*).

AIDS Information & Counseling
1380 Zhongshan Xilu, Hongqiao Lu, Hongqiao (6437 0055). Metro Hongqiao Lu. **Open** 8.30am-5pm Mon-Fri. **No credit cards.**

Shanghai Venereal Disease Association *196 Wuyi Lu, Changning (6251 1807). Metro Zhongshan Park.* **Open** 7.45am-7pm Mon-Fri; 7.45am-4.45pm Sat; 7.45-11am Sun. **No credit cards.**

Traditional Chinese medicine

See pp169-70.

Helplines

Lifeline Shanghai
6279 8990. **Open** noon-8pm daily. English-speakers are almost always available.

ID

Chinese citizens are expected to carry their photo ID with them at all times. Foreigners should carry a passport or a photocopy of the passport's information page and the page with the China visa.

Insurance

Make sure you have adequate health and travel insurance before travelling to Shanghai, as China has no reciprocal agreements with other countries. *See also p219* **Health**.

Internet

Most hotels offer internet services for a fee. Top-end joints usually offer free broadband access to anyone with their own laptop (as does bar/restaurant **Arch**, *see p123*). Otherwise, there are internet cafés on every corner, although most (especially the 24-hour ones) are gaming dens.

An hour's surfing in such places can be as cheap as RMB 2. Take ID with you.

Wireless connections have begun to catch on in the city so travellers with laptops can access the net at locations like Xintiandi (*see pp74-5*) and Element Fresh (*see p102*).

Cyber Bar & Café

77 Jiangning Lu, by Nanjing Xilu, Jingan (6217 3321). Metro Shimen Yilu. **Open** 24hrs daily. **Rates** RMB 5/hr. **No credit cards.** **Map** p249 D4.
An all-night bang-bang arcade atmosphere. Computers have noise-reducing headsets but what's the point when staff play mandopop at high volume?

O'Richard's Bar & Restaurant

2nd floor, Pujiang Hotel, 15 Huangpu Lu, by Garden Bridge, the Bund (6324 6388 ext 175). Metro Henan Lu. **Open** 8am-2am daily. **Rates** RMB 10/hr. **No credit cards.** **Map** p243 K3.
One of the few internet bars that caters to foreign tastes – surf with Tsingtao beer and plates of noodles.

Shanghai Library

1555 Huaihai Zhonglu, by Gaoan Lu, French Concession (6445 5555). Metro Hengshan Lu. **Open** 8.30am-8.30pm daily. **Rates** RMB 8/hr. **No credit cards.** **Map** p246 B7.

One of the few cyber cafés where you will see elderly people doing research online. No drinks or smoking are allowed and you must show a passport or library card to use one of the 24 terminals. Some sites, such as Hotmail, are periodically blocked.

Worldwide Network

555 Jiangsu Lu, by Yuyuan Lu, Jingan (6212 2933). Metro Jiangsu Lu. **Open** 8.30am-10.30pm Mon-Sat. **Rates** RMB 5/hr. **No credit cards.** **Map** p248 A5.
Attracts a teenage crowd and can get noisy and smoky during afternoons and evenings but is less busy during school hours.

Language

Chinese has many different dialects. For example, in Hong Kong people speak Cantonese, while in Shanghai they speak Shanghainese. The standard version of Chinese is called Mandarin or Putongua. For those who do not read Chinese characters there is a romanised alphabet called Pinyin.

English is not widely understood outside of top hotels and businesses. If you need to travel around the city, get a copy of the address written in Chinese and show it to the driver. Most business

---

Upwardly mobile

Mobile users in Shanghai have a new useful directory service at their fingertips. GuanXi is a wireless locator service. The way it works is that the user texts a venue name, for example 'Kommune,' via SMS to 885074. They then immediately receive a reply that states the address, directions on how to get there, the nearest cross road to the venue and its phone number. (The response to Kommune might read 'Kommune Café, No.6-7, Lane 210, Taikang Lu, near end of Sinan Lu, turn right 200m walk down Lane 210 50 metres on the left, 6466 2416.')

Guanxi also offers the users the option of receiving the information in Chinese, so that it can be shown to a taxi driver. There are over 10,000 venues in the GuanXi database, covering entertainment, shopping and tourist locations and the information is constantly updated.

GuanXi

Send SMS requests to 885074. **Rates** RMB 1-RMB 2 per request.

Directory

cards have Chinese and English addresses listed on them and are a valuable tool for getting around. *See also p230* **Vocabulary**.

Left luggage

Luggage can be left at Pudong International Airport (*see p214*) and Hongqiao Airport (*see p214*). Shanghai Railway Station (6354 3193) and Shanghai South Railway Station (6317 9234) also have left luggage services that charge RMB 20 for four hours or RMB 80 per day. Many better hotels can often arrange long-term luggage storage for their guests.

Legal help

For help finding a lawyer and basic information on Chinese law call the **Jun He** law firm (Suite 2501, Shanghai Kerry Centre, 1515 Nanjing Xilu, by Tongren Lu, Jingan, 5298 5488, junhesh@junhe.com).

For more information, *see also p219* **Embassies & consulates**.

Libraries

Shanghai Library

1555 Huaihai Zhonglu, by Gaoan Lu, French Concession (6445 5555). Metro Hengshan Lu. **Open** 8.30am-8.30pm daily. **Map** p246 B7.
The Shanghai Library is the largest of its kind in China. It has an outstanding collection of Chinese books, both antique and modern. The selection of foreign-language books is limited. The library also houses an art gallery and an internet café (*see p222*).

Lost property

To report a crime contact the English-speaking police hotline (6357 6666). For items left in taxis look at the receipt and use the contact number on the back to trace the vehicle. Hotel concierges can also be of assistance in tracking down lost belongings. If a passport

is lost, contact the relevant consulate immediately (*see p219*).

For Pudong International Airport lost property call 6834 6324; for Hongqiao Airport lost property call 6268 8899 ext 42071.

Media

Magazines

Shanghai has a multitude of free English-language magazines that have useful city listings. The two most popular are *City Weekend* (www.cityweekend.com.cn) and *that's Shanghai* (www.thatsshanghai.com). Both are monthlies. Other regular titles include *Shanghai Talk*, *Metrozine* and *Quo*. Pick them up for free at cafés, bars and restaurants around town, including branches of Starbucks.

Due to appear on the city's newsstands some time in late 2004 (ie you've got to pay for this one) is the monthly *Time Out Shanghai*, which will be in Chinese but with an English-language supplement.

Newspapers

Shanghai newsstands offer two main English-language newspapers, the locally produced *Shanghai Daily* (www.shanghaidaily.com) and the Beijing-printed *China Daily* (www.chinadaily.com.cn). There's also the *Shanghai Star* (www.shanghai-star.com.cn), which comes out on Tuesday and Friday and is a reliable arbiter of what's going on in arts, eats and local politics. The Chinese-language *People's Daily* can be read in English at www.english.peopledaily.com. The *Oriental Morning Post* includes an English-language supplement on Friday.

Newspaper editorial is scrutinised by the government necessitating self censorship.

For information on where to buy international newspapers and magazines, *see p136*.

Radio

The **BBC World Service** can be picked up at 17760, 15278, 21660, 12010 and 9740 kHz. The **Voice of America** (VOA) is at 17820, 15425, 21840, 15250, 9760, 5880 and 6125 kHz. For tuning information for the BBC go to www.bbc.co.uk/worldservice/tuning/ and for VOA go to www.voa.gov.

Television

News in English is shown at 10pm Mon-Sat on the Shanghai Broadcast Network (SBN). A cultural magazine in English, *Citybeat*, airs at 10pm on Sunday.

English-language news is also shown on English-speaking channel CCTV 9 at 4pm, 7pm and 11pm on weekdays and at noon on weekends. Most top-end hotels usually have at least CNN, ESPN, HBO and Star World.

Money

The monetary unit in China is the **RMB** (*renminbi*) also known as the *yuan* (written) or *kuai* (spoken). Bills come in denominations of RMB 100, 50, 10, five, two and one. Coins come in a variety of lower denominations including five, two and one *jiao* (10 *jiao* equals RMB 1).

Exchange rates fluctuate marginally but are generally stable at around RMB 8.3 to the dollar or RMB 15 to the pound sterling.

Note that few countries recognise RMB, so change any leftover cash at the airport as you leave. Bring receipts to prove that the amount you want to change back is less than the amount first changed into RMB.

ATMs

ATMs are not widely available and they may not accept foreign cards even if they display the Interact logo.

HSBC provides some of the more reliable ATMs, including at the following locations:

HSBC the Bund *15A Zhongshan Dongyilu, by Jiujiang Lu, the Bund.* Map p243 J4.
HSBC Hong Kong Plaza *Hong Kong Plaza, 282 Huaihai Zhonglu, by Huangpi Nanlu, Xintiandi.* Map p244 F6.
HSBC Shanghai Centre *Shanghai Centre, 1376 Nanjing Xilu, by Tongren Lu, Jingan.* Map p248 C4.
HSBC Tower *101 Yincheng Donglu, by Pudong Dadao, Pudong* Map p243 L4.

Banks

ABN AMRO *28th floor, Jinmao Tower, 88 Shiji Dadao, Pudong (5049 9303). Metro Lujiazui.* **Open** 10am-noon, 2-5pm Mon-Fri. Map p243 L4.
Bank of China *200 Yincheng Zhonglu, by Lujiazui Lu, Pudong (3883 4588). Metro Lujiazui.* **Open** 9am-5pm Mon-Fri. Map p243 K4.
China Construction Bank *1632 Yincheng Donglu, by Lujiazui Lu, Pudong (5888 0000). Metro Lujiazui.* **Open** 9am-5pm Mon-Fri. Map p243 K4.
Citi Bank *20th floor, Marine Tower, 1 Pudong Dadao, by Shiji Dadao, Pudong (5879 1200). Metro Lujiazui.* **Open** 9am-5pm daily. Map p243 L4.
HSBC *101 Yincheng Donglu, by Pudong Dadao, Pudong (6841 1888). Metro Lujiazui.* **Open** 9am-5pm daily. Map p243 L4.

Bureaux de change

If you want to change cash or travellers' cheques, there are two desks just beyond customs at the airports. In the city itself only certain banks, including those listed above, offer this service. Money can be changed at most hotel reception desks, although the service is restricted to hotel guests.

Blackmarket money changers are often found at Xiangyang market, on the Bund or outside banks. Some established money changers even do business insides bank premises next to the official money-changing counters. Blackmarket traders offer slightly better rates than the banks but there's no receipt and no comeback if you're shortchanged.

Credit cards

China has a limited infrastructure in place for use of credit cards. They are most commonly accepted at four- and five-star hotels and high-end restaurants. Be wraned, though: an extra four per cent handling fee is usually charged on all credit card transactions. Visa and Mastercard are the most widely accepted; American Express and Diners Club are also recognised, but less commonly so.

Lost/stolen credit cards

AmEx *6279 8082.*
Mastercard *10 800 110 7309.*
Visa *6323 6656.*

Tax

A 15 per cent surcharge is added on to the bill at hotels. There is a departure tax of RMB 50 for local flights and RMB 90 for international flights, both paid at the airport.

Natural hazards

There are limited natural hazards in Shanghai. The occasional typhoon has swept through the city causing minor floods and wind damage. Warnings will appear in the Chinese media. At present there is no English-language warning system, but the **English-language weather forecast** hotline is 121. For the **China Meteorological Administration** go to www.cma.gov.cn/ywwz/.

Air pollution varies depending on location. For details of air quality go to www.envir.online.sh.cn/index. asp. Mosquitoes are an annoyance during the summer months but repellent is readily available.

Opening hours

Opening hours are as in the West. Museums are usually open seven days a week.

Banks 9am-5pm Mon-Fri. (Some banks open seven days a week.)
Bars 11am/noon-2am daily.
Businesses 9am-6pm Mon-Fri.
Municipal offices 8am-5pm Mon-Fri. (Some offices may close for one hour at lunchtime.)
Post offices 9am-6pm daily.

Police

Police stations can be identified by a red light and a sign that says 'Jingcha'. Police wear a dark navy uniform. There are numerous private security guards throughout the city who do not enforce the law but wear a similar uniform to the local police. Traffic crossing guards armed with shrill whistles are also a prominent feature at every major road junction in Shanghai – disobey them at your peril.

Police stations

Hangpu Police Sub-bureau *174 Jinling Dongu, by Henan Nanlu, Old City (5358 0089). Metro Henan Lu.* Map p242 H5.
Renmin Square Policemen Admin *499 Nanjing Xilu, by Chengdu Lu, Renmin Square (6386 2999). Metro Renmin Park or Square.* Map p249 F4.

Postal services

The Chinese mail service is reliable and its staff honest, if slightly surly. International mail is processed promptly, but domestic mail can be slow. Postcards to any destination around the world cost RMB

4.50. Letters under 20 grams to Europe, Australia and North America cost RMB 6. Letters over 20 grams are charged an additional RMB 1.80 per 10 grams. Packages cost RMB 18 for 100 grams, then RMB 15 for every additional 100 grams. It's advisable to write the address in both English and Chinese.

There is a post office in every district – call 6325 2070 or go to www.chinapost.gov.cn to find local addresses. The main post office (*see below*) is north of Suzhou Creek and as such is not particularly convenient for most visitors. More usefully sited branch post offices include the one at the **Shanghai Centre** (1376 Nanjing Xilu, by Tongren Lu, Jingan) and one at **Xintiandi** shopping plaza. Both have English-speaking staff.

See also p217 **Couriers**.

Main post office

276 Beisuzhou Lu, by Sichuan Beilu, the Bund (6393 6666). Metro Henan Lu. **Open** 24hrs daily. **Map** p243 J2.

Property

Finding a home

The number of agencies targeting foreign clients here has ballooned in recent years. Although most are legit there are lots of unlicensed agencies too, so exercise caution.

The only legislative requirement of the Shanghai Municipal Government is that foreigners register at the relevant Foreign Affairs Police station (*see below*) within 72 hours of signing a lease on any property.

Changning *1171 Yuyuan Lu (6251 1688).*
Haungpu *Jinling Lu (6328 0123).*
Hongkou *Minhang Lu (6324 2200).*
Jingan *Nanjing Xilu (6247 1600).*
Jinshan *135 Zhujing Lu (5731 7301).*
Luwan *Jianguo Zhonglu (6473 5330).*
Pudong *1500 Yangao Lu (5899 0990).*

Real estate agents

Phoenix Property Agency

Yujia Building, 1336 Huashan Lu, by Pingwu Lu, French Concession (6240 4052/www.shanghai-realty. net). **Open** 9am-5pm Mon-Fri. **Map** p246 A6.
Established in 1999 and noted for its nose for unique properties. The website provides extensive listings.

Space

Suite 204, 30 Donghu Lu, by Xinle Lu, French Concession (5403 3338/ www.space.sh.cn). Metro Changshu Lu. **Open** 9am-5pm Mon-Fri. **Map** p246 C6.
Space specialises in high-end residential property. The online property search engine is up to date and useful for finding properties in a variety of budgets and locations.

Types of housing

Apartments

This generally means apartment buildings with individually owned flats. They are largely tenanted by local Chinese families due to convenient locations and reasonable prices. Prices for these properties in the city centre are in the order of $50-$500 per month.

New buildings

High-rise developments with Western standards and amenities. Dependent upon layout, size and location prices range from $450 to $2,500 per month.

Old houses

This category encompasses free-standing houses, townhouses or old lane houses. These properties are over-subscribed, and prices range from $500 to $40,000 per month.

Serviced apartments

These often offer concierge services and/or hotel quality facilities and are generally the only places available for short-term lease. Apartments range from studios to six-bedroom affairs and prices range from

$900 to $3,000 per month (three- to four-star hotel quality), through to $1,800 to $30,000 per month (five-star hotel quality).

Villas

Generally located on the outskirts of town in the Hongqiao, Xuhui and Pudong districts. Expect gardens, service-oriented management, security and a high standard of facilities – and prices in the order of $2,000 to $20,000 per month.

Precautions

A few things to be aware of:
● Any property that has a management company will have a monthly management fee. Check with your agent to see if this is a separate payment or whether it is included in the negotiated rent.
● Test to see that you can run your air-conditioners at the same time as the microwave and other appliances. If in doubt, insist that your agent includes an opt-out clause in your lease.
● Determine which parts of the house being shown to you are for private and which parts are for common use.

Religion

Religion is still a sensitive topic in the People's Republic. While long-established religions such as Christianity, Islam and Buddhism are visible and recognised (Judaism seems to be a border line case), it is always acknowledged that the Communist Party is the highest power in the land (*see p67* **Religious rights**).

Steer clear of sensitive topics such as Falun Gong or religious freedom in Tibet.

Buddhist

Jingan Temple *1686 Nanjing Xilu, by Wanghang Lu, Jingan (6256 6366/www.shjas.com). Metro Jingan Temple.* **Map** p248 C5.

Longhua Temple *Lane 2853 Longhua Lu, Longhua (6457 6327). Metro Longcao Lu.* **Map** p240 C4.
Temple of the City God *249 Fangbang Zhonglu, by Anren Jie, Old City.* **Map** p245 J6.

Catholic

All Saints' Church *425 Fuxing Zhonglu, by Danshui Lu (6385 0906). Metro Huangpi Lu.* **Services** 7.30am, 9.30am, 7pm Sun. **Map** p247 F7.
Dongjiadu Lu Catholic Church *185 Dongjiadu Lu, by Wanyu Jie, Old City (6378 7214).* **Services** 7am Mon-Sat; 6.30am, 8.30am Sun. **Map** p245 K8.
More Memorial Church *316 Xizang Zhonglu, Jiujiang Lu, Renmin Square (6322 5029). Metro Renmin Park or Square.* **Services** 7am, 9am, 2pm, 7pm daily. **Map** p242 G4.
Shanghai Grace Church *375 Shaanxi Beilu, by Weihai Lu, Jingan (6253 9394). Metro Shimen Yilu.* **Services** 7.30pm Wed; 9am Sat; 9am, 7pm Sun. **Map** p249 D5.
St Joseph's Church *36 Sichuan Nanlu, by Jinling Donglu, Old City (6336 5537).* **Services** 7am daily; 6am, 7.30am Sun. **Map** p243 J5.
St Ignatius Cathedral *158 Puxi Lu, by Caoxi Beilu, Xujiahui (6438 2595). Metro Xujiahui.* **Services** 6.15am Mon-Fri; 6.15am, 6pm Sat; 6.15am, 10am, 6pm Sun. **Map** p246 A10.
St Peter's Church *270 Chongqing Nanlu, by Fuxing Zhonglu, Xintiandi (6467 8080). Metro Huangpi Nanlu.* **Services** 5pm Sat; 10.30am Sun. **Map** p247 F7.

Jewish

Jewish Community of Shanghai *62 Changyang Lu, by Zhoushan Lu, Hongkou (6541 5007). Bus 22, 37.*

Muslim

Jinxing Mosque *No.117, Lane 77, Fulu Lu, Pinliang, Yangpu (6541 3199).*

Protestant

Hengshan Community Church *53 Hengshan Lu, by Wulumuqi Lu, French Concession (6437 6576). Metro Hengshan Lu.* **Services** 4pm Sun. **Map** p246 B8.

Safety

Shanghai is an extremely safe city. Crime against foreigners is negligible and what little occurs tends to be limited to pickpocketing. Female travellers can usually move about independently without harassment.

Smoking & spitting

Shanghai is a smoker's paradise. Cigarettes are inexpensive and smoked by all. Feel free to light up anytime, anywhere. Enquiries after non-smoking areas in a bar or restaurant will be met with much amusement.

Spitting is the most beloved non-spectator sport in town. From a mild spittle to a full-on, lung-rattling expectorant cough, it is a prevalent and revolting habit. The belief that it is healthy to expel noxious fluids from the body may have something to do with spitting's popularity. The habit was actively discouraged during the SARS outbreak of 2003 and gobbing was indeed on the wane for a time, but it since appears to have made a tremendous comeback.

Study

Chinese-language schools

Creative Methodology

8C Xinan Building, 200 Zhenning Lu, by Yuyuan Lu, Jingan (6289 4299/www.talkingchina.com). Metro Jinagsu Lu. **Rates** RMB 45/hr for small group classes (5 students); RMB 125/hr for individual classes. **No credit cards. Map** p248 A5.
The centre offers eight different levels of classes in addition to business Chinese, Shanghai dialect and Mandarin for Cantonese speakers. Tutoring is by bilingual teachers from a variety of respected Shanghai universities.

Ease Mandarin

Room 101, No.2, Lane 25, Wuxing Lu, by Kangping Lu, French Concession (5465 6999/www.ease mandarin.com). Metro Hengshan Lu. **Rates** RMB 80-150/hr (depending upon class size). **No credit cards. Map** p246 B8.
One of the most popular schools for expats wanting to study Mandarin. Friendly, helpful and dedicated teachers make the programme effective and engaging. Classes incorporate speaking, writing and reading.

Learning Mandarin Centre

Room 6012, 887 Huaihai Zhonglu, by Ruijin Erlu, French Concession (6431 6104/www.l-e-c.net). Metro Shanxi Nanlu. **Rates** RMB 110/hr. **Credit** MC, V. **Map** p247 E6.
In a convenient central downtown location, this school focuses on teaching English to Mandarin speakers but also offers classes for students wanting to study Mandarin.

Mandarin Centre

16 Songyuan Lu, by Hongqiao Lu, Hongqiao (6270 7668/www. mandarin-center.com/index.asp). Metro Hongqiao. **Rates** RMB 2,500-11,000 per 2- to 5-month term. **Credit** AmEx, MC, V. **Map** p240 B3.
Offers morning, afternoon and evening classes in a popular location for expats in the Hongqiao area. Classes range from two-, three- and five-month programmes. Instructors follow a traditional approach to teaching Chinese as the centre is affiliated with Fudan University.

Telephones

Dialling & codes

The country code for China is 86 and the city code for Shanghai is 021. Drop the prefix zero when dialling from overseas. Domestic calls require the city code but they are not necessary within Shanghai.

For outgoing international calls, dial the international access code, 00, followed by the country code, the area code and the local telephone number. The US and Canada country code is 1; the UK 44; Australia 61; and for New Zealand 64.

Useful city codes

Hangzhou *0571.*
Moganshan *0572.*
Nanjing *025.*
Putuoshan *0580.*
Suzhou *0512.*

Public phones

Chinese public phones take prepaid phone cards, available for RMB 20, RMB 30, RMB 50 and RMB 100. Users of public phones can make domestic and international calls. The latter type can be pricey – over RMB 10 a minute. The local rates are RMB 0.20 for three minutes; calls longer than three minutes are charged RMB 0.10 for every six seconds.

Operator services

Local directory assistance *114.* **International enquiries & reverse-charge/collect calls** **AT&T** *6391 0391.* **Global One** *10817/6279 8538.* **MCI** *10817.* **Sprint** *2890 9887.*

Telephone directories

To order a copy of the *Yellow Pages* call 5385 4017.

Operator Assisted Yellow Pages *96886.*

Phonecards

Internet calling cards (or 'IP' cards), widely available in Shanghai, are an economical option for overseas calling. The access codes for US phone card users are: Sprint (10-813); MCI (10-812); and AT&T (10-811).

Mobile phones

The two mobile phone providers in Shanghai are China Mobile and China Unicom. Both use the GSM system. China Mobile uses GPRS phones and China Unicom uses CDMA phones. China Mobile is the larger of the two but Unicom has lower rates. Mobile users from Japan and North America should check that their roaming service will operate in China.

Both providers offer pre-pay and billed services. With the pre-pay system users can purchase a SIM card, put it into any GSM phone and add value to the account with a prepaid card. The billed system requires Chinese ID.

Local prepaid phone cards and SIM cards can cut the cost of mobile use in Shanghai.

They are priced at RMB 100 and are sold at newsstands and convenience stores (try Parkson Department Store, 918 Hauihai Zhonglu, by Ruijin Erlu, French Concession). Incoming and outgoing calls are charged by the minute.

Faxes

Most hotels are willing to accept incoming faxes for guests. Faxes can be sent from hotel business centres or the front desk and are charged at around RMB 10 per page.

Time

China does not operate daylight-saving time.

Tipping

Hotel restaurants and other high-end, foreigner-aimed places usually add a 15 per cent surcharge to the bill. Everything else is at your discretion. Tour guides usually expect to be tipped.

Toilets

Public toilets are available throughout the city but standards vary tremendously. They charge a marginal fee and also sell tissues, feminine hygiene products and cosmetic items. The squat toilet is the most common type in these facilities but some have a Western-style commode. Hotels, bars and restaurants have Western-style toilets.

Tourist information

The main tourist office in Shanghai is the **Shanghai Tourist Information Service Centre** (303 Moling Lu, south exit of Shanghai Railway Station, 6353 9920, www.tourinfo.sh.cn). A tourist helpline (6252 0000, open

10am-9pm daily) has some English-speaking operators. The tourist offices themselves offer a limited selection of free information in English – the services tend to be geared toward local Chinese needs rather than international travellers. Concierges at top hotels offer a much higher standard of customer service.

There is a tourist bureau in every district – the following are among the best (although that's not saying much):

Jingan District Tourist Information & Service Centre *1699 Nanjing Xilu, by Wulumuqi Beilu, Jingan (3214 0042). Metro Jingan Temple.* **Open** 9am-5.30pm daily. **Map** p248 B5.
Luwan District Tourist Information & Service Centre *127 Chengdu Nanlu, by Huaihai Zhonglu, French Concession (5382 7330). Metro Huangpi Nanlu.* **Open** 9am-9pm daily. **Map** p247 E6.
Pudong New Area Tourist Information & Service Centre *168 Lujiazui Lu, by Yincheng Lu, Pudong (6875 0593). Metro Lujiazui.* **Open** 9am-6pm daily. **Map** p243 L4.
Yuyuan Tourist Information & Service Centre *Yu Bazaar, 159 Jiujiaochang Lu (6355 5032).* **Open** 9am-8pm daily. **Map** p245 J6.

Visas & immigration

All visitors to China require a visa. These are obtained through a Chinese embassy or consulate. Most tourists are issued with a single-entry visa, valid for entry within three months of issuing and good for a 30-day stay. Processing times and fees vary. In the UK the cost is £30 and you need to allow three working days for processing. Two passport photos are required for the application. A next-day express service is available for twice the standard fee.

Business visas are usually multiple entry and valid for three to six months from the date of issue. They allow the visitor to stay for the full specified period. These visas

Directory

Average climate

	Temp (°C)	Temp (°F)	Humidity (%)	Rainfall (mm)	Sunshine (hrs)
January	7-9	45-48	18	45-50	131
February	8-10	46-50	22	60-65	158
March	12-14	54-58	27	80-85	58
April	18-20	65-68	48	90-95	159
May	23-25	74-78	54	110-115	180
June	27-29	80-84	73	160-165	103
July	31-33	88-92	76	140-145	96
August	31-33	88-92	75.5	140-145	99
September	27-29	81-84	73	5	145
October	22-24	72-76	52	55-60	104
November	16-18	61-65	45	50-55	112
December	10-12	50-54	25.5	40-45	186

require a letter of invitation letter from the host business orcorporation.

For more information on current visa regulations and application procedures check the following websites:

UK citizens
www.chinese-embassy.org.uk.
US citizens
www.china-embassy.org.
Canadian citizens
www.chinaembassycanada.org/eng/.

Visa extensions of 30 days are easy to get. They take three days to process and cost RMB 160 for holders of British passports and RMB 125 for Americans. Extewnsions are available from the Public Security Bureau (PSB) just north of the Bund:

PSB *333 Wusong Lu, by Kunshan Lu, Hongkou (6357 7925).* **Open** 9-11.30am, 1.30-4.30pm Mon-Sat. **Map** p243 J2.

Long-term residence

Long-term residency requires a 'green card' or residence permit. The paperwork for a green card requires at least ten passport photos – one to go with each of the ten completed forms necessary for the application. It's a five-step process beginning with the acquisition of your intial

tourist visa (*see p227*). Beyond this you need a certificate of health, an employment visa and a work permit: only then you can you apply for the green card. Employers should help you with the process.

For the **health certificate**, the required examinations and tests may be done in your home country but it's much easier to do it in Shanghai. There is a new, efficient and clean testing facility (1701 Hami Lu, 6268 6171, open 8.30am-11am, 1.30-3pm Mon-Sat). Get there early (by 8am) and you should be out within the hour. To take a 'health exam' you'll need: a copy of your passport plus a copy of the photo and China visa pages, two passport photos and RMB 700. The exam includes blood tests for STDs, chest X-rays, a sonogram, vision test and general health queries.

For the **employment visa** you need an invitation letter from your company, your company employment license and your newly-obtained health certificate.

For the **work permit** (or 'red book') you'll need your employment application letter and CV, the contract you've signed with your company, your health certificate, your

passport (plus photocopies of the photo page) and three passport photos.

Finally, for the **residence permit** (green card) you will need the completed application form, the original and a photocopy of your entire (!) passport, two passport photos, your health certificate, your original work permit and a photocopy, and a copy of your company's business license. The green card is valid for twelve months.

Water

Don't drink the tap water. However, bottled water is widely available.

Weights & measures

China uses the metric system.

1 kilometre = 0.62 miles
1 metre = 1.09 yards
1 centimetre = 0.39 inches
1 kilogram = 2.20 pounds
1 gram = 0.035 ounces
1 litre = 1.76 pints
0 degrees Celcius = 32 degrees Fahrenheit

What to take

Everything you are likely to need can be found in Shanghai, although it may take some searching to find it. Prices may be slightly more expensive for foreign or imported goods. Although most medications, from aspirin to Zoloft, are available in China it's wise to bring all essentials with you – important medication may not be available here, and foreign prescriptions will not be accepted at pharmacies unless endorsed by a local, certified practitioner.

When to go

Climate

The weather is a major factor in planning a visit to Shanghai. There are times of the year when its high humidity can be seriously debilitating, making a visit to the city distinctly uncomfortable. A summary of what to expect during the year follows, but bear in mind that the weather in Shanghai can be very unpredictable.

Spring (March to mid May) is often pleasant and is one of the best times to visit weather-wise, although some of the heaviest rainfall is recorded during this time. Bring a light jacket or sweater for the evenings, which can be cool. Spring is also the time of fresh blooms so it's great for visits to the Yu Gardens and the gardens of Suzhou.

Summer (late May to mid September) is hot, hot, hot and stiflingly humid. Ironically, you'll probably still need to bring an extra layer for when you're indoors, as shops, restaurants, bars and hotels tend to crank up the air-conditioning to icy levels. Summer is also prime festival time (see pp148-152).

Autumn (late September to early December), along with spring, is generally the best time to visit Shanghai; temperatures are comfortably warm, and humidity drops to a bearable level. Sunny days and clear skies are relatively common.

Winter (mid December to February) gets chilly, windy and cloudy, so you need to bring extra layers of clothing. Although the temperature rarely drops below zero, it seems much colder due to the humidity – this is really not a good time to be around Shanghai, although the New Year festivities bring a little colour and warmth.

Public holidays

Many Shanghai public holidays are festival days dependent on the lunar calendar, so each year the dates change; for more information, see p148.

New Year's Day 1 January
Chinese Lunar New Year three days in January/February
Good Friday & Easter Monday March/April
Labour Day 1 May
Mid Autumn Festival September
China National Day 1 October
Christmas Day 25 December
Boxing Day 26 December

Women

Shanghai is a very safe city for women. There is minimal harassment and crime rates are low. Women can travel independently at night, but it's still sensible to exercise caution.

Some useful women's groups in Shanghai include:

American Women's Club 6415 9801.
Australian Women's Social Group 6415 9475.
Brits Abroad 6466 1948.
Expatriates Professional Women's Society epws2001@yahoo.com.

Working in Shanghai

Expect to spend about three months searching for a job. The following websites are all good starting points:

www.chinahr.com
www.monster.com
www.competencechina.com
www.nexus-partners.com

Many temporary jobs in China for English-speakers actually pay quite well. Typically, these jobs include voice recording, writing, teaching English or even modelling. Wages generally start at RMB 100 per hour and are paid in cash. Contracts for this type of work are uncommon. Although it is illegal, some foreigners work on this basis until getting a full-time job. The police rarely monitor this type of activity but significant fines can be levvied on anyone who is caught out.

Internships are a good way into the system if you have limited China-based work experience. Many consulates, US or European companies offer internships. These positions can and do often turn into paid employment upon completion.

Work visas

To apply for a work visa you need:

● A passport with at least six months' validity and at least one blank page.
● One completed visa application form with one additional passport photo.
● A visa notification issued by the authorised Chinese unit, and a work permit issued by the Chinese Labour Ministry/ Foreign Expert's Licence issued by the Chinese Foreign Expert Bureau. A visa notification issued by the authorised Chinese unit or proof of kinship is required for spouese or accompanying family members.

Allow three to four days for processing the documents. For more information, go to www.molss.gov.cn.

Directory

...ple speak ...(*see p222*)
Langu... it's substantially different in pronunciation from Mandarin and Cantonese, with several sounds that are not found in any other Chinese dialect. The bulk of the vocabulary is the same, but there are lots of variations and unique words and phrases. It's considered a coarse and uncultured dialect, unsuited to formal occasions. In such cases, people typically switch to Mandarin, which is the city's second language.

Grammatically, Chinese is easier than many languages. There are no tenses – Chinese words have only one form. Suffixes are used instead to denote tenses. There are no comparative adjectives. The most challenging part of learning Chinese is often the tones, as each sound has four different inflections, each of which can change the meaning of a word. Even for the Chinese, the various tones only avoid confusion up to a certain point: complete understanding is gained from the context.

In the written language, characters take the place of an alphabet. A character can be a word or part of a word, but normally a word consists of two or more characters. There are about 20,000 characters in a normal Chinese word processor. For those who do not read characters there is a romanised alphabet called Pinyin. However Chinese rarely understand it when spoken by non natives. Note that not all consonants in Pinyin are pronounced as in English:

c	like the 'ts' in 'hits'
q	like the 'ch' in 'chase'
r	like the 's' in 'measure'
x	like the 'sh' in 'shop'
z	like the 'dz' in 'duds'

Phrases

my name is...	*wo jiao...*
my last name is...	*wo xing...*
I am	*wo shi*
American	*meiguo ren*
British	*yingguo ren*
Australian	*aodaliya ren*
European	*ouzhou ren*
hello	*ni hao*
goodbye	*zai jian*
thanks	*xie xie*
how are you?	*ni zhenming yang*
you're welcome	*bu keqi*
sorry	*dui bu qi*
correct/right	*dui*
incorrect/wrong	*bu dui*
don't want	*bu yao*
don't have	*meiyou*
I don't know	*wo bu zhi dao*
I don't understand	*wo bu mingbai*
please speak more slowly	*qing shuo de man yidian*

Getting around

Is this taxi free?	*zhei che la ren ma?*
turn left	*zuo guai*
turn right	*you guai*
go straight	*yi zhi zou*
stop the vehicle	*ting che*
I want to go to	*wo yao qu*
hotel	*da jiu dian*
airport	*fei ji chang*
train station	*huo che zhan*
metro	*di tie zhan*
this place (point)	*zhe ge difang*
I want to return home	*wo yao hui jia*

Shopping

how much is it?	*duo shao qian?*
too expensive	*tai gui le*
cheaper?	*pianyi dian?*
too big	*tai da*
too small	*tai xiao*
please give me a receipt	*qing gei wo fapiao*

Eating & drinking

beer	*pijiu*
water	*shui*
English tea	*yinguo cha*
bill	*mai dan*

telephone	*dian hua*
bar/pub	*jiuba/jiuguan*
café	*kafeiguan*
restaurant	*canguan*

Dates & times

Monday	*xing qi yi*
Tuesday	*xing qi er*
Wednesday	*xing qi san*
Thursday	*xing qi si*
Friday	*xing qi wu*
Saturday	*xing qi liu*
Sunday	*xing qi tian*
morning	*zao shang/shang wu*
afternoon	*xia wu*
evening	*wan shang*
today	*jin tian*
tomorrow	*ming tian*
yesterday	*zuo tian*
day after tomorrow	*hou tian*
day before yesterday	*qian tian*

Numbers

zero	*ling*
one	*yi*
two	*er*
three	*san*
four	*si*
five	*wu*
six	*liu*
seven	*qi*
eight	*ba*
nine	*jiu*
ten	*shi*

Emergency phrases

There's an emergency!
zheshi jinji qingkuang
Please can you help me?
ni neng buneng bang wo ge mang

| I lost my passport | *wo de huzhao diu le* |
| I need to see a doctor | *wo yao kan bing* |

Call an ambulance!
qing jiao jingcha jiuhuche

| Fire! | *huo!* |
| Police! | *jing cha!* |

Mobile phones

I'd like to buy a phone card *wo ziang mai dianhua ka*
phone charger *dianhua chongdianqi*
mobile phone for hire *zuyong yidong dianhua*
prepaid mobile *yufu yidong dianhua*

Directory

Further Reference

Memoirs

Jung Chang *Wild Swans* (1992)
A moving memoir that spans three
turbulent generations of women in
China, beginning with the dying
stages of Imperial China and ending
with Tiananmen Square.
Nien Cheng *Life and Death in
Shanghai* (1987) Cheng, accused of
being a British spy, was put under
house arrest in 1966 and jailed. On
release she was told her daughter
had committed suicide; in reality she
was beaten to death by Red Guards.

Non-fiction

Stella Dong *Shanghai: The Rise
and Fall of a Decadent City* (2000)
The tabloid version of high-jinks and
low life as played out in the Shanghai
of the 1920s and '30s.
Lynn Pan *In Search of Old
Shanghai* (1982) Pan waxes historical
on Shanghai's glory days. The text is
by area as opposed to chronological
but criminally undermined by the
lack of an index.
Harriet Sergeant *Shanghai* (1991)
Compiled from first-hand interviews
Sergeant vividly portrays life in the
1920s and '30s living with the 'whore
of the orient'.

Fiction

JG Ballard *Empire of the Sun* (1984)
Part fiction, part autobiography, the
story of a young boy separated from
his parents in wartime Shanghai and
interned by the Japanese. A chilling
meditation on body, mind and the
things people do to survive.
Tom Bradby *The Master of Rain*
(2002) Thriller set in 1920s Shanghai
pitting a young Englishman against
Chinese gangsters and the allure of a
Russian whore.
Bo Caldwell *The Distant Land of
My Father* (2001) Young girl leaves
millionaire dad behind in Shanghai.
Dad interned by Japanese, loses all,
travels to America, reunites with
daughter. Aww.
Kazuo Ishiguro *When We Were
Orphans* (2000) An Englishman
raised in Shanghai returns to find the
dark truth about the deaths of his
parents. No happy endings.
André Malraux *Man's Fate* (1933)
Malraux's characters pierce the
quandaries of ideology and loyalty
posed by the early days of the
Cultural Revolution.

Mian Mian *Candy* (2003) Semi-
autobiographical tale of a Shanghai
'bad' girl that has picked up lots of
attention. Sex, drugs and brand
names are mixed with unconvincing
literary references.
Anchee Min *Becoming Madame
Mao* (2000) Patchy but brave attempt
to get inside the mind of China's very
own Lady Macbeth.
Wei Hui *Shanghai Baby* (2002)
Semi-autobiographical tale of the
other Shanghai 'bad' girl, which
again has picked up lots of attention.
More sex, drugs and brand names
are mixed with more unconvincing
literary references.

Code 46 (Michael Winterbottom,
2003) Set in a future Shanghai and
starring Tim Robbins and Samantha
Morton. Worth watching because
Shanghai has never looked more
magical and mysterious.
The Empire of the Sun (Steven
Spielberg, 2001) Adaptation of JG
Ballard's novel. Epic, tragic,
sweeping, and beautifully shot,
partly in Shanghai itself.
Jasmine Women (Hou Yong, 2004)
Visually stunning tale about three
generations of Shanghai women,
superbly acted by Zhang Ziyi and
Joan Chen.
The Lady from Shanghai (Orson
Welles, 1947) Nothing to do with
Shanghai at all – the closest it gets is
Rita Hayworth talking Mandarin in
San Francisco's Chinatown. We
include it here because we love it.
Pavilion of Women (Ho Yim,
2001) Melodramatic wartime tale of
interracial love between an American
missionary and a married Chinese
woman, based on the novel by Pearl
Buck. Actors Willem Dafoe and Luo
Yan do their best in this US-Chinese
co-production, but the story plays out
like a bad daytime TV soap opera.
Shanghai Express (Josef von
Sternberg, 1932) The story of
kidnapped foreigners travelling the
Beijing-Shanghai line. None of it was
shot in China but it's Dietrich at her
best, von Sternberg at his best, plus
Anna May Wong in all her glory.
Shanghai Panic (Andrew Cheng,
2001) No-budget underground film
about a group of Shanghai drop-outs
and their sex lives. It starts out
downright dystopian but ends up
being about the power of friendship.
Suzhou River (Lou Ye, 2000)
Somewhat surreal tale of lost love
and betrayal, set on the industrial
banks of Suzhou Creek. Modern film
noir Shanghai style.

Shanghai Story (Peng Xiaolian,
2004) A wonderfully subtle film
about a group of feuding Shanghai
siblings brought back together
around their ailing grandmother.
Shanghai Surprise (Jim Goddard,
1986) Madonna (a missionary nurse)
and Sean Penn (a fortune hunter) get
sucked into Shanghai's underworld.
Uh! Ow! That was the sound of our
sides splitting.
Shanghai Triad (Zhang Yimou,
1995) Classic gangster pic set in
1930s Shanghai, described by some
as China's *The Godfather*. Not quite,
but definitely worth a look.

Assorted artists *Fanyin Music
Box* (2003) Twelve tracks by nine
Shanghai bands showcase
everything from pop to rock to metal
to grunge.
Crystal Butterfly *Mystical Journey*
(2004/2005) This repeatedly
postponed debut album by one of
Shanghai's oldest and most famous
bands promises ethereal rock strains
rooted in influences like U2 and the
Cure, but with a Shanghainese twist.
The Honeys *On the Street* (2002)
Debut album of long-time local pop-
rock favourites runs the gamut from
fast, catchy tunes to soaring ballads.
Night Bus *Night Bus* (2004) New
group serves up perky pop-rock with
jazzy influences.
Chen Lirong *Old Shanghai
Gramophone* There are loads of
remakes of Old Shanghai classics,
mostly with bombastic martial music
and Cultural Revolutionary Opera
vocal trills. This one takes a more
'80s/'90s tack, reimagining the old
jazz favourites with heavily
synthesised oompah beats.
Shanghai Jazz *Musical Seductions
from China's Age of Decadence
(Assorted artists)* Jazz musos
currently working in Shanghai
contribute to a lively collection of
jazz faves from Old Shanghai.
Li Xianglan *Fragrance of Night*
(2003) One of Shanghai's most
enduring anthems from its 1930s
heyday. This album compiles the
original version of Li's signature
ditty and 16 other tracks.
Ian Widgery *The Original
Shanghai Divas Collection* Take the
top Chinese pop stars from the '20s
and '30s and remix with uptempo
grooves and laid-back break beats
for one of the hippest CDs in town.
Xiao Yao *Lost Topic* (2004) Singer-
songwriter Xiao mixes hard beats
and electronica into surprisingly
pleasant melodies.

Index

Note: page numbers in **bold** indicate section(s) giving key information on topic; *italics* indicate photos.

Advertisers' Index

Please refer to the relevant sections for contact details

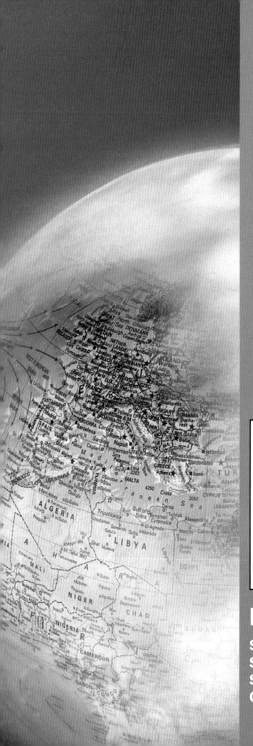

Place of interest and/or entertainment	▨
Railway station	▨
Park	▨
Hospitals/universities	▨
Hotels	▨
Area name	JINGAN
Bars	◎
Restaurants	●
Metro station	Ⓢ
Motorway	═══
Raised highway	═══

Maps

Shanghai Overview

see pp248-9

see pp246-7

A | **B** | **C**

1
2
3
4

QILIANSHAN LU

ZHENBEI LU
ZHENBEI LU

GUANGZHONG LU

Circus World

HUTAI LU

LINGSHI LU

GUANGZHONG LU

GONGHE XINLU

Zhabei Park

Shanghai West Railway Station

XINCUN LU

JIAOTANG LU

XINCUN LU

PUTUO

LANGAO LU

GUANGSIN LU

HUTAI LU

Shanghai Railway Station

Shanghai Railway Station

TAOPU LU

ZHENBEI LU

CAOYANG LU

Zhongtan Lu

Zhenping Lu

HENGFENG LU

Hanzhong Lu

WUNING LU

Caoyang Park

WUNING LU

CAOYANG LU

Caoyang Lu

ZHONGSHAN BEILU

TIANMU LU

JIANGNING LU

Jade Buddha Temple

SHIMEN LU

JINSHAJIANG LU

Jinshajiang Lu

CAOYANG LU

CHANGSHOU LU

JINGAN

East China Normal University

ZHONGSHAN BEILU

WANHANGDU LU

Jingan Temple

BEIJING XILU

GONGHE XINLU

Changfeng Park

Aquaria 21

CHANGNING LU

Zhongshan Park

Changning Lu

CHANGNING LU

JIANGSU LU

Jiangsu Lu

NANJING XILU

Shimen Yilu

Zhongshan Park

Changning Stadium

YANAN ZHONGLU

Shanxi Nanlu

CHANGNING LU

Tianshan Park

Yanan Xilu

Changshu Lu

HUAIHAI ZHONGLU

RUIJIN ERLU

Fuxing Park

Hongqiao Airport

Shanghai Zoo

Cypress Hotel

HONGQIAO LU

Hongqiao Central Garden

Manpo Boutique Hotel

FUXING LU

FRENCH CONCESSION

CHONGQING NANLU

YANAN XILU

HONGQIAO LU

HUAIHAI ZHONGLU

Hengshan Lu

HENGSHAN LU

Marriott Hongqiao

HONGXU LU

Mausoleum of Soong Qingling

ZHONGSHAN XILU

Hongqiao Lu

ZHAOJIBANG LU

WUZHONG LU

Xujiahui

XIETU LU

HONGQIAO

YISHAN LU

XUJIAHUI

WUZHONG LU

YISHAN LU

Yishan Lu

Shanghai Stadium

Shanghai Stadium

ZHONGSHAN NANERLU

HUAN XI YI DA DAO

Guilin Park

CAOXI BEILU

Caoxi Lu

Longhua Temple

YISHAN LU

CAOBAO LU

Caobao Li

Kepu Park

LONGHUA

Huangpu River

HUMIN LU

Shanghai South Railway Station

Shanghai Botanical Gardens

LONGWU LU

JIYANG LU

Shanghai

250
253

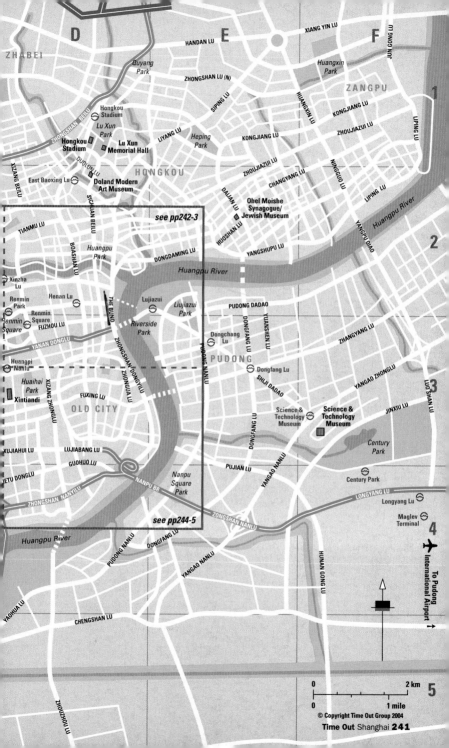

D E F

ZHABEI

HANDAN LU

XIANG YIN LU

JUN GONG LU

Quyang
Park

ZHONGSHAN LU (N)

Huangxin
Park

ZANGPU

SIPING LU

KONGJIANG LU

ZHOUJIAZUI LU

LIPING LU

1

Hongkou
Stadium

Lu Xun
Park

LIYANG LU

Heping
Park

KONGJIANG LU

ZHONGSHAN BEILU

East Baoxing Lu

Hongkou
Stadium

Lu Xun
Memorial Hall

HONGKOU

ZHOUJIAZUI LU

NINGGUO LU

XIZANG BEILU

DUOLUN LU

Doland Modern
Art Museum

SICHUAN BEILU

CHANGYANG LU

LIPING LU

Huangpu River

YANGPU QIAO

2

TIANMU LU

see pp242-3

DALIAN LU

Ohel Moishe
Synagogue/
Jewish Museum

HUOSHAN LU

YANGSHUPU LU

YANGPU QIAO

Huangpu
Park

BOASHAN LU

DONGDAMING LU

Huangpu River

Xinzha
Lu

Renmin
Park

Henan Lu

THE BUND

Lujiazui

Liujiazui
Park

PUDONG DADAO

YUANSHEN LU

ZHANGYANG LU

Renmin
Square

Renmin
Square

FUZHOU LU

Riverside
Park

ZHONGSHAN DONGLU

ZHONGHUA LU

PUDONG NANLU

Dongchang
Lu

DONGFANG LU

Dongfang Lu

PUDONG

SHJI DADAO

YANGAO ZHONGLU

3

LUO SHAN LU

YANAN DONGLU

Huangpi
Nanlu

XIZANG ZHONGLU

FUXING LU

Huaihai
Park

Xintiandi

OLD CITY

Science &
Technology
Museum

Science &
Technology
Museum

DONGFANG LU

JINXIU LU

Century
Park

XUJIAHUI LU

LUJIABANG LU

GUOHUO LU

Nanpu
Square
Park

PUJIAN LU

Century Park

YANGAO NANLU

LONGYANG LU

Longyang Lu

4

JIETU DONGLU

ZHONGSHAN NANLU

NANPU BR

PUDONG NANLU

ZONGSHAN NANLU

Maglev
Terminal

see pp244-5

Huangpu River

PUDONG NANLU

DONGFANG LU

YANGAO NANLU

HUNAN GONG LU

To Pudong International Airport

YAOHUA LU

CHENGSHAN LU

ZHOUZHOU LU

0   2 km

0   1 mile

© Copyright Time Out Group 2004

5

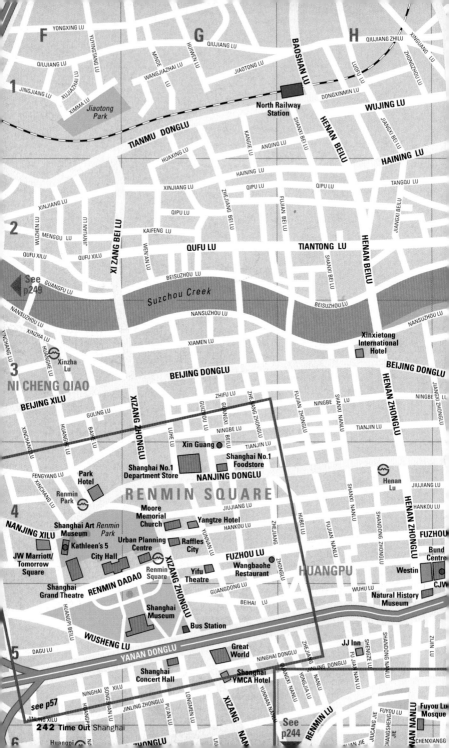

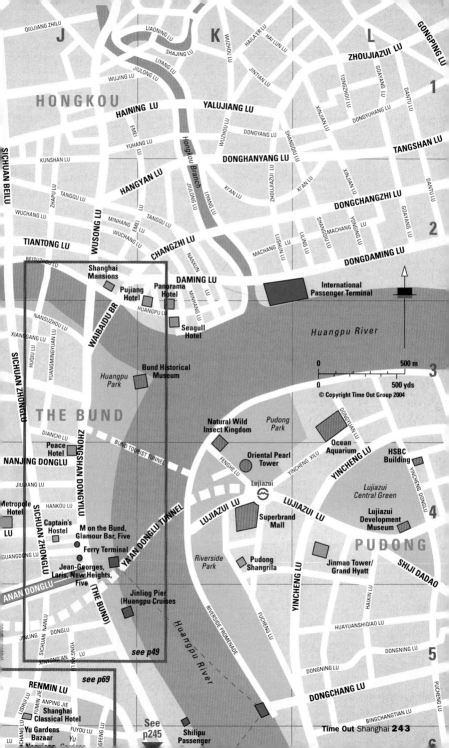

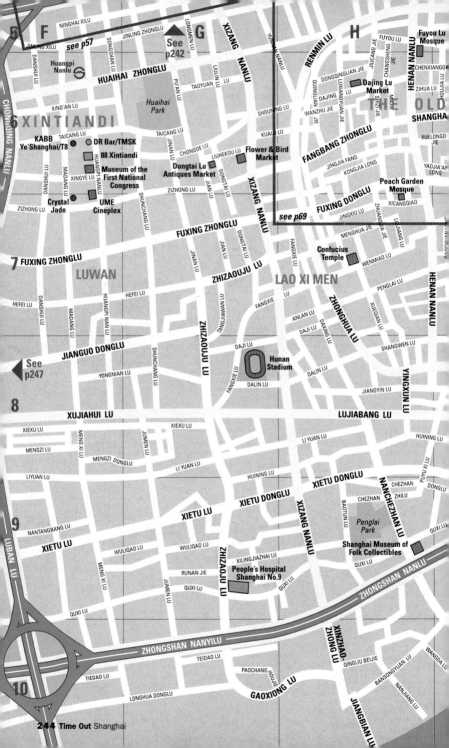

LISHU LU
FUMIN JIE
ANPING JIE
RENMIN LU
J
K
See
p243
DONGCHANG LU
L
PUCHENG LU
5

LU
FUYOU LU
BINGCHANGTIAN LU

JIUJIAOCHANG LU
Yu Gardens
Shilipu
Passenger
Terminal

SHANGCHENG LU

Nanxiang   Lubolang
Yu Gardens
Bazaar
ANREN
WUTONG LU
DANGFENG LU

QIXIN LU
6

CITY
OLD ST
FANGBANG ZHONGLU
YANGSHOU LU

ZHOUJIN LU
XIENZUO JIE

RONGCHANG LU
YANGJIADU LU

SANPAILOU LU
XUEYUAN JIE
GUANGQI LU
WAIKANGJIA
LAOTAIPING

ZOMGZI
LONG
FUXING DONGLU
XIYAQIE
LONG
MIEZHU JIE
LONG
XINMATOU
JIE

WEIFAN LU

WANGYUN LU
FUXING DONGLU
LAOXIN JIE
WALMA LU

XITANGJIA JIE
BAIDU LU

NANSHI
GUANGQI NAN LU
MEIJIA JIE
XUNDAO LU
MAOJIA LU
ZIXIA LU

ZHONGSHAN NANLU
XINMATOU JIE
PUDIAN LU
7

NINGHE LU
QIAOJIA LU
MIEZHU LU
BEISHIJIA LONG

YUJIA LONG
ZHUHANGMATOU JIE

HUANGJIA LU
XUNDAO JIE
WANGJIAMAOTOU LU
WANYU JIE
WANYUMATOU JIE

ZHONGHUA LU
DONGJIADU LU
XIGOUYU LONG
NANGU JIE
GONGYIMATOU JIE

DACHANG JIE
SANGYUAN JIE
Dongjiadu
Cathedral

KUALONG LU
DONGJIANGYIN
NANCANG JIE
Dongjiadu Lu
Fabric Market

HUINING LU
LIUSHI LU
DUOJIA LU
HUIGUAN JIE
HUIGUANMATOU JIE
8

HAINAN XILONG
CAOXIEWAN JIE

GUOHUO LU
HAICHAO
WALMA LU

PUYU LU

BANSONGYUAN LU
NANPU BRIDGE

Proposed Site
for 2010 Expo
PUDONG NANLU
9

Huangpu River
Nanpu
Square
Park

TANGNAN
JIAONAN LU

ZHONGSHAN NANLU

NANMATOU LU
SANLIQIAO LU
PUDONG NANLU
PUSAN LU
10

500 m
YINAN LU
SANLIQIAO LU

0
500 yds
XISANLIQIAO LU

© Copyright Time Out Group 2004
DONGFANG LU

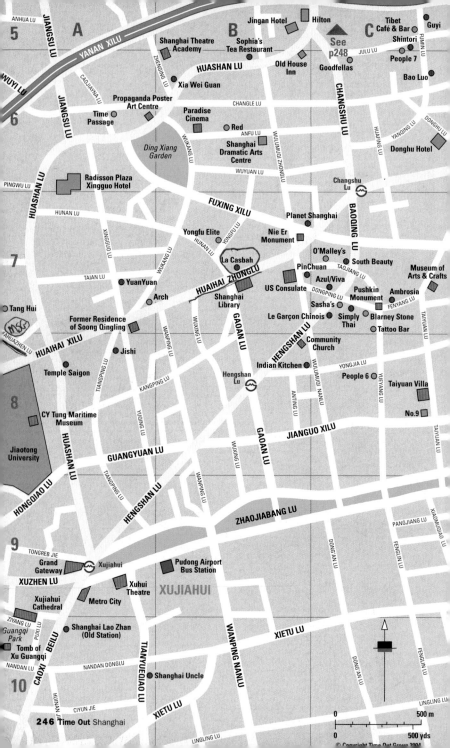

5

ANHUA LU

JIANGSU LU
WUYI LU
JIANGSU LU
HUASHAN LU
YANAN XILU

A

B

Jingan Hotel   Hilton

Shanghai Theatre   Sophia's
Academy   Tea Restaurant

HUASHAN LU   Old House
Inn   Goodfellas

See
p248

C

Tibet
Café & Bar   Guyi

Shintori

JULU LU   People 7

Bao Luo

FUMIN LU

6

Xia Wei Guan

Propaganda Poster
Art Centre

Time
Passage   Paradise
Cinema

CHANGLE LU

Red   ANFU LU

Ding Xiang
Garden   Shanghai
Dramatic Arts
Centre

WUYUAN LU

CHANGSHU LU

HUAFING LU

YANDING LU

DONGHU LU

Donghu Hotel

ZHENNING LU
CAOJIAXAN LU
WUKANG LU
WULUMUQI ZHONGLU

PINGWU LU

HUASHAN LU

Radisson Plaza
Xingguo Hotel

HUNAN LU   FUXING XILU

Changshu
Lu

BAOQING LU

7

HUASHAN LU
FAHUAZHEN LU
HUAIHAI XILU

Tang Hui

Yongfu Elite   Planet Shanghai

Nie Er
Monument

O'Malley's   South Beauty

Museum of
Arts & Crafts

Former Residence
of Soong Qingling   YuanYuan   Arch   La Casbah   PinChuan   Azul/Viva   Ambrosia

Shanghai
Library   US Consulate   DONGPING LU   Pushkin
Monument

FENYANG LU

Sasha's

Le Garçon Chinois   Simply
Thai   Blarney Stone

Tattoo Bar

TAIYUAN LU

XINGGUO LU

TAIAN LU

HUNAN LU

YONGFU LU

WANPING LU

WUXING LU

HUAIHAI ZHONGLU

GAOAN LU

HENGSHAN LU

WULUMUQI NANLU

TAOJIANG LU

TIANGPING LU

Jishi   Community
Church

8

Temple Saigon   Indian Kitchen   People 6   Taiyuan Villa

Hengshan
Lu   YONGJIA LU   No.9

CY Tung Maritime
Museum

Jiaotong
University   KANGPING LU

YUDONG LU   ANTING LU

HONGQIAO LU

HUASHAN LU

GUANGYUAN LU   GAOAN LU   JIANGUO XILU

TIANGPING LU

HENGSHAN LU

WANPING LU

WUXING LU

YUEYANG LU

TAIYUAN LU

XIAOMUQIAO LU

ZHAOJIABANG LU

PANGJIANG LU

9

TONGREB JIE

Grand
Gateway   Xujiahui   Pudong Airport
Bus Station

XUZHEN LU

Xuhui
Theatre   **XUJIAHUI**

Xujiahui
Cathedral   Metro City

DONG AN LU

FENGLIN LU

ZIYANG LU
PUXI LU
CAOXI BEILU
Guangqi
Park   Shanghai Lao Zhan
(Old Station)

Tomb of
Xu Guangqi

NANDAN LU   NANDAN DONGLU

TIANYUEQIAO LU

WANPING NANLU

XIETU LU

DONG AN LU

FENGLIN LU

10

Shanghai Uncle

CIYUN JIE

XIETU LU

LINGLING LU

HUNAN JIE

LINGLING LU

0   500 m

0   500 yds

246 Time Out Shanghai

© Copyright Time Out Group 2004

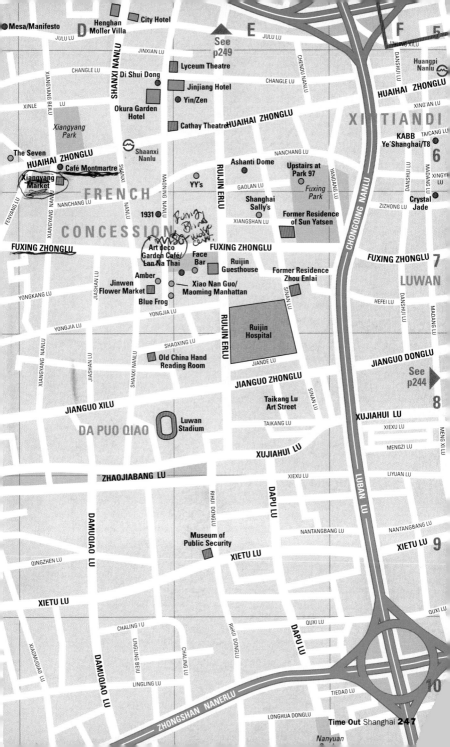

Mesa/Manifesto

Henghan
Moller Villa

City Hotel

D

E

F 5

JULU LU

JULU LU

See
p249

JINLING XILU

DANSHUI LU

Huangpi
Nanlu

JULU LU

JINXIAN LU

CHENDU NANLU

HUAIHAI ZHONGLU

CHANGLE LU

Lyceum Theatre

SHANXI NANLU

Di Shui Dong

CHANGLE LU

XING'AN LU

XINLE
LU

XIANGYANG BEILU

Jinjiang Hotel

XINTIANDI

Okura Garden
Hotel

Yin/Zen

KABB
Ye'Shanghai/T8

TAICANG LU

Cathay Theatre

HUAIHAI ZHONGLU

Xiangyang
Park

NANCHANG LU

MADANG LU

XINGYI
LU **6**

The Seven

HUAIHAI ZHONGLU

Shaanxi
Nanlu

Ashanti Dome

RUIJIN ERLU

Upstairs at
Park 97

YANDANG LU

DANSHUI LU

Crystal
Jade

Café Montmartre

SHANXI
NANLU

GAOLAN LU

Fuxing
Park

ZIZHONG LU

Xiangyang
Market

YY's

Shanghai
Sally's

MAONING NANLU

FENYANG LU

NANCHANG LU

XIANGYANG NANLU

**FRENCH
CONCESSION**

1931

Ruijin Bing
Wuse center

XIANGSHAN LU

Former Residence
of Sun Yatsen

FUXING ZHONGLU

LUWAN

FUXING ZHONGLU

Art deco
Garden Café/
Lan Na Thai

FUXING ZHONGLU

Face
Bar

Ruijin
Guesthouse

Former Residence
Zhou Enlai

HEFEI LU

DANSHUI LU

MADANG LU

Amber

Jinwen
Flower Market

JIASHAN LU

Xiao Nan Guo/
Maoming Manhattan

SINAN LU

Blue Frog

YONGKANG LU

YONGJIA LU

RUIJIN ERLU

Ruijin
Hospital

YONGJIA LU

JIASHAN LU

XIANGYANG NANLU

SHAOXING LU

SHANXI NANLU

Old China Hand
Reading Room

JIANDE LU

JIANGUO ZHONGLU

See
p244 ▶

JIANGUO DONGLU

8

JIANGUO XILU

SINAN LU

Taikang Lu
Art Street

XUJIAHUI LU

DA PUO QIAO

Luwan
Stadium

TAIKANG LU

XIEXU LU

MENG XI LU

MENGZI LU

DAMUQIAO LU

ZHAOJIABANG LU

XUJIAHUI LU

XIEXU LU

DAPU LU

LIYUAN LU

NANTANGBANG LU

NANTANGBANG LU

XIETU LU **9**

QINGZHEN LU

RIHUI DONGLU

Museum of
Public Security

XIETU LU

DAPU LU

QUXI LU

XIETU LU

CHALING LU

RIHUI DONGLU

DAPU LU

XIAODAMUQIAO LU

LINGLING BEILU

CHALING LU

10

DAMUQIAO LU

LINGLING LU

TIEDAO LU

ZHONGSHAN NANERLU

LONGHUA DONGLU

Nanyuan

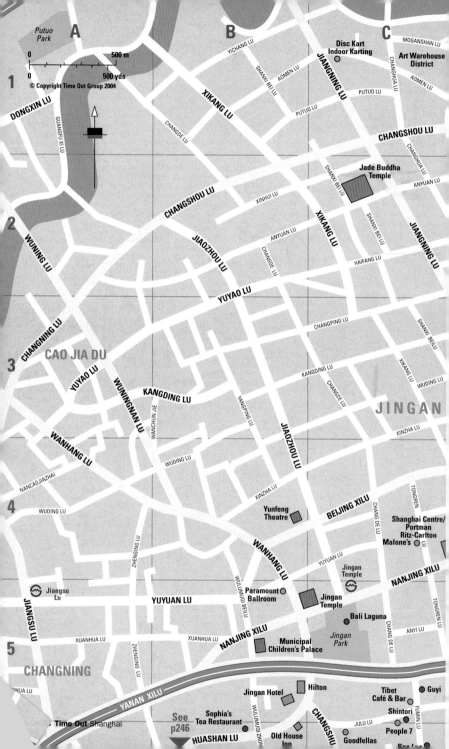

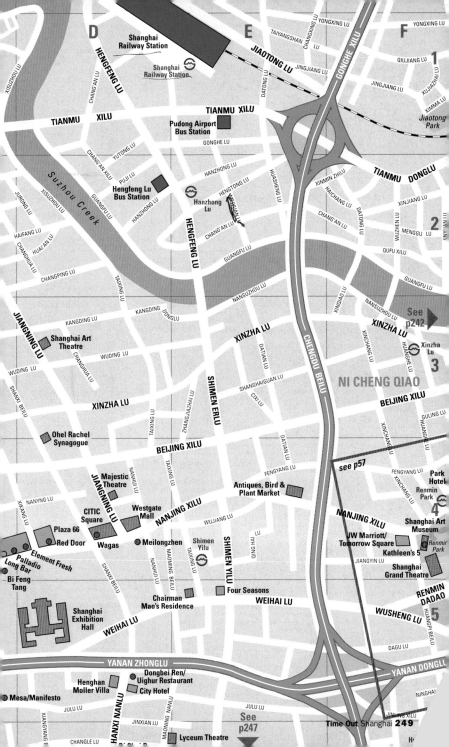

Street Index

Chinese Translations

THE BUND 外滩

Bund Centre 外滩商贸
Bund Historical Museum 外滩历史博物馆
Bund Museum 外滩博物馆
Bund Tourist Tunnel 外滩人行观光隧道
Chinese Post Office 邮政局大楼
Garden Bridge (Waibaidu) 公园桥(外白渡)
Huangpu Park 黄浦公园
M on the Bund 米氏餐厅
Metropole Hotel 新城饭店
Natural History Museum 自然博物馆
Shanghai Friendship Store 上海友谊商店
Shanghai Mansions 上海大厦
Suzhou Creek 苏州河
Three on the Bund 外滩三号

Streets 街道

Beijing Donglu 北京东路
Jiulong Lu 九龙路
Nanjing Donglu 南京东路
Yanan Donglu 延安东路
Zhapu Lu 乍浦路

RENMIN SQUARE & NANJING DONGLU 人民广场和南京东路

City Hall 大会堂
Great World 大世界
Hong Kong Shopping Centre 香港购物中心
Moore Memorial Church 沐恩堂
Shanghai Art Museum 上海美术馆
Shanghai Concert Hall 上海音乐院
Shanghai Grand Theatre 上海大舞台
Shanghai Museum 上海博物馆
Shanghai No.1 Department Store 上海第一百货公司
Tommorrow Square 明天广场
Urban Planning Centre 城市规划中心
Yifu Theatre 逸夫舞台

Streets 街道

Huanghe Lu 黄河路
Fuzhou Lu 福州路
Guangdong Lu 广东路
Renmin Dadao 人民大道
Xizang Zhonglu 西藏中路
Yanan Donglu 延安东路
Yunnan Nanlu 云南南路

JINGAN 静安

Antique, Bird & Plant Market	古玩、花鸟市场
Chairman Mao's Residence	毛泽东故居
Children's Palace	上海市少年宫
CITIC Square	中伩泰富广场
Jade Buddha Temple	玉佛寺
Jingan Park	静安公园
Jingan Temple	静安寺
Ohel Rachel Synagogue	摩西会堂
Plaza 66	恒隆广场
Shanghai Centre	上海商城
Shanghai Centre Theatre	上海商城剧院
Shanghai Exhibition Hall	上海展览中心
Westgate Mall	梅龙镇广场

Streets 街道

Maoming Beilu	茂名北路
Moganshan Lu	莫干山路
Nanjing Xilu	南京西路
Weihai Lu	威海路
Wujiang Lu	吴江路

OLD CITY 老城

Chenxiangge Nunnery	沉香阁
Cixiu Nunnery	慈修庵
Confucious Temple	孔庙
Dajing Lu Market	大镜路市场
Dajing Pavilion	大镜亭
Dongjiadu Cathedral	董家渡天主堂
Dongjiadu Lu Fabric Market	董家渡路布料批发市场
Fuyou Lu Market	福佑路市场
Fuyou Lu Mosque	福佑路清真寺
Hua Bao Building	华宝楼
Kuixing Pavilion	魁星楼
Nanpu Bridge	南浦桥
Peach Garden Mosque	小桃园清真寺
Shanghai Museum of Folk Collectibles	上海民间收藏陈列馆
Temple of the City God	城皇庙
White Cloud Taoist Temple	白云寺
Yu Gardens	豫园
Yu Gardens Bazaar	豫园小商品市场

Streets 街道

Anren Lu	安仁路
Dongjiadu Lu	董家渡路
Fangbang Zhonglu	方浜中路
Fuyou Lu	福佑路
Henan Nanlu	河南南路
Jiujiaochang Lu	旧校场路
Lishui Lu	里水路